The Non-Identity Problem and the
of Future People

David Boonin is Professor of Philosophy at the University of Colorado. He received his BA from Yale University and his PhD from the University of Pittsburgh. He taught at Georgetown University (1992–94) and Tulane University (1994–98) before taking up his current position at CU in 1998. He also held a visiting position for a semester as an Erskine Fellow at the University of Canterbury in Christchurch, New Zealand, in 2006. Boonin is the author of *Thomas Hobbes and the Science of Moral Virtue* (CUP, 1994), *A Defense of Abortion* (CUP, 2003), *The Problem of Punishment* (CUP, 2008), *Should Race Matter?* (CUP, 2011), *Beyond Roe: Why Abortion Should be Legal Even if the Fetus is a Person* (OUP, 2019), and *Dead Wrong: The Ethics of Posthumous Harm* (OUP, 2019) as well as a number of articles on such subjects as animal rights, euthanasia, same-sex marriage, and our moral obligations to past and future generations. He is also the editor of the *Palgrave Handbook of Philosophy and Public Policy* (Palgrave 2018), the co-author and co-editor, with his colleague Graham Oddie, of the popular textbook *What's Wrong?: Applied Ethicists and Their Critics* (OUP, 2009 (second edition)), and the current Editor of *Public Affairs Quarterly*.

Praise for *The Non-Identity Problem and the Ethics of Future People*

"For almost forty years, philosophers have searched for an explanation of why it is wrong for us to bring about the existence of worse- rather than better-off people. In this thorough and methodical book, David Boonin argues that this search is misguided. He systematically reviews all the explanations that have been offered (at least all I know of), and makes a strong case that they either fail to explain the assumed wrong or explain it in ways that have even more implausible implications than denying the wrong. Some books are seminal, opening up a new field or inquiry; this book could be called 'terminal,' cogently arguing that we abandon a search that has been pursued with great resourcefulness and tenacity. Boonin leaves us with a conclusion that many will find disturbing, but some will find liberating: that we face far fewer moral constraints in the creation of future people than we commonly suppose."

David Wasserman

"A model of philosophical reasoning . . . his argument is highly compelling. His negative arguments are thorough, clear, and insightful, and his positive arguments are illuminating. Anyone whose research relates to the non-identity problem—and given the interdisciplinary nature of the problem, that is a large number of people—would be well advised to read this book."

Molly Gardner, *Notre Dame Philosophical Reviews*

"important . . . argues for surprising and controversial conclusions"

Fiona Woollard, *Analysis*

"David Boonin's new book provides a wonderful opportunity to take a fresh look at what is perhaps the most important problem ever to arise within the area of population ethics. Brilliantly argued, perfectly organized, fascinating in content and accessible to a broad range of readers, *The Non-Identity Problem and the Ethics of Future People* marks a critical turning point in our efforts to understand the structure of moral law."

Melinda A. Roberts

"Throughout this careful examination, Boonin employs thoughtful case studies and thought experiments that serve to engage the reader in the analysis. The result is a book that is likely to put this philosophical quandary to rest . . . Essential."

Choice

The Non-Identity Problem and the Ethics of Future People

David Boonin

OXFORD
UNIVERSITY PRESS

UNIVERSITY PRESS

Great Clarendon Street, Oxford, OX2 6DP,
United Kingdom

Oxford University Press is a department of the University of Oxford.
It furthers the University's objective of excellence in research, scholarship,
and education by publishing worldwide. Oxford is a registered trade mark of
Oxford University Press in the UK and in certain other countries

© David Boonin 2014

The moral rights of the author have been asserted

First published 2014
First published in paperback 2020

Published in the United States of America by Oxford University Press
198 Madison Avenue, New York, NY 10016, United States of America

British Library Cataloguing in Publication Data

Data available

Library of Congress Cataloging in Publication Data

Data available

ISBN 978-0-19-968293-5 (Hbk.)
ISBN 978-0-19-886685-5 (Pbk.)

For my wife, Leah, and my children, Eli and Sadie

Preface

In early March 2013, the City of New York began putting up a series of public service announcements aimed at discouraging teenage pregnancy. In one particularly poignant example, a sweet little boy with a mournful expression and tears gently trickling down his face gazes directly at the viewer while the accompanying text reads: "I'm twice as likely not to graduate high school because you had me as a teen." The campaign sparked a bitter controversy over whether it inappropriately stigmatized teenage parents and their children. But lost in all the noise was the fact that the ad also quietly concealed a disturbing moral paradox.

The resentful words attributed to the little boy, after all, seem to imply that his chances of graduating from high school would have been better if his mother had waited until she was older before she became pregnant. But if his mother had waited until she was older before she became pregnant, this sweet little boy would never have existed. A different sperm and a different egg would instead have come together in the act of fertilization, and his mother would have conceived a different child as a result. Far from diminishing this little boy's chances of graduating from high school, then, his mother's act of getting pregnant as a teenager is precisely what made it possible for him to have any chance of graduating from high school at all.

The crying boy's plaintive lament is designed to convey the message that teenage mothers harm their children by conceiving when they are too young to raise their offspring in a fully responsible manner. But because the children they conceive as teenagers are not the same children as the children they would otherwise have conceived if they had waited to become parents until they were older, the claim that teenage mothers harm their children by conceiving them seems to be false. If this little boy was not harmed by his mother's choice to become a teenage parent, though, then what grounds can he have for complaining to her about it? And if he has no grounds for complaint, then why should we think that what she did was in any way wrong?

The puzzle that is generated by asking such questions is known as the non-identity problem. It arises in a surprisingly wide variety of contexts in which the choices that people make can have an effect on which particular people subsequently exist, and it has serious implications across a broad range of seemingly unrelated moral controversies, from the ethics of human cloning to the legitimacy of prohibitions on incest to our obligations to combat global warming to the debate over slave reparations. The case of the teenage mother and her disadvantaged child is simply one particularly vivid example of this vexing and far-reaching moral problem. Regardless of whether the ad campaign proved to be an effective means of combating teenage pregnancy, then, it at least did a nice job of highlighting the importance of solving the non-identity problem. And solving the non-identity problem is what this book attempts to do.

I first became interested in the non-identity problem when I encountered it as a graduate student in the early 1990s and I have continued to think about it on and off ever since. In 2008, I published an article on the subject in which I explained what the problem is, critically surveyed what I took to be the existing proposals for solving it, and offered a solution of my own. I was reasonably satisfied with the piece when it was finished, but it didn't take long after its publication for me to begin to realize how many other possible and potentially promising solutions I had overlooked, how much more would really have to be said to try to make my own approach to the problem seem viable, even how much more there was to say about what exactly the problem is in the first place and what a solution would have to accomplish in order to count as a genuinely satisfactory one. So I decided to write this book.

Articles about the non-identity problem have continued to appear at an increasing rate since it became a subject of philosophical inquiry in the mid-1970s, but this is the first book-length study devoted to its examination. I hope that it will provide a useful introduction to the problem for those who are coming to it for the first time as well as a valuable contribution to the literature for those who are already grappling with it. I have attempted to provide a clear and detailed explanation of what the problem is, why the problem matters, and what criteria a solution to the problem must satisfy in order to count as a successful one. In addition, before presenting my own solution to the problem in the final chapter, I have tried to offer an extensive and thorough critical survey of the existing literature on the subject.

Indeed, I suspect that some readers may find the critical survey that this book offers to be a bit too thorough. The current literature on the non-identity problem contains an extremely broad range of proposed solutions. My discussion of the literature is therefore somewhat lengthy. Many people who examine the problem seem to find only one or two approaches to be particularly promising and often find many of the rest to be easily dismissed. They might therefore expect a critical survey of the extant literature to go into detail about only a few possible solutions and to dispatch with most of the rest in just a few sentences each. The problem with this ideal is that while many people seem to think that there are only a few particularly promising approaches to solving the non-identity problem, there is very little agreement about which approaches are the promising ones and which are the ones that can easily be dismissed. As a result, I have tried as much as possible to engage in some detail with the literature as a whole. In a number of cases, I provide multiple objections to a particular solution. Readers who are convinced by my first objection in any given case and who are not particularly inclined to endorse the particular solution under consideration at that point should feel free to skim or pass over the rest of my discussion of that particular solution and move on to the discussion of the next one. I have attempted to render this approach a bit easier by removing parts of some of the longer discussions in the book and collecting them at the end in the form of a series of appendices. While these sections can be skimmed or ignored by those who do not find them to be of particular interest, however, I should stress that understanding at least some of my reasons for rejecting each of the solutions that I consider in Chapters 2–6 remains important, in part because all of the solutions I consider seem to me to merit consideration and in part because the results of the discussion in those chapters serve as the foundation for the defense of my own solution in Chapter 7.

I started working on this book in earnest in the spring of 2010, when I taught a graduate seminar on the ethics of sex and procreation. My first debt of gratitude is therefore to the students in that class, whose careful, detailed, frequent, and enthusiastic contributions to class discussion led me to spend over half the course on the non-identity problem and whose penetrating questions at every turn forced me to produce a tentative first draft of many sections of this book on the spot just as a way of trying to keep up with them. That fall, and for the next few falls after that, I also benefited from the opportunity to teach the non-identity problem for a few weeks to our incoming graduate students, and I would like to thank them, too, for their valuable critical feedback as I continued to develop my ideas.

Once I had a full manuscript to circulate, I was extremely fortunate to find a number of people who were interested in the problem and who generously provided me with comments and suggestions on a complete draft of the book. For their careful and time-consuming work, I am especially grateful to Eric Chwang, Rivka Weinberg, David Wasserman, Melinda Roberts, Christian Lee, Duncan Purves, Chelsea Haramia, Caleb Carr, Robyn Kath, and two anonymous reviewers for Oxford University Press. I would also like to thank Derek Parfit, Saul Smilansky, and David Benatar for comments on various parts of the manuscript, Michael Huemer, Claudia Mills, Michael Tooley, and Bob Pasnau for their helpful comments along the way, and Peter Momtchiloff for his support of the project at Oxford University Press.

As I tried to work out my thoughts on the subject over the last several years, I was also fortunate to have the opportunity to give a number of talks on different aspects of the problem at a variety of venues and I benefited greatly from the discussions that resulted. For this invaluable assistance, I am grateful to audiences at Oberlin College, the University of Calgary, the University of Alberta, the University of Canterbury (New Zealand), the University of Haifa, Hebrew University, Yale University, the University of California at Riverside, the University of Kansas, and the Arizona Workshop in Normative Ethics, as well as to audiences at several talks sponsored by the Center for Values and Social Policy at the University of Colorado.

A number of passages in this book first appeared in an earlier form in "How to Solve the Non-Identity Problem," *Public Affairs Quarterly*, vol. 22, no. 2 (2008), pp. 127–57. And much of Appendix B first appeared in a different form as "Better to Be," *South African Journal of Philosophy*, vol. 31, no. 1 (2012), pp. 10–25. I am grateful to the publishers of both journals for their permission to use that material here.

Finally, it is a great pleasure to have an excuse to acknowledge publicly how much I owe to my wife, Leah, and to my children, Eli and Sadie. This book is for them.

Contents (Short Version)

Contents (Expanded Version)

1

Five Plausible Premises and One Implausible Conclusion

Our actions sometimes have an effect not only on the quality of life that people will enjoy in the future, but on which particular people will exist in the future to enjoy it. In cases where this is so, the combination of certain assumptions that most people seem to accept can yield conclusions that most people seem to reject. When this happens, we have a problem. The problem appears to have been discovered independently in the late 1970s by Derek Parfit, Thomas Schwartz, and Robert M. Adams, and is now most closely identified with Parfit, whose 1976 article "On Doing the Best for Our Children" was among the first to report it, whose seminal 1984 book *Reasons and Persons* contains its fullest and most influential treatment, and whose work gave it the name by which it is now most commonly known: the non-identity problem.[1] This book is about that problem. In Chapter 1, I explain what the non-identity problem is, why the problem matters, and what criteria a solution to the problem must satisfy in order to count as a successful one. In Chapters 2 through 6, I use these criteria to argue against the many solutions to the problem that have thus far been proposed in the sizeable literature that the problem has generated. In Chapter 7, I defend a fundamentally different kind of solution.

1.1 What the Problem Is

The non-identity problem arises from a tension between the plausibility of certain general claims and the implausibility of certain specific conclusions that seem to follow from them. The problem is therefore best introduced by means of particular examples. Since the problem can occur in both a direct and an indirect form, I will begin with an example of each.

---

[1] See Parfit (1976a, 1976b, and 1984), Schwartz (1978, 1979), and Adams (1979). Another early statement of the problem appears in Bayles (1976: 297–8). See also Parfit (1982, 1983, 1986, 2011).

1.1.1 *The Direct Version*

Consider first the case of Wilma.[2] Wilma has decided to have a baby. She goes to her doctor for a checkup and the doctor tells her that there is some good news and some bad news. The bad news is that as things now stand, if Wilma conceives, her child will have a disability. The doctor cannot say precisely what the disability will be, but she can tell Wilma three things about it. First, it will be the kind of disability that clearly has a substantially negative impact on a person's quality of life. This could be because of features intrinsic to the disability itself, because Wilma's society discriminates against or fails to sufficiently accommodate people with the disability, or because of some combination of these reasons. Second, even if it is possible for a life to be worse than no life at all, this particular disability will clearly not be so serious as to render the child's life worse than no life at all. So while the disability will be considerably far from trivial, the child's life will nonetheless clearly be worth living. Finally, the disability will be irreversible. There will be no way to eliminate it or to mitigate its effects.

The good news is that Wilma can prevent this from happening. If she takes a tiny pill once a day for two months before conceiving, her child will be perfectly healthy. The pill is easy to take, has no side effects, and will be paid for by her health insurance. Fully understanding all of the facts about the situation, Wilma decides that having to take a pill once a day for two months before conceiving is a bit too inconvenient and so chooses to throw the pills away and conceive at once. As a result of this choice, her child is born with a significant and irreversible disability. For purposes of the example as I will use it throughout this book, I will stipulate that Wilma's child is incurably blind and that had Wilma taken the pills before conceiving, her child would instead have been sighted. I use the example of blindness here both because blindness is one of the most commonly employed examples in the literature on the non-identity problem and because while blindness is widely believed to be a quite serious disability, it is never viewed as so serious that it could plausibly make a person's life worse than no life at all. Readers who are skeptical of the claim that blindness is a particularly bad condition to be in can simply assume that it is not the blindness itself that makes things substantially worse for Wilma's child but rather her society's treatment of blind people. Or, if they prefer, they can simply substitute some other condition for blindness in the discussion that follows. What matters here is simply that whatever condition Wilma's child has, it is one that has a substantially negative impact on the child's quality of life, that it nonetheless leaves her child with a life that is clearly worth living, and that had Wilma simply taken the pills for two months before conceiving, her child would not have had this condition and would have enjoyed a substantially higher quality of life as a result.

With this understanding of the case in mind, it seems clear to most people that Wilma has done something morally wrong. But there is a seemingly sound

---

[2] This case is loosely based on Parfit's Handicapped Child case (1982: 118).

argument that apparently demonstrates that what Wilma has done is not morally wrong. The argument begins by pointing out that if Wilma takes the pill once a day for two months before she conceives, the child she conceives will not be the same child as the child she would conceive if she instead threw the pills away and conceived at once. This is because the sperm and egg that would come together if she conceives two months from now would be different from the sperm and egg that would come together if she conceives now and because which particular person she conceives is a function of which particular sperm and egg come together at conception. For purposes of illustration, it may help to suppose that if Wilma conceives now, she will have a girl and name her Pebbles, and that if she takes the pill once a day for two months before conceiving she will instead have a boy and name him Rocks. It is not the case, then, that whatever choice Wilma makes the same child will exist and will either be blind or not blind. Rather, either Pebbles will exist and be blind, or Rocks will exist and will not be blind. And Rocks is not identical to Pebbles.

It is not immediately obvious that this non-identity feature of Wilma's choice situation is morally relevant. But the argument that gives rise to the non-identity problem, and which I will refer to in this book as the non-identity argument, maintains that it is morally relevant for the following reason: when Wilma chooses to conceive at once rather than take the pills once a day for two months before conceiving, her choice does not make Pebbles worse off than she would otherwise have been. If Wilma had waited two months before conceiving, after all, then she would not have conceived Pebbles in the first place. She would instead have conceived Rocks. And since the significant and irreversible disability that Pebbles is born with does not cause Pebbles to have a life that is worse for her than never having been conceived at all, it follows that Wilma's choice does not make Pebbles worse off than she would otherwise have been. I will call this first premise of the non-identity argument P1.

P1: Wilma's act of conceiving now rather than taking a pill once a day for two months before conceiving does not make Pebbles worse off than she would otherwise have been

This claim is the foundation of the argument that gives rise to the non-identity problem.

The argument conjoins to this claim what seems to be a commonsense understanding of what is required in order for an act to harm someone, namely: if your act harms someone, then it makes that person worse off than they would have been had you not done the act. That this is a widely accepted view seems to be confirmed by the fact that if a person is accused of harming someone, it is standardly taken as a sufficient rebuttal to the claim if they can establish that they have not made their alleged victim worse off than they would otherwise have been. This claim can be represented more formally as what I will call P2.

P2: If A's act harms B, then A's act makes B worse off than B would otherwise have been

And from P1 and P2 we get

C1: Wilma's act of conceiving now rather than taking a pill once a day for two months before conceiving does not harm Pebbles

The argument then adds a further stipulation: that Wilma's act does not harm anyone other than Pebbles either. In many real life cases, of course, the addition of a disabled child to the world may well impose costs on someone. Having another blind child in the classroom, for example, is likely to require additional resources and thus to raise the total costs that must be borne by the taxpayers. But adding this stipulation to the argument is reasonable nonetheless. When people respond to the case by thinking that Wilma's act is morally wrong, after all, they do not say to themselves, "Oh, the poor taxpayers; what a terrible thing that Wilma has done to them."[3] Nor, in deciding whether they believe that Wilma has done something morally wrong, do they first require information about whether Wilma's choice will impose unwanted costs on any other third parties. Since it seems clear that their belief that Wilma has done something wrong is independent of any beliefs they might have about whether Wilma's act harms anyone other than Pebbles, it seems clear that what people believe is not simply that Wilma has done something morally wrong, but that Wilma has done something morally wrong even if she has not harmed anyone else. It therefore proves useful to stipulate that Wilma's act has not harmed anyone else and to see whether this stipulation will prevent us from justifying the conclusion that her act was morally wrong. In short, we have reason to accept, even if only for the sake of the argument, what I will call P3.

P3: Wilma's act of conceiving now rather than taking a pill once a day for two months before conceiving does not harm anyone other than Pebbles

And from P3 and C1, it follows that

C2: Wilma's act of conceiving Pebbles does not harm anyone

At this stage of the argument, a basic moral principle is invoked, one that most people seem to accept. In its simplest form, it is the idea of "no harm, no foul," the thought that if an act harms no one, then the act is not wrong. For purposes of analysis, however, it is useful to break this claim down into two parts: the claim that if an act harms no one, then it wrongs no one, and the claim that if an act wrongs no one, then it is not morally wrong. The first part maintains that if an act does not harm a particular person then that person has no legitimate moral claim against the act's being done. The second maintains that if an act is such that no particular person has a legitimate moral claim against its being done, then it is not wrong to do the act. That the "no harm, no foul"

---

[3] Though see Cooley (2007) for the claim that intentionally conceiving a disabled child is morally wrong because of the burdens it imposes on the business community. See also Rakowski (2002: 1413–14) and Shapiro (1996).

principle is widely accepted seems amply confirmed by considering how commonly people accused of having done something wrong respond by trying to show that their act didn't harm anyone and by how frequently those who believe that the acts prohibited by so-called victimless crime laws are wrong attempt to show that the acts in question really do harm someone.

With this basic moral principle in mind, the non-identity argument concludes as follows. First, we set out the first part of the "no harm, no foul" principle in what I will call P4.

P4: If an act does not harm anyone, then the act does not wrong anyone

From P4 and C2 it follows that

C3: Wilma's act of conceiving Pebbles does not wrong anyone

The argument then adds the second part of the "no harm, no foul" principle, what I will call P5.

P5: If an act does not wrong anyone, then the act is not morally wrong

From P5 and C3 we are then entitled to conclude that

C4: Wilma's act of conceiving Pebbles is not morally wrong

Because the conclusion represented by C4 seems so implausible, I will refer to it in this book as the Implausible Conclusion. The premises seem right. The premises entail the Implausible Conclusion. The Implausible Conclusion seems wrong. That's the problem.

1.1.2 *The Indirect Version*

The case of Wilma involves a choice that directly determines which particular person will exist after the choice is made. For this reason, I will refer to the version of the non-identity problem that is illustrated by such cases as the direct version of the problem. But there can also be cases in which a choice has consequences that initiate a complex chain of events that eventually have an equally decisive effect on which particular people exist after the choice is made. I will refer to the version of the problem that is illustrated by such cases as the indirect version of the problem. Here is an example.[4] A wealthy society is running out of the fossil fuels that have made its affluence possible, and it is choosing between two sources of energy to replace them. One option is a source of energy that would enable its current citizens to continue to enjoy a high standard of living and which would have no negative impact on future generations. The second option is a source of energy that would enable its current citizens to enjoy a slightly higher standard of living but which would generate a significant amount of toxic waste. The waste could be safely buried for a long period of time, but it

---

[4] This example is based on Parfit's Risky Policy case (1984: 371–2).

is known that after five hundred years, the waste would leak out and that of the millions of people who would be exposed to it, tens of thousands would be painlessly killed as a result once they reached the age of forty. Because the first option would generate no toxic waste, I will refer to it as the safe policy. Because the second option would expose a large number of people to the risk of premature death when the toxic waste leaks out five hundred years later, I will refer to it as the risky policy.

Although the difference in terms of the quality of life that the two policies would make possible for the current members of this society is relatively minor, over time it is enough to have a significant impact on a variety of choices that indirectly determine which people will be conceived in the somewhat distant future. The choice of one energy source over the other, for example, will eventually have an impact on how many children people decide to have and on when they decide to have them. It will also have an impact on where people decide to work, play, and live, all of which will have an impact on who they meet and when they meet them, which will in turn have an impact on who they decide to have children with, on whether they decide to have any children at all, and so on. For purposes of the example, I will stipulate that over time, the effects of these subtle differences will be enough to generate two entirely distinct sets of people: the set of people who will exist five hundred years from now if the safe policy is selected, and the completely different set of people who will exist five hundred years from now if the risky policy is selected.

Knowing that the risky policy will generate toxic waste that will eventually leak and painlessly kill tens of thousands of innocent people in the future, the current members of the wealthy society nonetheless decide to select that option because doing so will enable them to enjoy a slightly higher quality of life. As a result of their choice, the toxic waste that they create and bury leaks out five hundred years later and painlessly kills tens of thousands of innocent people once they reach the age of forty.

As in the case of Wilma, it will seem clear to most people that the members of the wealthy society have done something morally wrong. But, again as in the case of Wilma, there is a seemingly sound argument that apparently demonstrates that what the wealthy society has done is not morally wrong. Indeed, it is essentially the same argument. The innocent people who are killed as a result of the leaking toxic waste are not made worse off by the wealthy society's choice of the risky policy because if the wealthy society had instead selected the safe policy, those innocent people would never have existed in the first place. And living for forty years and then being painlessly killed is not worse than never living at all. If harming a person requires making them worse off than they would otherwise have been, then the wealthy society's selection of the risky policy does not harm the people who are later killed by the leaking toxic waste. Since the choice of the risky policy seems morally wrong regardless of whether it harms anyone other than the people who are later killed by the toxic waste, it is reasonable to assume for the sake of the argument that no one else is harmed by the choice of the risky policy either. This means that the wealthy society's choice of the risky policy, like Wilma's choice to throw away the pills and conceive at once, harms no one at all.

But if, as in that case, an act that harms no one wrongs no one and an act that wrongs no one is not morally wrong, then the wealthy society's act of selecting the risky policy rather than the safe policy is not morally wrong either. The premises again seem right. The conclusion again seems wrong. This is the non-identity problem again, this time in its indirect version.

The distinction between the direct and indirect version of the non-identity problem is important to note at the outset because at least some of the solutions to the problem that have been proposed in the literature turn out to work better for one version of the problem than for the other. A solution that appeals to the special obligations that parents have to their own children, for example, may be promising in the case of the direct version of the problem but irrelevant to the indirect version.[5] A fully satisfactory response should enable us to solve both versions of the non-identity problem.[6] But even if a given proposal turns out to solve only one version of the problem, that will still be a significant accomplishment. In Chapters 2 through 6, I will argue that none of the alternatives to my solution can solve either version of the problem. In Chapter 7, I will argue that my solution solves both.

1.1.3 Same Number Cases and Different Number Cases

Two additional ways in which non-identity cases can differ from one another also merit attention. The first arises from the distinction between what Parfit calls "same number" and "different number" cases.[7] Wilma, for example, is choosing between conceiving a child now and conceiving a child two months from now. The world will therefore contain the same number of people regardless of which option she chooses. The only difference is whether that number will include Pebbles or Rocks. This makes the case of Wilma a same number case. But suppose that Wilma was instead choosing between conceiving blind twins now or a single sighted child two months from now. In that case, her choice would determine not just which people would exist in the future but how many people would exist. That would make the case a different number case.

The distinction between same number and different number cases can also be applied to the case of the wealthy society. When I refer to that case in the rest of this book, I will assume that no matter which of the two energy policies the wealthy society chooses, in five hundred years the earth will contain ten billion people. The difference will be which ten billion people will exist and whether tens of thousands of them will be killed by leaking toxic waste when they turn forty. This makes the case of the

---

[5] See, e.g., section 2.2.

[6] In saying this, I do not mean to suggest that a fully satisfactory response must apply the same solution to both versions of the problem. A hybrid response that identifies one solution that solves the direct version and a second and distinct solution that solves the indirect version would still be fully satisfactory. But the point remains that the distinction between the two versions of the problem matters because if a particular solution only works on one version of the problem, the solution by itself cannot constitute a fully satisfactory response to the non-identity problem.

[7] Parfit (1984: 356).

wealthy society a same number case as well. But we could instead suppose, for example, that if the wealthy society chooses the safe policy there will be ten billion people five hundred years from now and no leaking toxic waste and that if it chooses the risky policy there will be more than ten billion people five hundred years from now, tens of thousands of whom will be killed by leaking toxic waste. That would make the case a different number case.

The distinction between same number and different number cases is important for the same reason that the distinction between the direct version of the non-identity problem and the indirect version is important: some solutions turn out to work better in one kind of case than in the other. Different number cases, in particular, introduce complications that are not present in same number cases. A consequentialist solution that explains why it would be wrong for Wilma to conceive a blind child rather than a sighted child, for example, might not be able to produce satisfactory results in the case where Wilma chooses between conceiving blind twins and conceiving a sighted child.[8] As in the case of the distinction between the direct and indirect versions of the non-identity problem, a fully satisfactory response to the problem should produce satisfactory results in both same number and different number cases. But, again as in the case of that distinction, if a given proposal turns out to solve only the same number version of the problem, that will still be a significant accomplishment. In Chapters 2 through 6, I will argue that none of the alternatives to my solution is successful even in same number cases. Since a solution to the non-identity problem cannot succeed in different number cases if it cannot succeed in the simpler same number cases, I will not explicitly discuss different number cases in those chapters. In Chapter 7, I will argue not only that my solution solves both the direct and the indirect version of the non-identity problem, but that it is successful in both same number cases and different number cases.

1.1.4   Bad Condition Cases and Bad Event Cases

A final distinction is less frequently noted in the literature. This is the difference between cases that involve the creation of people who are already in bad conditions and cases that involve the creation of people to whom bad things subsequently happen. If Wilma makes the choice that is a bit better for her, she will conceive a child who is blind rather than a different child who would have been sighted. Blindness, we are assuming, is a bad condition to be in, but we need not assume that any bad things will subsequently happen to her blind child as a result of Wilma conceiving her that wouldn't also have happened to her sighted child if she had conceived him instead. If the current members of the wealthy society make the choice that is a bit better for them, then five hundred years later there will exist a particular set of ten billion people rather than a different set of ten billion other people. None of the ten billion people who exist will

---

[8] See, e.g., section 6.1.

be in a bad condition as a result of the wealthy society's choosing the risky policy. But tens of thousands of them will subsequently be killed by the leaking toxic waste when they reach the age of forty, while no one would have been subsequently killed by leaking toxic waste if the wealthy society had chosen the safe policy. The case of Wilma is therefore a bad condition case while the case of the wealthy society is a bad event case.[9]

Most examples of the direct version of the non-identity problem in the literature involve bad condition cases and most examples of the indirect version involve bad event cases. But there is no necessary connection between the two distinctions. Suppose that the leaking toxic waste in the case of the wealthy society would not kill tens of thousands of people in the future, but would instead alter the time at which the people exposed to it later conceived and cause them to conceive blind children rather than sighted children. In that case, the wealthy society example would be a bad condition case rather than a bad event case. Similarly, if Wilma's conceiving now rather than two months from now would have no effect on the health of the child she would conceive but would somehow cause Wilma's body to produce a toxic substance that would leak out decades later and inevitably kill her grown child, then the case of Wilma would be a bad event case rather than a bad condition case.

The difference between bad condition cases and bad event cases, then, is indeed an additional distinction. And it is important for the same reason that the distinction

---

[9] Strictly speaking, the non-identity problem could arise in cases that are neither bad condition cases nor bad event cases. Suppose, for example, that if Wilma conceives now her child will be perfectly typical in every respect but that if she takes the pill once a day for two months before conceiving, her child will be extraordinary in ways that will lead him to live a much better life than the life of a typical person. In this case, if Wilma conceives now she does not create a child in a bad condition or a child to whom bad things will happen, but she still makes things significantly worse for her child than they would have been if she had waited. And this seems to be enough to generate the non-identity problem.

While the distinction between bad condition cases and bad event cases is therefore not exhaustive, I will set aside these further sorts of cases for two reasons. First, while the claim that Wilma's act is not morally wrong in the original version of the story strikes most people as highly implausible, the claim that her act is not morally wrong in this version of the story strikes many people as perfectly plausible and indeed true. So while the non-identity argument entails that Wilma's act is not morally wrong in the revised version of the story just as it does in the original version, it is less clear that its having this implication generates a serious problem in the revised version. Second, while there are solutions to the non-identity problem that might work in bad condition cases but not apply to bad event cases and solutions that might work in bad event cases but not apply to bad condition cases, it is hard to imagine a solution that would work in this further kind of case without working in more typical cases. It therefore requires no separate consideration.

Finally, it might seem that there could be significantly more worrisome examples that are neither bad condition cases nor bad event cases. Suppose, for example, that we adopt a policy that leads people in the future to have a much lower quality of life than they would otherwise have even though they do not suffer from any bad conditions like blindness and our act does not cause any bad events to happen to them like being killed by leaking toxic waste. In this case, unlike the modified version of the Wilma case, most people would probably agree that our act was morally wrong and that the case therefore generated a genuine problem. I am inclined to think that such cases should be considered as a version of the bad condition case. If people are born into a world with problematically limited resources, for example, then this should be viewed as a bad condition to be born into even if it is a condition of the world and not of their bodies. But even if this does represent a genuinely problematic non-identity case that is neither a bad condition case nor a bad event case, the point remains that there is no reason to consider it independently because any solution that would work in typical cases would work in this case as well.

between the direct and indirect version and between same number and different number cases is important: some solutions turn out to work better in one kind of case than in the other. An account on which your act can harm someone by causing them to incur a loss even if the act does not make them worse off than they would otherwise have been, for example, may prove successful in bad event cases but inapplicable to bad condition cases.[10] As in the case of the distinctions between the direct and indirect version and between same number and different number cases, a fully satisfactory response to the non-identity problem should produce satisfactory results in both bad condition cases and bad event cases. But, again as in the case of those other distinctions, if a given proposal turns out to solve only one version of the problem, that will still be a significant accomplishment. In Chapters 2 through 6, I will argue that none of the alternatives to my solution is successful in bad condition cases or in bad event cases. In Chapter 7, I will argue not only that my solution solves both the direct and indirect version of the non-identity problem and that it is successful in both same number cases and different number cases, but that it is also successful in both bad condition cases and bad event cases.

In the end, then, there are eight kinds of case that can give rise to the non-identity problem: direct same number bad condition cases, direct same number bad event cases, direct different number bad condition cases, direct different number bad event cases, indirect same number bad condition cases, indirect same number bad event cases, indirect different number bad condition cases, and indirect different number bad event cases. The thesis of this book is that the solutions to the non-identity problem that are currently on offer fail to solve the problem in any of these kinds of cases and that my alternative solution satisfactorily solves the problem in all of them.

1.1.5 Worseness and Wrongness

Before moving on to consider what would be involved in trying to solve the non-identity problem in any of these cases, it is important to make one final point about just what the problem is supposed to be. I will put the point here in terms of the example of Wilma, but the same could be said about the case of the wealthy society or about any of the variants of either of these cases that I referred to in the previous two subsections. So notice first that in the case of Wilma, there are two distinct claims about her choice that an argument based on the non-identity of Pebbles and Rocks might attempt to force us to accept:

The Worseness Claim: Wilma does not make the morally worse choice
The Wrongness Claim: Wilma does not make a morally wrong choice

In some contexts, these two claims would be coextensive. Suppose that Wilma's choice was between killing a bunch of innocent people and not killing a bunch of innocent people. In that case, if she killed a bunch of innocent people, she would make

---

[10] See, e.g., section 3.2.

the morally worse choice and she would make a morally wrong choice. But it is not obvious that every time someone makes the morally worse choice they thereby make a morally wrong choice. If there are, as commonsense morality supposes, acts that are supererogatory, then there are acts that it is morally better to do than not to do but that are nonetheless not wrong not to do. A person who chooses not to do a supererogatory act rather than to do one, on this account, makes the morally worse choice, but does not make a morally wrong choice. If donating a kidney to a needy stranger would be supererogatory, for example, then choosing not to donate a kidney to a needy stranger would be morally worse than choosing to donate one but it would not be positively immoral.

Since making the morally worse choice and making a morally wrong choice need not amount to the same thing, it is important to be clear about what, precisely, the problematic claim is that the non-identity argument is supposed to force us to accept. Is the Implausible Conclusion that generates the problem supposed to claim that Wilma's act is not morally wrong? Or is it supposed to claim that Wilma's act is not morally worse than the alternative? Is the non-identity problem a problem about worseness or a problem about wrongness?

Parfit's discussion in *Reasons and Persons* is not entirely clear on this point.[11] In the context of one of the cases he discusses, for example, he says that the problem is that we think the potential mother in question "ought" to wait and conceive later.[12] In other places, he says that we would have an "objection" to her choice not to wait to conceive.[13] These locutions seem more like the kind of thing we would say if we thought it would be positively immoral for the woman to conceive now than the kind of thing we would say if we merely thought it would be better for her to wait, though strictly speaking they seem consistent with either view.[14] At still other points, he simply says that she would have a moral reason to wait. This seems more like simply saying that it would be morally better for her to wait, though it is consistent with the view that it would be positively immoral for her not to do so.

But when he identifies a principle that he thinks might be able to ground a partial solution to the problem, the principle that Parfit introduces is cashed out in terms of worseness rather than in terms of wrongness. This is what Parfit calls "The Same Number Quality Claim" or simply Q: "If in either of two possible outcomes the same number of people would ever live, it would be *worse* if those who live are worse off, or have a lower quality of life, than those who would have lived."[15] Parfit writes that although

Q is plausible, it does not solve the Non-Identity Problem. Q covers only the cases where, in the different outcomes, the same number of people would ever live. We need a claim that covers cases where, in the different outcomes, different numbers would ever live. The Non-Identity Problem can arise in these cases.[16]

---

[11] In subsequent correspondence with the author (August 18, 2011), Parfit clarifies that he intended to claim that it is a problem in both senses.

[12] Parfit (1984: 358).   [13] Parfit (e.g. 1984: 359).   [14] See also Parfit (1982: 117, 119).

[15] Parfit (1984: 360, emphasis added).   [16] Parfit (1984: 361).

Although he does not explicitly claim that Q does solve the non-identity problem in same number cases, this claim is implied by the fact that the only reason he gives for saying that Q does not solve the problem across the board is that it does not apply to different number cases. Since Q makes a claim about worseness but not about wrongness, Q could solve the non-identity problem in same number cases only if the problem is avoiding the Worseness Claim. It could not solve the non-identity problem in same number cases if the problem is avoiding the Wrongness Claim because Q does not say anything about wrongness. This strongly suggests, though again does not strictly entail, that Parfit thinks of the problem in terms of worseness rather than in terms of wrongness.

Perhaps Parfit does not think there is an important difference here. But this would be a mistake. The non-identity argument poses a problem because it generates a conclusion that strikes most people as implausible from premises that strike most people as plausible. To the extent that commonsense moral beliefs oppose both the claim that Wilma does not make the morally worse choice and the claim that Wilma does not make a morally wrong choice, an argument for either claim would suffice to pose a serious problem. But while the argument presented in section 1.1.1 makes clear how one can seem to be forced into accepting the Wrongness Claim by arguing only from premises that strike most people as quite plausible, there is no parallel argument for accepting the Worseness Claim.[17] In order for an argument to convince us that the Worseness Claim was true, we would have to replace the "no harm, no foul" principle embodied by P4 and P5 of the non-identity argument with something importantly different. Instead of saying that if the choice of one act over another harms no one, then the act is not morally wrong, the argument would have to depend on the claim that if the choice of one act over another harms no one, then the act is not the morally worse of the two choices. But the latter claim, unlike the former claim, is not a part of commonsense morality. Indeed, commonsense morality clearly rejects it. As already noted, commonsense morality recognizes the category of supererogatory acts. If such acts exist, then there are many cases in which you can choose between two acts, neither of which harms anyone and neither of which is morally wrong, but one of which is nonetheless morally better than the other. And if one act is morally better than the other, then the other act must be morally worse.

While commonsense morality in ordinary cases does seem to endorse the claim that if the choice of one act over another harms no one then the choice is not morally wrong, then, it does not endorse the claim that if the choice of one act over another harms no one then it is not the morally worse of the two available choices. The

---

[17] This is not to say that there are no interesting arguments for the Worseness Claim. Some people have argued, for example, that one state of affairs cannot be worse than another unless it is worse for some particular person. This claim might be used to support the conclusion that the state of affairs in which Wilma conceives Pebbles is not worse than the state of affairs in which she conceives Rocks, which could in turn be used to support the claim that Wilma's act is not morally worse than the alternative that was available to her. But while this argument merits investigation, it is not a version of the non-identity argument.

non-identity argument can generate the non-identity problem, therefore, only when it is construed as an argument against the apparent wrongness of Wilma's choice, not as an argument against its apparent worseness. For the purposes of this book, then, this is how the non-identity problem will be understood.[18] When I refer to the Implausible Conclusion that gives rise to the problem, I will mean the claim that Wilma's act is not morally wrong, not the claim that Wilma does not make the morally worse choice. Indeed, for the purposes of this book, I will simply concede that it would have been morally better for Wilma to have waited and conceived Rocks. The problem is that even if we agree that it would have been better if she had waited, we seem unable to justify the claim that she did something positively immoral by failing to do so. And most people seem to think not only that Wilma could have made a better choice, but that her failing to do so was morally wrong.

To say that the non-identity problem is a problem about wrongness and not a problem about worseness, it is worth adding, is not to say that the presumed worseness of Wilma's choice cannot be used to account for its presumed wrongness. There are a number of ways in which we might try to show that Wilma's act is wrong by appealing to a principle on which an act is wrong because it produces a worse outcome. These approaches to solving the non-identity problem will be considered in Chapter 6. Rather, it is to say that the problem that such an argument would have to solve is the problem of accounting for the wrongness of Wilma's act, not the problem of accounting for its worseness. It is not the belief that Wilma's act is worse than the alternative that was available to her that gives rise to the non-identity problem. It is the belief that Wilma's act is morally wrong.

1.2 Why the Problem Matters

At this point, some readers may already be convinced that the non-identity problem is important. But other readers may not. They may agree that the argument that gives rise to the problem is interesting, but they may find themselves inclined to think of it more as a clever puzzle than as a serious matter worthy of sustained philosophical investigation. None of us, after all, seems likely to find ourselves in the position that Wilma or the wealthy society find themselves in. And the circumstances involved in the cases may seem so contrived that nothing larger turns on how we respond to them. So it might be thought that we have no reason to be concerned by the apparent difficulty of accounting for the presumed moral wrongness of the choices that Wilma and the wealthy society make. Before subjecting the non-identity problem to a sustained

---

[18] I will therefore set aside any proposed solutions to the problem that construe the problem exclusively in terms of worseness. Rachels, for example, attempts to solve the problem by appealing to a particular principle of hedonic well-being on which it would be "hedonically better" for Wilma to wait and conceive Rocks than to conceive Pebbles (2001: 221). But this response would solve the problem only if the problem were the problem of accounting for the claim that conceiving Pebbles is the worse choice. And the real problem is that of accounting for the claim that it is positively immoral for Wilma to make that choice.

philosophical investigation, then, it is worth saying a few words about why the significance of the problem cannot be so easily dismissed.

1.2.1 Practical Applications

One reason that the non-identity problem is important is that despite its esoteric appearance, it has a direct bearing on a number of important moral dilemmas that confront us in the real world. One hotly contested topic in the area of bioethics, for example, concerns the moral status of research that aims to develop the ability to successfully clone human beings. Virtually all of the arguments against the moral permissibility of conducting such research have the following general structure: if a human clone is produced, this will cause significant negative consequences for the clone, and the causing of these significant negative consequences renders it morally wrong to attempt to produce the clone for whom the consequences would be negative. A common version of this argument maintains that evidence from non-human mammalian cloning shows that many of the human beings who would be produced by cloning would have serious physical disabilities.[19] Other versions point to the psychological difficulties that clones would likely encounter as a result of the unusual family dynamics they would almost certainly confront or because of the anxieties they would likely experience about their individuality and identity.[20]

But none of these arguments against the development of human cloning technology maintains that the life of a clone would be so bad that it would be worse than no life at all. And assuming that it would not be worse than no life at all, the non-identity problem threatens to undermine all of these arguments against cloning research at once.[21] A couple that was choosing between producing a child by cloning or by natural reproduction, after all, would be in a position that was relevantly similar to that of Wilma. If they decided to clone and, as a result, created a disabled child rather than a child who

---

[19] See, e.g., Kass (2001: 683–4), the President's Council on Bioethics (2002: 89–93).

[20] See, e.g., Kass (2001: 684), the President's Council on Bioethics (2002: 101–4).

[21] Greene (2004) makes this point at least in the case of the arguments based on psychological harm. See also Roberts (1998: 179–216), Burley and Harris (1999), and, more briefly, Elsner (2006: 597–8) and Lane (2006: 129–31). Relatedly, Heller (1998) argues that the non-identity problem undermines those arguments against cloning based on traditional Christian principles that are grounded in a concern for the well-being of the resulting clone. To say that the non-identity problem undermines the major arguments against cloning is not to insist that as long as the problem remains unsolved we must conclude that developing human cloning technology is not wrong. There may be other arguments against cloning that are not affected by the problem. In addition, one could argue that in the absence of a consensus about how to solve the problem, we should adhere to a kind of precautionary principle that would err on the side of not engaging in cloning. Davidson argues for this kind of approach in the case of applying the non-identity problem to the subject of climate change in particular: even if our failing to reduce carbon emissions is relevantly similar to the wealthy society's choosing the risky policy, and even if we have no good response to the non-identity argument's claim that it is not wrong for the wealthy society to choose the risky policy, we should nonetheless adhere to an approach "in which climate damage is treated *as if* it were a wrongful harm to future generations" (2008: 482). Since the appeal to such a precautionary principle offers guidance in the absence of a consensus about how to solve the problem rather than a solution to the problem itself, I will not consider the merits of this approach here.

was not disabled, for example, the disabled child would not be made worse off by their choice than it would otherwise have been because if they had decided to conceive by natural reproduction rather than by cloning, the disabled child would not have existed at all. Some other child would have existed instead and that other child would not have been disabled. The argument that seems to show that Wilma's act is not morally wrong would therefore seem to show that their act was not morally wrong either. And if their act would not be morally wrong, then the most common arguments against permitting the development of human reproductive cloning technology would have to be rejected.

Cloning research represents one instance in which the direct version of the non-identity problem has important practical implications. There are many others. Couples are often urged to undergo genetic screening before they attempt to conceive, for example. But at least in cases where the genetic conditions in question would clearly leave any child they might conceive with a life that is not worse than no life at all, the common belief that it would be wrong for them not to undergo such screening is threatened in the same way that the arguments against developing human cloning technology are threatened. If failing to undergo genetic screening leads the couple to conceive a child with such a defect, after all, their failure will not have made the child worse off because if they had instead undergone the screening and acted on it, that child would not have existed in the first place.[22]

A recent study of in vitro fertilization, to take one more biotechnological example, reports that 3 percent of the clinics that perform the procedure have allowed prospective parents to use genetic screening to select in favor of deliberately implanting embryos with a selected for disability, with deafness in cases of deaf parents apparently being the most common example.[23] Most people believe that it is immoral for parents to deliberately create a deaf child when they could easily create a hearing child instead,[24] but the non-identity problem threatens to undermine their position as well. The parents who deliberately create a deaf child rather than a hearing child in this manner,

---

[22] This result might also generate constitutional problems for laws that would prevent couples from conceiving in such circumstances (see, e.g., Dillard (2010a)). Relatedly, McCarthy (2001: 304) applies the non-identity problem to the controversy over sex selection and argues that the practice can't be opposed on the grounds that it is bad for the resulting child because the resulting child would not otherwise have existed. Delaney (2011) applies the problem to the controversy over genetic enhancement and argues that the considerations that give rise to the non-identity problem can be used to justify the claim that genetically enhancing a person who would otherwise exist as an ordinary person without the enhancement can be wrong in cases where selecting a particular sperm and egg in order to create a person with precisely the same genetic characteristics would not be wrong. And Cohen argues that the non-identity problem raises problems for those arguments for prohibiting sperm-donor anonymity that depend on the claim that children are harmed by being deprived of information about their genetic parents (2011: 461–5; 2012: 435–42; 2013: 46–7).

[23] Smolensky (2008: 300). See also Spriggs (2002) for an account of, and reactions to, a deaf couple who successfully worked to find a deaf sperm donor so that they could conceive a deaf child. Anstey (2002) argues against both selecting for and selecting against deafness.

[24] Jonathan Glover, for example, refers to "screening to ensure that only a disabled child would be conceived" as "monstrous" (2007: 438).

after all, do not make that child worse off than that child would otherwise have been.[25] Indeed, depending on one's view of personal identity, the non-identity problem could also threaten to undermine the claim that it would be wrong to genetically manipulate an embryo after it was selected in order to cause that particular embryo to develop into a disabled child rather than into a non-disabled child.[26]

The features that give rise to the direct version of the non-identity problem in cases involving genetic screening, in vitro fertilization, and cloning research, moreover, appear in a variety of more mundane contexts. A number of women have chosen to become single mothers in recent years, for example, prompting a common complaint that their acts are immoral because children are better off being raised by two parents rather than one.[27] Opponents of same-sex couples who become parents through pregnancy or surrogacy arrangements typically object that children are better off with a mother and a father rather than with two of one and none of the other.[28] Elderly men who become fathers are often criticized because they will not be around long enough to play a meaningful role in their children's lives. Older women who try to conceive are frequently subject to the same kind of criticism, along with the additional concern that older women are more likely to give birth to children with birth defects such as Down syndrome.[29] Indeed, some countries have prohibited or restricted fertility treatments for older women for precisely this reason.[30] Girls who become mothers at a very young

---

[25] For this reason, Smolensky argues that disabled children who are brought into existence in this manner should not be allowed to later sue their parents for damages (2008: 301, 321, 335–6, 344). See also Pattinson (1999: 23–6). Similarly, Taylor (2010: 81–2) uses the non-identity problem to undermine the case for a legal prohibition on making such choices. Lillehammer (2005: 34–7) offers a tentative defense of the claim that such choices are not morally wrong, at least in the case of deafness, though for objections to Lillehammer's argument, see Shaw (2008). Fahmy (2011) does not quite defend the moral permissibility of the practice but she does argue that it is difficult to identify a satisfactory argument against it. And Hope and McMillan (2012: 22–4, 27–9) argue that even though the choice that parents make in such cases may well be wrong, the non-identity problem still establishes that their doctors should accede to their wishes since it shows that their choice does not harm anyone and since doctors should respect patient autonomy in such cases (though for a pointed response to their argument, see Roberts (2012)).

[26] Smolensky (2008) argues that the non-identity problem does not apply in such cases on the grounds that the same person will be born regardless of whether the genes of the developing embryo are manipulated. If that is the case, then the child is harmed by being caused to be disabled rather than not disabled. See Cohen (2008: 351–9) for a skeptical response to Smolensky on this point. If personal identity is a function of a person's precise genetic makeup, then even a relatively minor genetic alteration of the embryo might be enough to result in a different person's being born. And if that is the case, the non-identity problem will arise after all: tampering with the embryo to cause a disability will not harm the person who is born because that person would not have existed had the genetic manipulation not taken place. Hammond (2010: 163–5) also considers how the non-identity problem might apply to cases involving genetic manipulation.

[27] Bernstein notes that the non-identity problem threatens to undermine this kind of argument against single motherhood (2006: 225 n. 208). See also Wax (1996: 530–3).

[28] Robertson (2004: 332–3, 345–7) and Trent (2006: 1162–3) note how the non-identity problem threatens to undermine this kind of position.

[29] Relatedly, Goold and Savulescu (2009: 55–6) show that the non-identity problem weakens arguments against the practice of allowing healthy young women to have their eggs frozen for later use when those arguments appeal to claims about potential harm to the resulting children.

[30] France, for example, prohibited post-menopausal pregnancies in 1994, and the British woman who gave birth to twins at the age of sixty in a highly publicized case had to go to Italy to receive fertility treatment because her case was rejected by a British ethics committee (Fisher and Sommerville (1998: 218)). De Wert

age are often criticized because they will not be able to give their children as good an upbringing as they could provide if they waited until they were older.[31] Religious people are often told that it is wrong to marry outside of their faith at least in part because it is confusing for children to be raised in a household where two religions are practiced rather than one. Similar considerations are sometimes raised as arguments against marrying outside one's racial or ethnic group. And prohibitions against incest are frequently defended on the grounds that incestuous partners are more likely to conceive children with disabilities.[32] None of these is an unusual or exotic case. Many of them are quite familiar. And in all of them, the common argument for the wrongness of the choice in question is an argument for the wrongness of creating a child whose life is not worse than no life at all and who would not exist if the choice had not been made. The argument that seems to show that Wilma's act is not morally wrong therefore seems to show that none of these acts is morally wrong either. Indeed, the more one reflects on the fragility of the circumstances that lead to any particular act of conception, the more one sees the non-identity problem as virtually ubiquitous in cases involving even the most ordinary reproductive decisions.

On the plausible assumption that at least some non-human animals have at least some moral standing, moreover, the direct version of the non-identity problem also turns out to be of practical importance in resolving a number of debates about how it is permissible to treat them. Many popular arguments against various forms of animal breeding, for example, or against developing the technology to produce hybrids of different animal species, turn on the claim that the techniques are, or would be, bad for the animals that result from their employment. But, at least in cases where the animals in question have lives that are clearly not worse than no life at all, such arguments again run into the same problem that arises in the case of Wilma. If the use of a particular contested breeding technique results in the existence of a less happy animal than would otherwise have been produced, the technique still will not have harmed that less happy animal because if the technique had not been used, the less happy animal would not have existed in the first place.[33] As in the case of human beings, the problem can arise in the context of advanced reproductive technology but, again as in the case of human beings, the problem can also arise in more mundane contexts. A number of people have criticized those who breed bulldogs, for example, on the grounds that bulldogs have been bred to select for features that cause them to suffer from a variety of health problems. But someone who breeds bulldogs rather than golden retrievers does not make the bulldogs worse off than they would otherwise have been because if the breeder had bred golden retrievers instead, the bulldogs would not have existed at all.

argues that the "welfare of the prospective child" provides "compelling reasons" not to provide fertility treatment to couples over sixty (1998: 237).

[31] See Parfit (1984: 358–9).

[32] Peters (2009: 329) notes the connection between the non-identity problem and prohibitions on incestuous marriage. See also Chambers (2009: 146 n. 39) and Cohen (2011: 447–8).

[33] See, e.g., Streiffer (2008), Palmer (2011).

The story about the wealthy society may seem even more far-fetched than the story about Wilma. And so it may seem that the indirect version of the non-identity problem is practically irrelevant even if the direct version is not. But even the indirect version of the non-identity problem turns out to have important implications about a number of controversial moral issues. The problem can be applied, for example, to questions about our obligations to conserve resources now, or to reduce carbon emissions, on behalf of distant generations.[34] It can even arise in such mundane contexts as debates over tax policy. Many people think that significantly lowering tax rates for ourselves is wrong when doing so passes a greater tax burden along to future generations. But since significantly lowering our tax rates would predictably change people's behavior in ways that would over time lead to the conception of different people, the future people who would pay higher taxes as a result of our choice would not otherwise exist and so would not be harmed by our passing a greater tax burden on to future generations rather than a lesser burden.[35]

And the indirect version of the problem creates important difficulties when we attempt to answer questions about obligations that we might have to rectify injustices that were committed in the past. Consider, for example, the question of whether the United States owes reparations to the current generation of black Americans because of the injustices that were committed against earlier generations of black Americans through the institutions of slavery and Jim Crow. One of the most forceful arguments in defense of reparations appeals to the claim that contemporary black Americans suffer lingering negative consequences as a result of these earlier wrongful actions. But on the assumption that the lives of contemporary black Americans are nonetheless not worse than no life at all, the indirect version of the non-identity problem threatens to undermine this argument in the same way that the direct version threatens to undermine the arguments against developing human cloning technology.[36] A descendant of slaves who makes a claim for reparations, after all, is not worse off than he would have been had slavery never been practiced. Had slavery never been practiced, his ancestors would not have conceived at the same time, with the same people, and in the same numbers, and so had slavery never been practiced, the descendant of slaves would not exist at all. Even if one insists that an intellectual puzzle must have significant practical

[34] See, e.g., Parfit (1984: 361–4), Vanderheiden (2006), and Page (2006: 132–60). Similarly, see Crespi (2007, 2008) for an application of the non-identity problem to the morality of disposing of radioactive waste by dumping it in the ocean. Relatedly, Crespi (2010a) argues that the non-identity problem also renders the ongoing debate over the social discount rate largely irrelevant. And Crespi (2010b) argues convincingly that the non-identity problem also wreaks havoc with the ability to apply traditional techniques of cost-benefit analysis to identity-affecting policy decisions. The analysis of such cases in the familiar terms of how much the future people would be willing to pay to enjoy the benefits or to avoid the burdens of a particular social policy is undermined when whether the future people in question will exist in the first place depends on which policy is selected.

[35] For a similar point about the difficulties posed by the non-identity problem for assessing the effects on future generations of fiscal policy more generally, see Doran (2008: 264–5).

[36] See, e.g., Boonin (2011: 106–9), Meyer (2006: 407–10).

implications in order for it to be worth taking the time to try to resolve it, then, trying to solve the non-identity problem is well worth the trouble.

1.2.2 Theoretical Implications

But let's suppose that I have been mistaken about this and that the non-identity problem has no bearing at all on any issue of practical significance. Suppose, for example, that there turn out to be morally relevant differences between the cases of Wilma and the wealthy society on the one hand and all of the issues of practical consequence that I have referred to on the other. Even if this is so, the non-identity problem is still of great significance. This is because even if it puts no pressure on any of our beliefs about actual practical matters, it puts a great deal of pressure on some of our most widely accepted theoretical beliefs. And we cannot ignore a challenge to our theoretical beliefs merely because the challenge leaves our practical beliefs intact. If it turned out that a set of widely accepted beliefs jointly entailed that it would be permissible to kill human beings as long as they were over ten feet tall, for example, the fact that no human beings are over ten feet tall would do nothing to blunt the force of the thought that something was seriously wrong with at least one of those widely accepted beliefs and that it would be important to determine which of those beliefs it was.

Suppose, then, that no one will ever be in Wilma's position or in any position relevantly similar to it. But suppose also that theoretical beliefs that you currently accept entail that it would not be morally wrong to make the choice that Wilma makes if anyone ever did find themselves in Wilma's position. And suppose further that you agree that this result is quite implausible. In that case, you have good reason to worry about your theoretical beliefs. And that is the position that most people find themselves in when they first encounter the non-identity problem.

The theoretical beliefs that are thrown into question, moreover, are far from trivial. If we are right in thinking that Wilma acts immorally, then we must be wrong about what it is for a condition to make a person worse off, wrong about the relationship between making a person worse off and harming a person, wrong about the relationship between harming a person and wronging a person, or wrong about the relationship between wronging a person and doing something wrong. Any one of these would represent a significant mistake. If we are making one of them, it is thus an important matter to determine which one it is. And so solving the non-identity problem would remain an important theoretical task even if it were not also an important practical one.

1.3 Requirements for Solving the Problem

The non-identity problem arises because five plausible premises entail what I have called the Implausible Conclusion. Since if all five premises are true the Implausible Conclusion must be true as well, the only way to avoid the Implausible Conclusion would be to reject at least one of the premises. A successful solution to the non-identity problem, it therefore seems, must give us a reason to reject one of the premises of the non-identity argument. But not just any kind of reason for rejecting a premise will do. There are, in particular, three constraints that such a reason must satisfy in order for it to be capable of grounding a satisfactory solution to the non-identity problem.

1.3.1 The Independence Requirement

First, the reason provided for rejecting a given premise of the non-identity argument must be independent of the fact that rejecting the premise would enable us to avoid the Implausible Conclusion. I will refer to this as the independence requirement. P2, for example, maintains that in order for an act to harm a person, the act must make that person worse off than they would otherwise have been. One way to justify rejecting this premise would be to provide a counterexample: a case in which it was clear that a given act did harm a particular person but also clear that the act did not make that person worse off than they would have been had the act not occurred. A number of possible cases of this sort will be considered in Chapter 3. If any of them prove successful, they will provide a reason to reject P2 that in no way depends on the fact that rejecting P2 would enable us to avoid the Implausible Conclusion. The reason would be a good reason to reject P2, that is, even if P2 played no role in generating the non-identity problem. It would therefore satisfy the independence requirement. But suppose instead that someone denied P2, admitted that they could find no plausible counterexample to it, and offered as a reason for rejecting P2 the fact that if P2 is false then we can avoid the conclusion that Wilma's act is not morally wrong. In that case, the reason given for rejecting P2 would depend on the fact that we wish to avoid the Implausible Conclusion. It would therefore fail to satisfy the independence requirement.

The independence requirement imposes a reasonable constraint on a satisfactory solution to the non-identity problem because any reason for rejecting a particular premise that fails to satisfy the requirement fails to give a reason to reject that premise in particular. The fact that rejecting P2 would enable us to avoid the Implausible Conclusion, for example, gives us no reason to reject P2 rather than P1, because it is equally true that rejecting P1 would enable us to avoid the Implausible Conclusion, and it is true for the same reason: that doing so would deprive the non-identity argument of one of its premises. A solution to the non-identity problem must do more than simply tell us to reject some premise or other of the non-identity argument. To note that one of the premises of the argument must be rejected in order to avoid the Implausible Conclusion is simply to state the fact that gives rise to the problem, not to solve the problem. A solution to the problem must tell us which particular premise to reject if the solution is going to help us to avoid the Implausible Conclusion. And no reason for rejecting a premise that fails to satisfy the independence requirement can do this.

A reason for rejecting a premise that does satisfy the independence requirement, moreover, can ground a successful solution to the non-identity problem precisely because it can reveal just where the flaw in the non-identity argument lies. If there really is a convincing counterexample to the claim that harming a person requires making that person worse off than they would otherwise have been, for example, then that counterexample provides a reason to reject P2 in particular, not simply a reason to reject some premise of the non-identity argument or other. And if there is a good reason to reject P2 in particular, then there is a good reason to reject the argument that gives rise to the Implausible Conclusion.

1.3.2 The Robustness Requirement

In order to underwrite a successful solution to the non-identity problem, then, a reason for rejecting a given premise of the non-identity argument must be independent of the fact that rejecting the premise would enable us to avoid the Implausible Conclusion. But while a reason's being independent in this sense is necessary in order for it to solve the non-identity problem, it is not sufficient. Even if a reason is good enough to justify rejecting one of the argument's premises, it might not be good enough to justify rejecting the argument's conclusion. This is because some of the premises of the non-identity argument might turn out to be stronger than they have to be in order to justify the argument's conclusion.

P4, for example, maintains that if an act does not harm a person, then the act does not wrong that person. Suppose that there turn out to be cases in which attempting to harm a person wrongs that person even if the attempt to harm the person fails. If this is so, then there are counterexamples that provide an independent reason to conclude that P4 is false. But while the wrongness of failed attempts to harm people would be enough to show that P4 is false, it would not be enough to show that it is, as it were, false enough. This is because there is no reason to think that Wilma's act involves a failed attempt to harm Pebbles or anyone else. The proposed counterexample to P4, that is, could be accommodated simply by revising P4 to say that if an act neither harms anyone nor involves attempting to harm anyone, then the act does not wrong anyone. And the route from this revised version of P4 and the original versions of the other premises of the non-identity argument to the Implausible Conclusion could be preserved simply by adding a further premise to the non-identity argument pointing out that Wilma's act does not involve attempting to harm anyone either.

A proponent of a solution based on the proposed counterexample to P4 might refuse to accept the further premise. Such a critic might simply stipulate that in choosing to conceive now rather than take the pills once a day for two months, Wilma was attempting unsuccessfully to harm her child. Perhaps Wilma had not taken the time to consider the fact that delaying conception would cause her to conceive a different child and so acted on the mistaken belief that by conceiving now she could make Pebbles worse off than Pebbles would otherwise be. Nothing about my original presentation of the case excludes this possibility. And if we accept this stipulation, then the reason for rejecting P4 that is provided by cases in which an act is wrong because it involves attempting to harm someone will indeed be a good enough reason to reject the claim that Wilma's act is not morally wrong. Wilma's act will be wrong even though it harms no one because it involves wrongly attempting to harm someone.

But appealing to this further stipulation about Wilma's act would clearly be an unsatisfactory way to solve the non-identity problem. The Implausible Conclusion that is generated by the five premises of the non-identity argument maintains that Wilma's act as I have described it is not morally wrong. It does not claim that Wilma's act as I have described it could not be morally wrong even if we added further facts about it to the case. There are a number of further facts that could be added to the case that might well make her act wrong. We could add, for example, that her act was in violation of a democratically adopted law that she is morally obligated to obey, or that it ran counter to God's command, or that it broke a promise she had made. The non-identity problem is a problem precisely because Wilma's act seems to be morally wrong even in the absence of any such further facts. In order to solve the non-identity problem, then, a reason for rejecting a given premise must be a good enough reason to reject the Implausible Conclusion itself, not merely to reject a qualified version of the Implausible Conclusion that adds a further fact about Wilma's act and then uses that further fact to show that Wilma's act would be morally wrong. And the reason for rejecting P4 that is based on the claim that an act can wrong a person without harming that person by attempting to harm that person would clearly be unable to do this.

In order to underwrite a successful solution to the non-identity problem, then, a reason for rejecting a given premise of the non-identity argument must be strong enough to warrant rejecting any weakened version of the premise that would still be strong enough to generate the unqualified version of the Implausible Conclusion. I will refer to this as the robustness requirement. If a reason for rejecting a particular premise is not sufficiently robust, it will show that the non-identity argument as I have initially formulated it is mistaken, but it will not prevent a suitably revised version of the argument from yielding the very same Implausible Conclusion. And since the problem posed by the non-identity problem arises precisely from the fact that a set of plausible premises seems to entail that conclusion, any reason for rejecting a particular premise that is not sufficiently robust will be unable to ground a successful solution to the non-identity problem.

1.3.3 The Modesty Requirement

In order to underwrite a successful solution to the non-identity problem, then, a reason for rejecting a given premise of the non-identity argument must be independent and it must be robust. But it must not be too robust. In particular, it must not be so robust that it generates implications that are even more implausible than the Implausible Conclusion that the reason is deployed to help us avoid. I will refer to this as the modesty requirement. A cure to the non-identity problem, according to this final requirement, must not be worse than the disease.

P5, to take one more example, maintains that if an act does not wrong anyone, then the act is not morally wrong. Suppose a reason is given to believe that there is a certain property that an act can have that is sufficient to render the act morally wrong even if the act does not wrong anyone. The reason for believing in such a property would provide independent support for the claim that P5 is false. Suppose further that the property picked out by the reason was a property of Wilma's act of conceiving Pebbles in particular. In that case, the reason would also be strong enough to establish that Wilma's act was morally wrong. It would therefore satisfy both the independence requirement and the robustness requirement. But suppose, in addition, that the property picked out by this reason was a property of every human action. In that case, the reason for thinking that Wilma's act is morally wrong would be a reason for thinking that every human action is morally wrong. And the claim that every human action is morally wrong is clearly more implausible than the Implausible Conclusion's claim that Wilma's act is not morally wrong. A response to the non-identity problem that appealed to this reason would therefore fail to satisfy the modesty requirement. The cure would be worse than the disease.

The modesty requirement constitutes a reasonable constraint on a satisfactory solution to the non-identity problem because considerations about intuitive plausibility are precisely what give rise to the problem in the first place. Anyone who rejects the modesty requirement because they do not think that the implausible implications of a particular solution should count against it, that is, should not be bothered by the fact that the non-identity argument entails the Implausible Conclusion and so should not think that the non-identity argument generates a problem to begin with. The conclusion that is entailed by the non-identity argument, after all, is not self-contradictory. Nor can it be shown to be false as an empirical matter. The only reason the non-identity argument gives rise to the non-identity problem is that the argument's conclusion seems so implausible. Since the problem that stands in need of a solution is the problem of trying to avoid being stuck with an implausible conclusion, a reason for rejecting one of the argument's premises that commits us to an even more implausible conclusion cannot ground a satisfactory solution to the problem. If the only way to justify the claim that Wilma's act is morally wrong turns out to commit us to the claim that every human action is morally wrong, for example, then the non-identity problem will turn out to be an even bigger problem than it might at first seem, not a smaller one.

Whether a particular implication of a particular solution is sufficient to establish that the solution fails to satisfy the modesty requirement is a function of how implausible the particular implication is and how implausible the Implausible Conclusion is. It is difficult to justify the assertion that one particular claim is more implausible than another other than by simply appealing to the claim that most people will find it to be so. In the chapters that follow, then, whenever I claim that a particular solution fails to satisfy the modesty requirement, I will try to show that the solution has implications that I believe will strike most people as more implausible than the Implausible Conclusion. I will do this in part because the fact that most people would find a particular claim to be more implausible than the Implausible Conclusion strikes me as providing at least some support for the thesis that the claim really is more implausible than the Implausible Conclusion. But I will also do it because even if a particular reader denies the probative value of such collective judgments as a general matter, that reader will still be more likely to find a particular claim to be more implausible than the Implausible Conclusion if it is a claim that most people would find to be more implausible than the Implausible Conclusion. As long as you find a particular implication of a particular solution to be more implausible than the Implausible Conclusion, then, you should take that implication to establish that the solution fails to satisfy the modesty requirement even if you do not take the fact that most people would share your judgment to provide further support for this conclusion.

Regardless of whether the fact that most people would endorse a particular judgment gives the reader more reason to accept the judgment or simply gives me more reason to expect that the reader will already accept the judgment, establishing that a particular solution fails to satisfy the modesty requirement will ultimately involve two things: identifying particular implications of the solution that really will strike most people as highly implausible and providing reasons to think that the Implausible Conclusion is less implausible than that. I take up the first task in a variety of places throughout Chapters 2 through 6 and reserve the second for the defense of my own solution in Chapter 7. In this sense, the success of my arguments against a number of other solutions to the non-identity problem is at least in part contingent on how successful the defense of my own solution is and the defense of my own solution rests at least in part on my arguments against the other solutions. Chapter 7 completes my case against the solutions that are discussed in Chapters 2 through 6, that is, and the analysis I provide of those solutions in Chapters 2 through 6 serves as the foundation for the defense of my own solution in Chapter 7.

At this point, a critic of the modesty requirement might well ask: when you assert that most people would find a particular claim to be highly implausible, how do you know that your assertion is true? The answer is: I don't. I might be wrong. But this doesn't mean that my assertion is unreasonable or that my appealing to it is objectionable. Two brief examples may help to explain why. Consider first a case in which a woman must choose between conceiving a blind child and conceiving no child at all, and in which she knows that the blind child's life would clearly be worth living and that her act of conceiving it would have no effects on the well-being of anyone else. And suppose that she decides to conceive the child because she has a slight preference to do so. Now consider a case in which a woman who already has two sighted children must choose between conceiving a third sighted child or conceiving no more children at all, and in which she knows that the third sighted child's life would clearly be worth living and that her act of conceiving it would have no effects on the well-being of anyone else. And suppose that this woman decides not to conceive the third sighted child because she has a slight preference not to have any more children.

At a number of points in Chapters 2 through 6, I will argue that a particular solution to the non-identity problem entails that it would be positively immoral for the woman in the first case to conceive a blind child rather than to conceive no child at all or entails that it would be positively immoral for the woman in the second case to decline to conceive a third child. Whenever I do this, I will claim that most people will find these implications to be highly implausible and that this helps to show that the solution in question fails to satisfy the modesty requirement. Similarly, when I present and defend my own solution in Chapter 7, I will at one point return to both cases and use the claim that these implications are highly implausible as one way of helping to reveal the plausibility of my own solution. These various parts of my argument throughout the book will depend in part on the claim that most people will in fact find these two implications to be highly implausible. Do I really know that most people will find these two implications to be highly implausible? I do not. But I do have some reasons to think that they will.

One reason arises from having taught the non-identity problem to hundreds of students at various levels over well more than a decade as well as from having discussed it with a number of colleagues and with audience members at a number of talks I have given on the subject over the years. Whenever I teach the subject, I start by presenting my students with a case like that of Wilma and by asking for a show of hands to see how many of them think her act is morally wrong and how many do not. In a typical group of about thirty students, all or perhaps all but one or two usually raise their hand when I ask if they think her act is morally wrong. At some point during the discussion that follows, I always ask for a show of hands to see how many of them think that it would be wrong to conceive a blind child when the alternative is conceiving no child at all and when conceiving the blind child would have no effect on the well-being of anyone else. As far as I can recall, I have never had a single student raise their hand in response to this question, and when students have made comments about the case, they have tended to say not just that they find the claim that such an act would be wrong to be implausible, but that they find it to be outrageous or absurd. My experience asking about the second case has been similar, although from time to time I have had a student or two who think that the woman really would be obligated to have the third child in that case. And my experience posing these questions to colleagues and to audience members at talks has been essentially the same. So one reason I think that most people will share these judgments is that most people I have talked to so far have.

A second reason to think that most people will find these two implications to be implausible arises from having read a great deal of the literature on the non-identity problem and on some related issues. Within the literature on the non-identity problem itself, my impression is that the vast majority of people who express an intuitive judgment about either of these kinds of cases express the view that the acts in question would not be morally wrong. Indeed, when these sorts of cases come up in the literature, they tend to be used in the same way that I will mostly use them here: to show that a particular approach to the problem has an unacceptable implication. In addition, although this is not usually stated explicitly, those who endorse the judgment that these implications are unacceptable often leave the impression that they are confident in appealing to these judgments in part because they, like me, have had the experience of having most of the people they discuss the cases with agree with them. And this is so even in some of the literature that does not directly deal with the non-identity problem. There is, for example, an extensive body of work on the question of whether there is a moral asymmetry between deliberately creating a child who will have a miserable life and deliberately refraining from creating a child who will have a wonderful life. Philosophers who have weighed in on the subject have offered potentially powerful defenses of both positive and negative answers to this question, but while their conclusions often differ sharply, their discussions are almost always framed by a shared background assumption: that the commonsense view of the matter is that it is seriously wrong to deliberately create a miserable child but not at all wrong to decline to create a perfectly happy child. The fact that this characterization of the commonsense view of that issue goes essentially uncontested when the issue is discussed in the literature provides some evidence that most people do have this reaction to this particular pair of cases. And the view that it is not wrong to refrain from creating the happy child in this case is relevantly similar to the view that it is not wrong for the woman in my second case to refrain from conceiving a third child. So a second reason I think that most people will share the judgments about the women's actions in my two cases is that most people I have read on these subjects so far have, and it seems like most of the people they have talked to have, too.

A third reason to think that most people will find it highly implausible to claim that it would be wrong for the woman in my first case to conceive a blind child rather than no child and wrong for the woman in my second case to decline to conceive a third child arises from the fact that I myself find these claims to be highly implausible. This is not to say that my own intuitions are an infallible indicator of the intuitions that most other people will have. Sometimes my responses to a particular case do seem to render me an outlier. But as a general matter, my experience has been that when I find myself having a clear and strong moral intuition about a particular case, most of the people I end up discussing the case with or whose views of the case are presented in the relevant literature seem to have the same reaction to it that I do. This general sense that my intuitions tend to be in the mainstream, then, combined with the near uniformity with which I have encountered agreement with them over the years in the case of these two particular examples, leads me to think that it is reasonable to suppose that most people will, in fact, agree with them. And I have tried to limit my appeal to intuitions in this book as much as possible to examples about which this is true.

All of this is consistent, of course, with the possibility that I am wrong. Perhaps a more careful, rigorous, and systematic study of the sort that experimental philosophers have recently been conducting would reveal that, when biasing factors that I might be unaware of are removed from the cases, most people really do think that it would be wrong to conceive a blind child when the alternative was conceiving no child at all and that most people really do think that it would be wrong to decline to conceive a third child who would be quite happy simply because one had a slight preference not to have any more children. Or perhaps such a study would establish that people simply have no stable intuitions about such cases one way or the other and that their reactions can just as easily be manipulated in either direction by employing a variety of framing devices and other techniques of suggestion. I do not purport to have conducted such experiments or to know what the results of such experiments would be. And so while I believe that there are good reasons to accept the assertions I make in the chapters that follow when I claim that most people would find a particular implication of a particular solution to be highly implausible, I acknowledge that these good reasons might turn out to be outweighed by other and even better reasons. In short, I might be wrong.

But, of course, any of the arguments that I make in this book might turn out to be wrong, regardless of whether they involve an appeal to people's intuitions. And the same is true, as far as I can tell, about pretty much any argument in pretty much any book. So this limitation on the force of my appeal to people's intuitions, significant as it may be, provides no particular reason to doubt that the modesty requirement imposes a reasonable constraint on a satisfactory solution to the non-identity problem or to dismiss the particular claims that I make in the chapters that follow when I argue that a particular solution to the problem fails to satisfy this requirement. It simply shows that these claims that I make, like any other claim I make in this book, merit scrutiny, and that there are strategies that one could employ in attempting to defeat them. And that would presumably be true of the claims made in any book worth reading, or at least in any book worth reading on the non-identity problem.

The non-identity problem arises from the tension between five plausible premises and one implausible conclusion.

P1: Wilma's act of conceiving now rather than taking a pill once a day for two months before conceiving does not make Pebbles worse off than she would otherwise have been
P2: If A's act harms B, then A's act makes B worse off than B would otherwise have been
P3: Wilma's act of conceiving now rather than taking a pill once a day for two months before conceiving does not harm anyone other than Pebbles
P4: If an act does not harm anyone, then the act does not wrong anyone
P5: If an act does not wrong anyone, then the act is not morally wrong
C: Wilma's act of conceiving Pebbles is not morally wrong

If you do not find these premises to be particularly plausible or the conclusion to be particularly implausible or if you are so skeptical about the reliability or probative value of intuitions more generally that you are not particularly bothered to find that your views here are inconsistent, then the non-identity problem may not be a problem for you. But if, as seems to be the case for most people, all five of these premises strike you as quite plausible, the conclusion strikes you as quite implausible, and you think that your views about the premises and the conclusion really should be rendered consistent with each other, then you should feel the force of the non-identity problem and want to find a satisfactory solution to it.

Solving the non-identity problem seems to require finding a way to avoid the Implausible Conclusion. And finding a way to avoid the Implausible Conclusion, in turn, seems to involve a kind of balancing act. What is needed is an argument that independently undermines a particular premise of the non-identity argument, that is strong enough to undermine any revised version of the premise that would be sufficient to generate the same problem in a different form, and that is weak enough to avoid generating any further problems that are even bigger than the problem it sets out to solve. The question raised by the non-identity problem is whether there is such an argument. The rest of this book is an attempt to answer that question.

2

Rejecting the First Premise

The first premise of the non-identity argument maintains that Wilma's act of conceiving now rather than taking the pill once a day for two months before conceiving does not make Pebbles worse off than she would otherwise have been. This claim seems difficult to deny. If Wilma had not conceived when she did, then Pebbles would not have existed. And Pebbles's life is clearly not worse than no life at all. Since Wilma's act caused Pebbles to exist rather than not exist and since existing is not worse for Pebbles than not existing, Wilma's act did not make things worse for Pebbles than they would otherwise have been. While the truth of P1 may initially seem to be beyond doubt, however, a number of objections can nonetheless be raised against it. The goal of this chapter is to identify them and to consider whether any of them can be used as the basis for a satisfactory solution to the non-identity problem.

2.1 The Incoherence Objection

One objection to P1 maintains that it requires us to make a kind of comparison that is impossible to make. In order to accept the claim made by P1, on this account, we must be able to compare how things are for Pebbles when she exists and is blind with how things are for Pebbles when she does not exist. But in order for us to be able to compare these two conditions in terms of their being better or worse for Pebbles, the objection claims, they must both be conditions of Pebbles. And non-existence is not a condition of Pebbles in the case where Pebbles does not exist. Saying that Pebbles is non-existent in that case is just another way of saying that there is no Pebbles. And if there is no Pebbles, then there is no condition of Pebbles to compare to the alternative. The objection, in short, rests on two claims: that we cannot coherently make judgments about whether existing or not existing is better or worse for Pebbles, and that coherently making such judgments is necessary in order for P1 to be true. I will refer to the objection that arises from the conjunction of these two claims as the incoherence objection.

I am inclined to think that both claims made by the incoherence objection are false. My reasons for being inclined to think this are contained in Appendix A. But while I am inclined to think that both claims made by the objection are false, I am not sufficiently confident of this assessment to depend on it as a basis for rejecting the objection. So let's suppose, at least for the sake of the argument, that both claims made by the objection are true: that the statement that existing is better or worse than not existing really is incoherent and that the truth of P1 really does require that the statement be coherent. If both of these claims are true, then the incoherence objection to P1 should be accepted and the claim that P1 is true should be rejected for that reason. But even if this is so, the incoherence objection will still fail to ground a satisfactory solution to the non-identity problem. This is because, as I emphasized in section 1.3.2, in order to solve the non-identity problem, it is not enough to give a reason for rejecting one of the premises of the argument that gives rise to the problem. The reason for rejecting the premise must also be strong enough to justify rejecting any variants of the premise that might allow the problem to simply reappear in a slightly altered form. This is what I referred to as the robustness requirement. And the reason for rejecting P1 provided by the incoherence objection cannot satisfy the robustness requirement even if it does turn out to give us a sufficiently independent and modest reason to deny that P1 is true.

The reason for this is simple: if the purported incoherence of the comparison between existence and non-existence prevents us from affirming P1's claim that Wilma's act does not make Pebbles worse off than she would otherwise have been, then it will at the same time, and for the same reason, prevent us from affirming the claim that Wilma's act does make Pebbles worse off than she would otherwise have been. If the incoherence objection shows that P1 does not say something that is true, that is, it also shows that it does not say something that is false. It simply shows that it doesn't say anything intelligible at all. If that is so, then even if we accept the objection to P1, we cannot coherently claim that Wilma's act makes Pebbles worse off than she would otherwise have been. And if we cannot coherently claim that Wilma's act makes Pebbles worse off than she would otherwise have been, then the reasons for rejecting P1 provided by the incoherence objection will not be robust enough to solve the non-identity problem.

If P2 is correct in maintaining that if A's act harms B, then A's act makes B worse off than B would otherwise have been, after all, then the following modified version of P2 must also be correct: If A's act harms B, then the sentence "A's act makes B worse off than B would otherwise have been" is coherent. If the incoherence objection to P1 is accepted, we have reason to reject P1 and to accept in its place the following modified version of P1: The sentence "Wilma's act of conceiving now rather than taking a pill once a day for two months before conceiving does not make Pebbles worse off than she would otherwise have been" is not coherent. And these modified versions of P1 and P2 entail that Wilma's act does not harm Pebbles just as surely as the original versions of P1 and P2 do: if Wilma's act harms Pebbles, then the comparative sentence must be coherent, but the comparative sentence is not coherent, so Wilma's act does not harm Pebbles. Regardless of what we conclude about the coherence of the comparison between existence and non-existence and about its relevance to the truth of P1, then, our conclusions will not be robust enough to block the move to the claim that Wilma's act does not harm Pebbles. And if they can't block that move, then whatever they may imply about the truth of P1, they can't do enough to ground a satisfactory solution to the non-identity problem.

2.2 The *De Re/De Dicto* Objection

Let's now assume that the claim made by P1 is coherent. Even if P1 is coherent, it might still be false. One reason for thinking that P1 is false arises from the complaint that I have to this point unfairly misrepresented its content. The point of P1, after all, is to claim that Wilma's act of conceiving now rather than taking the pills for two months before conceiving does not make her child worse off. To help to make the point more vividly, I have given her child a name so that we have a clear and specific point of reference. But, a second objection to P1 maintains, this substitution of terms is illicit. If we represent P1 as saying that Wilma's act does not make "her child" worse off, rather than saying that it does not make "Pebbles" worse off, on this account, we will better represent the argument's starting point. And if we do this, the objection maintains, we will also see that the claim made by P1 is, at least in one crucial respect, false.

The problem with P1, on this account, can perhaps best be seen by putting it in terms of the familiar *de re/de dicto* distinction. The claim that Wilma wants to marry the tallest man in Bedrock, for example, could mean two different things: that there is a particular man that Wilma wants to marry who happens to be the tallest man in Bedrock (the *de re* reading) or that she wants to marry whatever man turns out to satisfy the description "the tallest man in Bedrock" (the *de dicto* reading). Similarly, the claim that Wilma's act does not make her child worse off is subject to two interpretations: the *de re* claim that her act does not make the particular child that she does conceive worse off than that particular child would otherwise have been, and the *de dicto* claim that her act does not make whatever person turns out to satisfy the description "her child" worse off than whatever person would otherwise have turned out to satisfy the description "her child" would have been. But, this objection then points out, the *de dicto* interpretation of this claim is false. In the *de dicto* sense, Wilma's act really does make her child worse off than her child would otherwise have been. Her act makes it the case that "the child that Wilma conceives" is blind rather than that "the child that Wilma conceives" is sighted, and this makes it the case that "the child that Wilma conceives" is worse off in the *de dicto* sense. Pebbles, in short, can truthfully say to Wilma "you made your child worse off than your child would otherwise have been in the *de dicto* sense. I am your child, and so the person you made worse off in the *de dicto* sense is me."[1] And if Wilma's act really did make her child worse off in this *de dicto* sense, then there is at least one interpretation on which P1 turns out to be false.

The proponent of this objection is surely correct to maintain that P1 is false on the *de dicto* reading. But this concession is not enough to solve the non-identity problem. The

---

[1] Hare makes this point (2007: 523).

significance of P1, after all, is that it helps to justify the further claim that since Wilma's act does not harm her child, it does not wrong her child. An objection to P1 that fails to block the move from the facts about Wilma's act to the claim that Wilma's act does not wrong her child is not robust enough to solve the non-identity problem. And simply noting that P1 is true in the *de re* sense but false in the *de dicto* sense is not enough to block that move. The claim that P1 is false in the *de dicto* sense will be robust enough to solve the non-identity problem only if we add to it the further claim that if Wilma's act harms her child in the *de dicto* sense then it wrongs her child. And this further claim should be rejected.

It might at first seem a simple matter to demonstrate that this further claim is false.[2] Suppose, for example, that Wilma decided to adopt a blind child when she could instead have adopted a sighted child. This choice would not harm her child in the *de re* sense, since it would not make the particular child that she adopted blind rather than sighted. But her choice would harm her child in the *de dicto* sense, since it would make it the case that the child who is correctly referred to as "her child" is blind rather than sighted. It would clearly be absurd to think that Wilma's act of adopting a blind child wronged her child in virtue of the fact that it harmed her child in the *de dicto* sense. This would clearly seem to show that harming someone merely in the *de dicto* sense does not wrong them. And this, in turn, would clearly seem to show that the *de re/ de dicto* objection to P1 is ultimately unsuccessful. Even if Wilma's act of conceiving Pebbles does harm her child in the *de dicto* sense, this reason for rejecting P1 will not be robust enough to block the move to the conclusion that Wilma's act does not wrong her child, and will thus not be robust enough to solve the non-identity problem.

As Caspar Hare has pointed out, however, things are not so simple: "it does not follow from the fact that *de dicto* betterness is not always morally significant that it is never so."[3] Even if we provide a great number of examples in which making someone worse off in the *de dicto* sense proves to be morally irrelevant, this may not be enough to show that it is not relevant in the case of Wilma and Pebbles in particular. And, in fact, Hare goes on to give an example in which he claims that "it is appropriate to expect people to care about making things *de dicto* better in some ways" and to claim that cases like that of Wilma and Pebbles are relevantly similar to this case. Before we can confidently reject the solution based on the *de re/de dicto* objection to P1, then, we must consider the argument that Hare constructs around the following example:[4]

The Safety Officer. Tess is a state safety officer, whose job it is to regulate those features of the automobile that protect its occupants in the event of a collision—air bags, crumple zones, and so forth. Noticing that people in her state are not wearing safety belts, she implements some tough new regulations and, a year later, is pleased to discover evidence that they have been effective,

---

[2] And it did at first seem a simple matter to me. See Boonin (2008: 134). Parfit also dismisses the objection quite quickly (1984: 359–60).

[3] Hare (2007: 516).   [4] Hare (2007: 516).

that the severity of injuries sustained in automobile accidents has been reduced as a result of people belting up. She gives herself a pat on the back.

In the Safety Officer case, Tess's new regulations clearly seem to make things better for accident victims. But now suppose it turns out that the regulations affect not just the severity of the injuries that occur, but the identity of the drivers who suffer them. Suppose, for example, that the regulations have an effect on how long it takes each person to start their car, which in turn affects the time at which they reach various intersections, red lights, and so on, with the result that the people who would have been in an accident had the regulations not taken effect now avoid the accidents they would otherwise have been involved in and some people who would have avoided being in accidents had the regulations not been implemented instead end up being involved in an accident that they would otherwise have avoided. In that case, Hare imagines a critic complaining to Tess as follows: you didn't make things better for the accident victims; you made things worse for them. After all, if your regulations had not been implemented, those accident victims would not have been in accidents in the first place. And it is not better to be in an accident than not to be in an accident. It is worse. So you have done a bad job.

If a critic of Tess were to register such a complaint, Hare counts on us to agree that Tess would be entitled to respond as follows: "Yes, what I did was *de re* worse for last year's accident victims. . . [but making things *de re* better for them was not my job]; my job was to make things *de dicto* better for the health of last year's accident victims."[5] Suppose, for example, that without the regulations Jack but not Jill would have had an accident and that Jack would have suffered 10 units of harm and that because of the regulations Jill but not Jack had an accident and that Jill suffered 5 units of harm. In that case, Tess's regulations did not make "the accident victim" better off in the *de re* sense. The accident victim in the *de re* sense is Jill and Jill is not better off than she would otherwise have been. But Tess's regulations did make "the accident victim" better off in the *de dicto* sense. The accident victim in the *de dicto* sense is whoever ended up having the accident. And because of Tess's regulations, whoever that person turned out to be suffered a less serious injury than whoever that person would otherwise have turned out to be would have suffered. Since it seems clear that Tess's regulations did, in fact, make things better in the morally relevant sense, and since they made things worse in the *de re* sense but better in the *de dicto* sense, the Safety Officer case seems to be one in which the *de dicto* sense is morally relevant rather than the *de re* sense.

If we ask why it is the *de dicto* sense rather than *de re* sense that is morally relevant in the Safety Officer case, moreover, Hare maintains that the most reasonable answer turns out to be one that applies to cases like that of Wilma as well. On Hare's account, there are two features of the Safety Office case that render the *de dicto* sense morally relevant.[6] First, Tess has a special role that makes it appropriate for her to be partial

---

[5] Hare (2007: 517–18, emphasis added).   [6] Hare (2007: 519).

to a certain group of people—accident victims—and to have her special concern for the health of that group of people guide her behavior. Second, due to the non-identity nature of her choice situation, it is impossible for her concern for the health of that group of people in the *de re* sense to guide her behavior. Whatever she does will be *de re* worse for the health of the people who actually get in accidents, so the only way that her concern for accident victims can guide her behavior is by focusing on the impact of her decisions on their well-being in the *de dicto* sense. In short, because of Tess's special responsibilities, she should be guided by a special concern for accident victims in particular and because of the non-identity nature of her choice situation, this concern can only express itself in the *de dicto* sense.

But both of these kinds of consideration seem to apply equally to the case of Wilma. Wilma, like Tess, has a special role that makes it appropriate for her to be partial to a certain group of people—in this case, her own children. And due to the non-identity nature of Wilma's choice situation, again as in the case of the non-identity nature of Tess's choice situation, it is impossible for Wilma's concern for that group of people in the *de re* sense to guide her behavior. Whichever choice Wilma makes, it will not be *de re* worse for the person she chooses to conceive, so the only way that her concern for the well-being of her children can guide her choice about which child to conceive is by focusing on the impact of her decision on the well-being of her child in the *de dicto* sense. As Hare puts it, "before her child is conceived, if concern for the health of her child is to play a role in guiding at least some of the choices that affect her child (as it should) it must be expressed *de dicto*—as a concern that things be *de dicto* better for the health of her child."[7] And, as we have already seen, in the *de dicto* sense, P1 of the non-identity argument turns out to be false: Wilma's act of conceiving now rather than taking the pill once a day for two months before conceiving does make her child worse off than her child would otherwise have been in the *de dicto* sense. And that, on the solution that Hare offers, explains why Wilma's act is morally wrong.[8]

There are two problems with Hare's example and thus with Hare's solution.[9] The first problem arises from the fact that Tess's claim that "my job is to make things *de dicto* better for the accident victims" can itself be understood in two ways. On one interpretation, the claim that the *de dicto* sense is relevant in the Tess case is plausible, but on that interpretation, Wilma's act of conceiving Pebbles does not make her child *de dicto* worse off. On the other interpretation, Wilma's act of conceiving Pebbles does make her child *de dicto* worse off, but on that interpretation, it is not plausible to say that the *de dicto* sense is relevant in the Tess case. The case of Tess thus fails to identify a morally relevant sense in which P1 of the non-identity argument is false.

---

[7] Hare (2007: 520, italics added). Malek defends the same objection (Unpublished-a).

[8] The same basic position is also defended by Wolf (2009) and Haramia (2013) and seems to be briefly endorsed by Govier (1979: 110–11), MacLean (1983: 196), Kumar (2003: 113–4), Davis (2008: 265–6), and Havstad (2010: 75–6) as well. See also Green (1997: 7–9), Partridge (2002: 81–3), Velleman (2008), Malek (2008: 124–5), Malek and Daar (2012: 5, 6–7), and Coons (2012).

[9] For further objections to Hare's argument, see also Wasserman (2008) and Urbanek (2010: 133–9).

When put in terms of the case of Jack and Jill, the first interpretation of Tess's *de dicto* claim can be put like this: either Jack will be in an accident or Jill will be in an accident, and whoever it turns out to be, Tess's job is to make sure that the person who is in the accident suffers less harm than would have been suffered by the person who would otherwise have been in the accident. The second interpretation can be put like this: either Jack will be in an accident or Jill will be in an accident, and whoever it turns out to be, Tess's job is to make sure that the person who is in the accident ends up having a higher level of health after the accident than the person who would otherwise have been in the accident would have ended up having after the accident.

To understand this distinction and its significance in undermining Hare's solution, a specific example may prove useful. So suppose that as things now stand, neither Jack nor Jill has been involved in an accident and that Jack has a health level of 100 units and Jill has a health level of 80 units. Tess has to choose between Policy 1 and Policy 2. If she chooses Policy 1, Jack will be in an accident and suffer a loss of 10 units of health. If she chooses Policy 2, Jill will be in an accident and suffer a loss of 5 units of health. We can represent the options available to Tess here as follows:

	Policy 1	Policy 2
Jack	has an accident; drops from 100 units to 90	does not have an accident
Jill	does not have an accident	has an accident; drops from 80 units to 75

Which policy should Tess choose?

On the first interpretation of the *de dicto* claim, Tess should focus on the magnitude of the harm that the accident victim—whoever that turns out to be—would suffer. If Jack is in an accident, he will lose 10 units of health. If Jill is an accident, she will lose 5 units of health. Losing 5 units of health is a smaller harm than losing 10 units of health, and so Tess should choose Policy 2, the policy on which Jill is in the accident. If Tess selects Policy 2, then things will be better in the *de dicto* sense for the accident victim in the sense that the accident victim will suffer less harm than the accident victim would otherwise have suffered. On the second interpretation of the *de dicto* claim, Tess should instead focus on the level of health that the accident victim—whoever that turns out to be—will enjoy after the accident. If Jack is in an accident, he will be reduced from 100 units of health to 90 units of health. If Jill is in an accident, she will be reduced from 80 units of health to 75 units of health. 90 units of health is greater than 75 units, and so Tess should choose Policy 1, the policy on which Jack is in the accident. If she selects Policy 1, then things will be better in the *de dicto* sense for the accident victim in the sense that the accident victim will end up having a higher level of health after the accident than would otherwise have been enjoyed by the accident victim after the accident.

It is clear that Tess should choose Policy 2. Her job is to reduce the severity of the accidents that occur, not to increase the severity of the accidents by redirecting them onto healthier people who will as a result be better off after the accidents they have than the other people would have been after the accidents that they would have had. And, indeed, Hare himself is quite clear about this in his presentation of the case. He writes that Tess "is pleased to discover evidence that [her new regulations] have been effective, that the severity of injuries sustained in automobile accidents has been reduced as a result." He does not insist that Tess would be entitled to be pleased to discover evidence that her regulations had made accident victims better off simply by redirecting accidents onto healthier people. So even Hare agrees that the claim that the *de dicto* sense is morally relevant in the case of Tess is true on the first interpretation of that claim but false on the second.

But this, in turn, means that Hare's solution to the non-identity problem is unsuccessful even if we agree with his claim that Wilma should be concerned with the *de dicto* sense in just the same way that Tess should be. Tess's duty is to minimize the harm that will be suffered by whatever person turns out to occupy the role of accident victim, not to ensure that whatever person turns out to occupy that role ends up as healthy as possible. So if Hare is right in saying that the case of Wilma is morally symmetric with the case of Tess, then we should say the same thing about Wilma. If Wilma really does have the same kind of *de dicto* moral duty that Tess has, that is, then Wilma's duty is not to redirect her conception decision in order to ensure that after she conceives the person who occupies the role of her child will be doing better than would otherwise have been the case. That would be like Tess redirecting accidents onto healthier people and thus selecting Policy 1. Rather, assuming that Hare is correct in maintaining that the cases of Tess and Wilma are morally on a par, Wilma's duty is simply to minimize the harm that will be incurred by whatever person turns out to occupy the role of her child. If Wilma really does have the same moral obligation that Tess has, that is, then Wilma's decision procedure should involve asking the following questions: If I conceive a blind child now, how much harm will my act of conceiving that child cause to that child? If I instead conceive a sighted child later, how much harm will my act of conceiving that child cause to that child? If the act of conceiving one child will cause less harm to that child than the act of conceiving the other would cause to the other, Wilma should conclude, then I am morally required to conceive that child because I have a special obligation to protect my child from harm.

But the non-identity problem arises in the first place precisely because neither of Wilma's choices will cause any harm at all to the particular child that she conceives. And so her act of conceiving Pebbles is consistent with the only reasonable *de dicto* interpretation of the moral principle that we can extract from the Safety Officer case. In the relevant sense in which Tess is concerned to make things *de dicto* better for accident victims, Wilma's act of conceiving Pebbles does not make her child *de dicto* worse off. And so even in the *de dicto* sense that turns out to be morally relevant in the case of Tess, P1 of the non-identity argument still proves to be true. And since P1 still proves to be true in the morally relevant sense, even if it proves to be false in a morally irrelevant sense, the reason for rejecting P1 that arises from the *de re/de dicto* distinction fails to be robust enough to solve the non-identity problem.

I've argued so far that even if Hare is correct in maintaining that Wilma has the same *de dicto* moral duties to her child that Tess has to accident victims, this fails to show that Wilma's act of conceiving Pebbles makes Pebbles worse off in a morally relevant sense. But let's now suppose that I'm wrong about this and that if the two cases really are morally symmetric, then Wilma's act really does make her child worse off in a morally relevant sense. Even if this is so, there is a second reason to reject Hare's solution: the best explanation of why Tess has the *de dicto* moral obligations that she has does not entail that Wilma has the same *de dicto* moral obligations in the first place. Hare's explanation of the basis of Tess's obligations has implications that are even more implausible than the Implausible Conclusion, and an alternative explanation that avoids those implications does not apply to Wilma. In order to establish that Wilma's act is morally wrong, that is, the solution based on the *de re/de dicto* distinction will end up creating bigger problems than it will solve. The *de dicto* cure will be worse than the non-identity disease. As a result, even if the solution were able to satisfy the robustness requirement, it would still fail to satisfy the modesty requirement.

Hare's explanation of the grounds of Tess's *de dicto* moral obligations appeals to two facts about Tess: that she has a special obligation to be partial to a particular group of people and that due to the non-identity nature of her choice situation, her concern for that group of people cannot be expressed in the *de re* sense. If these facts suffice to account for Tess's obligation to promote the interests of accident victims in the *de dicto* sense, Hare argues, then since the two facts also apply to cases like that of Wilma and her children, they suffice to generate the same obligation for Wilma to promote the interests of her children in the *de dicto* sense. But the claim that Tess's obligations are generated by the two facts that Hare appeals to has implications that are even more implausible than the Implausible Conclusion.

Suppose, for example, that I have just received my license to practice medicine and am in the process of establishing my first practice. At the moment, I have no patients, but because the town I have moved to has long suffered from a shortage of doctors, I am immediately inundated with requests from people who would like me to be their doctor. In fact, I have twice as many applications as I can accept and am trying to decide which of the applicants to take on as patients. The two features that Hare appeals to in order to explain Tess's *de dicto* obligations apply equally to this case. As a doctor, I have a special obligation to be partial to a particular group of people—my patients. And in deciding which people to accept as patients, I can't be guided by *de re* considerations. Anyone I accept as a patient will be *de re* better off as a result of my taking them on, and so *de re* considerations can't tell me whom to accept as a patient. But this means that if Hare's explanation of the source of Tess's obligations is correct, then I am morally obligated to decide which people to take on as patients by appealing to *de dicto* considerations. In deciding which people to take on as patients, that is, I should be guided by the *de dicto* concern for what would be best for the health of "my patients." And this means that I must choose the healthier people to accept as patients. This result is clearly more implausible than the Implausible Conclusion. And since this account of the basis of Tess's obligations is needed in order for Hare's claim about the content of Tess's obligations to entail that Wilma's act is morally wrong, a solution based on the case of Tess is incapable of satisfying the modesty requirement.

There is, moreover, a much more straightforward explanation of the source of Tess's obligations: Tess has an obligation to reduce the severity of automobile accidents because Tess has agreed to take on such an obligation as part of her professional responsibilities. This alternative explanation appeals to a consideration, the fact that Tess has agreed to do something, whose moral salience is at least as compelling as the considerations that Hare's explanation appeals to. The explanation based on consent, moreover, avoids the problem that Hare's explanation runs into in the case of the doctor. Since I have not agreed to guide my decision about which people to take on as patients by appealing to *de dicto* considerations, the consent-based explanation of Tess's *de dicto* obligations does not entail that as a doctor I have parallel *de dicto* obligations. And the consent-based explanation can avoid the same kind of problem that will also arise for Hare's explanation in many other contexts in which a person has a professional obligation to be partial to his clients once he takes them on as clients: bodyguards, therapists, teachers, members of the clergy, babysitters, day care workers, and so on. In all of these cases, the person in question has an obligation to be partial to the members of a certain group, *de re* considerations cannot help the person decide which people to make a part of that group, and so Hare's explanation would entail that the person has a *de dicto* obligation to take on as clients those who are already doing better. For all of these reasons, the consent-based account of the source of Tess's *de dicto* obligations is superior to the account that Hare provides.

But if the consent-based explanation really is the better account of the origin of Tess's obligations, then Hare's solution must again be rejected. Wilma has not agreed to take *de dicto* considerations into account in deciding which child to conceive. And so the reason that Tess must take *de dicto* considerations into account does not entail that Wilma must do so. My first objection to Hare's solution maintained that even if the case of Tess does establish that Wilma has to take *de dicto* considerations into account in the way that Tess does, this does not mean that P1 of the non-identity argument is false in a morally relevant sense. But as it turns out, the case of Tess does not establish that Wilma has to take *de dicto* considerations into account in the first place. For both of these reasons, the *de re/de dicto* solution to the non-identity problem must be rejected.

2.3 The Metaphysical Objection

A third way of objecting to P1 appeals to a metaphysical claim about the relationship between genetic identity and personal identity. Suppose that we call the particular sperm and egg that came together in the conception of Pebbles $Sperm_1$ and Egg_1, and call the particular sperm and egg that would instead have come together in the conception of Rocks if Wilma had waited two months before conceiving $Sperm_2$ and Egg_2. P1 maintains that Wilma's act of conceiving Pebbles does not make Pebbles worse off than she would have been if Wilma had waited two months before conceiving. The reasons for accepting this claim are that if Wilma had waited two months before conceiving, she would instead have conceived Rocks, and that Rocks is not the same person as Pebbles. And the reason for accepting the claim that Rocks is not the same person as Pebbles is grounded in the fact that $Sperm_1$ and Egg_1 are not the same sperm and egg as $Sperm_2$ and Egg_2. P1, in short, seems to depend on the claim that genetic identity is necessary for personal identity. If the sperm and egg whose fusion gave rise to you had never come together, on this account, then you would never have existed.

This metaphysical claim is widely accepted and deeply plausible. But it can be challenged. If genetic identity is not necessary for personal identity, then it is at least possible that Pebbles and Rocks will turn out to be one and the same person, a person who will either be conceived now as a blind girl or two months later as a sighted boy. There is, moreover, at least one version of such an account on which this result would be not simply possible, but true. If we fix Pebbles's personal identity not by saying that she is essentially the result of the coming together of $Sperm_1$ and Egg_1 but by saying that she is essentially the result of Wilma's conception decision, then whether Wilma conceives now or two months later, whether it is $Sperm_1$ and Egg_1 or $Sperm_2$ and Egg_2 that are brought together in the process, the result will be one and the same person. And if that is the case, then by conceiving Pebbles as a blind child now, Wilma really does make the person she conceives worse off than that very person would otherwise have been. Pebbles would otherwise have been Rocks, on this account, and Rocks would not have been blind. Indeed, making use of a version of the kind of account of identity across possible worlds developed by David Lewis, at least one philosopher has recently argued that this metaphysical claim can be used to solve at least some versions of the non-identity problem.[10] If Rocks turns out to

---

[10] Wrigley (2006; 2012). Kamm (2000–1: 72) also notes the possibility that one could deny P1 by denying the metaphysical claim and appeals to Robert Nozick's closest continuer account of personal identity. Kobayashi defends the same kind of solution by appealing to a very different holistic metaphysical view (1998: 170, 181–2). Although the details of these accounts differ from those of Lewis's account, the same basic problems noted in the text will arise if these other accounts are used to try to solve the non-identity problem: in order for them to really entail that Pebbles and Rocks are one and the same person they will have implications that are even more implausible than the Implausible Conclusion and since they depend on the assumption that Pebbles and Rocks are one and the same person they cannot solve the problem if there is genuine non-identity between the two and so cannot satisfy the robustness requirement.

Meachem (2012) offers a similar solution that, like Wrigley's, appeals to a counterpart account of the sort proposed by Lewis. But Meachem's version avoids the problem created by treating Pebbles and Rocks as one and the same person because it does not insist that they should be viewed as one and the same person in all

be the counterpart of Pebbles in the world in which Wilma takes the pill for two months before conceiving, for example, then Rocks is the appropriate reference point for talking about who Pebbles would have been if Sperm$_1$ and Egg$_1$ had never been brought together.

I am inclined to think that a solution to the non-identity problem that is based on this sort of metaphysical claim cannot satisfy the modesty requirement. This is partly because the claim that you would still have existed even if the sperm and egg that came together in your conception had never come together strikes me as considerably more difficult to believe than the claim that it is not morally wrong for Wilma to conceive Pebbles. But it is also because the metaphysical claim underlying this solution produces even more implausible implications in variations on the case of Wilma.

Consider, for example, a different number version of the story in which Wilma is told that if she conceives now she will conceive a blind girl whom she will name Pebbles but that if she takes the pill once a day for two months before conceiving she will conceive sighted twins whom she will name Chip and Stone. In this case, the result of Wilma's conception choice if she waits two months is two distinct people, Chip and Stone. A proponent of the metaphysical objection to P1 could respond to this case in two ways. One would be to insist that Chip and Stone would both be the same person as the person that Wilma would conceive if she conceives now. This would enable the proponent of the solution to explain why it would be wrong for Wilma to conceive now. Conceiving now would make Pebbles worse off than she would otherwise be since she would otherwise be both Chip and Stone, each of whom are sighted. But since Chip and Stone are two distinct people, and thus not identical to each other, the claim that Pebbles is identical to both of them is much harder to believe than is the Implausible Conclusion. The other way that a proponent of the metaphysical objection to P1 could respond would be to concede that Pebbles will not exist if Wilma does not conceive now in the different number version of the case while continuing to maintain that Pebbles will exist as Rocks if Wilma does not conceive now in the same number version of the case. This makes the metaphysical claim the position appeals to less difficult to accept, but it entails that although it would be wrong for Wilma to conceive Pebbles when her alternative was to conceive a single sighted child, it would not be wrong for Wilma to conceive Pebbles when her alternative was to conceive two sighted children. And this result is also more implausible than the Implausible Conclusion.

A second variant of the case of Wilma poses further problems for the metaphysical objection to P1. It arises from an example provided by Josh Parsons that is meant to

contexts. In some contexts, Meachem concedes, the appropriate counterpart relation would not identify Rocks as the counterpart of Pebbles. It is just that "the counterpart relation that we should use when making moral judgments" is one on which Rocks is treated as the counterpart of Pebbles, the result of which is that when we ask, morally speaking, how Pebbles would have been doing had Wilma waited two months before conceiving, the answer is that she would have been doing better as a sighted boy (2012: 270). But Meachem provides no reason to think that this is the appropriate counterpart relation to use when thinking about such situations morally other than the fact that if we do so, we get the result that Wilma's act is morally wrong (at least if we combine it with a principle on which harming Pebbles makes Wilma's act wrong). This sort of solution is therefore incapable of satisfying the independence requirement.

show that P1 of the non-identity argument need not depend on genetic essentialism after all.[11] Suppose that Wilma is told that if she conceives now she will conceive a blind girl whom she will name Pebbles and that if she takes a pill once a day for an entire year and then conceives, she will conceive a sighted boy whom she will name Rocks. It might at first seem that this case is not relevantly different from the original version of the Wilma story, and that the proponent of the metaphysical objection to P1 could therefore again simply maintain that Pebbles and Rocks would be the same person. And if Pebbles and Rocks really would be the same person, then Wilma would make this person worse off by conceiving the person now as blind Pebbles rather than later as sighted Rocks. But even if we are willing to accept this metaphysical claim in the original version of the Wilma story, it would be much harder to accept it in this version. This is because, as Parsons points out, the fact that the two conceptions would take place a year apart means that Wilma could in fact conceive both Pebbles and Rocks.

As with the different number version of the case of Wilma, a proponent of the metaphysical objection to P1 could respond to this case in two ways. One would be to insist that Pebbles and Rocks really would be the same person in this case. But since Pebbles and Rocks could both exist at the same time in this case, it is much harder to believe that they are one and the same person than it is to simply accept the claim that it would not be wrong for Wilma to conceive Pebbles in the original version of the story. The other would be to concede that Pebbles will not exist if Wilma waits a year before conceiving in this version of the story while continuing to maintain that Pebbles will exist as Rocks if Wilma waits two months before conceiving in the original version of the story. This would make the metaphysical claim the position appeals to less difficult to accept, but it entails that although it would be wrong for Wilma to conceive Pebbles when her alternative was to conceive a single sighted child in two months, it would not be wrong for Wilma to conceive Pebbles when her alternative was to conceive a sighted child in a year. And this result, too, is more implausible than the Implausible Conclusion. For all of these reasons, I am therefore inclined to think that a solution to the non-identity problem that is based on the metaphysical objection to P1 cannot satisfy the modesty requirement.

Even if I am mistaken about this, however, there is still a more fundamental problem with the metaphysical solution. The problem is that the solution cannot satisfy the robustness requirement. The reason for this is that the non-identity problem is ultimately a moral problem, not a metaphysical problem. The problem arises because most people, when presented with a case like that of Wilma, respond with a very strong conviction that the act in question is morally wrong. When they think about a case like that of Wilma, moreover, most people do not view it through the lens of the kind of metaphysical system developed by Lewis. What they think is that it is wrong for Wilma to conceive a blind child now rather than a sighted child later even if we assume that the sighted child really would be a different person. When I introduced the robustness

---

[11] Parsons (2003: 148, 150).

requirement in section 1.3.2, I said that in order to satisfy the requirement, a reason for rejecting a given premise of the non-identity argument must be strong enough to prevent a modified version of the argument from producing the same Implausible Conclusion. The Implausible Conclusion says that Wilma's act of conceiving Pebbles rather than Rocks is not morally wrong. But what this really means for most people is that Wilma's act of conceiving Pebbles rather than Rocks is wrong even if Pebbles and Rocks really would be different people. And the metaphysical objection to P1 can do nothing to show that this claim is false. It can help account for the wrongness of Wilma's act if Pebbles and Rocks turn out to be one and the same person and Wilma's choice turns out not to really be a non-identity choice. But it can't help account for the wrongness of Wilma's act if Pebbles and Rocks turn out to be different people and her choice turns out to be a genuine non-identity choice. And so even if it were modest enough to satisfy the modesty requirement, a solution based on the metaphysical objection to P1 would still fail to be robust enough to satisfy the robustness requirement.

2.4 The Equivocation Objection

P1 claims that Wilma's act of conceiving Pebbles does not make Pebbles worse off than she would otherwise have been. Part of the reason this claim seems so difficult to deny is that, by stipulation, the disability that Pebbles is born with is clearly not so bad as to prevent her life from being worth living. And if Pebbles's life is clearly worth living, then how could she be made worse off by living it than she would otherwise have been? A fourth objection to P1, however, maintains that things are not so simple. It does this by appealing to a distinction between two things that might be meant by the claim that a particular life is not worth living. This objection to P1 has been pressed by Janet Malek.

Following an argument first put forth by David Benatar,[12] Malek points out that the claim that a particular life is worth living is ambiguous. It could mean that the life is worth continuing but it could also mean that the life is worth creating. She then argues that the quality of life required to make a life worth living in the second sense is higher than that required to make a life worth living in the first. If this is so, then there could be lives that are worth continuing but not worth creating. And this, in turn, reveals a sense in which P1 could turn out to be false. As Malek puts it:

As a result of the discrepancy between a life worth continuing and a life worth conceiving, there are some cases in which a child whose life is worth continuing is worse off than if he had never existed (because he does not have a life that was worth conceiving). While it is true that the interests of a child whose life is worth *conceiving* cannot be lowered by his own conception, it is not true that the interests of a child whose life is merely worth *continuing* are not lower than

¹² See Benatar (2000: 175–7).

they otherwise would have been. Therefore, if the phrase "a life worth living" means "a life worth continuing," [then P1] is false.[13]

The key question, then, is why we should think that some levels of well-being are such that a life lived at that level would be worth continuing but nonetheless not worth creating. Malek offers two arguments in defense of this claim, but neither is successful.

Malek's first argument is based on the claim that it takes more to justify ending a life than it takes to justify not creating a life.[14] This is a reasonable starting point. In general, it is difficult to justify killing someone and easy to justify not creating someone. Malek takes it that this claim supports the conclusion that some lives that are worth continuing are not worth creating. Her reasoning seems to run as follows: the threshold at which a life is worth continuing is relatively low, so it takes a relatively strong justification to end it. The threshold at which a life is worth creating is relatively high, so it takes a relatively weak justification to decline to start it. If this is right, then the mere fact that a life is worth continuing is not enough to show that it would have been worth creating. If a given life would not have been worth creating, then it may well be worse than no life at all even if it would be worth continuing if it were created. And if it would be worse than no life at all in this sense in the case of Pebbles, then P1 would turn out to be false after all.

The problem with Malek's first argument is that there is a better explanation for the asymmetry the argument rests on, and the better explanation fails to support her objection to P1. The better explanation is that it is relatively hard to justify killing a person because people have a right to life and relatively easy to justify not creating a person because merely possible people have no right to be conceived. This alternative explanation is better than Malek's both because of the plausibility of the distinction it appeals to and because it can account for our judgments in certain cases where Malek's explanation cannot.

Suppose, for example, that you know that if you conceive a child today the child will go on to enjoy an extraordinarily wonderful life. Most people will agree that you could justify your decision not to conceive the child simply by appealing to the fact that you don't want to. The rights-based account explains why it is so easy for you to justify your decision: the person you would create if you conceive today has no claim against you that you help bring him or her into existence. But Malek's explanation cannot account for this judgment. On her account, the reason it is relatively easy to justify not conceiving a child in general is that the threshold at which a life is worth creating is relatively high. But this does nothing to explain why it is still relatively easy to justify not conceiving a child even in cases where the life in question would clearly fall well above that threshold.

Or suppose that a person already exists, that he is suffering an absolutely miserable life with no possibility for improvement, but that he nonetheless explicitly tells you

---

[13] Malek (Unpublished-b: 6).   [14] See also Benatar (2000: 177).

that he does not want you to kill him. Most people will agree that it would be very hard to justify killing this person. Certainly you could not justify it simply by appealing to the fact that you wanted to kill him. The rights-based account explains why it is so hard for you to justify killing this person: even though his quality of life is extremely low, his right to life and refusal to consent to being killed generates a very strong reason against killing him. But Malek's explanation cannot account for this judgment. On her account, the reason it is relatively hard to justify killing a person in general is that the threshold at which a life is worth continuing is relatively low. But this does nothing to explain why it is still relatively hard to justify killing a person without their consent even in cases where the person's life clearly falls below that threshold.

Malek's second argument appeals to the common belief that death is bad for a person in a way that not existing prior to conception is not bad. As Malek puts the argument:

Although death is generally viewed as a bad thing, people are rarely troubled by preconception nonexistence. Because the "bad" of death must be figured into evaluations of whether a life is worth continuing, the threshold at which a life is judged to be worth continuing must be lower than the threshold at which it is judged to be worth conceiving.[15]

Prior to creating a person, that is, there is only one good thing about creating them: the welfare that they will enjoy if they exist. The fact that creating them will protect them from never existing, as it were, is not a further good thing about creating them. If they never exist, their not existing will not be bad for them. But after a person has already been created, there are two good things about continuing their life: the welfare they will enjoy if they continue to exist and the fact that continuing their life will protect from death, which is a bad thing for them. The badness of death, on this account, provides an extra reason for extending a person's life, a reason that does not exist in the case of merely creating someone's life. If that is correct, then there again seems to be a reason to think that there can be lives that are worth extending but not worth creating. And if that is correct, then there again seems to be a reason to reject P1.

But whether the badness of death for a person raises a problem for P1 depends on why, exactly, death is bad for a person. And on the most natural account of why death is bad for a person, Malek's objection to P1 proves to be unsuccessful. On that account, death is bad for a person because it deprives the person of the valuable future experiences he would otherwise have enjoyed. But this means that death is bad for the person only if those future experiences would have been good for him to have. If death deprives a person only of experiences that it would have been bad for him to have, such as unrelenting, excruciating suffering, then the death is not bad for that person. This is the commonsense view of the matter.

But if this view is correct, then we should say precisely the same thing about whether a person's life would be worth creating in the first place. If the future experiences that an already existing person would enjoy are good enough to make his premature death

---

[15] Malek, (Unpublished-b: 5).

bad for him, then if those very same experiences would also be enjoyed by a not yet existing person, they should also be good enough to make that person's life worth creating. If they are good enough to be bad to lose, that is, then they are good enough to be worth obtaining in the first place. And if they are good enough to be worth obtaining in the first place, then they are good enough to be worth creating the person who would have them. In the end, then, Malek's second argument, like her first, fails to justify the claim that there is a range of cases in which a person's life would be worth continuing but not worth creating. And as a result, both of her arguments fail to raise a problem for P1 of the non-identity argument.

I have argued so far that Malek's arguments fail to establish that there are cases in which a child whose life is worth continuing is worse off than if he had never existed. But let's now suppose that I have been mistaken about this and that there really are such cases. Even if this is so, the existence of such cases will not be enough to solve the non-identity problem. This is because it will show only that there are some cases in which P1 is false, not that there are no cases in which P1 is true. And as long as there are some cases in which P1 is true, the objection based on the distinction between lives that are worth creating and lives that are worth continuing will fail to be robust enough to solve the non-identity problem. If Malek's arguments are successful, that is, then there will be at least some conditions that are so bad that it would not be worth creating a life with that condition even though it would be worth continuing a life with it. In such cases, P1 of the non-identity argument would turn out to be false. But this would provide no reason to think that every case that generates the non-identity problem involves such a condition and so no reason to think that there are no cases in which P1 of the non-identity argument would turn out to be true.

Imagine, for example, a person whose quality of life is so low that it is just barely worth continuing. If it were even just a tiny bit lower, the life would no longer be worth living at all. In this case, if Malek's arguments are correct, we ought to say that while a life in that condition is worth continuing, it is not worth creating. A person already living such a life would be better off continuing to live, that is, but they would have been better off still if they had never come into existence in the first place. The non-identity problem will not arise in such a case on this account. The act of creating such a person will be wrong because it will make that person worse off than they would otherwise have been. The non-identity problem in that case will be dissolved because P1 will be false.

As I have already noted, I am skeptical about this claim. If the person's quality of life, however low, is good enough that it is bad for him to lose it, it still seems good enough that it would not be worse for him to gain it in the first place. But even if we are willing to say in some such cases that the person is worse off coming into existence, surely we will not be willing to say it about all of the cases that can be used to generate the non-identity problem. Indeed, we would surely not be willing to say it in the case of Wilma and Pebbles. Our judgment of the quality of life of a typical blind person is not simply that the person's life is just barely worth continuing, but that it was worth creating in the first place. You might encounter a person with an extremely low quality of life and think that they would have been better off not existing, but it is extremely unlikely that you would think this of a person simply because the person was blind. Even if Malek's arguments prove to be successful, then, they can underwrite a solution to the non-identity problem as I have formulated it only if we agree that being blind is so terrible that a blind person is worse off being brought into existence than never existing at all. And this claim is sufficiently implausible to prevent any solution that depends on it from satisfying the modesty requirement.

2.5 The Asymmetry Objection

A final objection to P1 arises from the claim that there is an important asymmetry between pleasure and pain. This objection is pressed by David Benatar in his provocative 2006 book *Better Never to Have Been*,[16] and if it can be sustained, it would establish that Wilma's act of conceiving Pebbles really does make Pebbles worse off than she would otherwise have been, even if everything that I have said so far in this chapter has been correct.

Benatar grounds his argument in the intuitive response that he expects most people to have to a variety of cases. Consider, for example, what I will call the Blessed Couple and the Cursed Couple. The Blessed Couple knows that if they conceive a child, the child's life on the whole will contain a million units of pleasure and zero units of pain. The Cursed Couple knows that if they conceive a child, the child's life on the whole will contain zero units of pleasure and a million units of pain. It is difficult to resist the thought that there is an important moral asymmetry between the two cases and that while it would be wrong for the Cursed Couple to conceive the Cursed Child, it would not be wrong for the Blessed Couple not to conceive the Blessed Child. If there really is such an evaluative difference between the Blessed Couple and the Cursed Couple, moreover, there must be some general principle that accounts for it. Benatar's strategy is to identify the general principle that he thinks best accounts for the difference and then to show that this principle has important implications for, among other things, the question of whether Wilma's act of conceiving Pebbles makes Pebbles worse off than she would otherwise have been.

Benatar presents the general principle he appeals to as a set of four claims:[17]

(1) the presence of pain is bad
(2) the presence of pleasure is good
(3) the absence of pain is good, even if that good is not enjoyed by anyone

---

[16] For an earlier version of the argument, see Benatar (1997). For a related argument, see Weinberg (2008). The discussion that follows is a modified version of Boonin (2012).

[17] Benatar (2006: 30).

(4) the absence of pleasure is not bad unless there is somebody for whom this absence is a deprivation

A few clarifications are in order before we turn to the question of why we should accept this set of claims and what, if anything, it implies about the case of Wilma and Pebbles.

I take it that (1) and (2) are straightforward and uncontroversial. They assert that pain in itself is a bad thing and that pleasure in itself is a good thing. It should be clear, moreover, in what sense they are to be taken to be bad in itself and good in itself: they are bad or good for someone, namely the person who experiences them. But (3) and (4), and the asymmetry between them, require a bit more attention. Let me begin with (4). The claim that the absence of pleasure is not bad unless there is somebody for whom this absence is a deprivation suggests (although it does not strictly entail)[18] that the absence of pleasure is, in fact, bad, when it is the deprivation of pleasure for a particular person. This may sound as if Benatar means to say that the absence of pleasure in such a case is bad in itself, in the way that the presence of pain is bad in itself, but several pages later he clarifies that

when I say that [the absent pleasure that is a deprivation of a particular person] is bad, I do not mean that it is bad in the same way that the presence of pain is bad. What is meant is that the absent pleasure is relatively (rather than intrinsically) bad. In other words, it is *worse* than the presence of pleasure.[19]

This suggests that we can restate (4) as follows:

(4) the absence of pleasure is *worse than* the presence of pleasure only if there is somebody for whom this absence is a deprivation

which in turn suggests that we can restate (3) as follows:[20]

(3) the absence of pain is *better than* the presence of pain even if there is nobody for whom the absence of pain is a benefit

And this, in turn, raises a question about (3).

Unlike (1) and (2), which make claims about something's being good or bad *simpliciter*, (3) and (4) make relational claims about one thing's being better or worse than another. (4) makes a claim that one thing is worse than another only in the case where the same person exists in both scenarios that are being compared. It says, for example, that Larry existing without pleasure is worse than Larry existing with pleasure. This claim raises no particular difficulty about what is meant by one thing's being worse than

---

[18] The absence of pleasure as a deprivation might be good, for example, if the person deserves to be deprived of the pleasure. I will follow Benatar in ignoring such potential complications.

[19] Benatar (2006: 41).

[20] This is not to insist that Benatar would not also endorse the claim that that absence of pain is intrinsically good under such conditions, but for purposes of explicating and analyzing the argument, it will prove to be simpler to render (3) and (4) parallel in this respect.

another. The former scenario is presumably worse than the latter because it is worse for Larry. But (3) makes a claim about one thing's being better than another not just in the kind of case where the same person exists in both scenarios being compared, but also in the kind of case where the person exists in one scenario and doesn't exist in the other. It maintains not only that Larry existing without pain is better than Larry existing in pain, that is, but also that there being no pain because there is no Larry is better than Larry existing in pain. The former claim again raises no particular difficulty about what is meant since in that case Larry existing without pain is presumably better than Larry existing in pain because it is better for Larry. But the latter claim does raise a problem: how can Larry's not existing at all be better for Larry than Larry's existing in pain? For one condition to be better than another for Larry seems to require that both conditions be conditions of Larry, and it is a familiar point that non-existence is not a condition that characterizes Larry when Larry doesn't exist. Saying that Larry is non-existent is just another way of saying that there is no Larry, and so no condition of Larry at all.

Benatar offers two responses to this problem,[21] but I will focus here only on one. Following Feinberg, Benatar points out that it seems perfectly intelligible to say of some existing person that he would be better off dead. This seems intelligible, on Benatar's account, not because it means that if he dies he will then be in a condition that is better for him than his current condition, but because it simply means that from the point of view of his own well-being, he should prefer not to exist at all rather than to exist in his current condition. When (3) maintains that the absence of pain is better than the presence of pain even if there is nobody for whom the absence of pain is a benefit, then, the relational claim can be understood in this sense. Just as it can make sense to say of a particular person that it is better for him that he no longer exist than that he continue to exist given that his existence involves a certain amount of pain, so it can make sense to say of a person who would otherwise have existed that it is better—and better *for him*—not to exist than to exist in a certain amount of pain.[22] Of course, we can identify the already existing person in whose interest it is to cease existing while we cannot identify the particular person who would have existed and who would have been worse off for having existed. But, at least on Benatar's account,

we can still say that whoever that person would have been, the avoidance of his or her pains is good when judged in terms of his or her potential interests. If there is any (obviously loose) sense in which the absent pain is good *for* the person who could have existed but does not exist, this is it.[23]

With all of this in mind, then, we can restate Benatar's set of claims more precisely as follows:

(1) the presence of pain is intrinsically bad
(2) the presence of pleasure is intrinsically good

[21] See Benatar (2006: 21–2).   [22] Benatar (2006: 30–1).   [23] Benatar (2006: 31).

(3) the absence of pain is better than the presence of pain if either (a) there is an actual person whose interests are better served by the absence of the pain or (b) the presence of the pain would require the existence of a person who would not otherwise exist and whose potential interests are better served by the absence of the pain

(4) the absence of pleasure is worse than the presence of pleasure only if there is an actual person whose interests are better served by the presence of the pleasure

Since the four claims together maintain that the presence of pleasure and pain are symmetric with respect to intrinsic goodness and badness but that there is an asymmetry between the absence of pleasure and pain with respect to the relational properties of being better than and worse than, I will refer to the conjunction of these four claims as Benatar's Relational Asymmetry Principle (RAP).

Why should we think that the Relational Asymmetry Principle is true? The answer, according to Benatar, is that accepting the principle provides the best way for us to make sense of our intuitions about cases like the Blessed Couple and the Cursed Couple. If the Cursed Couple conceives, there will be a child existing in pain rather than no child at all. According to RAP (3b), the absence of pain is better than the presence of pain if the presence of the pain would require the existence of a person who would not otherwise exist and whose potential interests are better served by the absence of the pain. And so RAP implies that by conceiving the Cursed Child, the Cursed Couple would make things worse for that child. If the Blessed Couple decides not to conceive, there will be no child at all rather than a child existing with pleasure. According to RAP (4), the absence of pleasure is worse than the presence of pleasure only if there is an actual person whose interests are better served by the presence of the pleasure. Since if the Blessed Couple does not conceive there will be no such actual person, this means that if the Blessed Couple does not conceive the Blessed Child, they will not make things worse for that child. RAP, in short, seems to entail that what the Cursed Couple does by conceiving makes things worse for the Cursed Child while what the Blessed Couple does by refraining from conceiving does not make things worse for the Blessed Child. And this, in turn, seems to provide a natural explanation for why it is wrong for the Cursed Couple to conceive but not wrong for the Blessed Couple not to conceive.

Let's suppose for the moment that RAP is true. What would it entail about Wilma's act of conceiving Pebbles? We have been assuming that despite her disability, the life of Pebbles will clearly contain more good than bad. To make this perfectly clear for the sake of the example, let's suppose that if Wilma conceives Pebbles, Pebbles's life on the whole will contain 500,000 units of pleasure and only 20,000 units of pain. Intuitively, it should seem clear that Pebbles would not be made worse off by being conceived in this case. But RAP seems to show that this assessment is mistaken.

Following Benatar, we can think about what RAP would imply about the case of Wilma by considering the relevance of the pain that Pebbles would suffer and the relevance of the pleasure that Pebbles would enjoy independently. With respect to the

20,000 units of pain that Pebbles will suffer if Wilma conceives her, RAP entails that Pebbles existing will be worse for Pebbles than Pebbles not existing. RAP (3b) maintains that the absence of pain is better than the presence of pain even if there is no actual person who is benefited by the absence of pain. So, with respect to the choice between existing and not existing, the 20,000 units of pain that Pebbles would suffer count against bringing Pebbles into existence. Even though it is true that if Pebbles is not conceived there will be no actual person who is benefited by the absence of the 20,000 of units of pain, RAP (3b) maintains that the absence of pain still makes it better for Pebbles that she not exist than that she exist.

With respect to the 500,000 units of pleasure that Pebbles will enjoy if Wilma conceives her, however, the implications of RAP are crucially different. In particular, the principle entails that in this respect, Pebbles existing will not be better for Pebbles than Pebbles not existing. RAP (4) maintains that the absence of pleasure is worse than the presence of pleasure only if there is an actual person whose interests are better served by the presence of the pleasure. But in the case of Pebbles, the absence of the 500,000 units of pleasure would be the result of the absence of any actual Pebbles to be deprived of it. So, with respect to the choice between existing and not existing, the 500,000 units of pleasure that Pebbles would enjoy if she were conceived do not make it better for Pebbles that she exist than that she not exist.

The result of combining these two considerations is as follows. With respect to the 20,000 units of pain, non-existence is better for Pebbles than existence. With respect to the 500,000 units of pleasure, existence is not better for Pebbles than non-existence. So non-existence has one advantage for Pebbles over existence—it avoids the badness of Pebbles suffering pain—but existence has no advantage for Pebbles over non-existence—the fact that Pebbles would enjoy pleasure makes existence no better for her than non-existence because the absence of pleasure is not worse for Pebbles than the presence of pleasure when there is no actual Pebbles to be deprived of the absent pleasure. If non-existence has an advantage over existence for Pebbles and existence has no advantage over non-existence for Pebbles, then non-existence is better for Pebbles than existence. If Wilma conceives Pebbles, she will cause the worse thing to happen from the point of view of the interests of Pebbles. Relative to non-existence, she will not be better off as a result of the 500,000 units of pleasure. But relative to non-existence, she will be worse off as a result of the 20,000 units of pain. So Wilma will make Pebbles worse off by conceiving her. P1 of the non-identity argument is therefore false, and we can solve the non-identity argument by appealing to the claim that Wilma's act is wrong because it harms Pebbles.

There are a number of reasons to reject this solution. First, it fails to satisfy the modesty requirement. The argument it appeals to entails that every act of conceiving a person harms that person as long as the person's life will contain at least some pain. Since the life of every person contains at least some pain, this means that the argument entails that every person who is conceived is harmed by being brought into existence. This implication is more implausible than the Implausible Conclusion that the solution would help us to avoid. If we can establish that it is wrong for Wilma to conceive Pebbles only by showing that it is wrong for anyone to conceive anyone, this will show that the non-identity problem is an even bigger problem than it seemed, not a smaller one. The asymmetric cure is worse than the non-identity disease.

Second, the argument the solution rests on is not strong enough to satisfy the robustness requirement. This is because the argument that entails that Wilma would harm Pebbles by conceiving her also entails that Wilma would harm Rocks by conceiving him. Since Wilma's choice is between conceiving Pebbles and conceiving Rocks, and since Benatar's argument entails that either choice would harm the person she conceives, the fact that conceiving Pebbles would harm the person she conceives provides no reason to think that it would be wrong for Wilma to conceive Pebbles. Benatar's argument, that is, might show that it would be wrong for Wilma to conceive Pebbles rather than to conceive no one, but it cannot show that it would be wrong for Wilma to conceive Pebbles rather than to conceive Rocks. And it is the difficulty of justifying the latter claim that gives rise to the non-identity problem.

I suspect that these two problems will strike most readers as sufficient grounds for rejecting a solution to the non-identity problem that is based on Benatar's argument. Indeed, for most people the first problem will likely seem enough on its own. For those who are not convinced of this, though, as well as for those who are simply interested in Benatar's position, I want to add that there is an even bigger problem with such a solution: it ultimately fails to satisfy the independence requirement. This is because Benatar's argument depends on his claim that the Relational Asymmetry Principle provides the best explanation for the moral asymmetry between cases like that of the Blessed Couple and the Cursed Couple and because this claim can be undermined on independent grounds. My argument for this claim is somewhat lengthy. It is contained in Appendix B. Readers who are already convinced that a solution to the non-identity problem that is based on Benatar's position should be rejected and who are not particularly interested in the position itself may want to simply ignore this appendix. For those who are not yet convinced that Benatar's solution should be rejected or who at least remain interested in Benatar's project, the appendix provides an additional reason to reject Benatar's argument and thus to reject the prospect of solving the non-identity problem by means of it. Whether because of the reasons contained in the appendix or simply for the reasons stated here, while Benatar's argument offers an intriguing challenge to P1 of the non-identity argument, it is ultimately no more able to ground a satisfactory solution to the non-identity problem than are any of the other available objections to P1. If we are going to avoid the Implausible Conclusion by rejecting one of the premises of the non-identity argument, we will have to look elsewhere.

3

Rejecting the Second Premise

The first premise of the non-identity argument maintains that Wilma's act of conceiving Pebbles does not make Pebbles worse off than she would otherwise have been. I argued in Chapter 2 that no reason for rejecting P1 can ground a satisfactory solution to the non-identity problem. So let's now suppose that P1 is true. Does this mean that Wilma's act does not harm Pebbles? It does if we accept the additional claim that if A's act harms B, then A's act makes B worse off than B would otherwise have been. This claim constitutes the second premise of the non-identity argument, and I will refer to the account of harm that it embodies as the Counterfactual Account of harm. If, as P1 maintains, Wilma's act does not make Pebbles worse off than she would otherwise have been and if, as P2 maintains, harming a person does make that person worse off than they would otherwise have been, then Wilma's act does not harm Pebbles. And if Wilma's act does not harm Pebbles, then we can start to see why there is a problem accounting for the presumed wrongness of Wilma's act.

The Counterfactual Account is the commonsense account of harm. If I vandalize your car and you are asked why you think that my act has harmed you, you are likely to reply by pointing to the various ways in which my act has made you worse off than you would have been had I not vandalized your car. If you demand compensation for the harm that my act has caused you and you are asked what you think would be a fair amount, moreover, you are likely to describe a settlement that would leave you no worse off than you would have been had I not done what I did. The goal of compensating you for the harm done to you, that is, seems to be to erase the harm to the extent that doing so is possible. And if erasing the harm done to you amounts to restoring you to the condition that you would now be enjoying had my act not occurred, then the harm itself seems to amount to my making you worse off than you would have been had my act not occurred in the first place. Finally, if I complain that your act of scratching your nose has harmed me, you are likely to appeal to the claim that your act did not in any way make me worse off than I would otherwise have been as a way of rebutting my complaint. In all of these contexts, the Counterfactual Account seems to provide the clearest and most natural way to make sense of our commonsense beliefs about harm. And so it seems reasonable to accept the Counterfactual Account of harm unless a better alternative comes along.[1]

---

[1] Thomson has recently defended a more complex version of the Counterfactual Account on which if

Indeed, our commonsense beliefs about harm seem to support an even stronger claim than the one made by the Counterfactual Account. The Counterfactual Account claims that an act's making someone worse off than they would otherwise have been is necessary in order for the act to harm that person. It does not claim that making the person worse off than they would otherwise have been is also sufficient for the act to harm that person. But it is difficult to think of a case in which we would be inclined to say that an act had made a particular person worse off than they would otherwise have been and yet not be inclined to say that the act had harmed that person.[2] And so our commonsense beliefs can probably be used to establish an initial presumption in favor of the stronger claim that making a person worse off than they would otherwise have been is both necessary and sufficient for harming that person.

Assessing this stronger claim, however, will not be necessary for our purposes. The non-identity argument requires only the claim that making a person worse off than they would otherwise have been is a necessary condition for harming them in order to

A's act harms B, then A's act causes B to be in a particular state and prevents B from being in some other state that would have been better for B in at least some respect (2011: 448). It is not clear to me that the cases Thomson appeals to in arriving at this result justify favoring her account over the simpler version of the Counterfactual Account that I have labeled P2 (Thomson cites a case in which villain C throws acid in victim A's eyes and bystander B subsequently sprays a neutralizer into A's eyes which prevents A from becoming fully blind but results in A's having dim vision. Thomson's version of the Counterfactual Account produces the intuitively correct result here: that C harmed A but B did not. But the simple Counterfactual Account seems to produce the same result: C's throwing the acid in A's eyes did make A worse off than A would have been if C had not thrown the acid, and B's spraying the neutralizer in A's eyes did not make A worse off than A would have been if B had not sprayed the neutralizer). But even if we accept this more complicated version of the account, the result will still be that Wilma did not harm Pebbles by conceiving her. As Thomson herself notes in the context of a slightly different case, there is no state better for Pebbles than blindness that Wilma's act of conceiving Pebbles prevented Pebbles from enjoying (2011: 451). And the same will hold of the case of the wealthy society: although selecting the risky policy causes the toxic waste to later leak which in turn causes some future people to be killed, there is no state that is better for them than this that adopting the policy prevents them from enjoying.

[2] Bradley (2012: 397) suggests that the following sort of case generates a problem for the claim that making someone worse off than they would otherwise have been is sufficient for harming that person: suppose that I consider giving you some new golf clubs that you would enjoy and then I decide not to do so. The claim that making you worse off than you would otherwise have been is sufficient for harming you entails that I have harmed you by refraining from giving you the golf clubs and that result strikes Bradley as implausible. But the claim that A's *act* harms B if and only if A's act makes B worse off than B would otherwise have been need not entail that I harm you in this case since my not giving you golf clubs is not clearly an act of mine. We might well say that my omitting to give you golf clubs harms you, but I am inclined to think that this implication is not particularly implausible. If I decline to give you a pill that I have in my pocket that would prevent you from suffering a great deal of pain, for example, I think most people would find it perfectly plausible and even natural to say that I have harmed you by withholding the medicine. The benefit that you are deprived of from not getting the new golf clubs may be trivial by comparison, but that means only that the harm to you from not getting the golf clubs would be trivial in that case, not that it would be no harm at all. In addition, the parallel implication strikes me as perfectly plausible in the case of benefiting someone. If I am considering filing a lawsuit against you and you know that I would have a very good chance of winning a large amount of money from you if I did, then you would probably find it natural to feel a great sense of relief if I decide not to go ahead with the action and to feel that my decision to refrain from suing you has benefited you (for an additional response to the objection, see Klocksiem (2012: 293–5)). So I am inclined to think that making worse off is both necessary and sufficient for harming. But as I note in the text below, this stronger claim is not necessary in order to sustain the non-identity argument.

justify the move from the claim made by P1, the claim that Wilma's act does not make Pebbles worse off than she would otherwise have been, to C1, the claim that Wilma's act does not harm Pebbles. As a result, I will continue to formulate the Counterfactual Account in terms of providing a necessary condition for harming someone rather than a necessary and sufficient condition. So understood, the account may initially seem to be so strongly supported by our commonsense beliefs and practices that it may be difficult to imagine what the alternatives are. But there are, in fact, a number of alternatives worth considering. The goal of this chapter is to consider those alternatives and to assess their implications for solving the non-identity problem.

It may help to organize our discussion of the possible alternatives to the Counterfactual Account of harm if we begin by noting two features of the Counterfactual Account itself. First, the Counterfactual Account of harm is fundamentally comparative: to say that an act harms a person involves identifying two distinct states of affairs and then comparing them in terms of one's being worse than the other for the person in question. Second, the Counterfactual Account employs a particular baseline in making the comparison: it asks whether the state of affairs that results from performing the act is worse for the person in question than the state of affairs that would have resulted had the act not been performed. This is why the account is not simply comparative, but counterfactually comparative.

Given these two features of the Counterfactual Account, there are three ways in which we could try to develop an alternative account of harm. First, we could preserve the fundamentally comparative structure of the Counterfactual Account but substitute a different comparative baseline. Rather than saying that if A's act harms B then it makes B worse off than B would otherwise have been, that is, we could say that if A's act harms B then it makes B worse off than some other point of comparison. Second, we could change the fundamentally comparative structure of the account itself and replace it with one on which comparative considerations play some role in the analysis of harm while non-comparative considerations play some role as well. Finally, we could abandon comparative considerations altogether and maintain that the best analysis of harm is entirely non-comparative. I will consider the first kind of alternative in section 3.1, the second kind in section 3.2, and the third kind in section 3.3.

Before turning to the alternatives to P2, however, it is worth briefly considering one kind of case that might seem to pose a problem for the Counterfactual Account itself. This is the kind of case in which an act kills a person. Suppose, for example, that Norm is an ordinary person with a reasonably happy future ahead of him and that I kill him painlessly in his sleep. Intuitively, it seems clear that my act harms Norm. But it might seem that the Counterfactual Account is incapable of accounting for this judgment. This is because if I kill Norm, then there is no Norm to be worse off than he would have been had I not killed him. And if there is no Norm to be worse off than he would otherwise have been, then my act of killing Norm does not make it the case that Norm is worse off than he would otherwise have been. The Counterfactual Account will therefore entail that my act of killing Norm does not harm him.

I am inclined to think that the case of Norm does not pose a genuine problem for the Counterfactual Account. This is because I am inclined to think that the claim that "A's act makes B worse off than B would otherwise have been" does not entail the claim that "after A's act, B exists in a state that is a worse state for B than the state in which B would otherwise have existed." In typical cases of harm, making B worse off than he would otherwise have been does involve causing B to subsequently exist in a worse state than that in which he would otherwise have existed. If I vandalize your car, or punch you in the nose, or steal your wallet, I leave you in a worse state after my act than you would otherwise have been in, and it is precisely because of this that my act makes you worse off than you would otherwise have been. But death is not a typical case of harm. There is therefore no reason to think that it must involve making its victim worse off in the same way that typical harms do. And once we recognize this, we can see that the Counterfactual Account is capable of accounting for the harm of death after all.

When I kill Norm, I do not cause him to be in a state that it is worse for him to be in, but I do make him worse off than he would otherwise have been. By killing Norm and depriving him of the reasonably happy future he had ahead of him, I make his life as a whole go less well for him. Causing Norm's life as a whole to go less well for him makes Norm worse off. It is true that after Norm is dead there is no Norm for whom things have been made worse by his life's being shortened. But it is nonetheless also true that Norm is worse off living a shorter life than living a longer life and that my act of killing him causes him to live the shorter life rather than the longer life. My act of killing Norm therefore makes Norm worse off by causing him to live a worse life. He is not worse off once he is dead, but he is nonetheless worse off living the shorter life than he would have been had he lived the longer life that he would otherwise have lived. The fact that killing Norm does not put him in a worse state, then, does not show that killing Norm does not make Norm worse off than he would otherwise have been. It shows only that killing Norm does not make Norm worse off than he would otherwise have been by putting him in a worse state than he would otherwise have been in. But killing Norm does make Norm worse off than he would otherwise have been despite the fact that it does not put him in a worse state than he would otherwise have been in. It makes Norm worse off than he would otherwise have been by making Norm live a life that is less good for him than the life that he would otherwise have lived would have been. And because this is so, the Counterfactual Account of harm can successfully account for the fact that the act of killing Norm harms him. Or so it seems to me.[3]

Because I'm inclined to think that killing Norm really does make Norm worse off than he would otherwise have been, I'm inclined to think that the case of Norm poses no problem for the Counterfactual Account as I have stated it. But if it turns out that I am mistaken about this, we can easily reformulate the account to avoid this problem. We can do this by saying that if A's act harms B, then A's act makes *B's life* worse for B than it would otherwise have been. This formulation of the Counterfactual Account

---

[3] Feldman defends this kind of account (1991: 218–20). See also Purves (Forthcoming).

has the same implications that the original formulation has in typical cases of harm because vandalizing your car, punching you in the nose, and stealing your wallet all make your life worse for you than it would otherwise have been. It also clearly entails that killing Norm harms him since killing Norm makes Norm's life overall worse for him than it would otherwise have been. Even if we are convinced that making Norm's life worse than it would otherwise have been does not entail making Norm himself worse off than he would otherwise have been, and so are convinced that the original formulation of the Counterfactual Account entails that killing Norm does not harm him, this revised version of the account will be able to avoid this problem. And the revised formulation of the Counterfactual Account is just as good as the original formulation for the purposes of generating the non-identity problem: Wilma's act of conceiving Pebbles does not make Pebbles's life worse for her than it would otherwise have been just as it does not make Pebbles herself worse off than she would otherwise have been. I find this alternative formulation of the Counterfactual Account more awkward and less intuitive than the one I started with, and since modifying the original formulation also strikes me as unnecessary, I will continue to characterize the Counterfactual Account in terms of A's act making B worse off. But in reading what follows, those who agree that killing Norm makes his life as a whole go worse but deny that this means that it makes Norm himself worse off can simply substitute the formulation on which the Counterfactual Account is cashed out in terms of A's act making B's life worse for B than it would otherwise have been and this should have no effect on the substance of any of the relevant arguments. The objections that I will raise against those solutions to the non-identity problem that are based on rejecting P2 of the non-identity argument will not be affected by the answer to the question of which formulation of P2 we should accept if we do not reject P2. Having attended to this initial concern about the Counterfactual Account, then, let us turn to the alternatives.

3.1 Non-counterfactual Comparative Accounts of Harm

One kind of alternative to the Counterfactual Account of harm arises from the thought that while the account might be correct in picturing harm as a fundamentally comparative matter, it might nonetheless be mistaken in taking as its comparative baseline the state of affairs that would have resulted had the act in question not been performed. The challenge in developing an alternative comparative account lies in identifying and motivating the alternative baseline. The challenge in using such an alternative account to solve the non-identity problem lies in showing that the account can justify the claim that Wilma's act wrongfully harms Pebbles. I am skeptical about whether the first challenge can be met. But even if it can, I am confident that the second cannot.

3.1.1 The Temporal Account

Perhaps the most natural alternative baseline refers to how things were before the act in question took place. The result of substituting this temporal baseline for the counterfactual baseline employed by the Counterfactual Account is what I will call the Temporal Account of harm.

TA: If A's act harms B, then A's act makes B worse off than B was before A's act

The Temporal Account gets it right in simple cases just as the Counterfactual Account does. When I vandalize your car, for example, my act clearly harms you. The Counterfactual Account produces this result because my act makes you worse off than you would otherwise have been. The Temporal Account produces the same result because my act also makes you worse off than you were before I vandalized your car. Similarly, when you scratch your nose, your act clearly does not harm me. The Counterfactual Account produces this result because your act does not make me worse off than I would otherwise have been. But the Temporal Account again produces the same result: your act also does not make me worse off than I was before you scratched your nose. As a result, the Temporal Account seems to be at least as good as the Counterfactual Account.

In addition, there is one kind of case in which the Temporal Account seems to prove superior to the Counterfactual Account. This is the kind of case in which an act makes you worse off than you were before but does not make you worse off than you would otherwise have been. Consider the following example.[4]

The Two Hit Men: Mr. Bad orders Hit Man 1 to shoot and kill you. Hit Man 1 doesn't always follow his orders, so Mr. Bad orders Hit Man 2 to shoot and kill you if Hit Man 1 fails to shoot and kill you. Hit Man 2 always follows his orders. As it happens, though, Hit Man 1 shoots and kills you and Hit Man 2's orders prove to be unnecessary.

It seems clear that Hit Man 1 harms you when he shoots and kills you. And the Temporal Account produces the correct result in this instance. Hit Man 1's act of shooting you makes you worse off than you were before he shot you. But the Counterfactual Account seems to produce the wrong result this time. Hit Man 1's act of shooting you does not make you worse off than you would have been if Hit Man 1 had not shot you because if Hit Man 1 had not shot you then Hit Man 2 would have shot you instead. The Temporal Account seems to get it right in all the cases that the Counterfactual Account gets right, then, and it also seems to get it right in a kind of case that the Counterfactual Account seems to get wrong. As a result, it seems that we should reject the Counterfactual Account of harm. And since the Counterfactual Account of harm

---

[4] This is a modified version of an example given by Hanser (2008: 436). Thomson presents some similar cases as problems for the Counterfactual Account, though not in favor of the Temporal Account (2011: 446–7). Woollard (2012: 684) and Bradley (2012: 396) have also recently appealed to similar cases in arguing against the Counterfactual Account. See also Carter (2002: 93).

represents P2 of the non-identity argument, it seems that we can solve the non-identity problem by rejecting P2.

I'm inclined to think that a proponent of the Counterfactual Account should simply bite the bullet here and deny that Hit Man 1's act harms you. This is because I'm inclined to think that the case of the two hit men is relevantly similar to other cases that seem, at least to me, to pose no problem for that account. Suppose, for example, that Philip is trapped on a runaway trolley. The trolley is about to smash into a brick wall, which will kill him instantly. You can prevent this from happening by pulling a switch before the trolley approaches a branch in the line. If you pull the switch, the trolley will be diverted and will instead smash into a second brick wall, which will also kill Philip instantly and at the exact same moment that the first wall would have killed him. You pull the switch. As a result, Philip is killed by smashing into the second brick wall rather than the first. Did your act of pulling the switch harm Philip? It seems clear that it did not.

Now let's change the trolley case a bit. If you don't pull the switch, the trolley will run over a booby-trap in the line which will cause a gun to fire at Philip, killing him instantly. If you do pull the switch, the trolley will be diverted and will instead run over a second booby-trap which will cause a second gun to fire at Philip, killing him instantly. You pull the switch. As a result, Philip is killed instantly by a bullet from the second gun rather than by a bullet from the first gun. Did your act of pulling the switch harm Philip? Again, it seems clear that it did not. What if we change the switch to a trigger? That doesn't seem to make a difference either.

But now the case of you and Philip seems to be on a par with the case of Hit Man 1 and you. In both cases, the victim will be killed by the firing of a certain gun if the agent does not pull the trigger and the victim will be killed by the firing of a different gun if the agent does pull the trigger. It seems clear that your pulling the trigger in the trolley case does not harm Philip. This supports the claim that Hit Man 1's pulling the trigger in the hit men case does not harm you.[5] And if Hit Man 1's pulling the trigger does not

---

[5] A critic might point to a difference between the trolley case and the hit men case. In the trolley case, the sequence of events that results in Philip's death has already been initiated. Your pulling the trigger simply diverts the already initiated causal chain from playing itself out in one way to playing itself out in another. But in the hit men case, Hit Man 1's pulling the trigger initiates the chain of events that results in your death. Perhaps we don't think that your act harms Philip because we think that diverting an already existing sequence of events can't count as harming someone while initiating a new sequence of events can. If that's what explains our reaction to the trolley case, then the claim that your pulling the trigger doesn't harm Philip in that case fails to support my claim that Hit Man 1's pulling the trigger doesn't harm you in the two hit men case.

But the difference between initiating and diverting a chain of events doesn't seem to explain our reaction to the case of you and Philip. After all, suppose that if the trolley continues on its current track, it will softly land on a giant pillow and that if you pull the switch the trolley will be diverted and will instead smash into a brick wall, which will kill Philip instantly. In this case, we would clearly say that your pulling the switch does harm Philip, despite the fact that in this case your pulling the switch merely diverts an already initiated chain of events. The reason we think your pulling the trigger doesn't harm Philip in the original version of the story, then, is not that your act is one of diverting an already existing chain of events. Rather, the reason is simply that Philip is going to die at the same time and in the same manner whether you pull the trigger or not. But that is equally true of the case of Hit Man 1 and you. And that is why Hit Man 1's pulling the trigger does not harm you.

harm you, then the case of the two hit men fails to provide a genuine counterexample to the Counterfactual Account of harm. Indeed, since the Temporal Account entails that Hit Man 1's pulling the trigger does harm you, I'm inclined to think that rather than providing a reason to favor the Temporal Account over the Counterfactual Account, the case of the two hit men actually provides a good reason to favor the Counterfactual Account over the Temporal Account.

A second kind of case that makes it plausible to deny that Hit Man 1 harms you by pulling the trigger is the kind of case in which a person's act causes something bad to happen to you while preventing someone else from causing something even worse to happen to you. Consider this example:

Ticket Preventer: The meter by your parked car has expired and a police officer is just about to discover this. If he does, he will write you a ticket that will cost you $25. Just before the traffic officer discovers that your meter is expired, a friend of yours walks by and notices the situation. She does not have any change with her, but she notices that you left your door unlocked and that there is change sitting in your cup holder. She takes four quarters out of your car and feeds the meter. As a result, you have one less dollar in your car, and you do not get a $25 ticket.

It would clearly be odd to say that your friend's act harms you in this case. The reason it would be odd to say this is that although her act causes something bad to happen to you—it causes you to lose a dollar, and that's a bad thing—having the bad thing happen is necessary in order prevent something even worse from happening. It seems implausible to say that your friend's act harms you, that is, because even though it does cause a bad thing to happen to you, it also causes you to be better off than you would otherwise have been. But while the fact that you are made even better off than you would otherwise have been by your friend's act makes the harmlessness of her act particularly striking, the reason that the fact is relevant is simply that her act did not make you worse off than you would otherwise have been. An act that makes you better off, that is, is simply a particularly conspicuous example of an act that does not make you worse off. If all the police officer was going to do was take a dollar from your car and put it in the meter, then if your friend took the dollar and put it in the meter first, her act wouldn't make you better off. But the fundamental reason for thinking that her act did not harm you in the original version of the case would remain: her act did not harm you because although it caused something bad to happen to you, it did not make you worse off than you would otherwise have been since the bad thing was going to happen to you either way. This seems to me to be the intuitively correct thing to say about the revised version of the ticket preventer case. If your friend took the quarters out of your car and used them to feed the meter because she knew that the police officer would do the very same thing in a minute if your friend didn't do so first, it seems highly unlikely that you would complain that your friend's act had harmed you. But this revised version of the ticket preventer case, like the case of Philip and the trolley, is structurally symmetric with the case of the two hit men. And so again, upon reflection, it seems to me that Hit Man 1 really does not harm you when he shoots you and that the case therefore favors the Counterfactual Account rather than the Temporal Account. Mr. Bad clearly harms you by initiating a chain of events that will leave you worse off than you would have been had he not issued his orders, but given that he has issued his orders, and that Hit Man 2 will shoot you if Hit Man 1 fails to, Hit Man 1's act itself does not harm you.

Finally, it may also be worth noting that the claim that Hit Man 1's act does not harm you seems to be supported by the presumption that there should be symmetry between what we say about harm and what we say about benefit. Suppose that you need to borrow a pen, that Nice Man 2 is about to lend you his pen and that just as he is about to do so, Nice Man 1 pushes him out of the way so that he can lend you his pen instead. It would seem odd to say that Nice Man 1's act of lending you his pen rather than letting Nice Man 2 lend you his pen in any way benefits you. In the same way, at least upon reflection, it should seem odd to say that Hit Man 1's act of shooting you rather than letting Hit Man 2 shoot you harms you.

It's possible, of course, that my reaction to the case of the two hit men is mistaken. And so it's possible that the case really does provide some reason to favor the Temporal Account over the Counterfactual Account.[6] Even if that is so, however, there is an even stronger reason to favor the Counterfactual Account over the Temporal Account. The reason is grounded in cases in which an act does not make you worse off than you were before but does make you worse off than you would otherwise have been. Suppose, for example, that you are seriously ill, that someone is about to bring you some medicine, that I intercept them and prevent them from delivering it to you, and that as a result you continue to suffer for many weeks before recovering rather than recovering right away.[7] In this case, it is clear that my act of preventing you from receiving the medicine harms you. But while my act does make you worse off than you would otherwise have been, it does not make you worse off than you were before. The Counterfactual Account therefore produces the correct result in this case while the Temporal Account produces the incorrect result. And since it strikes me as considerably more clear that I harm you by keeping you from getting the medicine you need in this case than it is that Hit Man 1 harms you by causing you to be shot by his gun rather than by the gun of Hit Man 2, it seems to me that this reason for favoring the Counterfactual Account over the Temporal Account strongly outweighs the purported reason for favoring the Temporal Account over the Counterfactual Account, if indeed the case of the two hit men provides any such reason at all.

But suppose that I am wrong about all of this and that we really should favor the Temporal Account over the Counterfactual Account. Even if this is so, this result cannot help us solve the non-identity problem. If we reject P2 of the non-identity argument and replace it with the Temporal Account of harm, we will be able to simply

---

[6] Though see Klocksiem (2012: 295–6) for a different way of reconciling this kind of case with the Counterfactual Account that also strikes me as quite reasonable.

[7] This point is made by Hanser (2008: 429).

modify P1 and keep the non-identity argument as a whole intact. Even if a solution to the non-identity problem that depends on the Temporal Account to justify reject-ing P2 can satisfy the modesty requirement, then, it will nonetheless fail to satisfy the robustness requirement. As it stands, P1 maintains that Wilma's act does not make Pebbles worse off than she would otherwise have been. But the reason for thinking that P1 is true is equally a reason to endorse what I will call

P1': Wilma's act does not make Pebbles worse off than she was before

P1 is true because if Wilma had not conceived Pebbles, then Pebbles would not have existed and P1 compares Pebbles being blind with Pebbles not existing. But Pebbles also did not exist before Wilma's act of conceiving her, and so the truth of P1' will rest on precisely the same comparison: the comparison between Pebbles being blind and Pebbles not existing. If Pebbles is not worse off being blind than not existing in the case of P1, then Pebbles is not worse off being blind than not existing in the case of P1'. And P1' conjoined with the Temporal Account of harm produces precisely the same result that P1 conjoined with the Counterfactual Account of harm produces: since Wilma's act does not make Pebbles worse off than the relevant baseline on either version of the argument, Wilma's act of conceiving Pebbles does not harm Pebbles on either version of the argument. And so even if the Temporal Account shows that P2 is false, it does not show that it is, as it were, false enough.

3.1.2 The Moralized Account

A second alternative to the counterfactual baseline takes normative considerations into account. It compares the results of an act not with how things would otherwise have been or with how things used to be, but with how things ought to be. The result of substituting this moralized baseline for the counterfactual baseline employed by the Counterfactual Account is what I will call the Moralized Account of harm.[8]

MA: If A's act harms B, then A's act makes B worse off than B should have been

The Moralized Account, like the Temporal Account, gets it right in the simple cases that initially seemed to favor the Counterfactual Account. In the case where I van-dalize your car, for example, I should have refrained from doing so. The Moralized Account correctly entails that my act of vandalizing your car harms you because my act makes you worse off than you should have been. In the case where you harmlessly scratch your nose, on the other hand, your act is not morally wrong. The Moralized Account correctly entails that your act of scratching your nose does not harm me. Your act does not make me worse off than I should have been.

In addition, and again like the Temporal Account, there is one kind of case in which the Moralized Account seems to prove superior to the Counterfactual Account. This

---

[8] Morriem, for example, proposes an account of harm on which "a person P is harmed at time T in respect R if his condition regarding R is worse than it should have been at time T" (1988: 23, emphases altered).

is the kind of case in which an immoral act causes something to happen that is not as bad as what in fact would otherwise have happened but that is worse than what should instead have happened. Here is an example.[9]

Angry Alastair: Angry Alastair sees you walking across campus and becomes even angrier. He really wants to tear your arms off. If he doesn't do that, he will slap you in the face. Although the urge to tear your arms off is extremely strong, he manages to resist the temptation and instead merely slaps you in the face.

It seems clear that Angry Alastair harms you when he slaps you in the face. And the Moralized Account produces the correct result in this instance. The right thing for Alastair to have done when he saw you walking across campus would have been to refrain from attacking you altogether, and by slapping you in the face, he made you worse off than you would have been had he refrained from attacking you altogether as he should have done. He therefore made you worse off than you should have been. But the Counterfactual Account seems to produce the wrong result this time. Alastair's act of slapping you in the face does not make you worse off than you would have been if he had not slapped you in the face because if he had not slapped you in the face he would instead have torn your arms off, and that would have made things even worse for you. The Moralized Account seems to get it right in all the cases that the Counterfactual Account gets right, then, and it also seems to get it right in a kind of case that the Counterfactual Account seems to get wrong. As a result, we again seem to have a reason to reject the Counterfactual Account of harm. And since the Counterfactual Account of harm represents P2 of the non-identity argument, we again seem to be in a position to solve the non-identity problem by rejecting P2.

As with the case of the two hit men, I am again inclined to think that a proponent of the Counterfactual Account should simply bite the bullet here. This is because I'm inclined to think that the case of Angry Alastair is relevantly similar to other cases that seem, at least to me, to pose no problem for that account. Suppose, for example, that the police officer in the original version of the ticket preventer case comes across your car before your friend gets there and that as he is about to write the $25 ticket, he instead decides to give you a break by taking the dollar in change from your car to feed the meter on your behalf. If there is no way that the police officer is going to simply leave your car there without either ticketing it or feeding the meter with your quarters, then it seems as clear to me in this case as it does in the original version of the ticket preventer case that the act of taking the change from your car and putting it in the meter does not harm you. And it again seems plausible to say this precisely because the alternative would have made things even worse for you. But this modified version of the ticket preventer case is structurally symmetric with the case of Angry Alastair: if his slapping you in the face really is the only thing that

---

[9] This is a modified version of an example given by Norcross (2005: 166), though Norcross does not present it as an argument for the moralized account.

will in fact prevent Alastair from tearing your arms off, then his slapping you in the face does not really harm you precisely because it does not make you worse off than you would otherwise have been. And so I'm inclined to think that Angry Alastair does not really harm you when he slaps your face and that the case therefore fails to provide a genuine counterexample to the Counterfactual Account. Indeed, as with the case of the two hit men and the Temporal Account, I'm inclined to think that the case of Angry Alastair not only fails to favor the Moralized Account over the Counterfactual Account but positively favors the Counterfactual Account over the Moralized Account.

It's again quite possible, of course, that my reaction to the case of Angry Alastair is mistaken. And so it's quite possible that the case really does provide some reason to favor the Moralized Account over the Counterfactual Account. Even if that is so, however, there is an even stronger reason to favor the Counterfactual Account over the Moralized Account. The reason is grounded in cases in which an act does not make you worse off than you should have been but does make you worse off than you would otherwise have been. And such acts occur whenever harmful acts are morally justified. If I shoot you in self-defense or as part of the prosecution of a just war, for example, or if I send you to prison as a morally justified instance of deserved punishment, then my act makes you worse off than you would otherwise have been. But on the assumption that my act is not morally wrong, my act does not make you worse off than you should have been. Since my act is morally justified, it makes you exactly as well off as you should have been. The Moralized Account therefore entails that these acts do not harm you while the Counterfactual Account entails that they do harm you. And since it strikes me as far more clear that I harm you by shooting you or sending you to prison in these cases than it is that Angry Alastair harms you by slapping you in the face when doing so prevents him from tearing your arms off, it seems to me that the reason for favoring the Counterfactual Account over the Moralized Account strongly outweighs the purported reason for favoring the Moralized Account over the Counterfactual Account, if indeed the case of Angry Alastair provides any such reason at all.

But suppose I am wrong about all of this and that we really should favor the Moralized Account over the Counterfactual Account. Even if this is so, this result cannot help us solve the non-identity problem. If we reject P2 of the non-identity argument and replace it with the Moralized Account of harm, we will again be able to modify P1 and keep the argument as a whole on track. So a solution to the non-identity problem that uses the Moralized Account to justify rejecting P2 will fail to satisfy the robustness requirement, just as a solution that appeals to the Temporal Account to justify rejecting P2 fails to satisfy it. As it stands, P1 maintains that Wilma's act does not make Pebbles worse off than she would otherwise have been. But the reasons for thinking that P1 is true provide a foundation for endorsing what I will call P1'':

P1'': Wilma's act of conceiving Pebbles does not make Pebbles worse off than she should have been

The truth of P1" follows from the nature of the two options available to Wilma and the principle that ought implies can. Wilma can either conceive Pebbles as a blind child or not conceive Pebbles at all. Those are the only two possible options. Since ought implies can, these two options are the only possible candidates for what Wilma ought to do. Either one or the other of them is the right act, or both of them count as a right act. But neither of these options is better for Pebbles than Pebbles being conceived as a blind child. So whatever the morally right act or acts turn out to be, Wilma's act of conceiving Pebbles as a blind child does not make Pebbles worse off than she should have been. And P1" conjoined with the Moralized Account produces precisely the same result that P1 conjoined with the Counterfactual Account produces: Wilma's act of conceiving Pebbles does not harm Pebbles.

The reasons for thinking that P1" is true, moreover, point to a more general reason to deny that any purely comparative alternative to the Counterfactual Account can be used to solve the non-identity problem.[10] Any such account must say that if A's act harms B, then it makes B worse off than B was or would be in some other scenario. But in the case of Wilma, there are only two possible scenarios available to her: the one in which Pebbles is blind and the one in which Pebbles does not exist. Pebbles existing and being blind is not worse for Pebbles than either of these, and so any comparative account that entails that Wilma's act harms Pebbles must take as its baseline a state of affairs that Wilma could not possibly bring about. Pebbles existing and being blind is worse than Pebbles existing and being sighted, for example, and so an account on which the relevant baseline is one in which Pebbles exists and is sighted will entail that Wilma harms Pebbles by causing Pebbles to exist and be blind.[11] But any such account will by its very nature have unacceptable implications. Helping an incurably blind person cross the street, for example, could turn out to harm that person because it would leave the person worse off than they would be if you instead magically cured their blindness. Any solution based on such an account would therefore fail to satisfy the modesty requirement. If the non-identity problem

---

[10] Feinberg, for example, at one point considers an account on which "A [wrongfully] harms B only if his wrongful act leaves B worse off then [sic] he would be otherwise *in the normal course of events insofar as they were reasonably foreseeable in the circumstances*" (1987: 153, emphasis in original). This account is meant to address a possible problem caused by such cases as that in which a taxi driver negligently injures a passenger thereby causing him to miss a flight that, it later turns out, would have killed him. I'm inclined to think that such cases are better handled by appealing to what I call the Short-term Counterfactual Account in section 3.3.1, but even if the view that Feinberg considers is accepted, it can't be used to solve the non-identity problem. Wilma's act, after all, does not make Pebbles worse off than she would otherwise be in the normal course of events as they were reasonably foreseeable to Wilma either. It makes Pebbles precisely as well off as Wilma foresaw she would be.

[11] Markie (2005: 301-2) seems to endorse this view. Similarly, Dillard (2010a: 10-11) suggests that we can solve the non-identity problem by appealing to the notion of a "threshold harm," on which Pebbles is harmed by being brought into existence with a quality of life that falls below a prescribed threshold even if the life is not really worse than no life at all (see also DeCamp (2012: 37)). But if living as a blind person falls below this threshold, then it will again be the case that Wilma did not make Pebbles any worse off than she could possibly have been.

is to be solved by rejecting P2, then, the Counterfactual Account of harm will have to be replaced by an account that has a different structure, and not just a different baseline.

3.2 Hybrid Accounts of Harm

One way to change the structure of our account of harm is to make it more complicated. Rather than treating "A's act harms B" as the immediate subject of analysis, we could treat "B is harmed" as more fundamental and then analyze the harmfulness of A's act in terms of the relation between A's act and B's being harmed.[12] This kind of two-part analysis generates the possibility of an account of harm that is neither purely comparative nor purely non-comparative. If an account has this structure and is comparative at one level but non-comparative at the other, I will refer to it as a hybrid account of harm. Before considering the possible merits of a purely non-comparative account of harm, then, we should first consider whether such a hybrid account might provide the basis for a satisfactory solution to the non-identity problem.

3.2.1 The Comparative/Non-comparative Account

Let's begin with the approach on which B's being harmed is understood comparatively but A's harming B is understood non-comparatively. To say that B's being harmed is comparative is to say that B's being harmed involves something happening to B that makes B worse off relative to some baseline. Perhaps the event makes B worse off than he was before, or than he would have been if the event had not occurred. Matthew Hanser has endorsed a version of this kind of account on which "harms paradigmatically consist in losses of 'basic goods.' The power of sight, for example, is a basic good for a human, so *losing* the power of sight is a harm."[13] To employ this kind of analysis as part of a hybrid account of harm, this comparative claim about B's being harmed must be combined with a non-comparative claim about the relation between B's being harmed and A's harming B. Perhaps the simplest version of such a claim would be to say that A's harming B amounts to A's causing B to be harmed. This claim about what it is for A to harm B is non-comparative. It doesn't compare the results of A's act with the results of some other possible act of A's. It just says that A's act harms B if it has a certain kind of consequence, regardless of what the alternatives to A's act were and regardless of what the consequences of the alternatives were.

In many cases, of course, merely being the cause of a consequence is not enough to be morally responsible for bringing it about, and so when we come to consider whether an act wrongfully harms someone, we may need to revise the non-comparative component to take this fact into account. Perhaps the simplest way of doing this would be to

---

[12] Hanser has endorsed this kind of account. See Hanser (2008: 421; 2009: 181).
[13] Hanser (2009: 186). See also Hanser (2011: 462).

say that the claim that A's act harms B amounts to the claim that A's act makes A at least partly responsible for B's being harmed. This is the version of the non-comparative element of the analysis that Hanser endorses: "A harms B if and only if his actions make him at least partially *responsible* for a harm suffered by B."[14] Bracketing off the question of whether a given harmful act is also one that the agent is morally responsible for causing, however, it is probably best to let the analysis of harm itself rest at a more general level. The result of combining the general non-comparative claim about A's harming B with the general comparative claim about B's being harmed is what I will refer to as the Comparative/Non-comparative Account, since it treats the comparative element as the more fundamental. The account can be put as follows:

C/NA: If A's act harms B, then A's act causes B to suffer a comparative harm

This Comparative/Non-comparative Account offers an alternative to the Counterfactual Account that differs not just in terms of the relevant baseline, but in terms of its structure. The question is whether this alternative account can help us solve the non-identity problem.

The answer is that it cannot and the reason for this is simple. The Comparative/Non-comparative Account of harm treats B's being harmed comparatively. But Pebbles is not harmed comparatively. No event occurs that makes Pebbles worse off than she was before, than she would otherwise have been, or than she would be on any other plausibly relevant baseline. And since Pebbles is not comparatively harmed, there is no comparative harm for Wilma to have non-comparatively caused Pebbles to suffer. On Hanser's version of the Comparative/Non-comparative Account, this is so because Pebbles does not suffer the loss of a basic good. The ability to see may be a basic good, but Pebbles never has that good to begin with, and so never suffers the loss of it. Indeed, Hanser himself acknowledges that his particular account of harm is unable to account for the presumed wrongness of acts like Wilma's: "*losing* the power of sight is a harm. Merely *lacking* the power of sight, by contrast, is not a harm."[15] But the same problem will arise for any version of the Comparative/Non-comparative Account. As we saw in section 3.1, there is no relevant baseline on which Pebbles existing and being blind counts as worse for Pebbles. As a result, there is no plausible account on which Pebbles suffers a comparative harm, and thus no plausible account on which Wilma non-comparatively causes Pebbles to suffer a comparative harm.

Before moving on to consider a second kind of hybrid account of harm, however, it is important to note that Hanser thinks that his version of this first kind of hybrid account can at least solve the non-identity problem in what I referred to in section 1.1.4 as bad event cases, like the case of the wealthy society. If the current members of the wealthy society adopt the risky policy today and as a result hundreds of years in

---

[14] Hanser (2009: 182). Martin and Baertschi also seem briefly to endorse this kind of approach (2012: 12–13).

[15] Hanser (2009: 186). See also Hanser (1990: 69).

the future a number of people are killed by leaking toxic waste when they turn forty, the wealthy society's act of selecting the risky policy now does turn out to harm those future people, at least on Hanser's version of the Comparative/Non-comparative Account. When those future people are killed by the leaking waste, an event occurs that makes them comparatively worse off in the sense that they suffer the loss of those basic goods that their being alive had to that point been enabling them to enjoy. Because Hanser's version of the Comparative/Non-comparative Account employs a temporal comparative account of being harmed, it follows that when they suffer the loss of these basic goods, they are harmed. And because this harm is caused by the actions of the current members of the wealthy society, actions for which they are presumably responsible, the current members of the wealthy society harm the people who are later killed by the leaking waste by adopting the policy that leads to the waste leaking out and killing them. Even if the Comparative/Non-comparative Account can't solve the non-identity problem in bad condition cases like the case of Wilma, then, it looks like it can at least solve the problem in bad event cases like the case of the wealthy society. And so the Comparative/Non-comparative Account might offer a solution to at least one part of the non-identity problem, even if it cannot solve the problem as whole.[16]

While the Comparative/Non-comparative Account does entail that the current members of the wealthy society harm those future people by adopting the risky policy, however, this turns out to provide a reason to reject the account itself rather than to endorse the solution that the account would offer to the bad event version of the non-identity problem. This is because the account entails that the current members of the wealthy society harm the people who are killed as a result of their adopting the risky policy only because the account includes as a harm the loss of a good that the people were enjoying in the first place only because adopting the policy led to their having the good. If the wealthy society had not adopted the risky policy, that is, the people who were later killed by the leaking waste would not have had lives to lose to begin with. But counting such losses as a harm, let alone as a morally wrongful harm, has implications in other cases that are even more implausible than the Implausible Conclusion. In order to construe the Comparative/Non-comparative Account in a way that enables it to entail that the wealthy society harms the people killed by the risky policy, that is, the account must be construed in a way that prevents it from satisfying the modesty requirement.

Suppose, for example, that Ray was born with a condition that prevents him from seeing, and that there is a procedure, but only one procedure, that a doctor could perform that would enable Ray to see. The procedure would correct the condition that

---

[16] Vanderheiden seems to make the same suggestion, though not as explicitly, in arguing that conservation policies are justified as a means of preventing us from causing harm to future people even if those people do not yet exist and it has not yet been determined which future people will exist (2006: 346, 350, 351). See also Carter (2001: 444). To the extent that Vanderheiden's and Carter's solutions turn out to be a version of Hanser's solution, they are vulnerable to the same objection I raise against Hanser's solution. Locke (1987: 135) can also be understood as briefly defending this kind of solution.

prevents Ray from seeing, but it would also have a side effect. The side effect would result in Ray's very slowly developing an infection. This infection would cause Ray to lose his vision forty years after the operation took place. In order for the Comparative/Non-comparative Account to entail that the wealthy society harms future people by adopting the risky policy, it must take the loss of a good that a person enjoyed only because a particular act caused the person to enjoy the good in the first place, and consider that loss of the good to be a comparative harm even if the loss of the good is caused by the very same act that caused the initial presence of the good. But this means that in order to use the Comparative/Non-comparative Account to solve the bad event version of the non-identity problem, it must be understood in a way that entails that the doctor harms Ray by performing the procedure on him. The procedure, after all, causes the infection that causes the loss of vision forty years later and the loss of vision counts as a comparative harm that is caused by the procedure even though the vision whose loss constitutes the harm existed in the first place only because the procedure was performed. But the claim that the doctor harms Ray by performing the procedure is clearly implausible. And in order to use the Comparative/Non-comparative Account to show that the wealthy society does not merely harm the people killed by the leaking waste but wrongfully harms them, the account will also have to entail that the doctor does not merely harm Ray, but wrongfully harms Ray. This implication is even harder to believe, and harder to believe than the claim that Wilma's act of conceiving Pebbles is not morally wrong. Since the Comparative/Non-comparative Account of harm has implications that are even more implausible than the Implausible Conclusion, the attempt to solve even just the bad event version of the non-identity problem by means of appealing to it fails to satisfy the modesty requirement.[17] Rather

---

[17] In correspondence with the author, Hanser suggests that the objection grounded in the case of Ray can be overcome by simply accepting the implication that the doctor's act harms Ray but denying that this means that the doctor's act wrongfully harms Ray. In particular, Hanser appeals to the following difference between the case of Ray and the case of the wealthy society: in the case of Ray, the harmful loss caused by the doctor's act is a byproduct of the means that the doctor employs in order to confer a significant benefit on Ray, a benefit that he is responsible for conferring on Ray. But in the case of the people who are killed by the leaking toxic waste hundreds of years in the future, the harmful loss caused to them by the wealthy society's adoption of the risky policy is not in any sense a byproduct of the means that the wealthy society employed in order to confer a benefit on those people that they are responsible for conferring on them. We can block the move from the claim that the doctor's act harms Ray to the conclusion that the doctor's act wrongs Ray, then, by saying that a harm to a particular person can be morally justified if it is the byproduct of an attempt to confer a greater benefit on that person. And since this would justify the harm caused to Ray but not the harm caused to the people killed by the leaking toxic waste, the result seems to be that a rejection of P2 that is grounded in an appeal to the Comparative/Non-comparative Account of harm can satisfy both the robustness requirement and the modesty requirement after all.

The problem with this response to the objection that is grounded in the case of Ray is that the response assumes that the reason that it is permissible for the doctor to harm Ray by performing the procedure is that the harm to Ray is the byproduct of an attempt to make things better for Ray overall. But what is really relevant to the permissibility of performing the procedure on Ray is not that doing so will make things better for Ray, but simply that doing so will not make things worse for Ray. Consider, for example, the following variation on the case: Ray is blind and is currently asleep. He will wake up in five hours. If I snap my fingers right now, his blindness will be cured but a noxious gas will unavoidably be released causing him to lose his vision an hour before he wakes up. So regardless of whether I snap my fingers right now, Ray will never have

than providing the grounds for at least a partial solution to the non-identity problem, then, the Comparative/Non-comparative Account ends up providing the grounds for no solution at all.

3.2.2 The Non-comparative/Comparative Account

I've argued so far that the Comparative/Non-comparative Account of harm can't be used to solve the non-identity problem. What about a hybrid account that is developed the other way around? This second kind of hybrid account would understand B's being harmed non-comparatively but would treat A's harming B comparatively. To say that B's being harmed is non-comparative is to say that B's being harmed amounts to B's being put in a bad condition. In one sense, this understanding of being harmed may still involve making a comparative claim. To be in a bad condition, for example, might be cashed out in terms of being in a condition that falls below a specified threshold, in which case being harmed would involve a comparison between B's condition and that threshold. But the claim is nonetheless non-comparative in the sense that is relevant here: B would be harmed by being in that bad condition regardless of how that condition compared with any other conditions, if any, that B might otherwise or previously have been in. In order to use this non-comparative account of B's being harmed as part of a hybrid account of harm, we would then have to combine it with a comparative account of A's harming B. To say that A's act harms B in the comparative sense would be to say that A's act harms B if it causes B to suffer more non-comparative harm, where this might mean more than B would otherwise have suffered or more than B previously suffered. The result of combining these two claims is what I will refer to as the Non-comparative/Comparative Account of harm. The account can be put as follows:

N/CA: If A's act harms B, then A's act causes B to suffer more non-comparative harm

---

vision when he is awake. In this version of the case, I have no moral reason to snap my fingers. So it would clearly not be wrong for me to decline to snap my fingers. But suppose that I would get a little pleasure from snapping my fingers. It seems clear, at least to me, that doing so would be perfectly permissible. Snapping my fingers would have no effect whatsoever on any conscious experience that Ray would ever have. It is therefore extremely difficult to believe that snapping my fingers would be morally wrong. But in this version of the case, Hanser's account of harm entails that my snapping my fingers will harm Ray because it will cause Ray to lose his vision, and the harm will not be the byproduct of an attempt to make things better for Ray. Ray will be no better off having the ability to see for a few hours while he is asleep than he would be if he never had the ability at all. If, as seems clear to me, it would nonetheless be permissible for me to snap my fingers in this case, this must be because it is permissible to do an act that causes someone to lose a good that the act causes them to possess in the first place as long as the act does not make them worse off. The act need not make them positively better off. It must simply not make them worse off. And this is enough to prevent Hanser's account of harm from solving the non-identity problem even in bad event cases. Even if the harm that the present members of the wealthy society cause the future people to incur when the future people are killed by the leaking toxic waste is not the byproduct of an attempt to make things better for the future people, it is still the case that it is the byproduct of an act that does not make things worse for them. And so even if we accept the claim that the wealthy society harms the future people by selecting the risky policy, we will not be justified in concluding from this that they wrongfully harm them.

This account, too, offers an alternative to P2 that differs in structure from the Counterfactual Account of harm. And so this account, too, raises the question of whether it could help us solve the non-identity problem.

The answer in this case at first appears to be considerably more promising. It seems reasonable to suppose that blindness is a bad state for someone to be in. So it seems reasonable to suppose that on the non-comparative account of B's being harmed that is employed by this second hybrid account of harm, Pebbles is harmed by being put in this state. If A's harming B is comparative in the way that this second hybrid account says it is, moreover, then it seems clear that Wilma's act results in Pebbles suffering more of this non-comparative harm: more than Pebbles would otherwise have suffered and more than she suffered prior to Wilma's act. Pebbles suffers the harm of being put in a blind state if Wilma conceives Pebbles, but Pebbles does not suffer the harm of being put in a blind state if Wilma does not conceive Pebbles and she did not suffer the harm of being put in a blind state before Wilma conceived her. Here, then, for the first time, we have a rival to the Counterfactual Account of harm that really does seem to entail that Wilma's act of conceiving Pebbles harms Pebbles.

The problem with appealing to the Non-comparative/Comparative Account of harm as a way of solving the non-identity problem is not that the account would not solve the problem if we accepted it. The problem is that we have good reason not to accept it. The reason arises from three facts. The first is that all people who exist are non-comparatively harmed in many ways over the course of their existence: they end up enduring conditions that are bad for them to be in. The second is that if a particular person who might exist in fact never exists, then that person will never suffer any non-comparative harm at all. The third is that a person who does exist never suffers any non-comparative harm before they exist. It follows from these three facts that any couple that considers conceiving a child will cause the child to suffer more non-comparative harm by conceiving it than by not conceiving it: more than it suffered before it existed and more than it would have suffered if it had never existed. This, in turn, means that the Non-comparative/Comparative Account of harm entails that every act of conception harms the person who is conceived. This conclusion, as I noted in the discussion of Benatar's argument in section 2.5, is more difficult to accept than the Implausible Conclusion we are trying to avoid. And this, in turn, means that a solution to the non-identity problem that is based on the Non-comparative/Comparative Account of harm will fail to satisfy the modesty requirement that a successful solution to the problem must satisfy.

A defender of the Non-comparative/Comparative Account might respond to this problem by trying to render the claim that everyone who conceives a child harms the child by conceiving it less counterintuitive. They might do this by saying that while the couple harms the child by causing all of the non-comparative harms it suffers, the couple also benefits the child by causing all of the non-comparative benefits that it enjoys, and by allowing that as long as the benefits outweigh the harms, there's nothing wrong about the couple conceiving. The Non-comparative/Comparative Account, so understood, would simply be making a claim about what it is to be harmed in a particular respect, not a claim about what it is to be harmed all things considered.

But if the Non-comparative/Comparative Account is understood in this way, then while it may prove to be a sufficiently modest account of harm to be plausible, it will prove too modest to solve the non-identity problem. The claim that Wilma's act of conceiving Pebbles harms Pebbles will simply mean that Wilma's act causes the bad conditions that Pebbles endures as well as the good conditions that Pebbles enjoys. And if the fact that the benefits to the child outweigh the harms to the child is enough to make it not wrong for conception to take place in ordinary cases, then it will be enough to make it not wrong for Wilma to conceive Pebbles, too. Whether the Non-comparative/Comparative Account is taken to be an account of all things considered harm or of something else, then, it cannot provide a satisfactory solution to the non-identity problem. If it is robust enough to solve the problem it is not modest enough to be plausible and if it is modest enough to be plausible it is not robust enough to solve the problem.

3.3 The Non-comparative Account of Harm

I have argued so far that attempts to solve the non-identity problem by replacing the Counterfactual Account of harm with some other comparative of account of harm or with a hybrid account of harm that combines comparative and non-comparative elements are unsuccessful. The alternative accounts of harm are either unacceptable on independent grounds or fail to entail that Wilma's act harms Pebbles or both. A final and more radical departure from the Counterfactual Account denies that there must be any comparative element to harm in the first place. What I will call the Non-comparative Account need not deny that the considerations pointed to by the Counterfactual Account successfully identify a sufficient condition for harming someone. The account can allow that if A's act makes B worse off than B would otherwise have been, then that may be enough to ensure that A's act harms B. But the Non-comparative Account denies that such considerations provide a necessary condition for harming someone. It denies that from the claim that A's act harms B it follows that A's act makes B worse off than B would otherwise have been. And this, as we have seen, would be enough to warrant rejecting P2 of the non-identity argument.

The Non-comparative Account seeks to accomplish this by identifying a particular way in which an act can harm a person without making that person worse off. And it does this, in effect, by combining the non-comparative elements of the two hybrid accounts of harm we have already discussed and rejected. Like the first hybrid account, the Non-comparative Account treats A's harming B as A's causing B to suffer a harm. Like the second hybrid account, the Non-comparative Account treats B's suffering a harm as B's being in a bad state. The result of combining these two elements is an act that causes a person to be in a bad state. Treating this as a sufficient condition for harm rather than as a necessary condition, the Non-comparative Account of harm can therefore be put as follows:

NA: A's act harms B if A's act causes B to be in a bad state

The basic idea underlying this account is intuitively plausible: some states are bad for a person to be in, and an act that causes a person to be in such a state thereby harms that person. Pain, for example, is bad. An act that causes a person to be in a painful state harms that person for that reason. In addition, the Non-comparative Account produces the correct answers in the simple cases that initially seemed to motivate the Counterfactual Account. If I vandalize your car, for example, my act makes you worse off than you would otherwise have been, but it also causes you to be in a bad state. Your scratching your nose does not make me worse off than I would otherwise have been, but it also doesn't cause me to be in a bad state.

Indeed, since the Non-comparative Account only purports to identify a sufficient condition for harm while the Counterfactual Account purports to identify a necessary condition, the Non-comparative Account can often appeal to the Counterfactual Account itself to respond to what might otherwise seem to be counterexamples. If I steal a dollar from a billionaire, for example, it might seem reasonable to say that I harm her without causing her to be in a bad state. Since my stealing the dollar presumably makes the billionaire at least a little bit worse off than she would otherwise have been, this result might seem to favor the Counterfactual Account over the Non-comparative Account. But the Non-comparative Account does not insist that it is impossible to harm someone without causing them to be in a bad state. It simply says that causing someone to be in a bad state is one way that you can harm them. Making them worse off than they would otherwise have been might be another. And so the claim that I harm the billionaire by stealing a dollar from her even though doing so does not put her in a bad state is consistent with the Non-comparative Account of harm.

Finally, the Non-comparative Account, unlike many of the other alternatives to the Counterfactual Account, entails that Wilma's act of conceiving Pebbles really does harm Pebbles. We are assuming that blindness is a bad state to be in and Wilma's act of conceiving Pebbles causes Pebbles to be in this bad state. Since the Non-comparative Account maintains that causing someone to be in a bad state is sufficient for harming them, the Non-comparative Account therefore entails that Wilma's act of conceiving Pebbles harms her. The Non-comparative Account, in short, would justify rejecting P2 of the non-identity argument in a way that would genuinely block the move from P1's claim that Wilma's act does not make Pebbles worse off than she would otherwise have been to C1's claim that Wilma's act does not harm Pebbles. And doing this would be enough to solve the non-identity problem.

There are two problems with trying to use the Non-comparative Account to solve the non-identity problem in this way. Both problems arise from cases in which an act causes a person to be in a state that is bad, but not as bad as the state the person would have been in if the act had not been performed. Here is an example.[18]

Surgery: You are unconscious and suffering from a swollen appendix. A surgeon can perform an operation on you but must make a decision about whether to do so before you wake up and so she cannot secure your consent. If she does not perform the operation, you will wake up in great deal of abdominal pain and will die in a matter of hours. If she does perform the operation, she will save your life, but you will wake up with some mild post-operative pain. The surgeon decides to perform the operation.

Two things seem to be clear about this surgery case. First, the doctor's act of operating on you does not harm you. If anything, her act clearly benefits you by saving your life and reducing the amount of pain you will suffer when you wake up. Second, the doctor's act of operating on you is not morally wrong. If anything, it would have been morally wrong for her not to operate on you.

But the Non-comparative Account of harm, and the attempt to use that account to solve the non-identity problem, seems to have problems accounting for both of these judgments. The doctor's act causes you to experience post-operative pain, and post-operative pain is a bad state to be in. Since the Non-comparative Account says that an act harms you if it causes you to be in a bad state regardless of whether the state is worse than the state you would otherwise have been in, the Non-comparative Account seems to entail that the doctor's act harms you. The Non-comparative Account is an account of harm, of course, not an account of wrongness. But as an account of harm, it will help to solve the non-identity problem only if it can ground an account of wrongful harm. The claim that Wilma's act of conceiving Pebbles harms Pebbles will help to solve the non-identity problem only if harming Pebbles in this way is morally wrong. Even if we are willing to bite the bullet and accept the claim that the doctor's act of operating on you really does harm you, then, it seems that we will also have to bite an even bigger bullet and accept the claim that the doctor's act of operating on you wrongfully harms you. But this claim is clearly more implausible than the Implausible Conclusion. And so a solution based on the Non-comparative Account of harm clearly seems unable to satisfy the modesty requirement. The Non-comparative cure looks much worse than the non-identity disease.

As a result, there are two distinct challenges facing a proponent of the solution based on the Non-comparative Account of harm. First, the defender of the solution must defend the Non-comparative Account itself by showing that it is reasonable to accept the claim that the doctor's act of operating on you harms you. Second, the defender of the solution must explain how the fact that Wilma's act non-comparatively harms Pebbles can make Wilma's act of conceiving Pebbles morally wrong while the fact that the doctor's act non-comparatively harms you does not make the doctor's act of operating on you morally wrong. In subsection 3.3.1, I will discuss the first challenge. In subsection 3.3.2, I will discuss the second. In both cases, defenders of the

---

[18] This is a modified version of an example given by Harman (2004: 91).

Non-comparative Account have offered some potentially powerful arguments. But in both cases, I will argue that they are ultimately unsuccessful.

3.3.1 Arguments for the Non-comparative Account of Harm

The most important defense of the Non-comparative Account of harm is that of Elizabeth Harman, in her 2004 article "Can We Harm and Benefit in Creating?" and her 2009 follow-up "Harming as Causing Harm."[19] Harman puts the account in general terms as follows: "an action harms someone if it causes the person to be in a bad state."[20] And while she does not provide a detailed account of what makes a state a bad one to be in,[21] the examples she gives in setting out her position should suffice for our purposes: "One harms someone if one causes him pain, mental or physical discomfort, disease, deformity, disability, or death."[22]

Harman provides two arguments in defense of this account: a negative argument and a positive argument. The negative argument offers a reason to reject what Harman takes to be the most compelling argument in favor of the Counterfactual Account. This is the argument based on examples like the surgery case, which Harman presents as follows:[23]

Surgery: A doctor cuts a hole in my abdomen in order to remove my swollen appendix. Cutting open my abdomen causes me pain (as I recover); but if the operation had not been performed, I would have suffered worse pain and died very soon.

As noted above, cases like this seem to provide clear support for the Counterfactual Account over the Non-comparative Account. It seems clear that the doctor's act does not harm the patient in this case, that the Counterfactual Account justifies this conclusion in an intuitively satisfying manner, and that the Non-comparative Account unacceptably entails that the doctor harms the patient by saving the patient's life.

But Harman rejects the foundation of this argument, the assumption that it is intuitively obvious that the doctor does not harm the patient in this case. What is really clear, Harman maintains, is simply that what the doctor does is morally permissible. And the claim that the doctor's act is morally permissible does not provide a good reason to favor the Counterfactual Account over the Non-comparative Account. A defender of the Non-comparative Account can simply maintain that while the doctor's act does harm the patient, the act is nonetheless permissible despite the strong presumption against causing harm because not performing the act will result in even greater harm to the patient.[24] And so, on Harman's account, cases like surgery fail to

---

[19] See also Shiffrin (1999) discussed below. Woollard (2012) endorses the claim that this kind of account of harm can offer a partial solution to the problem. See also Meyer (2004: 308–9), Dillard (2007: 53–4), Herstein (2009: 1207–10), and DeCamp (2012: 37).

[20] Harman (2009: 139).

[21] Though Harman does note that, if pressed, she is "willing to offer one: bad states are those states that are worse in some way than the normal healthy state for a member of one's species" (2009: 139).

[22] Harman (2009: 139). See also: "An action harms a person if the action causes pain, early death, bodily damage, or deformity to her, even if she would not have existed if the action had not been performed" (2004: 93).

[23] Harman (2004: 91).   [24] Harman (2004: 91).

justify endorsing the Counterfactual Account over the Non-comparative Account. The intuition suggesting that such cases do not involve harmful acts can be successfully explained away, and the claim that is needed in order to do so can be as easily accommodated by one account as by the other.

There are two problems with Harman's attempt to reconcile the Non-comparative Account with our intuitions about the surgery case. Before considering them, however, it is important to note an ambiguity in Harman's treatment of the case itself: what, precisely, is the bad state that the doctor's act causes in virtue of which we are supposed to think that the doctor's act harms the patient? In her description of the case in her original 2004 paper, Harman refers to the fact that the doctor's act causes post-operative pain, which seems to suggest that this is the source of the harm. But a few lines later, she says that the doctor "harms me because he causes significant damage to my body." This suggests that causing there to be a hole in the abdomen, rather than causing there to be post-operative pain, is what accounts for the claim that the doctor's act is harmful. Similarly, in her 2009 paper, she writes that the doctor "causes me pain and he physically injures me," without making clear which of these results is supposed to account for the claim that the doctor's act is harmful.[25] It might at first seem that either understanding of the case would be sufficient for Harman's purposes. But, in fact, neither version of the case can ground a successful version of her argument, though for different reasons.

Suppose first that the bad state that the doctor's act causes is the bodily damage that results from her making an incision in the patient's abdomen. To avoid confusion about the purported source of the harm, we might focus on a variant on Harman's case in which the doctor must cut a hole in the patient in order to save the patient but in which pain medication will prevent the patient from suffering any post-operative discomfort. I will refer to this as the hole without pain version of the surgery case. In this sort of case, the Non-comparative Account entails that the doctor's act harms the patient since it causes the patient to be in a bad state. But there is a problem with using this kind of case as a means of testing the ability of the Non-comparative Account to accommodate the intuitions that drive people to reject that account in favor of the Counterfactual Account when they consider cases like surgery. The problem is that in the hole without pain version of the case, the Counterfactual Account also entails that the doctor's act harms the patient. Cutting a hole in the patient's abdomen, after all, is not the same thing as removing the patient's appendix. The cutting is one act. The removing is another. Cutting a hole in the patient's abdomen, moreover, is an act that in and of itself leaves the patient worse off than she would otherwise have been. Making the patient worse off by causing the hole in her abdomen is permissible, of course, provided that it is done in order to then remove the swollen appendix. But this is consistent with the recognition that the act of causing the hole in the abdomen is an act that in itself makes the patient worse off and that, according to the Counterfactual

---

[25] Harman (2009: 139).

Account, the act is therefore harmful. And so in the hole without pain version of the example, the surgery case does not generate the intuition that Harman's response is supposed to explain away. Her reason for focusing on the surgery case in the first place, that is, is that it is supposed to be a problem case for the Non-comparative Account: a case where most people will be inclined to think that no harm has been done and where the Counterfactual Account will support that view but where the Non-comparative Account will entail that harm has been done in a seemingly problematic way. Her negative argument can succeed only if it is aimed at a version of the case that really does seem to support the Counterfactual Account over the Non-comparative Account in the first place, that is, and the hole without pain version of the surgery case does not do that.

Suppose on the other hand that the bad state that the doctor's act causes is the post-operative pain. To avoid confusion about the purported source of the harm, we might focus on a second variant on Harman's case in which the doctor can treat the condition without cutting or disfiguring the patient's body but in which the patient will suffer from some post-operative pain. Let's suppose that the doctor can somehow remove the appendix simply by inserting a device into the patient's mouth and that doing so will later cause the patient to endure a moderate headache. I will call this the pain without hole version of the surgery case. In this version of the surgery case, unlike in the hole without pain version, the Non-comparative Account and the Counterfactual Account really do yield different results. Since the post-operative pain caused by the doctor's act is a bad state for the patient to be in, the Non-comparative Account again entails that the doctor's act harms the patient. But since Harman stipulates that the patient would have been in even greater pain upon awakening had the procedure not been performed, the Counterfactual Account entails that the doctor's act does not harm the patient. The patient is not worse off experiencing the moderate post-operative headache than she would have been had she instead been experiencing the even more severe abdominal pain that would have resulted had the operation not been performed. And since the doctor's act in the pain without hole version of the surgery case does not make the patient worse off than she would otherwise have been, the Counterfactual Account entails that the doctor's act does not harm her in this case. This makes the pain without hole version of the case a fair test for Harman's negative argument. Most people will be inclined to say that the doctor has not harmed the patient on this construal of the case, and Harman can try to provide a credible account of why people would initially be inclined to say this, an account that is ultimately consistent with favoring the Non-comparative Account over the Counterfactual Account.

But in the pain without hole version of the surgery case, the divergent results that render it a fair test case ultimately favor the Counterfactual Account rather than the Non-comparative Account. And, contrary to Harman's suggestion, they do so independent of any intuitions that we may have about the permissibility of the doctor's act. The reason it is implausible to say that causing the post-operative pain in the pain without hole case means that the act harmed the patient is not that saying so would imply that the act was morally impermissible. The reason it is implausible is simply that the pain did not make the patient worse off than she would otherwise have been. That our intuitions about the permissibility of the doctor's act in this version of the case are irrelevant to this assessment can be seen by assuming that it is morally permissible for fully informed, mentally competent adults to harm themselves, and by then looking at a case where a person treats himself in a manner that is structurally similar to the way that the doctor treats her patient in the pain without hole version of the surgery case.

Suppose, for example, that you have a headache that is currently causing you 100 units of pain. You are a mentally competent adult, and you know the following: if you do nothing, you will continue to experience 100 units of pain for the next hour, after which the pain will suddenly end. If you instead swallow a little pill that you have in your hand, the pain will end immediately. The pill, though, has one side effect: thirty minutes after taking it, it causes a headache that generates 10 units of pain and lasts for five minutes. You take the pill, the headache immediately ends, and thirty minutes later you experience the 10 units of pain for five minutes that are caused by the pill's side effects. Did your act of swallowing the pill harm you?

In this case, our intuitions about whether the act harms you cannot be confused by our intuitions about whether the act is permissible. Since the act is clearly permissible whether it harms you or not, if it seems clear to us that the act does not harm you, this cannot be simply because it seems clear to us that the act is permissible. And in this case it does seem clear, at least to me, that the act does not harm you. It does cause you to experience a 10 unit headache for five minutes that you would not otherwise experience. But if you were not experiencing the 10 unit headache during those five minutes, you would instead be experiencing a different 100 unit headache. That fact alone, independent of any questions about the permissibility of your taking the pill, seems sufficient to justify concluding that you do not harm yourself by taking the pill even though you do cause yourself a five-minute 10 unit headache that you would not otherwise experience. Since it seems clear that you do not harm yourself by taking the pill and that the Counterfactual Account produces the correct result in this case while the Non-comparative Account produces the incorrect result, the headache case provides a reason to favor the former account over the latter. And since the headache case is structurally symmetric with the pain without hole construal of the surgery case, this in turn shows that Harman's attempt to diffuse the force of the surgery case is unsuccessful: we think that the doctor does not harm the patient in that version of the case not because we think the doctor does not wrong the patient, but because the doctor does not make the patient worse off than the patient would otherwise have been.

This result points to two problems with Harman's negative argument. One is that the argument fails to diffuse the force of the thought that the Counterfactual Account is more plausible than the Non-comparative Account. If the purported harm caused by the doctor's act is the hole in the patient's abdomen, then the result produced by the Non-comparative Account is plausible only because it is the same result that is produced by the Counterfactual Account. If the purported harm caused by the doctor's act is the post-operative pain, then the result produced by the Counterfactual Account is different from the result produced by the Non-comparative Account and is more plausible than the result produced by that account. And the result produced by the Counterfactual Account is more plausible in that case precisely because the post-operative pain that the doctor's act causes the patient does not make the patient worse off than she would otherwise have been.

The second problem with Harman's negative argument is that the implications of the Non-comparative Account are plausible only in the hole without pain version of the case, but it is the pain without hole version that is relevantly similar to the cases that generate the non-identity problem. The Non-comparative Account seems plausible in the hole without pain version of the case only because on that construal of the case, the doctor's causing the patient to be in a bad state makes the patient temporarily worse off as a means of ultimately making her better off. This is like a case where a parent spanks a misbehaving child out of the belief that this will help the child learn how to treat other people which in turn will help the child flourish in the future. Even if the spanking does prove beneficial to the child in the long run for this reason, it nonetheless remains plausible to say that the spanking harms the child because the painful bad state it causes makes the child worse off than he would otherwise have been in the short run.

But the cases that give rise to the non-identity problem are fundamentally different from both the spanking case and the hole without pain version of the surgery case in this respect. When Wilma causes Pebbles to be in a bad state by causing Pebbles to exist and to be blind, she does not do something that makes Pebbles temporarily worse off than she would otherwise have been as a means of helping to make Pebbles better off than she would otherwise have been in the long run. If Wilma chooses to conceive Pebbles, it causes Pebbles to be in a bad state, but there is no point in time at which being in this bad state makes Pebbles worse off than she would otherwise have been at that time. This makes the Wilma case relevantly like the pain without hole version of the surgery case rather than like the hole without pain version. It is precisely because, on the pain without hole version of that case, there is no point in time at which the patient is worse off as a result of the doctor's act than she would otherwise have been at that time that it remains implausible to think that the doctor's act harms the patient on that version of the case. And so even if there is a version of the surgery case about which the Non-comparative Account provides a plausible assessment, it is not a version that can help us solve the non-identity problem. In order to use the Non-comparative Account to solve the non-identity problem, that is, that account must be understood as the claim that an act harms a person if the act causes that person to be in a bad state even if there is never a point in time at which the person is worse off as a result of the act. And nothing that Harman says about the surgery case helps to make this claim plausible regardless of whether the purported harm in that case is the hole or the pain.

Since this is the most serious problem with Harman's negative argument, and since as we will see below there is a parallel problem with her positive argument, it is worth briefly elaborating on what the problem is by putting the problem more explicitly in terms of the non-identity argument itself. P2 of that argument maintains that if A's act harms B, then A's act makes B worse off than B would have been had A not done the act. The Non-comparative Account purports to give us a reason to reject P2. But a reason for rejecting P2 will be robust enough to help solve the non-identity problem only if it forces us to modify P2 in a way that will block the move to C1's claim that Wilma's act does not harm Pebbles. And Harman's negative argument in defense of the Non-comparative Account cannot do this. Since Harman's argument establishes that the Non-comparative Account is plausible, if it establishes this at all, only in the hole without pain version of the surgery case, it can only support, at most, a crucially restricted kind of counterexample to P2. This is the kind of case in which A's act harms B and in which A's act does not make B worse off than B would have been in the long run but does make B worse off than B would have been in the short run. And this limitation on the scope of the counterexample means that even if we were to find Harman's attempt to show that the surgery case does not support the Counterfactual Account to be compelling, it would only force us to retreat to the claim that the surgery case supports a modified version of that account. This modified version is what I will refer to as the Short-term Counterfactual Account:

STCA: if A's act harms B, then A's act makes it the case that there is at least some point in time at which B is worse off than B would have been had A not done the act even if in the end B is made better off overall by the act than B would have been had A not done the act

The Short-term Counterfactual Account is consistent with the claim that the doctor's act harms the patient in the hole without pain version of the surgery case, since the patient is temporarily made worse off by the doctor's initial incision, and that is the only construal of the case on which the result produced by the Non-comparative Account is plausible.

But if a reason for rejecting the original Counterfactual Account gives us no reason to reject the Short-term Counterfactual Account, then it cannot ground a solution to the non-identity problem. This is because, as noted above, the Wilma case is relevantly like the pain without hole version of the surgery case rather than the hole without pain version. There is no point in time at which Pebbles is worse off than she would otherwise have been as a result of Wilma's act of conceiving her, just as there is no point in time at which the patient is worse off than she would otherwise have been as the result of the doctor's act in the pain without hole version of the surgery case, but there is a point in time during which the patient is worse off than she would otherwise have been as a result of the doctor's act in the hole without pain version of that case. As a result, even if we abandon the claim that the surgery case supports the original Counterfactual Account, we can still generate the non-identity problem by making two simple changes to the non-identity argument. First, we can replace P2 of the argument, the original Counterfactual Account of harm, with what I will call P2', the Short-term Counterfactual Account. Second, we can take P1, which says that Wilma's act of conceiving Pebbles does not make Pebbles worse off than she would otherwise have been, and replace it with what I will call P1':

P1': Wilma's act of conceiving Pebbles does not make it the case that there is at least some point in time at which Pebbles is worse off than she would otherwise have been

P1' is true for the same reason that P1 is true: if Wilma conceives Pebbles, Pebbles will be blind but she will not be worse off than she would be if she did not exist. And P1' and P2' entail C1 for the same reason that P1 and P2 entail C1: in both cases, the first premise points out that Wilma's act does not make Pebbles worse off in a way that the second premise claims to be necessary in order for harm to occur. Since P1' is true, and since P1' and P2' entail C1, forcing us to abandon P2 for P2' cannot help us solve the non-identity problem. In the end, then, Harman's negative argument is unsuccessful. It fails to show that our intuitions about the surgery case do not support the Counterfactual Account. And even if it did show that, it could not show that they do not support the Short-term Counterfactual Account. And since P1' is true, the Short-term Counterfactual Account is good enough to preserve the non-identity argument. I am inclined to think that Harman's negative argument fails to satisfy the independence requirement because I am inclined to think that it fails to undermine the case for the original Counterfactual Account, but even if it does satisfy that requirement, it clearly fails to satisfy the robustness requirement. A reason for rejecting the original Counterfactual Account of harm that is not a reason for rejecting the Short-term Counterfactual Account is not a strong enough reason to block the move from the basic facts about Wilma's act to the conclusion that Wilma's act does not harm Pebbles. And even if Harman's negative argument succeeds in diminishing our confidence in the original Counterfactual Account, it provides no reason to reject the Short-term Counterfactual Account.

What about Harman's positive argument? Harman's positive argument for the Non-comparative Account rests on two cases that she claims

illustrate that the following claim is true: An individual can be harmed by an action and can have legitimate complaint about the action—indeed, she can be impermissibly harmed by the action—although she does not wish (nor should she wish) that the action had not occurred, and although the action makes her better off than she would otherwise be.[26]

There are several components to this claim, some of which are more relevant to the moral principle that Harman conjoins with the Non-comparative Account rather than to the Non-comparative Account itself, but I will focus here on the question of whether the two cases at least support the portion of her claim that maintains that a person "can be harmed by an action. . . although the action makes her better off than she would

---

[26] Harman (2004: 99).

otherwise be." If this claim is true, then P2 of the non-identity argument is clearly false. And if the reason this claim is true is that the people in the cases are caused to be in a bad state even though they are not made worse off than they would have been had the acts not been performed, then the cases will also establish that the Non-comparative Account is true.

The two cases are what Harman refers to as Rape and Nazi Prisoner:[27]

Rape: A woman is raped, becomes pregnant, and ends up raising the child. The woman is remarkably able to separate the trauma of the rape from her attitude to the child, and they have a normal and healthy parent–child relationship. The woman's life is better, due to the value to her of the relationship with her child, than it would have been if she had not been raped, even taking into account the trauma of the rape. This woman loves her child. She does not wish that she had not been raped, because if she had not been raped, then her child would not exist.

Nazi Prisoner: A man was imprisoned in a Nazi concentration camp, where he suffered many harms. But his experience in the camp enriched his character and deepened his understanding of life, such that overall his life was better than it would have been had he not been imprisoned in the camp. He does not wish that the Nazis had not imprisoned him, because he so values what he gained from this experience.

Harman claims that these two cases "show that [the Counterfactual Account of harm] is fundamentally misguided." But do they?

One reason to be skeptical of this claim is that it is not clear that the victims in these cases are harmed by the acts that wrong them. Perhaps the acts wrong them despite the fact that the acts benefit them. And if the victims are not harmed by the acts that wrong them, then the fact that the Counterfactual Account entails that they are not harmed by the acts poses no problem for that account. One reason for doubting that the victims are harmed by the wrongful acts in these cases is set out in the first part of Appendix C. But since I am not sufficiently confident that this reason suffices to overturn Harman's argument, I will assume here that the rape and Nazi prisoner cases really are cases in which the person in question is harmed. Even if this is so, there is a problem with Harman's use of these cases that prevents her positive argument from grounding a satisfactory solution to the non-identity problem.

The main problem with Harman's positive argument for the Non-comparative Account parallels the second problem that I raised for her use of the surgery case in her negative argument for that account. As we saw in that context, the Non-comparative Account can be used to solve the non-identity problem only if it is understood as the claim that an act harms a person if the act causes that person to be in a bad state even if there is never a point in time at which the person is worse off as a result of the act. This is so because while the acts in non-identity cases do cause a person to be in a bad state, they do not cause it to be the case that there is a point in time at which the person in question is worse off then they would otherwise have been at that time. Wilma's act

---

[27] Harman (2004: 99).

causes Pebbles to be blind, for example, but there is no point in Pebbles's life at which this makes things worse for her than they would have been at that point if Wilma had not conceived her. And so an argument for rejecting P2 that rests on our being forced to accept the Non-comparative Account can help to solve the non-identity problem only if accepting the Non-comparative Account forces us not just to reject P2 and the Counterfactual Account, but also to reject what I called P2' and referred to as the Short-term Counterfactual Account: the claim that if A's act harms B, then A's act makes it the case that there is at least some point in time at which B is worse off than B would have been had A not done the act even if in the end B is made better off overall by the act.

The surgery case failed to establish that the Non-comparative Account is true in the sense required to undermine P2' because the only version of that case on which it is plausible to think that the doctor's act harms the patient proved to be the hole without pain version on which the doctor's act of making the incision makes the patient temporarily worse off as a means of later making the patient better off. But the rape and Nazi prisoner cases also fail to establish that the Non-comparative Account is true in a sense that is sufficiently robust to warrant rejecting P2' and for precisely the same reason. Even if we agree that the acts harm the people in question in these two cases, these are clearly cases in which an act makes a person much worse off in the short run but better off in the long run. The immediate consequences of the rape make the rape victim much worse off at that time than she would otherwise have been at that time while some of the long-term consequences of the rape later make her better off overall than she would otherwise have been. And the immediate consequences of being imprisoned in the concentration camp make the Nazi prisoner much worse off at that time than he would otherwise have been at that time while some of the long-term consequences of that experience later make him better off overall than he would otherwise have been. Surely if we react to these cases by agreeing that the people are harmed by the acts in question, it is in virtue of the fact that the acts make the people so much worse off than they would otherwise have been at least in the short run. Indeed, Harman herself comes close to inadvertently acknowledging this when she refers to "the harm to someone of *going through these experiences*."[28] Going through the horrible experience itself clearly makes the rape victim and the concentration camp prisoner worse off than they would otherwise have been during the time that the experience was happening. This is why the Short-term Counterfactual Account of harm can account for the claim that the victims are harmed in these cases. And so even if they prove to be counterexamples to the original Counterfactual Account of harm, the rape and Nazi prisoner cases can do nothing to undermine the Short-term Counterfactual Account. And the Short-term Counterfactual Account is sufficiently robust to generate the non-identity problem.

---

[28] Harman (2004: 100).

Even if we agree that the acts harm the people in question in these two cases, then, the cases will do nothing to show that causing a person to be in a bad state can harm a person in cases where there is no point in time at which the person is made worse off as a result of the act. To do that, Harman would have to provide cases in which an act does not make a person worse off than they would otherwise have been at any point in time subsequent to the act and in which we nonetheless respond to the case by agreeing that the act clearly harmed the person. The rape and Nazi prisoner cases do not do this, since those cases clearly involve short-term harm, and the fact that it is so difficult to imagine any case that could do this only serves to reinforce the conclusion that we have already come to: that the inclination to say that the acts are harmful in the rape and Nazi prisoner cases is due entirely to the fact that they do make the victims worse off than they would otherwise have been, at least in the short run. Since the rape and Nazi prisoner cases can therefore do nothing to show that the Short-term Counterfactual Account is false even if they do show that the original Counterfactual Account is false, and since the Short-term Counterfactual Account is just as good as the original Counterfactual Account for purposes of demonstrating that Wilma does not harm Pebbles by conceiving her, the rape and Nazi prisoner cases cannot ground a successful solution to the non-identity problem. As with the case of Harman's negative argument, I am inclined for the reasons presented in the first part of Appendix C to think that the rape and Nazi prisoner cases that underwrite her positive argument fail to provide an independent reason to accept the Non-comparative Account over the Counterfactual Account and that any argument for rejecting P2 that is based on our response to the cases therefore fails to satisfy the independence requirement. But even if the reasons provided by those cases do turn out to undermine the original Counterfactual Account, they clearly fail to undermine the Short-term Counterfactual Account. And so even if the reasons for rejecting P2 provided by Harman's positive argument do turn out to satisfy the independence requirement, they are clearly not strong enough to satisfy the robustness requirement.

Harman can also be understood as providing a second positive argument for the Non-comparative Account, one that refers back to the surgery case. "Seeing that the doctor harms me," she says of that case, "enables us to see why surgery is a last resort and is not to be undertaken lightly—we must be quite sure the harm is justified before proceeding."[29] If the claim that the Non-comparative Account enables us to see why surgery is a last resort is meant to be understood as the claim that the Non-comparative Account can account for this judgment, then the claim is correct but does not constitute an argument for that account over the Counterfactual Account. If the claim is meant to be understood as the claim that choosing the Non-comparative Account rather than the Counterfactual Account enables us to account for this judgment, then the claim would count as an argument against the Counterfactual Account. But understood in this way, the claim is false. The Counterfactual Account can also account for

---

[29] Harman (2009: 139).

this judgment. Suppose, after all, that there is an available alternative to performing the surgery. Suppose, for example, that the doctor can choose between giving the patient a tasteless pill that has no side effects, and performing an operation that will result in a hole in the patient's abdomen and post-operative pain. In that case, choosing to perform the surgery rather than to give the patient the pill will make the patient worse off than she would otherwise be and the Counterfactual Account will entail that doing so would harm her. Since there is a strong moral presumption against harming people, the Counterfactual Account of harm therefore provides a strong moral presumption against performing the surgery when there is a less invasive alternative available. On either interpretation of the claim that the Non-comparative Account enables us to see why surgery is a last resort, then, the claim provides no reason to favor that account over the Counterfactual Account. To the extent that the claim is meant to provide an additional positive argument in defense of the Non-comparative Account, it is therefore no more successful than the first positive argument or the negative argument.

3.3.2 Arguments for the Wrongness of Non-comparatively Harming

I have argued so far that Harman's arguments for the Non-comparative Account of harm are unsuccessful. They fail to undermine the Counterfactual Account of harm, and even if they succeeded in undermining it, they would not be strong enough to undermine the short-term version of that account, and thus not robust enough to help us solve the non-identity problem. In addition, I believe that there is a further kind of reason to reject the Non-comparative Account beyond the problems generated for it by the surgery case. This reason is spelled out in the second part of Appendix C. But let's suppose that I am mistaken about all of this and that the Non-comparative Account of harm really is correct. If the Non-comparative Account is correct, then Wilma's act of conceiving Pebbles really does harm Pebbles despite the fact that it does not make Pebbles worse off than she would otherwise have been in the short term or in the long term. Even if this is so, however, the fact that Wilma's act harms Pebbles will help to solve the non-identity problem only if harming a person in this sense is morally wrong. And it is open to the critic of Harman's solution at this point to simply concede that Wilma's act harms Pebbles but to maintain that the act is not morally wrong because the benefits that it enables Pebbles to enjoy outweigh the harms associated with the condition that it inflicts on her.

The Non-comparative Account, after all, doesn't just entail that Wilma's act of conceiving Pebbles harms Pebbles because it causes her to be in a bad state. It also entails that the doctor's act of operating on you harms you because it causes you to be in a bad state, whether that state is the hole or the pain. But even if we are willing to accept the claim that the doctor's act harms you, we will surely reject the claim that the harmfulness of the doctor's act makes her act wrong. And the most natural basis for rejecting that claim would clearly seem to be the fact that the harm the doctor's act causes you is greatly outweighed by the benefits the act enables you to enjoy. If this is what accounts for the fact that the doctor's harmful act is not wrong, assuming that we agree that the doctor's act is harmful in the first place, then it will also entail that Wilma's harmful act is not wrong, since the benefits that Pebbles is able to enjoy as a result of Wilma's act of conceiving her greatly outweigh the harms to Pebbles caused by the act. The challenge facing the proponent of the Non-comparative Account of harm who wants to use that account to solve the non-identity problem, then, is to develop an alternative account of why the doctor's harmful act is not morally wrong and to show why the moral principle that this alternative account appeals to does not entail that Wilma's harmful act is also not morally wrong. In the absence of such an account, any attempt to solve the non-identity problem by appealing to the Non-comparative Account of harm will entail that the doctor acts wrongly when she saves the patient's life. And since this claim is even less plausible than the Implausible Conclusion that the account is trying to help us avoid, any solution based on such an account will fail to satisfy the modesty requirement. Several attempts have been made to respond to this challenge by providing such a principle, but none of them is successful.

3.3.2.1 HARMAN'S DEFENSE

Perhaps the most important representative of the Non-comparative Account here is again Harman. I will begin by focusing on the formulation of the moral principle she appeals to in her 2004 paper and will consider her revised version of the principle after raising an objection to the initial version. The initial version of Harman's principle consists of two parts. The first part maintains that the fact that an act would harm a person provides a powerful reason in favor of the claim that the act would be morally impermissible. The basic idea here is that there is a strong moral presumption against causing people to be in bad states. The second part of the principle maintains that the fact that an act would also benefit the person it would harm is not enough to outweigh this reason and render the act morally permissible, even if the benefits would be greater than the harms for the affected person. In particular, if the same sort and amount of benefit could instead be conferred on someone else without causing that other person the corresponding harms, then the fact that the harmful act would also cause greater benefits is not enough to render the act morally permissible. The basic idea here is that the beneficial consequences of performing an act that will harm someone can help to justify performing the harmful act only if the same sort of beneficial consequences can't also be produced by instead performing a different, non-harmful, act. As a result, we can put the moral principle that Harman appeals to in terms of what I will call the Alternative Possibility Principle:[30]

APP: The fact that a harmful act would cause a greater amount of benefit than harm to the harmed person is not enough to render the act morally permissible if there is an available alternative act that would harmlessly confer comparable benefits on someone else

[30] As Harman puts the principle in the earlier paper, "reasons against harm are so morally serious that the mere presence of greater benefits to those harmed is not in itself sufficient to render the harms permissible: when there is an alternative in which parallel benefits can be provided without parallel harms, the harming action is wrong" (2004: 93).

Note that the Alternative Possibility Principle provides neither a necessary nor a sufficient condition for a harmful act's being morally permissible. It does not maintain that the lack of an available harmless alternative act is enough to make it permissible to do the harmful act. Even if there is no such alternative available, the harmful act might still turn out to be wrong. Nor does the Alternative Possibility Principle insist that the lack of an available harmless alternative act is necessary in order for such an act to be permissible. Even if a harmless alternative act is available, there might turn out to be some kind of special consideration that would render it permissible in certain circumstances to choose the harmful act instead. What the principle does do is pick out one particular property and claim that this property is not sufficient for rendering the harmful act permissible. This is the property of causing an even greater amount of benefit to the person harmed by the act. The Alternative Possibility Principle maintains that this property cannot, by itself, render an otherwise impermissible harmful act morally permissible.

With these clarifications in mind, we can now see what the combination of the Alternative Possibility Principle and the Non-comparative Account of harm entails about the Wilma and surgery cases. Let's begin with the case of Wilma. The Non-comparative Account maintains that an act harms a person if the act causes that person to be in a bad state. On the assumption that blindness is a bad state for a person to be in, this means that Wilma's act of conceiving Pebbles harms Pebbles. But Wilma's act of conceiving Pebbles also benefits Pebbles by causing her to be in the good states that she gets to enjoy as a result of having been conceived. And on the assumption that blindness is not so bad that it makes a person's life worse than no life at all, the benefits that Wilma's act enables Pebbles to enjoy are greater than the harms that it inflicts on her. As noted above, it therefore seems natural to suppose that even if Wilma's act of conceiving Pebbles harms her, the harmfulness of Wilma's act could not account for the act's presumed wrongness. But the Alternative Possibility Principle maintains that the fact that a harmful act would cause a greater amount of benefit than harm to the harmed person is not enough to render the act morally permissible if there is an available alternative act that would harmlessly confer comparable benefits on someone else. And while Wilma's act benefits Pebbles more than it harms her, Wilma could have conferred the same kind and amount of benefit on some other child without causing that other child the harm of being blind. She could have done this by taking the tiny pill once a day for two months before conceiving and then conceiving a different child who would not have been blind. The Alternative Possibility Principle does not provide a necessary condition for a harmful act's being morally permissible. So it does not by itself entail that Wilma's act is morally impermissible. But the principle does pick out a property and claim that the property is not sufficient for rendering a harmful act morally permissible. This is the act's property of causing an even greater amount of benefit to the person harmed by the act. And if that property doesn't render Wilma's act morally permissible, it is difficult to imagine what other feature of the case could render the act permissible, given the strong moral presumption against harmful acts.

Let's now turn to the surgery case. The Non-comparative Account maintains that an act harms a person if the act causes that person to be in a bad state. On the assumption that pain and disfigurement are bad states for a person to be in, this means that the doctor's act of operating on the patient harms the patient. But the doctor's act of operating on the patient also benefits the patient by saving her life and it seems reasonable to suppose that the benefits she confers on the patient are therefore greater than the harms. The Alternative Possibility Principle maintains that the fact that a harmful act would cause a greater amount of benefit than harm to the harmed person is not enough to render the act morally permissible if there is an available alternative act that would harmlessly confer comparable benefits on someone else. In the case of Wilma, this meant that the benefits to Pebbles caused by Wilma's act were not sufficient to render Wilma's act of conceiving Pebbles morally permissible. This was because Wilma could have conferred the same amount and sort of benefits without doing the harmful act. But the surgery case is different in this respect. There is no way for the doctor to confer the benefits of saving a life in this case without causing some pain and disfigurement. There is therefore nothing about the Alternative Possibility Principle that prevents the benefits of the doctor's act from rendering the act morally permissible. The combination of the Alternative Possibility Principle and the Non-comparative Account of harm, in short, entails that Wilma's act harms Pebbles, that the harmfulness of Wilma's act cannot be justified by the benefits it causes, that the doctor's act harms her patient, but that the harmfulness of the doctor's act can be justified by the benefits it causes her patient. And that is precisely what a defender of the Non-comparative Account must establish in order to use that account to solve the non-identity problem. I have already argued that we should not accept the Non-comparative Account of harm in the first place. If we do accept that account, though, the question that remains is whether we have good reason to accept the Alternative Possibility Principle.

Harman can be understood as offering three arguments in support of this principle. The most direct argument is what she describes as "the intuitive thought behind" the principle:

The fact that an action harms someone provides a strong moral reason against acting; it is a reason that tells in favor of *refraining* as opposed to *performing the action*. If the action also benefits the harmed person, but performing the action is not the only way to provide such benefits—indeed, refraining from performing the action would provide similar benefits to someone—then considerations of benefit simply do not tell *in favor of acting* as opposed to *refraining from acting*.[31]

The fact that an act has a certain feature, in short, does not count in its favor if not doing the act has the very same feature.

---

[31] Harman (2009: 139–40). Note that the argument is presented in support of the modified version of her principle, but the argument in support of the principle remains the same.

The claim that Harman presents as the intuitive thought behind the Alternative Possibility Principle seems correct. But it does not support the principle. The reason for this is that the move from the intuitive thought to the principle requires a transition from a premise about one kind of reason to a conclusion about a second kind of reason. And once the distinction between the two kinds of reasons is made clear, the problem with moving from one to the other becomes clear as well.

The distinction I have in mind is between reasons to do an action and reasons to believe that doing the action would be morally permissible. Suppose, for example, that you need to use a car for the day, and that Andy and Bill each consent to let you borrow theirs. It is a bit more convenient for you to get to Andy's car than to get to Bill's car, and so you end up using Andy's car for the day. And now consider two questions. First, does the fact that Andy consented to let you use his car count in favor of your borrowing Andy's car rather than borrowing Bill's car? Here, the answer is clearly no. Bill also consented to let you use his car, and since both of them gave consent, the fact of consent provides no reason to choose one car rather than the other. Second, does the fact that Andy consented to let you use his car count in favor of the claim that borrowing his car would be morally permissible? Here, just as clearly, the answer is yes. It would be much harder to justify the permissibility of taking Andy's car for the day without his consent than to justify the permissibility of taking Andy's car for the day with his consent.

The case of Andy and Bill demonstrates that we are not entitled to move from the claim that "p is not a reason to do X" to the conclusion that "p is not a reason to believe that doing X is morally permissible": the fact that Andy consented to let you borrow his car is not a reason for you to borrow Andy's car rather than Bill's car, but it is a reason to believe it would be permissible for you borrow Andy's car rather than Bill's car. But Harman's first argument for the Alternative Possibility Principle requires precisely this kind of inference: the intuitive thought tells us that the fact that a harmful act would also benefit the person harmed is not a reason to choose to do that act when the alternative act would benefit someone else without harming them, but the Alternative Possibility Principle that is supposed to be supported by this thought does not say that the benefits to the harmed person are not a reason to do the act. It says that the benefits are not a reason to conclude that the act would be morally permissible. If all the principle said was that the benefits to the harmed person were not a reason to do the act, after all, then the principle would be unable to solve the non-identity problem even if we accepted it. The Implausible Conclusion that generates the problem maintains that Wilma's act of conceiving Pebbles rather than Rocks is not immoral, not that Wilma has a good reason to conceive Pebbles rather than Rocks. As a result, the intuitive thought that Harman appeals to fails to provide support for the moral principle she seeks to defend.

It might be objected that there is an important difference between the case of the borrowed car and the kinds of cases with which Harman is concerned. In the case of the borrowed car, there is something that counts in favor of the permissibility of borrowing each car—the consent given by the owner—and nothing that counts against it. But in the kinds of cases that the Alternative Possibility Principle is meant to apply to, there is something that counts in favor of the permissibility of each action—the benefit the action would cause to the person affected by it—but something that counts against the permissibility of only one of the actions: the act that would harm as well as benefit the person affected. And so it might be thought that the problem with moving from reasons to do a particular act to reasons to believe in the permissibility of doing a particular act that arise in the former case need not arise in the latter case.

This objection can be evaluated by modifying the car case so that it is parallel to the cases covered by Harman's principle. So suppose that in addition to the facts already mentioned, Bill owns two cars while Andy has only one. As a result, there will be no harm to Bill if you borrow his car for the day, but Andy will be significantly inconvenienced if you borrow his car. As in the original case, the fact that Andy consents to let you use his car is not a reason for you to choose borrowing his car over borrowing Bill's. But, again as in the original case, the fact that Andy consents to let you use his car is still a perfectly good reason in favor of the permissibility of your borrowing his car. It would certainly be more thoughtful of you to spare Andy the burden by instead borrowing Bill's car, but this does not mean that Andy's consent does not count in favor of the permissibility of borrowing his car. Andy's consent clearly still does count in favor of the permissibly of borrowing his car. And so the problem with the move from the intuitive thought to the Alternative Possibility Principle remains.

In addition to her direct appeal to the intuitive thought, Harman can be understood as offering two indirect arguments in support of the Alternative Possibility Principle. One argument is presented explicitly. This is the argument that appeals to the rape and Nazi prisoner examples. As noted above, Harman presents the cases not just as evidence that acts can harm a person even though they don't make the person worse off than they would otherwise have been, but as evidence that acts can be wrong *because* they harm a person even though they don't make the person worse off than they would otherwise have been. The cases, that is, were in part designed to show that "An individual can be. . . *impermissibly* harmed by [an] action. . . although the action makes her better off than she would otherwise be."[32] And if this is so, then even if it does not directly entail all of the details of the Alternative Possibility Principle, it at least establishes the principle's core claim: that the fact that a harmful act would cause a greater amount of benefit than harm to the harmed person is not enough by itself to render the act morally permissible.

But the rape and Nazi prisoner cases do not provide support for this claim. The reasons for this are parallel to the reasons provided in section 3.3.1 and in the first part of Appendix C for rejecting the claim that the rape and Nazi prisoner cases support the Non-comparative Account of harm itself. First, it is not sufficiently clear that the acts in question are harmful, and if they are not harmful, then they are not relevant to

---

[32] Harman (2004: 99, emphasis added).

the Alternative Possibility Principle. Second, and more importantly, even if we agree that the acts in question are harmful, the cases can at most establish that the fact that a harmful act would cause a greater amount of benefit than harm to the harmed person is not enough to render the act morally permissible in an importantly restricted range of cases: those cases in which the harmful act leaves the person worse off than they would otherwise be for at least some period of time. This quite modest claim does nothing to support the much stronger claim that the fact that a harmful act would cause a greater amount of benefit than harm to the harmed person is not enough to render the act morally permissible in cases where there would be no point in time during which the person is worse off than they would otherwise be as a result of the act being performed. It may well be reasonable, for example, to say that the purported long-term benefit to a child of spanking him for misbehaving does not justify the act of spanking him because the act objectionably makes him worse off in the short run than he would otherwise be. But even if this is so, it provides no support for the much stronger claim that the long-term benefit to a child of some other form of treatment would not justify the use of that form of treatment if it did not make the child worse off than he would otherwise be at any point in time. And it is the much stronger kind of claim that is needed in order to solve the non-identity problem. Since non-identity cases are cases of this latter sort and the rape and Nazi prisoner cases are cases of the former sort, the rape and Nazi prisoner cases are therefore unable to support a version of the Alternative Possibility Principle that is sufficiently robust to solve the non-identity problem.

Finally, although the argument is not presented explicitly and perhaps is not even intended by Harman to be suggested implicitly, it is worth noting that a defender of the Alternative Possibility Principle might appeal to the claim that the principle is justified precisely because it helps us to distinguish between the surgery case and the Wilma case. In both cases, an act causes someone to be in a bad state, and in both cases the act also causes a greater amount of benefit than harm. But Wilma had an alternative act available to her that would have harmlessly conferred comparable benefits on someone else while the doctor did not. There was an easy way for Wilma to confer the benefits made possible by living on a child without causing the child to be blind, that is, but there was no way for the doctor to confer the benefit of saving a patient's life without causing the bodily damage and post-operative pain. The Alternative Possibility Principle would account for the fact that Wilma's act was impermissible while the doctor's act was not, that is, and this fact might itself be taken as a reason to accept the principle.

The problem with appealing to this fact in support of the principle, though, is that it begs the question in favor of the solution that the principle is designed to support. It therefore fails to satisfy the independence requirement. If we assume that Wilma's act is wrong because it harms Pebbles, that is, then the fact that the principle would explain why the harmful act is not rendered permissible by its benefits would lend support to the principle. But we can't simply assume that the reason that Wilma's act is wrong is that it harms Pebbles because that is precisely what the argument based on the principle is trying to establish in the first place.

I have argued so far that we have no good reason to accept the Alternative Possibility Principle. In addition, we have one good reason to reject it. The reason is that it has implications that are more implausible than the Implausible Conclusion. Any solution based on the principle will therefore fail to satisfy the modesty requirement. Consider this case:

Ice Cream Sundae: You have just been given a delicious ice cream sundae but have decided that you do not wish to eat it. There are two children nearby who would each derive an immense amount of pleasure from eating it. Sally is sitting close to you while Ben is sitting on the far side of the room, so it would be a bit more convenient for you to give it to Sally. If you give the sundae to Sally, it will later cause her to have a short, mild stomach ache. If you give it to Ben, it will not cause him to have a stomach ache.

In this case, it seems clear that it would be morally permissible for you to give the sundae to Sally. But the Alternative Possibility Principle entails that doing so would be impermissible. If you give the sundae to Sally, after all, this will cause her some harm. And while it will also cause her a much greater amount of benefit, the Alternative Possibility Principle maintains that this fact does nothing to render the act permissible if you could harmlessly confer a comparable benefit on someone else. And since you could instead give the sundae to Ben without causing any harm at all, the Alternative Possibility Principle dictates that you must give the sundae to Ben. This result is more implausible than the Implausible Conclusion, and so a solution based on the principle that entails it will fail to satisfy the modesty requirement. Indeed, the same point can be made by considering a variation on Harman's surgery case. Suppose that as the doctor is about to save the patient's life, a second dying person is brought in. The doctor can save only one of the two, and if he saves the second patient, the procedure will cause no bodily damage or post-operative pain. In that case, the Alternative Possibility Principle entails that it would be morally impermissible for the doctor to perform the surgery on the first patient. The principle, that is, entails that the benefit of saving the first patient's life justifies the harm the procedure will cause only if there aren't any other people whose lives could be saved in some other, harmless, manner. And that result, too, is clearly implausible.[33]

Harman overlooked this problem in her 2004 paper, but in her 2009 follow up she acknowledges it and tries to overcome it. She begins by drawing a distinction between what she calls:[34]

4*. If an action harms someone, then the fact that the action also benefits the person harmed, and benefits him more than it harms him, is *ineligible* to justify the harm if *failing to perform the action* would similarly benefit someone.

---

[33] Hanser appeals to a similar case (2009: 183).
[34] Harman (2009: 139, italics in the original but boldface added).

and

4. If an action harms someone **who does not independently exist,** then the fact that the action also benefits the person harmed, and benefits him more than it harms him, is *ineligible* to justify the harm if *failing to perform the action* would similarly benefit someone.

4* is, in effect, a variant of what I have been referring to as the Alternative Possibility Principle. The only difference is that rather than saying that the benefits are not sufficient to render the harmful act permissible, 4* says that the benefits are not even eligible to render the act permissible. 4 is an importantly restricted version of 4*. It makes the same claim that 4* makes but only in cases in which the existence of the person who would be harmed by a given act is dependent on the act's being performed. Harman then argues that while cases like the ice cream sundae case do undermine what she calls 4*, they do not undermine 4. Cases like the ice cream sundae case and the variant on the surgery case involve acts that harm people who exist independently of the act's being performed and so cannot serve as counter-examples to 4. And since 4 is all that is needed to solve the non-identity problem, Harman can simply accept the change from 4* to 4 and preserve the soundness of her solution.

Harman recognizes the objection that will naturally arise at this point: that her modification of the principle she started with is entirely ad hoc. Without some independent justification for restricting the scope of 4* to that found in 4, that is, the justification for the claim needed to solve the non-identity problem will simply be that if we accept it, then we will be able to solve the non-identity problem. And this will leave her solution unable to satisfy what I have referred to as the independence requirement. Harman offers a response to this objection in her 2009 paper. I believe that her response is unsuccessful and my reasons for believing this are presented in the third part of Appendix C. But even if I am mistaken about this, the basic problems with her argument for accepting at least some version of the Alternative Possibility Principle remain. The intuitive thought behind the principle fails to support it, appealing to the fact that the principle would justify the distinction between the Wilma case and the surgery case begs the question in favor of the solution the principle aims to support, and if the rape and Nazi prisoner cases support the principle at all, they support its application only in a limited range of cases that do not apply to cases like Wilma or the wealthy society: cases where an act would make a person worse off than they would otherwise be in the short term while benefiting them overall in the long term. Even if Harman's analysis provides a foundation for justifying the claim that such acts are morally wrong, the analysis cannot be extended to the sorts of cases that generate the non-identity problem. Even if we accept Harman's defense of the Non-comparative Account of harm itself, then, and I have argued that we should not accept it, neither version of the moral principle she conjoins to that account can be used to ground a satisfactory solution to the non-identity problem.

3.3.2.2 SHIFFRIN'S DEFENSE

I have argued so far that Harman's Alternative Possibility Principle fails to provide a satisfactory route from the Non-comparative Account of harm to the conclusion that Wilma's act of conceiving Pebbles wrongfully harms Pebbles. But this does not mean that the Non-comparative Account cannot be used to solve the non-identity problem. It simply means that a successful solution based on that account would have to make use of a different moral principle. And Shiffrin proposed such an alternative in her important 1999 paper, "Wrongful Life, Procreative Responsibility, and the Significance of Harm."

Shiffrin's principle maintains that there is a morally relevant distinction between two kinds of benefit that might be conferred on a person in the course of harming them. One kind of benefit is what Shiffrin calls a "pure" benefit. This involves adding something good to someone's condition.[35] The other is what, following Hanser, I will call a "preventative" benefit.[36] This involves preventing something bad from being added to someone's condition or preventing them from having something good taken from their condition. If a child is about to eat a bowl of ice cream and you thoughtfully give him some chocolate syrup to put on top of it, for example, you have given him a pure benefit. If an anvil is about to fall on his head or someone is about to steal his bicycle and you prevent the bad thing from happening to him, you have given him a preventative benefit. The principle that appeals to this distinction maintains that preventative benefits can justify harmful acts in a way that pure benefits cannot.[37] For that reason, I will refer to it as the Preventative Benefit Principle. The principle can be put as follows:

PBP: A harmful act can be rendered permissible by the fact that it would confer a greater amount of preventative benefit on the person harmed by the act, but a harmful act cannot be rendered permissible by the fact that it would confer a greater amount of pure benefit on the person harmed by the act

The Preventative Benefit Principle does not maintain that every harmful act that confers greater preventative benefits is permissible. Such an act might be impermissible, for example, if the person performing the act had promised not to perform it. And the principle does not insist that no harmful act that confers only pure benefits is permissible. Such an act might be permissible, for example, if the person on the receiving end of the harm consents to it. But the principle does claim that one particular kind of reason for thinking that a harmful act would be permissible—the kind of reason that appeals to the fact that the harmful act would also confer greater benefits on the person harmed—is only a good reason if the benefit conferred would be a preventative benefit rather than a pure benefit.

---

[35] Shiffrin (1999: 124).   [36] Hanser (2009: 183). Shiffrin herself does not seem to give it a name.
[37] It is not always clear whether Shiffrin means to endorse the claim that it takes a greater amount of pure benefit than of preventative benefit to justify harming a person or the stronger claim that pure benefits are simply incapable of rendering it permissible to harm a person. But since only the stronger claim will suffice to solve the non-identity problem, I focus on that version of the claim here.

With these clarifications in mind, we can now see what the combination of the Preventative Benefit Principle and the Non-comparative Account of harm entails about the Wilma case and the surgery case. Let's begin with the case of Wilma. The Non-comparative Account maintains that an act harms a person if the act causes that person to be in a bad state. On the assumption that blindness is a bad state for a person to be in, as we have already seen, this means that Wilma's act of conceiving Pebbles harms Pebbles. But Wilma's act of conceiving Pebbles also benefits her by enabling her to have all the good things she enjoys in her life. And on the assumption that blindness is not so bad that it makes a person's life worse than no life at all, the benefits that Wilma's act confers on Pebbles are greater than the harms. As noted above, it therefore seems natural to suppose that even if Wilma's act of conceiving Pebbles harmed her, the harmfulness of Wilma's act could not account for the act's presumed wrongness. But the Preventative Benefit Principle maintains that the fact that a harmful act would cause a greater amount of benefit than harm to the harmed person can render the act permissible only if the benefit conferred on the harmed person is a preventative benefit. And while Wilma's act benefits Pebbles more than it harms her, it does so by conferring on Pebbles a pure benefit rather than a preventative benefit. Conceiving Pebbles, that is, does not protect Pebbles from something bad that would happen to her if she were not conceived. It simply enables her to have something good to enjoy: the good things she will experience in her life. The Preventative Benefit Principle does not provide a necessary condition for a harmful act's being morally permissible. So it does not by itself entail that Wilma's act is morally impermissible. But the principle does pick out a property that is not sufficient for rendering a harmful act morally permissible. That is the property of causing an even greater amount of benefit to the person harmed by the act if the benefit is a pure benefit. And if the fact that the benefits outweigh the harms doesn't render Wilma's harmful act morally permissible, it is difficult to imagine what other feature of the case could render it permissible, given the strong moral presumption against harmful acts.

Let's now turn to the surgery case. The Non-comparative Account maintains that an act harms a person if the act causes that person to be in a bad state. On the assumption that pain and disfigurement are bad states for a person to be in, as we have already seen, this means that the doctor's act of operating on her patient harms her patient. But the doctor's act of operating on her patient also benefits her patient by saving her patient's life and it therefore seems reasonable to suppose that the benefits she confers on her patient are greater than the harms. The Preventative Benefit Principle maintains that the fact that a harmful act would cause a greater amount of benefit than harm to the harmed person can render the act permissible if the benefit is a preventative benefit but not if it is a pure benefit. In the case of Wilma, this meant that the benefits caused by Wilma's act were not sufficient to render her act morally permissible. This was because the benefits that Wilma's act conferred on Pebbles were pure benefits. But the surgery case is different in this respect. The benefit that the doctor's act confers on her patient is the avoidance of the severe pain and imminent death that the patient would otherwise suffer. So there is nothing about the Preventative Benefit Principle that prevents the benefits of the doctor's act from rendering her act morally permissible. The combination of the Preventative Benefit Principle and the Non-comparative Account of harm, in short, entails that Wilma's act harms Pebbles, that the harmfulness of Wilma's act cannot be justified by the pure benefits it causes, that the doctor's act harms her patient, and that the harmfulness of the doctor's act can be justified by the preventative benefits it confers on her patient. And that is precisely what a defender of the Non-comparative Account must establish in order to use that account to solve the non-identity problem. I have already argued that we should not accept the Non-comparative Account of harm in the first place. If we do accept that account, though, the question again remains whether we have good reason to accept the Preventative Benefit Principle.

Shiffrin defends the principle by claiming that it offers the best account of the judgments we are likely to make in two particular pairs of cases. The first pair of cases is this:[38]

Drowning: Moe is drowning. If Larry does not rescue Moe, Moe will either die or suffer brain damage from oxygen deprivation. In order to rescue Moe, Larry will have to break Moe's arm. Larry rescues Moe. As a result, Moe is spared death or brain damage and has a broken arm.

Gold Cube: Richie Rich wishes to bestow a gift upon Average Joe. The only gift he can give is a cube of gold worth $5 million. The only way to give it to Joe is to drop it on him, which will break Joe's arm. Richie is unable to communicate with Joe ahead of time and so cannot secure Joe's consent. Richie drops the cube on Joe. As a result, Joe is $5 million richer and has a broken arm.

Shiffrin thinks that we will respond to these two cases as follows: Larry owes no compensation to Moe for breaking Moe's arm in the course of benefiting him, but Richie does owe compensation to Joe for breaking Joe's arm in the course of benefiting him. Since we don't owe compensation for permissibly harming people but do owe compensation for impermissibly harming people, and since the benefit Larry confers on Moe is a preventative benefit while the benefit that Richie confers on Joe is a pure benefit, this response to the cases seems to provide support for the Preventative Benefit Principle: preventative benefits can render harmful acts permissible in a way that pure benefits cannot.

I assume that everyone will agree that Larry owes no compensation to Moe for breaking his arm. It's less clear that most people will agree that Richie owes compensation to Joe for breaking his arm, partly because many people may think the act generates no duty of compensation in the first place and partly because they may think that some portion of the value of the gold cube could itself be taken to constitute the compensation owed to Joe. I'm inclined to think that one or the other of these responses is reasonable, and so I don't find it at all obvious that Richie would owe compensation to Joe. But let's suppose that neither of these responses is acceptable, and that Richie really does owe Joe compensation for breaking his arm. Even if this is true, it does not follow

---

[38] Shiffrin (1999: 125, 127). I have modified and shortened the cases.

that Richie's act was impermissible. Duties of compensation can arise from acts that are not morally impermissible. If I have to break into your unoccupied winter cabin in order to survive a snowstorm, to take a familiar example, many people will agree that it would be morally permissible for me to do so and that I would nonetheless owe you compensation for the damage I caused by breaking in. Similarly, one might think that Richie's act is morally permissible while thinking that Richie would nonetheless owe Joe compensation for the harm he caused by doing the permissible act.

But let's suppose that Richie's act really is morally impermissible. Even if this is so, the fact that Larry's harmful act is permissible while Richie's harmful act is impermissible will support the Preventative Benefit Principle only if that principle provides the best explanation of the difference in terms of permissibility between the two cases. And it does not. The difference between preventative and pure benefits marks one difference between the two cases. But there is a second difference. The second difference is that in the case of Larry and Moe, the harms and benefits are roughly commensurable: they are harms and benefits in terms of physical well-being. But in the case of Richie and Joe, the harms and benefits are far less easily compared: harms in terms of physical well-being and benefits in terms of financial well-being. I believe that it is this difference in terms of commensurability, rather than the difference between pure and preventative benefits, that does the work of making it seem that Richie's act is impermissible while Larry's is permissible, at least for those to whom this seems to be the case. And if the distinction between pure and preventative benefits is not doing the work in generating the moral difference between the cases, assuming that there is such a difference, then the cases themselves provide no support for the principle that rests on that distinction.

We can test the claim that it is the difference in terms of commensurability that accounts for the presumed difference in permissibility by revising one of the two cases so that the two cases continue to differ in terms of pure and preventative benefits but become comparable in terms of the commensurability or lack of commensurability of the harms and benefits. If after making such a change the two cases continue to seem different in terms of permissibility, this will count as evidence that the commensurability difference was irrelevant and that the difference between pure and preventative benefits was generating the difference in permissibility. But if the two cases now seem to become the same in terms of their permissibility, this will count as evidence that it was the commensurability difference that was driving our moral reaction to the original cases and that the difference between pure and preventative benefits had nothing to do with it.

One way we can do this is to take the pure benefits case and make it just like the preventative benefits case in terms of commensurability. In the case where Larry confers a preventative benefit on Moe by rescuing him, the harms and benefits seem commensurable. So we can change the case in which Richie's giving the gold cube to Joe confers a pure benefit on Joe by making it one in which the harms and benefits are also commensurable. Here is an example:

Two Cubes: Richie Rich wishes to bestow a gift upon Average Joe. The only gift he can give is a cube of gold worth $5 million. The only way to give it to Joe is to drop it on top of one of Joe's possessions: a much smaller gold cube that is worth $500. If Richie does this, Joe's small gold cube will be destroyed. Richie is unable to communicate with Joe ahead of time and so cannot secure Joe's consent. Richie drops the large gold cube on Joe's small gold cube, putting Joe in possession of the large gold cube and destroying the small gold cube. As a result, Joe now has a $5 million dollar gold cube rather than a $500 gold cube.

In this case, as in the original gold cube case, Richie confers a pure benefit on Joe. But in this case, unlike the original gold cube case, the harm that Richie causes is easily commensurable with the benefit he confers.

While it may seem plausible to many people to say that it would be wrong for Richie to break Joe's arm to give him the large gold cube in the original gold cube case, it is difficult to believe that many people will think it wrong for Richie to destroy Joe's much smaller gold cube in order to give him the much larger gold cube in the two cubes case. If you were to deposit an unexpected $5 million dollar gift into my bank account and if this were to result in my unavoidably being charged a $500 fee due to some particular feature of the transaction, for example, I doubt very much that anyone would think that you had wronged me by doing this to me or think that you now owed me $500 in compensation as a result. But if this is so, then Richie's act in the original version of the gold cube case was wrong, if it was wrong at all, not because the benefit it conferred was pure rather than preventative, but rather because the benefit it conferred was not sufficiently commensurable with the harm that it caused. And if this is the reason that Richie's act was wrong in the original gold cube case while Larry's act was not wrong in the drowning case, then the presumed difference between our moral judgments about those two cases provides no support for the Preventative Benefit Principle.

The other way to test the claim that it is the difference in commensurability that does the work in Shiffrin's cases rather than the difference between pure and preventative benefits is to take the preventative benefits case and make it just like the pure benefits case in terms of commensurability. For those who are interested, I provide such an example in Appendix D and argue that it, too, supports the claim that the difference in commensurability does the work in Shiffrin's cases and not the difference between pure and preventative benefits.

The second pair of cases that Shiffrin appeals to in support of the Preventative Benefit Principle appears in the following passage:[39]

[I]t seems wrong to break an unconscious patient's arm even if necessary to endow her with valuable, physical benefits, such as supernormal memory, a useful store of encyclopedic knowledge, twenty IQ points worth of extra intellectual ability, or the ability to consume immoderate amounts of alcohol or fat without side effects. At the least, it would be much harder to justify than inflicting similar harm to avert a greater harm, such as death or significant disability.

---

[39] Shiffrin (1999: 127).

Harming someone to give them a significant supernormal ability seems wrong in a way that harming them to prevent them from incurring a significant disability does not, that is, and since the former involves pure benefits while the latter involves preventative benefits, this kind of case again seems to support the Preventative Benefit Principle.

As with Shiffrin's first pair of cases, it is again not completely clear how widespread the intuitions that her argument depends on will prove to be. Let's suppose that John is an average person with average abilities, for example, and hold other things fixed by comparing the case where his arm is broken in order to give him twenty extra IQ points worth of intelligence with the case where his arm is broken in order to prevent him from losing twenty IQ points worth of intelligence. I suspect that a fair number of people will see the two cases as being morally on a par. But let's go ahead and assume that it would be impermissible to break John's arm in the first case but permissible to break it in the second. Even if this is so, the intuition that there is a difference in terms of permissibility in these two cases will support the Preventative Benefit Principle only if that principle provides the best explanation of the intuition. And it does not. The difference between preventative and pure benefits marks one difference between the two cases involving John. But as with Shiffrin's first pair of cases, there is again a second difference. The second difference this time turns on the fact that the pure benefits case involves putting John above what is viewed as the normal baseline while the preventative benefits case involves preventing John from falling below that baseline. People tend to put more weight on not falling below such a baseline than they put on being elevated further above it. I believe that it is this difference in terms of being above or below the normal baseline, rather than the difference between pure and preventative benefits, that does the work of making it seem that breaking John's arm to give him twenty extra IQ points is wrong while breaking his arm to prevent him from losing twenty IQ points is not, at least to those to whom things appear this way. And, as with the first pair of cases, if the distinction between pure and preventative benefits is not doing the work in generating the apparent difference in permissibility between the two cases involving John, then the cases provide no support for the principle that rests on that distinction.

We can test the claim that it is the difference in terms of taking place above or below the normal baseline that accounts for the presumed difference in permissibility by revising one of the two cases involving John so that they continue to differ in terms of pure and preventative benefits but become comparable in terms of clearly both taking place below or both taking place above the normal baseline. If after making such a change the two cases continue to seem different in terms of permissibility, this will count as evidence that the baseline difference was irrelevant and that the difference between pure and preventative benefits was generating the difference in permissibility for those who perceive such a difference. But if the two cases come to seem the same in terms of their permissibility, this will count as evidence that it was the baseline difference that was driving our reaction to the original cases, to the extent that we have the reaction that Shiffrin's argument presupposes, and that our reaction to those cases does nothing to support the claim that there is a morally relevant difference between pure and preventative benefits.

Since changing someone's level of intelligence may introduce complicating worries about whether we are also changing their identity, it will prove simpler to use a pair of cases that involve physical abilities that seem less intimately connected to identity. So suppose that we are instead talking about either giving someone enhanced vision or preventing them from suffering a deterioration of their vision. And suppose that we agree that in the case in which John has average vision, it would be wrong to break his arm to give him supernormal vision but not wrong to break his arm to prevent him from incurring a vision disability of comparable magnitude. In that case, we can change the pair of examples either by having both cases take place above the normal baseline or having both cases take place below it. In either event, the result seems to me to be that we will not think there is a difference in terms of the permissibility of the acts in question, even if we thought that there was such a difference in the original pair of cases. And if that's right, then Shiffrin's second pair of cases, like her first, ultimately fails to support the Preventative Benefit Principle.

Suppose first that we revise the cases so that both choices take place above the normal baseline. Here is an example:

Super Vision One: John has vision that is ten times better than normal vision. If you break his arm, you can improve his vision so that it will be twenty times better than normal vision.

Super Vision Two: John has vision that is twenty times better than normal vision. If you break his arm, you can prevent his vision from being reduced to the point where it is only ten times better than normal vision.

As with the original pair of examples in which John starts off as average, one of these cases involves harming John to confer a pure benefit and the other involves harming him to confer a preventative benefit. But unlike the original pair of examples, both of these cases clearly take place well above the normal baseline. We can thus use this pair of cases to see what is doing the work in generating our responses to the original pair of cases. To me, at least, the answer seems clear: there is no morally relevant difference between breaking John's arm in Super Vision One and breaking it in Super Vision Two. I am inclined to think that this is because the benefits of having vision that is twenty times better than normal rather than ten times better than normal are not great enough to warrant breaking someone's arm regardless of whether the benefit would come as a pure or a preventative one. But if I am wrong about that, and if the benefits really are great enough to justify breaking someone's arm, then they seem great enough to justify it regardless of whether the benefit would be pure or preventative. And so either way, when both cases clearly take place well above the normal baseline, the difference between pure and preventative benefits strike me, at least, as morally irrelevant.

The second way to revise the two cases is to have both of them take place below the normal baseline. The result would be a pair of cases like this:

Subnormal Vision One: John has vision that is twenty times worse than normal vision. If you break his arm, you can improve his vision so that it will be only ten times worse than normal vision.

Subnormal Vision Two: John has vision that is ten times worse than normal vision. If you break his arm, you can prevent his vision from being reduced to the point where it is twenty times worse than normal vision.

To me, at least, it seems clear that there is also no morally relevant difference between breaking John's arm in Subnormal Vision One and breaking it in Subnormal Vision Two. I am inclined to think that this is because the benefits of having vision that is only ten times worse than normal rather than twenty times worse than normal really are great enough to warrant breaking someone's arm regardless of whether the benefit would come as a pure or a preventative one. But if I am wrong about that, and if the benefits are not great enough to justify breaking someone's arm, then they seem not to be great enough to justify it regardless of whether the benefit would be pure or preventative. And so either way, when both cases clearly take place well below the normal baseline, the difference between pure and preventative benefits again strikes me, at least, as morally irrelevant. And if that's right then, again, the cases that Shiffrin appeals to fail to provide support for the distinction underlying the Preventative Benefit Principle.

I have argued so far that Shiffrin's examples fail to provide support for the Preventative Benefit Principle. But let's suppose that I have been wrong about this. Let's suppose that it would be wrong for Richie to drop the gold cube on Joe and wrong for us to break John's arm in order to improve his vision, and let's suppose that these acts would be wrong precisely because they would only be providing pure benefits rather than preventative benefits. Even if this is so, and even if we therefore accept Shiffrin's principle, the principle itself will be unable to help us solve the non-identity problem. This is because a problem arises when we try to extend the application of the principle from cases involving our treatment of people who already exist to cases involving the creation of new people.

If it is wrong for Richie to drop the gold cube on Joe even though doing so will be good for Joe on the whole, for example, this will have to be because it is wrong for Richie to treat Joe paternalistically. If it were permissible to treat Joe paternalistically, after all, then it would be permissible to harm him in order to produce even greater benefits for him regardless of the kind of benefits that would result. But this reason for thinking that it is wrong for Richie to harm Joe can't be used to justify the claim that it is wrong for Wilma to harm Pebbles by conceiving her. Even if we accept the Non-comparative Account of harm and agree that Wilma's act of conceiving Pebbles harms Pebbles, and even if we agree that the benefits that Wilma confers on Pebbles are pure rather than preventative ones and that the difference between pure and preventative benefits is relevant in the case of Richie and Joe, this will still fail to show that Wilma's act wrongfully harms Pebbles. At the time that Wilma conceives Pebbles, after all, Pebbles does not exist and so there is no one who is being treated paternalistically by Wilma when Wilma does what she does.

We can test the claim that the purported wrongness of harming a person in order to confer merely pure benefits on him depends on his being a person with the right not to be treated paternalistically, moreover, by looking at cases involving the treatment of young children. If in the case of young children we still think that a harmful act cannot be rendered permissible by its generating a greater amount of pure benefits, this will count as evidence that opposition to paternalism is not what accounts for our intuition in the case of Richie and Joe and that Shiffrin's principle can legitimately be extended from cases of harming adults to cases of harming by conception. But if in the case of young children we think that it is permissible to harm in order to confer merely pure benefits, this will count as evidence that the reason it is impermissible for Richie to harm Joe in order to confer merely pure benefits, if it really is impermissible for Richie to harm Joe in the first place, is that Joe is a competent adult human being who has a right not to be treated paternalistically. And this would mean that the Preventative Benefit Principle, even if it really does provide the best account of cases like the gold cube, cannot legitimately be extended to cases like that of Wilma.

And when we apply the principle to cases involving children, the results are clear: in the context of those relationships in which it is permissible for us to treat young children paternalistically, it is permissible for us to harm them in order to more greatly benefit them, even if the benefits are pure and not preventative. Here is a simple example:

Training Wheels: Bobby's parents want Bobby to learn how to ride a bicycle. He has been practicing with training wheels and has reached the point where the best way for him to learn to ride is to take the wheels off and try riding without them. Bobby's parents know that if they remove the training wheels and have him ride the bike, this will cause him to fall down and hurt himself a number of times before he masters the bike. But they also know that the benefits of being able to ride a bike will outweigh the costs he will incur in the process of learning to ride.

In the case of the training wheels, the benefits to Bobby are pure benefits rather than preventative ones. Learning to ride a bicycle does not prevent you from having bad things happen to you. It simply enables you to have more good things happen. But even though the benefits to Bobby are merely pure benefits, it is nonetheless clear that it is morally permissible for his parents to harm him as a means of conferring those benefits on him. It would not be permissible for Bobby's parents to force an unconsenting adult to learn to ride a bicycle even if the benefits of his learning to ride would also greatly outweigh the harms he would incur along the way, but it is surely permissible for them to inflict such harms on their own young child. This shows that even if we accept the Preventative Benefit Principle, and even if we agree that the principle shows that the pure benefits to Joe cannot justify Richie's act of harming Joe, the principle cannot be extended to the case of Wilma. Since Wilma's act does not involve treating a competent adult in an objectionably paternalistic manner, and since it is ultimately the paternalistic nature of Richie's act that renders it immoral if it is immoral at all, the reason for thinking that it is wrong for Richie to harm Joe in the process of benefiting him fails to show that it is wrong for Wilma to harm Pebbles in the process of benefiting her. We have good reason to reject the Preventative Benefit Principle, then, but even if we accept it, the principle itself is insufficiently robust to solve the non-identity problem.

I began this chapter by noting that while the Counterfactual Account of harm embodied by P2 of the non-identity argument may at first seem to be virtually unassailable, there are, in fact, a number of potentially powerful alternatives to that account that must be considered. Having now considered those alternatives, I remain inclined to believe that P2 is true. But even if P2 isn't true, there is no reason for rejecting it that can ground a satisfactory solution to the non-identity problem. Any alternative to the Counterfactual Account of harm will either have implications that are even more implausible than the Implausible Conclusion or will fail to entail that Wilma's act harms Pebbles or both. The rejection of P2 cannot ground a satisfactory solution to the non-identity problem, then, because if the reason given for rejecting it is modest enough to satisfy the modesty requirement it will be too modest to satisfy the robustness requirement, and if it is robust enough to satisfy the robustness requirement it will be too robust to satisfy the modesty requirement. As proved to be the case with P1, if we are going to avoid the Implausible Conclusion by rejecting one of the premises of the non-identity argument, we will have to look elsewhere.

4

Rejecting the Third Premise

The first premise of the non-identity argument maintains that Wilma's act of conceiving Pebbles does not make Pebbles worse off than she would otherwise have been. The second premise maintains that if A's act harms B, then A's act makes B worse off than B would otherwise have been. If both of these premises are true, then Wilma's act does not harm Pebbles. I argued in the last two chapters that neither of these premises can be rejected in a way that will ground a satisfactory solution to the non-identity problem. Any argument for rejecting either of them is either too weak to block the move to the conclusion that Wilma's act does not harm Pebbles or too strong to avoid entailing conclusions that are even more implausible than the Implausible Conclusion. If we are going to find a satisfactory solution to the non-identity problem, then, we will have to concede that Wilma's act does not really harm Pebbles and look for a solution elsewhere.

What about the third premise? P3 maintains that Wilma's act does not harm anyone other than Pebbles. If P3 is also accepted, it will follow that Wilma's act harms no one. And if Wilma's act harms no one, it will become even more difficult to justify the claim that her act is wrong. But why should we accept P3? In the real world, after all, it seems plausible to suppose that conceiving a blind child rather than a sighted child will impose extra burdens on at least some third parties, such as taxpayers who may well foot the bill for special assistance if the child attends a public school. The reason for accepting P3 despite this fact is simple. In deciding whether they think that Wilma's act is morally wrong, most people do not first stop to think about whether her act harms any third parties. This is because the belief that most people have that Wilma's act is morally wrong does not depend on her act's having negative consequences for any third parties. If her act really is wrong, that is, it is wrong even if it harms no one other than Pebbles. Since the belief that Wilma's act is wrong is really the belief that Wilma's act is wrong even if it does not harm anyone other than Pebbles, it will be a problem for our ability to vindicate this belief if we cannot show her act to be wrong without appealing to such secondary harms. It is thus no objection to P3 to point out that, in the real world, conceiving disabled children often does impose some further costs on at least some other people. The only way to reject P3 would be to claim not merely that it is contingently true that some other people are usually harmed by acts such as Wilma's, but rather that it is necessarily true that someone else always is. I am aware of only two ways in which P3 might be thus attacked and will consider them here in turn.

4.1 Harming Yourself

One possibility would be to insist that Wilma's act harms herself because it will be more difficult for her to raise a blind child than to raise an otherwise comparable sighted child. If Wilma's act harms Wilma, then P3 is false, and we can therefore block the move from P1 and P2 to the Implausible Conclusion even if Wilma's act really doesn't harm Pebbles.

There are two reasons to reject this kind of solution. First, there is no reason to insist that Wilma must harm herself by conceiving Pebbles. There are presumably a variety of distinctive burdens that the parent of a blind child typically incurs, but there may also be a variety of distinctive and compensating rewards. For the purposes of evaluating the argument, we can simply stipulate that this would be the case for Wilma. Suppose, for example, that Wilma has two sisters. One has a blind child and the other has a sighted child. Wilma has observed both sisters carefully over a long period of time and as a result reasonably believes that the two sisters are equally happy with their children. Neither would trade their child for the other. Having thought about it carefully, Wilma is confident that she will be just as happy regardless of whether she has a blind child or a sighted child. There is nothing incoherent about this scenario. But the claim that it would not be wrong for Wilma to conceive Pebbles under such circumstances will still strike most people as implausible. And if it would be wrong for Wilma to conceive Pebbles even if conceiving Pebbles did not harm Wilma, then the fact—if it is a fact—that conceiving a blind child would typically harm the parent of the blind child will be unable to account for the claim that conceiving the blind child would be wrong.

But suppose that I'm wrong about this and that it is necessarily the case that Wilma harms herself by conceiving a blind child rather than a sighted child. Even if this is so, there is a second reason that this fact cannot be used to account for the wrongness of Wilma's act. The reason is that the claim that Wilma harms herself by conceiving Pebbles rather than Rocks supports the claim that Wilma's act is morally wrong only if self-harmful acts are morally wrong. But even those who deny that we have any moral duties to ourselves will generally agree that Wilma's act is morally wrong. Given that Wilma's act seems to be wrong regardless of whether self-harmful acts are wrong, a successful account of the wrongness of her act must be independent of the claim that self-harmful acts are wrong. And a solution to the problem based on the claim that Wilma harms herself by conceiving Pebbles rather than Rocks cannot be made independent of that claim.

Finally, it is worth noting that if these two objections can be overcome, and if a solution based on the claim that Wilma's act harms herself really can be used to ground a successful solution to the direct version of the non-identity problem, it will still be unable to solve the indirect version. Even if Wilma harms herself by conceiving Pebbles, that is, the currently living members of the wealthy society clearly don't harm themselves by choosing the risky policy that results in thousands of people being killed by leaking toxic waste five hundred years later. Indeed, the members of the wealthy society benefit from choosing that policy.[1] A solution that works only in the case of the direct version of the non-identity problem would still be a significant achievement. But it is nonetheless worth noting how far short of a complete solution we would be even if the self-harming solution could be made to work in the case of Wilma.

4.2 Harming Possible People

The only other possibility that I am aware of appeals to the claim that by conceiving Pebbles, Wilma harms the child she would otherwise have conceived.[2] If she had not conceived Pebbles, after all, then two months later she would instead have conceived Rocks. And given some basic facts about human reproduction, conceiving Pebbles necessarily made it the case that Rocks would never be conceived. If Rocks were to be conceived, moreover, he would have a good life and would not be blind. From the point of view of his interests, then, things would be better if he were conceived than if he were not conceived. But if things would be better for Rocks if he were conceived than if he were not conceived, then it seems that things would be worse for Rocks if he were not conceived than if he were conceived. Making things worse for Rocks, moreover, amounts to harming him. And so, we might conclude, Wilma does harm someone by conceiving Pebbles. She harms Rocks.

There are three problems with this approach to rejecting P3. The first problem arises from the fact that harm requires a subject. Assuming that from the point of view of the interests of Rocks it is better for Rocks to exist than to not exist, if Wilma conceives Rocks, we can say that there is someone who has been made better off by her

---

[1] Some people have argued that we might harm ourselves by leaving future generations with impoverished lives because we identify our interests with theirs in some way (see, e.g., de Shalit (1997: 132–3)) or that by reducing the quality of life in future generations we might harm some of our contemporaries by sabotaging their future-oriented projects (e.g. Meyer (1997: 141–3, 151)). But such considerations cannot ground a sufficiently robust solution to the non-identity problem. This is because they cannot justify the claim that it would be wrong for the current members of the wealthy society to adopt the risky policy even if none of them identifies their interests with those of their descendants in any way and even if none of them has future-oriented projects that would be undermined by the subsequent leaking of the toxic waste.

[2] It might seem that there is another possible subject of harm: the set of Wilma's future children taken as a whole. Peters, for example, argues in a case like that of Wilma that "even though failure to substitute [e.g. Rocks for Pebbles] causes no apparent harm to any individual afflicted child as long as her life is worth living, the failure to avoid unnecessary human suffering is palpably harmful to the interests of the children so conceived as a class" (1989: 511) (see also Peters (1999: 398–9; 2004: 37) and Malek (2008:124)) and van der Zee and de Beaufort suggest that the "collective" can be a subject that is "afflicted by harm" in such cases where the collective refers to the "collective of potential persons" of a particular parent (2011: 452–3). But this kind of approach does not provide a genuine alternative. Saying that the "class" or "collective" is harmed reduces either to the *de re/de dicto* approach already discussed in section 2.2 or to the kind of consequentialist approach that is discussed in sections 6.1–6.3.

act, namely Rocks. But if Wilma does not conceive Rocks, then while we can still say that this makes things worse from the point of view of the interests of the person who would have existed if she had conceived Rocks, the fact remains that there isn't anyone who has been made worse off by her act. We could speak of possible Rocks, but "possible Rocks" is not a name that refers to a subject who exists and who has been harmed. "Possible Rocks" is simply an expression that refers to the claim that there could have been a subject who existed and who would have benefited from existing if he had existed. That is not enough to show that there is a subject who has been harmed by the fact that Rocks will never exist, and so is not enough to show that P3 is false.

But let's suppose that this first problem can be overcome and that it really does make sense for us to say that possible Rocks has been harmed by not being brought into existence. Even if this is so, there are two further reasons to reject the solution to the non-identity problem that is based on this claim. The first is that the claim is either too weak to solve the problem or too strong to avoid having implications that are more implausible than the Implausible Conclusion. Even if we agree that Wilma's act harms a possible person, after all, we can continue to maintain that it harms no actual persons. So we can simply modify P3 to read "Wilma's act of conceiving Pebbles does not harm any other actual people" and revise P4 to read "If an act does not harm any actual person, then the act does not wrong anyone" and the argument for the Implausible Conclusion will still go through. A solution based on the claim that Wilma has harmed possible Rocks by not conceiving Rocks will therefore fail to satisfy the robustness requirement. The only way to block this move would be to insist that harming merely possible people by not bringing them into existence is itself morally wrong. But this claim clearly has implications that are even more implausible than the Implausible Conclusion. Every instance of refraining from conceiving when one could have conceived would turn out to seriously wrong the possible person who would have been created. Even those who think that we have an obligation to reproduce do not think that we have an obligation to conceive every time we could do so nor do they think that the obligation is one that we have to the possible people themselves. And so in order to satisfy the robustness requirement, the solution would have to be so strong that it would be unable to satisfy the modesty requirement.

Finally, and perhaps more importantly, even if we agree that Wilma's act harms possible Rocks and that harming possible people is morally wrong, this would still not be enough to show that Wilma's act is morally wrong. This is because in order to conceive Rocks, Wilma would have to refrain from conceiving Pebbles and so would have to harm possible Pebbles. Her choice would therefore not be between conceiving Pebbles while harming possible Rocks and conceiving Rocks while harming no one. Rather, it would be between conceiving Pebbles while harming possible Rocks and conceiving Rocks while harming possible Pebbles. And once this becomes clear, it should become clear that the fact that conceiving Pebbles harms possible Rocks, if it does turn out to be a fact, would not be enough to show that conceiving Pebbles is morally wrong, and thus not enough to help us avoid the Implausible Conclusion.

Indeed, if we take seriously the claim that we harm possible people by not bring-ing them into existence, then Wilma faces the same sort of dilemma that any mother would face when forced to choose between harming one or the other of her two chil-dren. Suppose, for example, that Sophie has two children who are otherwise compa-rable except that one of them is blind, that both of her children are drowning, and that she can only save one of them. In this case, saving the blind child harms the sighted child and saving the sighted child harms the blind child. Presumably no one would say that it would be wrong for Sophie to save her blind child on the grounds that doing so would harm her sighted child. But that is precisely what we would be saying of Wilma if we said that it was wrong of her to conceive Pebbles because doing so harmed possible Rocks. And so, once again, a solution to the non-identity problem based on the claim that Wilma's act has harmed possible Rocks will prove to be too weak to do the job at all or too strong to do the job satisfactorily. Either way, it cannot serve as the basis for a successful solution to the problem. And since there seem to be no other credible ways of attempting to deny P3 besides the two that I have considered here, there seem to be no credible ways of solving the non-identity problem by denying P3 at all. As proved to be the case with P1 and P2, if we are going to avoid the Implausible Conclusion by rejecting one of the premises of the non-identity argument, we will once again have to look elsewhere.

5

Rejecting the Fourth Premise

The first three premises of the non-identity argument maintain that Wilma's act does not make Pebbles worse off than she would otherwise have been, that in order for an act to harm a person the act must make that person worse off than they would otherwise have been, and that Wilma's act does not harm anyone other than Pebbles. If these three premises are true, then Wilma's act does not harm anyone. I have not insisted in the previous chapters that all three of these premises are true. But I have argued that, for purposes of generating the non-identity problem, they are true enough: no solution to the problem that is based on an independently motivated rejection of any of these premises satisfies both the robustness requirement and the modesty requirement.

Let's now suppose that I have been right about this. If I have been right, then a solution to the non-identity problem must concede that Wilma's act does not harm anyone. One way a solution could do this would be to identify a property that can make an act wrong even if no one is wronged by the act and to show that Wilma's act has this wrong-making property. This possibility amounts to solving the problem by rejecting the non-identity argument's fifth premise, and will be examined in Chapter 6. Another way to do this would be to identify a way that an act can wrong a particular person even if it does not harm that person and to show that Wilma's act wrongs a particular person in this way. This amounts to solving the problem by rejecting the non-identity argument's fourth premise: the claim that if an act harms no one then it wrongs no one. That is the kind of solution that will be examined in this chapter.

In one sense, it is not difficult to come up with potential counterexamples to P4. There are many cases in which an act does not harm a person but is at least widely believed to wrong that person. If I point a gun at you and pull the trigger in an attempt to kill you, for example, it seems clear that I have wronged you even if the gun misfires and you are not harmed. The same seems to be true if I am not attempting to harm you when I pull the trigger but am nonetheless acting with a reckless disregard to the risk of harm that my act exposes you to. But while counterexamples such as these may provide reasons to reject P4, the reasons are not robust enough to help us solve the non-identity problem. This is because if we are forced to revise P4 so that it includes as wrong acts that unsuccessfully attempt to harm a person or that are done with reckless disregard for whether they will harm a person, we can simply point out that Wilma's act has neither of these further wrong-making properties.[1] Wilma does not choose to conceive now in order to cause harm to anyone. She chooses to conceive now in order to avoid the inconvenience of taking the pill once a day for two months before conceiving. And Wilma need not act with indifference to the possibility that her act will cause harm to anyone. We can stipulate that she decides to conceive now only because she has thought things through carefully and has determined that since her choice will not make anyone worse off than they would otherwise have been, her choice will not harm anyone. In asking whether we can solve the non-identity problem by rejecting P4, then, the question is not whether we can show that P4 is false. The question is whether we can show that it is false enough. Is there a way for an act to wrong a person without harming that person that can be used to help us avoid the Implausible Conclusion without producing even more implausible implications in other cases? Is there a reason to reject P4, that is, that will satisfy both the robustness requirement and the modesty requirement? This chapter attempts to answer that question.

5.1 Rights-based Arguments

One way that an act might be thought capable of wronging a person without harming that person arises from the claim that people have rights. If it is possible to violate a person's rights without harming them, it seems plausible to suppose that doing so would wrong them. And if it is possible to do an act that neither harms a person nor violates their rights but that generates in them a right that will subsequently be violated, it might seem plausible to suppose that that, too, would wrong them. This suggests two distinct rights-based arguments against P4 that might be offered as a way of solving the non-identity problem. It might be argued that Wilma's act is wrong because it violates someone's rights. Or it might be argued that Wilma's act is wrong because it generates a right in someone that will later be violated. Both arguments have had their defenders in the literature on the non-identity problem. I will consider their merits

---

[1] Weinberg and Hurley (Forthcoming) have recently argued that the non-identity problem can be solved by rejecting P4 in a way that is analogous to the case of torts for negligence. If I negligently expose you to the risk of harm, for example, I can be sued for wronging you even if on the whole you end up better off as a result of my behavior, as in a case where my negligent driving injures you but forces you to miss a plane that subsequently crashes and would have killed you. But there is a crucial difference between negligence cases and non-identity cases. In negligence cases, there is a person who has been wrongly exposed to the risk of harm. Because they have been wrongly treated, they have standing to sue. But in non-identity cases, there is no one who has been wrongly exposed to the risk of harm. It isn't simply that Wilma's act did not in fact make Pebbles worse off than she would otherwise have been. Wilma's act did not even subject Pebbles to a risk of being made worse off than she would otherwise have been. So the analogy with cases of wronging people by treating them negligently even in cases where they end up better off overall cannot be used to solve the problem. Kumar's example of the drunk driver who wrongs you by exposing you to the risk of harm even though he doesn't end up hitting you fails to gain traction for the same reason (2003: 103).

individually in the two subsections that follow and discuss a problem they both have in common in the subsection after that.

5.1.1 The Direct Version

The most straightforward rights-based solution to the non-identity problem begins with the claim that some acts are wrong because they violate a person's rights. If you have a right to life and I kill you, for example, then my act wrongs you because it treats you in a way that you have a right not to be treated. In typical cases, an act that violates a person's rights also harms that person. But it is not clear that all rights-violating acts must be harmful acts. If there are cases in which an act violates a person's rights without harming that person, then these cases will serve as counterexamples to P4. They will show, that is, how one can wrong a person without harming that person. And if it is possible to wrong a person without harming that person by violating that person's rights, then it seems possible that Wilma's act might wrong someone by violating someone's rights even if her act doesn't harm anyone. This is what I will refer to as the direct version of the rights-based solution.

If I break a promise to you, for example, or lie to you, or discriminate against you on the basis of your race, then many people would say that I have treated you wrongly, even if you suffer no harm as a result of my act and even if I knew ahead of time that you would suffer no harm. Doran Smolkin appeals to a case in which a doctor lies to her dying patient in order to ease the patient's suffering. The doctor's act can be wrong, Smolkin argues, because it violates a right that protects the patient's interest in maintaining self-determination and because acting against this particular interest may not be justified even if doing so does not leave the patient worse off in terms of promoting his interests overall. But if this is so, Smolkin suggests, then "there appears to be nothing necessarily implausible or even particularly unusual about saying that a person can have a legitimate complaint that some act violated her rights even though she may not have been better off had that act not been performed."[2] And if this is so, then there is no particular reason to doubt that Wilma's act might violate someone's rights even though her act leaves no one worse off than they would otherwise have been.

---

[2] Smolkin (1994: 319; 1999: 201). Velleman endorses a solution on which "a child has a right to be born into good enough circumstances" and claims that the right is violated in cases relevantly similar to that of Wilma (2008: 275). Jecker proposes a solution on which "a child has a... right not to be born with important opportunities foreclosed" and makes the same kind of claim about its implications (2012: 34). Woodward (1986) offers a similar argument. Holtug also suggests that the problem can be avoided by appealing to "deontological principles, e.g. to the effect that certain acts are wrong, even if they harm no-one," though he does not develop this suggestion (2003: 7). And although Steinbock and McClamrock put their claim that it would be wrong to conceive a seriously disabled child in terms of the act's being "unfair" to the child, the only two examples they give of wronging a person in a way that does not leave them worse off than they would otherwise be (a person is unjustly framed but later becomes rich and famous as a result and a person's plane is hijacked but he becomes a hero as a result) seem to render their position another version of the direct rights-based solution (1994: 19). See also Schiavone (2009: 316–17).

There are two problems with using cases like the lying doctor as a basis for solving the non-identity problem. In the case where the doctor lies to her patient, it is easy to identify the person whose right is violated by the act and it is easy to identify the right that is violated by the act. The person whose right is violated is the patient and the right that is violated is the right not to be lied to. The same is true in the other sorts of cases that writers such as Smolkin appeal to. But in the case where Wilma conceives Pebbles, it is hard to see whose right Wilma's act could be violating and even harder to see what right the act could be violating. There seem to be three possibilities, but none of them is satisfactory.

One possibility would be to say that Pebbles is the person whose rights are violated. There are two reasons to reject this suggestion. First, the act in question is Wilma's act of conceiving Pebbles and that act takes place before Pebbles exists. It is hard to see how an act can violate a person's rights if the person does not exist when the act takes place. A proponent of this first possibility might point to cases such as that in which someone plants a bomb under a child's house a few months before the child is conceived and in which the bomb explodes and maims the child several years later. This case might show that an act really can violate a person's rights before that person is conceived.[3] It is not clear that this case is best described as one in which the act of planting the bomb violates the child's rights. It seems at least as plausible to say that the act of planting the bomb causes something to happen later that violates the child's rights. If that is correct, then while this case might be used to help support the indirect version of the rights-based argument that I will discuss in the following subsection, it cannot support the direct version of the argument that I am concerned with here. And even if the case does show that an act can violate a person's rights before that person exists, it does this only by showing that an act can violate a person's rights before that person exists by initiating a sequence of events that results in something later happening to the person that violates that person's rights. Nothing bad happens to the child in that example, after all, until the bomb goes off. And it is even harder to see anything that happens to Pebbles as a result of Wilma's act of conceiving her that could plausibly count as violating Pebbles's rights.

The only possible candidate for a right of Pebbles that Wilma's act might cause to be violated, in fact, seems to be the right not to exist in, or to be caused to exist in, the condition that Pebbles exists in. Existing in that condition, after all, is the only thing that Wilma's act causes to happen to Pebbles.[4] But the only available reason for attributing

<hr />

[3] See, e.g., Elliot (1989: 160–2).

[4] A proponent of the rights-based solution might suggest that the right of Pebbles that Wilma's act violates is not a right to be in a certain kind of state or to be treated in a certain kind of way, but rather a right that Wilma make her decision according to a certain kind of criterion: one on which she must make the choice that is impersonally better, and so must choose to conceive a different child who will not be blind rather than conceive Pebbles, at least given the circumstances in which Wilma's choice must be made. But there are two problems with this suggestion. First, it seems ad hoc. What reason is there for agreeing that Pebbles has a right that Wilma make the impersonally better choice other than the fact that doing so would enable us to avoid the Implausible Conclusion? Second, appealing to this kind of right amounts to appealing to the claim that Wilma has an obligation to make the impersonally better choice. This kind of solution is

such a right to Pebbles seems to be that if we attributed such a right to Pebbles, we could account for the claim that Wilma's act is morally wrong. This, in fact, is the strategy that Smolkin seems to adopt. Smolkin writes that when he considers cases that are relevantly similar to that of Wilma, it seems to him

that what is principally objectionable about them is that future people in each of these cases were caused to have lives that were seriously defective. As a preliminary thesis, then, a future person has been wronged by some act A, if A was a necessary condition for her to come into being, and A resulted in her having a life that will in some serious sense be defective.[5]

He goes on to refine the claim so that the future person has a complaint "if and only if some act that was a necessary condition for her coming into being also resulted in her being unable to acquire to a sufficient degree one or more of the elements needed for well-being in a particular stage of life."[6] And if we cast this claim in terms of rights, we can say that Pebbles has a right that was violated by being conceived because being conceived was necessary for her coming into existence and resulted in her being unable to see.

But this defense of the direct version of the rights-based solution fails to provide a reason for attributing this right to Pebbles that is independent of the fact that doing so will enable us to avoid the Implausible Conclusion. It therefore fails to satisfy the independence requirement. Smolkin posits the existence of rights that are violated in the cases with which he is concerned, that is, because if the future people have such rights then this would justify the claim that the acts in question would wrong them, which in turn would justify the claim that the acts in question are wrong. If we reject P4 and say that conceiving such people violates their rights even though it doesn't harm them, then we can account for the wrongness of the acts that put them in that condition. But we can also account for the wrongness of the acts that put them in that condition if we reject any of the other premises of the non-identity argument. Smolkin's argument, then, gives us no reason to reject P4 in particular. It simply establishes that if we reject some premise of the non-identity argument, we can avoid the Implausible Conclusion. But that is something that we already knew. And without providing an argument for the claim that Pebbles has a right that Wilma violates that is independent of the fact that attributing such a right to her will enable us to solve the non-identity problem, we have no reason to accept the claim that Wilma violates Pebbles's rights by conceiving her.

Finally, the claim that Pebbles has a right not to exist in the state she is in has implications that will strike most people as even more implausible than the Implausible Conclusion. This is because if Pebbles has the right not to exist in this state, then she must have this right regardless of whether Wilma could instead have conceived a

---

treated separately in Chapter 6 and should be rejected for the reasons provided there (see especially sections 6.1–6.4).

[5] Smolkin (1999: 202).   [6] Smolkin (1999: 206).

sighted child if she waited a few months before conceiving. This means that it would have been wrong for Wilma to conceive Pebbles even if Wilma's only alternative had been conceiving no child at all. The implication that conceiving a blind child is wrong even if the alternative is conceiving no child at all will surely strike most people as even more implausible than the Implausible Conclusion. And so this feature of the claim that Pebbles has a right not to be conceived in a blind condition provides a good reason to conclude that a solution based on attributing this right to Pebbles cannot satisfy the modesty requirement.

A second way of developing the direct version of the rights-based argument would be to say that the person whose rights are violated is not Pebbles herself, but rather possible Pebbles. This proposal avoids the problem of having the rights violation taking place before the subject whose rights are violated exists. If it makes any sense at all to speak of possible Pebbles as existing in some sense, then the victim of the rights violation will already exist at the time that Wilma's act of conceiving Pebbles takes place. But this suggestion avoids the timing problem only by creating even bigger problems. First, it is not at all clear that it makes sense to attribute actual rights to merely possible people. Second, even if we thought that possible Pebbles really could have actual rights, what right would she have that Wilma could be understood to be violating? Since Wilma's act is the act that results in possible Pebbles being made actual, the only kind of right that Wilma could be understood to be violating would be the right of possible Pebbles not to be brought into existence as an actual person. But it is hard to imagine a reason that could be given for attributing such a right to possible Pebbles other than the fact that doing so would enable us to avoid the Implausible Conclusion. This means that a solution based on attributing this right to possible Pebbles would fail to satisfy the independence requirement.

Finally, even if an independent reason for attributing this right to possible Pebbles were uncovered, the claim that possible Pebbles has this right would again have implications that will strike most people as even more implausible than the Implausible Conclusion. This is because if possible Pebbles has the right not to be conceived, then she must have this right regardless of whether Wilma could instead conceive a sighted child if she waited a few months before conceiving. This means that it would be wrong for Wilma to conceive Pebbles even if Wilma's only alternative were conceiving no child at all. And the implication that conceiving a blind child is wrong even if the alternative is conceiving no child at all will again strike most people as even more implausible than the Implausible Conclusion.

The only remaining possibility seems to be to say that by conceiving Pebbles, Wilma violates the rights of the child she would otherwise have conceived, namely Rocks. This would mean that the subject whose rights Wilma violates is possible Rocks and that the right that she violates is the right that possible Rocks has to be made actual. But it is again difficult to imagine a reason that could be given for attributing such a right to possible Rocks that is independent of the fact that doing so would help us to avoid the Implausible Conclusion, and so again difficult to see how a solution based on such a claim could satisfy the independence requirement. The claim that possible Rocks has such a right, moreover, will again have implications that will strike most people as even more implausible than the Implausible Conclusion. If possible Rocks has the right to be conceived, after all, then it would seem that every possible child has the right to be conceived and that we violate some possible person's rights every time we are in a position to conceive a child and fail to do so. Even those who believe in a moral obligation to reproduce do not think that failing to reproduce violates the rights of the possible children who could have been conceived. And so a solution based on the claim that Wilma's act violates the rights of possible Rocks will fail to satisfy the modesty requirement as well.

Indeed, while all three versions of the direct rights-based solution fail to satisfy the independence requirement and the modesty requirement, this final version runs the risk of failing to satisfy the robustness requirement as well. If possible Rocks has a right to be conceived, after all, it is difficult to see why possible Pebbles wouldn't have a right to be conceived, too. Since Wilma can't conceive both of them, she is in a position in which no matter which choice she makes, she will violate someone's rights. And if that is so, then the fact that conceiving Pebbles means violating the rights of possible Rocks will not be enough to establish that conceiving Pebbles would be wrong. And so even if we reject P4 and agree that there are acts that wrong people by violating their rights without harming them, as in the case of the doctor who tells a comforting lie to her patient, there seems to be no way to exploit the revision of P4 that such examples justify as a way of solving the non-identity problem. The problem will simply reappear once we add the further claim that Wilma's act does not violate anyone's rights. And since this premise seems just as secure as the other premises that constitute the non-identity argument, the non-identity problem will remain invulnerable to the direct version of the rights-based solution.

5.1.2 *The Indirect Version*

Suppose I do an act that neither harms you nor violates your rights. It seems plausible to suppose that my act might nonetheless wrong you if it involves generating in you a right that you did not previously have and that I know will subsequently be violated. It seems plausible to suppose that this might be so, moreover, even if you are better off overall as a result of my doing the act than you would have been if I had refrained from doing it. And if this is so, then there is a second way that the claim that people have rights might be used to try to solve the non-identity problem. Rather than claiming that Wilma's act is wrong because it violates a right that someone already has at the time of her act, a solution might be grounded in the claim that Wilma's act is wrong because it generates a new right that will be violated at some point after her act. I will refer to this as the indirect version of the rights-based solution.

This indirect rights-based solution has been defended independently by James Woodward and Michael Tooley.[7] Both ground their positions in the response they

---

[7] Woodward (1986: 812–13) and Tooley (1983: 270–3; 1998: 119–22). See also Bruhl (2002: 417–21), Archard (2004: 404, 416), Caney (2006: 267–8), Vanderheiden (2006: 345), Markie (2005: 296, 303), and Elliot (1989: 163).

expect most people to have to cases in which you can either benefit someone while generating a right in them that will later be violated or refrain from benefiting them and refrain from generating any new rights in them. Suppose, for example, that I can either promise to mow your lawn and promise to paint your house, in which case I know that I will keep the first promise but break the second promise, or that I can promise to do neither task, in which case I know that I will do neither.[8] Given these choices, you will be better off if I choose the first option rather than the second, but many people will think that I would nonetheless wrong you by choosing the first option. If my choosing the first option really would wrong you, this seems to support the claim that an act can wrong you by generating in you a right that will later be violated even if the act leaves you better off than the alternative and even if the act itself does not violate any of your rights. And if this is so, then Wilma's act might prove to be wrong for the same sort of reason. If it is wrong to generate a right in an already existing person that will later be violated, after all, it seems plausible to suppose that it would also be wrong to generate a new right that will later be violated by creating a new person with a right that will later be violated. And so, on this account, we might be able to appeal to the importance of moral rights as a way of denying P4 without having to insist that Wilma's act itself violates anyone's rights. And this might enable us to identify a reason for rejecting P4 that is strong enough to satisfy the robustness requirement but still reasonable enough to satisfy the modesty requirement.

While the indirect version of the rights-based solution may in some respects represent an improvement over the direct version, however, there are a number of reasons to reject it as well. First, the solution rests on a questionable foundation. It assumes that in the case in which I make two promises to you knowing that I will break one of them, my act is wrong because it generates a right in you that will later be violated. Only if this is the reason that my act is wrong will the reason carry over to the case of acts that involve creating a new person with a right that will subsequently be violated. But there is a simpler explanation for the wrongness of my making the two promises: my act is wrong not because it generates a new right that you do not currently have and that will later be violated but because the act violates a right that you already have: the right not to be the subject of a false promise. The difference between these two explanations of the wrongness of my making the two promises is important. The first explanation implies that it is also wrong to create a new person with a right that will later be violated, since the act of creating such a person is also an act that generates a new right that will later be violated. But the second explanation does not have this further implication. On the second explanation, my act is wrong because it violates a right that you already have: the right not to have someone make a false promise to you. If this is the reason that my act of making the two promises is wrong, then the example does nothing to support the

---

[8] This is a version of the example that Woodward provides (1986: 810).

claim that an act can also wrong a person even if the act doesn't violate that person's rights. It is simply another example of an act that wrongs a person precisely because it does violate that person's rights. Without an independent reason to prefer the former explanation over the latter, then, we have no reason to accept the foundation of the indirect rights-based solution.

But suppose we accept the first explanation and agree that it would be wrong for me to make the two promises to you because it would be wrong for me to do an act that generates in you a right that will later be violated. Even if we accept this account, we presumably think that whether the fact that my act would generate a new right that will later be violated is enough to render my act immoral depends at least in part on the magnitude of the benefit you would receive from my performing the act. Suppose, for example, that you will soon die if I don't donate a kidney to you, and that I can either promise that I will give you a kidney and promise that I will paint your house, in which case I will keep the first promise but break the second promise, or that I can promise to do neither, in which case I will do neither. In this case, it seems clear that it would not be wrong for me to make both promises and then keep the first one, even though doing so would again generate in you a right that would later be violated. This suggests that even if the generation of a new right that will later be violated establishes a moral presumption against doing an act, the presumption can be overcome if there is a substantial enough difference in terms of the overall consequences between doing the act and not doing the act. Even if Wilma's act of conceiving Pebbles does prove to generate a new right in Pebbles that will later be violated, then, this will not be enough to show that her act was immoral. A solution that appealed to this principle would have to claim that the presumption against generating a right that will later be violated is so strong that it is not outweighed by the fact that without the act, Pebbles would not exist in the first place and so would not enjoy any of the goods that her life enables her to enjoy. And nothing about the case of the two promises provides support for such a conclusion. Indeed, if anything, the promise-breaking case involving the donated kidney establishes a powerful presumption against this conclusion. If it is not wrong to generate a right that will later be violated when doing so is necessary in order to save someone's life, then why should it be wrong to generate a right that will later be violated when doing so is necessary in order to give someone a life that would be worth saving in the first place?

But now let's suppose that both of these problems can be overcome and that Wilma's act really will be wrong if it turns out to generate a new right in Pebbles that will later be violated. Even if this is so, this will help to solve the non-identity problem only if we can identify a right that Wilma's act generates in Pebbles that will later be violated. And it is difficult to imagine what right that would be. Tooley suggests that Wilma's act can be shown to be wrong by appealing to a general principle such as this: "Every person has a right to an equal chance of enjoying those natural resources, both environmental and genetic, that a person living in his society might enjoy, and that make it possible for one to lead a satisfying life."[9] Wilma's act is wrong, on this account, not because the act itself violates anyone's rights, but because it generates a right in Pebbles that will not be satisfied, the right to the same chance of enjoying the ability to see that others in her society enjoy.

There are two problems with appealing to the existence of such a right as a way of solving the non-identity problem. First, it is not clear that there is a reason for attributing this right to people that is independent of the fact that doing so will help us to avoid the Implausible Conclusion. Tooley, at least, provides no such reason. This suggests that a solution based on the existence of such a right may have difficulty satisfying the independence requirement. Second, the claim that Wilma's act is wrong because it generates this right in Pebbles that will later be violated has implications that will strike most people as even more implausible than the Implausible Conclusion. If Pebbles has such a right, after all, then she has it regardless of whether Wilma could instead have conceived a sighted child. This means that a solution based on the appeal to this right can show that Wilma's act is wrong only by showing that it is wrong to conceive a blind child even if the alternative is conceiving no child at all.[10] Indeed, such a solution entails that it would be wrong to conceive any child who would enjoy less than an equal chance of enjoying the valuable genetic resources available in his society. It would thus be wrong to conceive even a sighted child who had significantly limited vision even if the alternative was conceiving no child at all. These implications will strike most people as more implausible than the Implausible Conclusion and thus provide good reason to conclude that a solution based on such a right does not satisfy the modesty requirement either.

The reasons for thinking that the particular right that Tooley appeals to cannot ground a satisfactory solution to the non-identity problem, moreover, seem to extend to any right that a proponent of the indirect rights-based approach might appeal to. In order to avoid entailing that it is immoral to conceive a blind child when the alternative is conceiving no child at all, any right will have to be such that every blind person has the right if and only if their parents could instead have conceived (or perhaps could easily have conceived) a different sighted child. But it is difficult to imagine any reason that could be given for positing the existence of a right with such a bizarre structure that is independent of the fact that if there were such a right, it would entail that it is wrong for Wilma to conceive Pebbles when she could easily conceive Rocks instead, but not wrong for her to conceive a blind child when the alternative would be conceiving no child at all. And in the absence of such a reason, any right that would be able to satisfy the modesty requirement would prove unable to satisfy the independence requirement. No such right, as a result, could ground a satisfactory solution to the non-identity problem.

[9] Tooley (1983: 272). See also Tooley (1998: 120).
[10] McMahan (2001: 456) also notes this problem.

A defender of the indirect version of the rights-based solution might concede that the solution fails in the case of Wilma, but maintain that it nonetheless succeeds in the case of the wealthy society. Indeed, while Woodward explicitly acknowledges that there may be no right that is violated in cases like that of Wilma,[11] he claims that there is a right that is violated in cases like that of the wealthy society: the right not to be killed.[12] Or, as he at one point puts the claim more precisely, it

seems plausible that the [people who are later killed by the leaking toxic waste], like other innocent people, have rights that others should not knowingly pursue policies that will kill, injure, or poison them or will create substantial risks of these results, at least when there is no weighty justification for such policies and alternative policies which involve no such risks are available.[13]

It is wrong for the wealthy society to adopt the risky policy, on this account, for the same reason that it would be wrong for me to make the two promises. As Woodward puts it, "it can be wrong to adopt a course of action which will both bring certain obligations into existence and make failure to meet them unavoidable, even though this course of action affects another's overall interests as favorably as any other course of action would."[14]

The problem with appealing to this right as a way of solving the indirect version of the non-identity problem concerns the content of the right itself. It can best be put in the form of a dilemma. If the right is simply a right not to be killed, then it is clear that selecting the risky policy will eventually cause that right to be violated in those who die as a result of the leaking toxic waste. But the claim that there is a right not to be killed in this unqualified sense has implications that are even more implausible than the Implausible Conclusion. Every time the government builds a new highway, for example, it knows that some people will die in accidents on that highway as a result of its decision. The claim that there is a right not to be killed in this unqualified sense would therefore entail that the people who are later killed on the highway have their rights violated by the construction of the highway and that it would be wrong for the government to build the highway as a result. A solution based on attributing to people this unconditional right not to be killed could satisfy the robustness requirement, then, but not the modesty requirement.

But suppose that we qualify the right not to be killed in order to avoid such problem cases. A natural way to do this would be to say that you have a right against a policy's being adopted that would result in your death or a substantial risk of your death unless there is a sufficiently good justification for adopting the policy. The qualifying clause would explain why your rights are not violated if you die as the result of the state's decision to build a highway in cases where there was a good enough reason to build the highway. It would therefore enable a solution based on the appeal to such a right to satisfy the modesty requirement. This seems to be the kind of thing that Woodward has in

[11] Woodward (1986: 815 n. 12; 1987: 808–9).   [12] Woodward (1987: 801, 808)
[13] Woodward (1986: 812).   [14] Woodward (1986: 813).

mind when he goes beyond appealing to the claim that the people who die as a result of the leaking toxic waste simply have a right not to be killed.

But if we qualify the right not to be killed in this way, then in order to show that the people who are killed by the leaking toxic waste have their rights violated, we will first have to give a reason to think that the wealthy society was not justified in adopting the risky policy. And the reason for thinking that the wealthy society was not justified in adopting the risky policy will have to be independent of the claim that adopting the policy led to the subsequent violation of their rights. The qualified version of the right not to be killed, that is, amounts to the right not to be killed as the result of the adoption of an unjustified policy. Adopting the risky policy will lead to a subsequent violation of this right, then, only if it is in fact an unjustified policy. And we cannot use the assumption that the policy is unjustified as a premise in arguing for the conclusion that the policy leads to a subsequent rights violation, because the claim that the policy is unjustified is precisely what the rights-based argument is trying to establish. The claim that the people who are killed by the leaking toxic waste have a right not to be killed by it, then, is either too strong to be plausible, or too weak to do the job. It fails to satisfy the modesty requirement or it fails to satisfy the robustness requirement. Either way, it fails to underwrite a satisfactory solution to the indirect version of the non-identity problem. In the end, then, the indirect version of the rights-based solution proves no more successful than the direct version.[15]

5.1.3 The Rights Waiver Argument

I have argued so far that neither the direct nor the indirect version of the rights-based solution can satisfactorily identify a right that is violated in non-identity cases. But let's now suppose that I have been mistaken about this. Let's suppose, for example, that Pebbles has a right not to be conceived, or not to be deprived of vision, and that the people who will exist in the future if the wealthy society selects the risky policy today will have a right not to be killed by the leaking toxic waste. Even if this is so, there is a further problem that undermines both versions of the rights-based solution. The problem arises from the fact that people can waive the rights that they have and that when they do, acts that would otherwise be morally wrong become morally permissible.[16]

Suppose, for example, that you have a right not to have your eyes cut out. Under normal circumstances, I would violate this right if I were to cut your eyes out. But suppose also that a diabolical villain has injected a lethal poison into your eyes, and that the only way for me to save your life is to cut your eyes out before the poison spreads to the rest of your body. In that case, you would presumably tell me that you were willing to waive your right not to have your eyes cut out. And once you waived this right, the right that you formerly had would no longer generate a moral objection to my cutting your eyes

---

[15] See Parfit (1986: 854–61) for a further critique of Woodward in particular.

[16] McMahan (1981: 127) raises this point. For a more detailed discussion of the waiver problem, see Page (2006: 145–50).

out. The explicit waiving of rights before a particular act is performed, moreover, is not always necessary in order for the waiver of rights to render the act morally permissible even if it would otherwise be morally wrong. Suppose, for example, that you are currently under heavy sedation and that the only way for me to save your life is to cut your eyes out before you can be revived and thus before you can explicitly waive your right against my doing so. In that case, it seems reasonable to suppose that you would agree to waive your right against my doing so right now if you could or that you will actually agree to waive your right after the fact if I go ahead and do so. These claims seem reasonable because it is reasonable to suppose that you would approve of my cutting your eyes out right now if you understood what was happening and that you will approve after the fact once you understand what happened. And these facts seem to be enough to prevent what would otherwise be a morally wrong act from being morally wrong. Even though you have not in fact waived your right not to have your eyes cut out, the fact that you would waive it now if you could or that you will waive it later when you can is enough to render my otherwise morally wrong behavior perfectly acceptable.

But if the hypothetical or subsequent waiver of rights is sufficient to render the right in question morally inert in the case of you and the diabolical villain, then it is also sufficient to render the right in question morally inert in non-identity cases—assuming that such a right exists in such cases in the first place. Even if Pebbles really does have a right not to be brought into existence as a blind person, for example, it is reasonable to suppose hypothetically that she would agree to waive her right against Wilma conceiving her if she could or to conclude that she actually will agree to waive her right after the fact if Wilma conceives her. These claims seem reasonable for precisely the same reason that it seems reasonable to suppose that you would agree or will agree to waive your right in the case of the diabolical villain and the lethal poison: blindness is presumably a bad condition to exist in, but it is not so bad that it is worse than not existing at all and so, on the whole, you will be glad that your eyes were cut out despite your loss of vision and Pebbles will be glad that she was conceived despite her lack of vision. And if Pebbles would or will waive her right not to be conceived under the circumstances in which Wilma conceives her, then the fact that she has a right not to be conceived under those circumstances—if it is a fact—cannot make it morally wrong for Wilma to conceive her.

Similarly, if the future people who will be killed by the leaking toxic waste if the wealthy society selects the risky policy now really will have a right not to be killed by the leaking toxic waste, it is reasonable to suppose hypothetically that they would agree to waive their right at the time that the wealthy society was making its choice if they could or to conclude that they actually will waive their right after the fact if the wealthy society chooses the risky policy. This seems reasonable because they, too, will be glad that they were conceived, even though they will die prematurely. And this means that the fact that they have a right not to be killed by the leaking toxic waste—if it is a fact— cannot make it morally wrong for the wealthy society to select the risky policy. Even if the objections that I have raised against the rights-based solution in the previous two subsections prove unsuccessful, then, the fact that people can waive their rights shows that neither the direct version nor the indirect version of the rights-based solution is strong enough to solve the non-identity problem. Even if I have been wrong in maintaining that the rights-based solution cannot satisfy both the independence requirement and the modesty requirement, it cannot satisfy the robustness requirement. I will refer to the argument that establishes this claim as the rights waiver argument.

Many readers may believe that I have already said enough to establish the soundness of the rights waiver argument. Those who think the argument merits a more detailed discussion may consult Appendix E, in which I respond to five objections that have been raised against it. Either way, if the rights waiver argument is correct, then we should reject both the direct and the indirect rights-based solution to the non-identity problem even if my previous objections to those solutions prove unsuccessful. In addition, accepting the rights waiver argument has one important further implication. It shows that an even more modest version of the rights-based solution should also be rejected. The versions of the solution that I have considered so far appeal to the claim that an act is morally wrong if it violates a right or if it generates a right that will later be violated. The more modest version of the rights-based solution allows that an act might sometimes be morally acceptable even if it violates a right or generates a right that will later be violated. It allows, for example, that it might not be wrong to violate a right if doing so would prevent a greater number of rights violations from occurring or would prevent an enormous decline in the overall amount of human well-being. But, this more modest solution maintains, if all else is equal, and if the only salient difference between two options is that one but not the other would violate someone's rights or would generate a right that would later be violated, then it is morally wrong to do that act that would violate the right or generate the right that would later be violated.[17] I will refer to this as the all else equal version of the rights-based solution.

The all else equal version of the rights-based solution has one significant advantage over the direct and indirect versions. Those versions of the solution entail that it would be morally wrong for Wilma to conceive a blind child even if her only alternative were conceiving no child at all. And this, as I pointed out earlier, will strike most people as even more implausible than the Implausible Conclusion. But the all else equal version of the rights-based solution does not entail this. The case in which Wilma must choose between conceiving a blind child and conceiving no child at all is not a case in which all else is equal. The fact that in this case the act that would violate a right or generate a right that would later be violated would also produce a child while the act that would not violate a right or generate a right that would later be violated would not produce a child might render it morally acceptable for her to do the act that would violate a right or generate a right that would later be violated in this case. And while the all else equal version of the rights-based solution is therefore more modest than the other versions,

---

[17] I am not aware of anyone who has defended this solution in print, but it has been suggested to me as a possible variant of the rights-based solution by Michael Tooley.

it can still appear to be robust enough to solve the non-identity problem. Wilma's act of conceiving Pebbles will be morally wrong, on this account, not simply because it violates a right or generates a right that will later be violated, but because there is no other respect in which the two options available to her are relevantly different and that would justify her choosing the act that violates a right or generates a right that will later be violated over the act that does not.

But the rights waiver argument shows that even this more modest all else equal version of the rights-based solution is unacceptable. This is because the principle that the solution appeals to has implications that are more implausible than the Implausible Conclusion in cases involving rights that would or will be waived. Suppose, for example, that Mike and Ike are drowning, that you can save only one of them, and that it would be a bit more convenient for you to save Mike rather than Ike because Mike is a bit closer to you. But suppose also that while Ike is drowning in a public swimming pool, Mike is drowning in a nearby swimming pool in his own back yard. In order to save Ike, that is, you would simply have to walk across some public property, but in order to save Mike, you would have to violate his right that people not trespass on his private property without his permission. And let's suppose that because he is drowning, Mike cannot hear you if you stand at the edge of his property and ask for permission to enter his back yard.

In this case, it is clear that Mike would waive his right against your trespassing on his property if he could or that he will waive that right after the fact if you save his life. And it is also clear that it would not be morally wrong for you to save Mike rather than Ike as a result of this. But the principle underlying the all else equal version of the rights-based solution cannot accommodate this judgment. That principle maintains that if all else is equal, and if the only salient difference between two options is that one but not the other would violate someone's rights or would generate a right that would later be violated, then it is morally wrong to do the act that would violate the right or generate a right that would later be violated even if the person in question would or will waive that right. Saving Mike would violate such a right since it would involve trespassing on Mike's property without his consent. Saving Ike would not since it would not violate any right. There is no other relevant difference between the two cases except that saving Mike would be a bit more convenient for you. The all else equal principle therefore entails that it would be wrong for you to save Mike, despite the fact that Mike clearly would or will waive his right that you not trespass on his property. This implication is even more implausible than the Implausible Conclusion. So the solution that appeals to the principle that has this implication cannot satisfy the modesty requirement that a successful solution to the non-identity problem must satisfy. Although the all else equal version of the rights-based solution is in one respect more modest than the direct and indirect versions of the solution, then, the rights waiver argument shows that it is still not modest enough.

A defender of the all else equal version of the rights-based solution might try to avoid this problem by modifying the all else equal principle. The modification would restrict the scope of the principle to cases involving rights that would not and will not be waived. This would make the principle substantially more plausible and would prevent it from entailing that it would be morally wrong for you to save Mike rather than Ike. But while this modification would enable the all else equal solution to satisfy the modesty requirement, it would prevent it from satisfying the robustness requirement. If the principle doesn't apply to cases in which a right would be or will be waived, then the rights waiver argument shows that it doesn't apply to the case of Wilma and Pebbles either. The rights waiver argument, after all, shows that Pebbles would waive or will waive whatever right Wilma's act of conceiving her would otherwise violate. And if the all else equal principle doesn't apply to the case of Wilma, then it can't show that Wilma's act is morally wrong. In the end, then, the rights waiver argument shows that the all else equal version of the rights-based solution is either too weak to solve the non-identity problem or too strong to do so. The all else equal version of the rights-based solution, like the other versions of the solution, should ultimately be rejected. Even if P4 is false because rights violations can render a harmless act morally wrong, this reason for rejecting P4 cannot ground a satisfactory solution to the non-identity problem.

5.2 Fairness-based Arguments

A second way that an act might be thought capable of wronging a person without harming them arises from the claim that some ways of treating a person are unfair. If it is possible to treat a person unfairly without harming them, then it seems plausible to suppose that doing so would wrong them. And if this is so, then it may seem plausible to suppose that Wilma's act might be wrong because it treats Pebbles unfairly even if it doesn't harm her. This suggests that a fairness-based argument might be offered against P4 as a way of solving the non-identity problem. Several writers have attempted to use Rawls's famous veil of ignorance to develop such a solution and I will begin with these before considering a few other fairness-based solutions.[18]

5.2.1 The Veil of Ignorance Principle

The basic idea behind the veil of ignorance can be brought out by considering a specific example. So suppose that you and I are members of a society in which most people are white and the rest are black. We are considering whether it would be morally acceptable for our society to adopt a practice on which white people are permitted to enslave black people. I am white and so from a self-interested standpoint I would prefer that the practice be permitted. You are black and so from a self-interested standpoint you would prefer that it be forbidden. If our society attempts to reach a consensus about what to do by having everyone favor what they think would be best for them, we will

---

[18] See especially Weinberg (2002) and Reiman (2007). Shaw briefly endorses the same kind of argument (2008: 412).

either be stuck at an impasse or the minority will be forced to accept the will of the majority. Neither outcome is morally acceptable. The veil of ignorance attempts to avoid this problem by directing us to cast our hypothetical votes in such cases for the option that we think would make things best for us in the absence of knowledge of particular facts about ourselves that seem to be morally irrelevant. Would I prefer to permit the practice or forbid it, for example, if I had to make my decision on self-interested grounds without knowing my own race and had to select and agree to a principle that would govern slavery in my society before finding out whether I was going to turn out to be one of the white people in that society or one of the black people? Presumably, my reasoning from such a perspective would look at least roughly like this: if I turn out to be white, I will be somewhat better off if slavery is permitted than if it is forbidden, but if I turn out to be black, I will be much worse off if slavery is permitted than if it is forbidden. Since from behind the veil of ignorance I don't know whether I will turn out to be black or white and have to select and agree to a principle governing slavery before I can find that out, the rational thing for me to do is to select and agree to the option with the best worse-case outcome for me. As a result, I should vote against permitting slavery. Everyone else who reasons from behind the veil of ignorance should reason in the same way, regardless of what their actual race turns out to be, and so everyone should agree that this would be the right thing to do. The veil of ignorance therefore helps us to arrive at a unanimous agreement to endorse what is clearly the intuitively correct answer, and it helps us to do this by appealing to an intuitively appealing account of fairness: it would not be fair to take advantage of morally irrelevant features like race in arriving at principles that would govern our treatment of each other.

We can think of this argument against permitting slavery as appealing to what I will call the Veil of Ignorance Principle, or Veil Principle for short:

VP: An act is morally wrong if it violates a rule that would be agreed to by people reasoning self-interestedly from behind a suitably defined veil of ignorance

In this particular case, the suitably defined veil of ignorance is one in which people do not know their race while they deliberate about whether the society that will be governed by their decision should permit race-based slavery. In other cases, the characteristics that the deliberators would have to be ignorant of in order to ensure that their deliberations produce a fair outcome might be different.

Slavery, of course, is a harmful practice. And the fact that it is harmful can presumably ground a satisfactory moral argument against it. But the fact that an act is wrong because it is harmful does not mean that the act cannot also be wrong because it is unfair. If slavery is also wrong independent of its harmfulness because it violates a rule that people reasoning self-interestedly would agree to from behind a suitably defined veil of ignorance, then other acts might be wrong because they violate such a rule even if those other acts are not harmful. Similarly, slavery presumably violates people's rights. And this, too, could ground a satisfactory moral argument against it. But the fact that an act is wrong because it violates someone's rights does not mean that the act cannot also be wrong because it is unfair either. If slavery is wrong not just because it violates rights but also because it violates a rule that people reasoning self-interestedly would agree to from behind a suitably defined veil of ignorance, then other acts might be wrong because they violate such a rule even if those other acts don't violate anyone's rights. If Wilma's act of conceiving Pebbles violates a rule that people reasoning self-interestedly would agree to from behind a suitably defined veil of ignorance, then, her act might prove to be wrong for this reason even if it does not harm anyone or violate anyone's rights. Assuming that the Veil Principle is correct, then, the question is whether Wilma's act really does violate such a rule. In order to answer this question, we must first determine what would count as a suitably defined veil of ignorance in this case.

5.2.1.1 THE ACTUAL PEOPLE APPROACH

The case of slavery posed a question of inter-racial fairness. It was therefore important to prevent the deliberators from taking unfair advantage of knowing what race they belonged to. The case of Wilma poses a question of inter-generational fairness. As a result, the most natural way to identify the suitably defined veil of ignorance for assessing principles that would govern that case is to prevent the deliberators from taking unfair advantage of knowing what generation they belong to. The people deliberating about Wilma's behavior, that is, should know that at some point in time they will be an actual member of the society that is to be governed by their decision, but they should not be able to know to which generation in that society they belong. This version of the veil of ignorance is natural because temporal location seems to be morally irrelevant in the same way that spatial location is morally irrelevant. The fact that one person is born sooner or later than another person should make no more difference than the fact that one person is standing to the left or to the right of another person in determining the extent to which their interests should be represented in a decision procedure that will produce principles affecting them both. Since this version of the veil stipulates that as a deliberator you know that you actually exist at some point in time, although you don't know at which point, I will call this way of applying the Veil Principle to the case of Wilma the actual people approach.

Let's suppose that the actual people approach is the correct way to apply the Veil Principle to the case of Wilma. What would this entail? Since Wilma decided to conceive Pebbles rather than Rocks, Wilma and Pebbles are people who will actually exist in one generation or another and Rocks is not. So Wilma and Pebbles are among the people whose interests must be represented from behind the suitably defined veil of ignorance and Rocks is not. As a deliberator behind the suitably defined veil of ignorance, that is, you must consider how any proposed principle would affect your interests if you turn out to be Wilma, Pebbles, or any other actual person whose life will be governed by the principle, but you need not consider how it would affect your interests if you turn out to be merely possible Rocks. Since the specific question we are trying to answer is whether Wilma's act of conceiving Pebbles rather than Rocks was morally wrong, the question we must ask is whether the deliberators in this case would agree to a rule that would permit a woman to make such a choice under such circumstances if the deliberators reasoned from behind a veil of ignorance understood in this way. This means that the deliberators must evaluate the merits of any proposed principle not only without knowing specific facts about themselves, but without knowing which temporal location they occupy. Given that the rule that they select will govern both the circumstances under which they may be conceived and the circumstances under which they may conceive others, that is, what would they say about a rule that permitted a woman to conceive a blind child rather than an otherwise comparable sighted child simply because doing so would be a little more convenient for her?

The answer to this question on this first approach to applying the Veil Principle is clear. From behind this version of the veil of ignorance, you should reason as follows: if I turn out to be a woman like Wilma, I will prefer adopting this rule to rejecting it. Adopting the rule will make things a bit more convenient for me, since it will permit me to conceive right away rather than taking a pill once a day for two months before conceiving. If I turn out to be a child like Pebbles, I will also prefer adopting this rule to rejecting it. Adopting the rule will make it possible for me to be conceived. If I turn out to be any other actual member of Wilma's society, I will be indifferent between adopting this rule and rejecting it since by stipulation acts such as that of Wilma's have no effects on anyone other than the woman and the child she conceives. So if I turn out to be someone like Wilma or someone like Pebbles after the veil of ignorance is lifted, I will prefer adopting the rule to rejecting it and if I turn out to be anyone else I will be indifferent between adopting the rule and rejecting it. Since adopting the rule will either leave me better off than rejecting it or at least no worse off adopting it than rejecting it, I should favor adopting it. Anyone else who will actually exist in the society to be governed by this decision should reason in the same way. And so they will all agree to accept a rule on which a woman in a situation like that of Wilma is permitted to make the kind of choice that Wilma makes. And since they will all agree to accept this rule, Wilma's act of conceiving Pebbles will turn out not to violate the Veil Principle.

If the interests of merely possible people like Rocks were also represented in the deliberations behind the veil, of course, things might turn out to look differently. Someone like Rocks, after all, would prefer to incur the minor inconvenience of having to delay conception when he was the one conceiving so that he could be one of the people who is actually conceived when his mother conceives. But the actual people approach to applying the Veil Principle does not include Rocks among the people whose interests are represented by the deliberators from behind the veil of ignorance. It includes only the interests of those people who at some point actually exist. And because Wilma chose to conceive Pebbles, Rocks is not among those people. So on this first approach to applying the Veil Principle to the case of Wilma, no matter which actual person's interests are represented, that person is better off if the rule is adopted than if the rule is rejected or is at least no worse off. As a result, this first approach to applying the Veil Principle to the case of Wilma cannot be used to justify the claim that Wilma's act is morally wrong.

A defender of the fairness-based approach to solving the non-identity problem might respond to this result by saying so much the worse for this first way of applying the Veil Principle to the case of Wilma. By limiting the people whose interests are represented behind the veil of ignorance to those who actually exist at some point, this critic might complain, the actual people approach to applying the Veil Principle unfairly biases the results in favor of the choices that people actually make. Wilma's decision to conceive Pebbles rather than Rocks turns out to be morally acceptable, on this account, only because Wilma in fact decided to conceive Pebbles rather than Rocks. And if a moral principle ends up endorsing the moral acceptability of an act simply because the act was performed, then the moral principle itself must clearly be rejected.

In one sense, this complaint about the actual people approach to applying the Veil Principle is warranted. If Wilma had decided to conceive Rocks rather than Pebbles, then the actual people approach would have identified Wilma and Rocks as among the people whose interests should be represented by the deliberators from behind the veil of ignorance and would have directed us to ignore the interests of merely possible people like Pebbles. And if we had then asked whether it was morally acceptable for Wilma to have conceived Rocks rather than Pebbles, the result would have been that this, too, was morally acceptable. If I turn out to be representing the interests of someone like Wilma I will favor allowing Wilma this choice, after all, if I turn out to be representing the interests of someone like Rocks I will favor allowing it, too, and if I turn out to be representing the interests of any other actual person I will be indifferent since by stipulation the choice in question will have no effect on me. It therefore seems that whatever procreative decision a person makes, the actual people approach to applying the Veil Principle will ensure that it is morally acceptable. And this result is unacceptable.

This response to the actual people approach to applying the Veil Principle is mistaken. The actual people approach does entail that it is not wrong for Wilma to conceive Pebbles and that it is not wrong for Wilma to conceive Rocks. But this is not because the approach is biased toward the choices that people actually make. Rather, it is because neither of Wilma's choices would be unfair to any of the people who would actually exist as a result of it. If a particular choice really would be unfair to someone who would actually exist as a result of it, the actual people approach would be able to register this fact and would deem the choice to be morally wrong as a result of it.

Suppose, for example, that Wilma were told that if she conceived Pebbles now then Pebbles would suffer a life of such unbearable agony that it would be far worse than no life at all and that if she waited two months and conceived Rocks, then Rocks would enjoy a perfectly satisfactory life. If Wilma conceived Pebbles in that case, the actual people approach would again dictate that the interests of Wilma and Pebbles be represented by the deliberators from behind the veil of ignorance along with the interests of all of the other actual people and that the interests of merely possible Rocks be ignored, but doing so this time would entail that Wilma's act was morally wrong. If I turn out to be Wilma, after all, I will only be slightly worse off if I have to endure the inconvenience of waiting a few months before conceiving, but if I turn out to be Pebbles on the version of the case where Pebbles's life would be far worse than no life at all, I will be much worse off if Wilma is allowed to conceive me than if she is required to postpone conception. Since from behind the veil of ignorance I don't know whether I will be someone like Wilma or someone like Pebbles, and since by stipulation any of the other people I might turn out to be would be unaffected by Wilma's decision, the rational thing for me to do is again to make the choice with the best worse-case outcome for me. The worse-case outcome for me if I choose the rule permitting Wilma to conceive Pebbles in this version of the case is that I turn out to be Pebbles and have to endure a life that is far worse than no life at all. The worse-case outcome for me if I choose the rule forbidding Wilma to conceive Pebbles in this case is that I turn out to be Wilma and suffer the mild inconvenience of postponing conception for a few months. Because the former outcome is much worse for me than the latter, I should choose to adopt the rule that would prohibit Wilma from conceiving Pebbles in this version of the case. And everyone else deliberating from behind the veil would reason in the same way. The actual people approach to applying the Veil Principle, therefore, does not simply endorse whatever procreative choice people actually make. If Wilma conceived Pebbles in this version of the case, the approach would entail that Wilma's act of conceiving Pebbles was morally wrong. The fact that the approach deems neither of Wilma's choices to be morally wrong in the original version of the case, then, does not show that the actual people approach simply approves of any procreative choice that people actually make. Rather, it shows that neither of Wilma's options in the original version of the story would treat any actual person unfairly while conceiving Pebbles in the version of the story in which this would cause Pebbles to endure a life that is far worse than no life at all would treat an actual person unfairly. There is therefore no reason to reject the claim that the actual people approach is the appropriate approach to applying the Veil Principle to the case of Wilma, and thus no reason to think that the Veil Principle can solve the non-identity problem.

5.2.1.2 THE ACTUAL AND POSSIBLE PEOPLE APPROACH

But let's suppose that the actual people approach really is mistaken in limiting those whose interests are represented by the deliberators behind the veil of ignorance to those people who actually exist at some point given that a certain choice was made. If this is so, the natural alternative is to add the interests of those people who will not actually exist but who would have existed had a different choice been made. In the case in which Wilma conceives Pebbles rather than Rocks, for example, the result would be that in deliberating behind the veil of ignorance I would know that in addition to the possibility that I will turn out to be Wilma or Pebbles or any other actual person in Wilma's society, I might also turn out to be Rocks and that I must make my decision without knowing which of these people I will turn out to be. Since this version of the veil stipulates that as a deliberator you know that you are an actual or possible person but you don't know which, I will call this way of applying the Veil Principle to the case of Wilma the actual and possible people approach.[19]

It is not at all clear that this alternative approach to applying the Veil Principle will produce the result that Wilma's act is morally wrong. From behind this revised veil of ignorance, I might well reason as follows. If I turn out to be Rocks, I will prefer a rule that prohibits Wilma from conceiving Pebbles, but if I turn out to be either Wilma or Pebbles I will prefer a rule that permits Wilma to conceive Pebbles, and if I turn out to be anyone else, I will be completely indifferent since by stipulation Wilma's choice in that case will have no effect on me. Since there is a two in three chance that once the veil is lifted I will find that I am someone who prefers the rule that permits Wilma to conceive Pebbles if I have any preference at all, it may well seem to follow that I should favor permitting Wilma to conceive Pebbles. By the same reasoning, of course, I will also prefer a rule that permits Wilma to conceive Rocks rather than Pebbles. But the point remains: merely adding possible people like Rocks to the set of people whose interests are represented by the deliberators who are reasoning self-interestedly from behind the veil of ignorance does not ensure the selection of a rule on which Wilma's act of conceiving Pebbles rather than Rocks will turn out to be morally wrong. A solution based on the actual and possible person approach to applying the Veil Principle may well therefore prove unable to satisfy the robustness requirement.

But more importantly, even if there is a route from the actual and possible people approach to the conclusion that Wilma's act of conceiving Pebbles is morally wrong, this result cannot be used to ground a satisfactory solution to the non-identity problem. This is because any solution that is based on this approach will fail to satisfy the independence requirement and the modesty requirement.

The actual and possible people approach fails to satisfy the independence requirement because there is no reason for deliberators reasoning self-interestedly from behind the veil of ignorance to consider the interests of merely possible people that

---

[19] Weinberg's argument at times seems to be grounded in the actual people approach. When she first describes the nature of the parties who would deliberate behind her version of the veil of ignorance, for example, she notes that "merely possible people do not have interests independent of their existence, so we need concern ourselves only with future actual people" (2002: 409) (see also 2002: 408, 422 n. 10). At other times, though, the interests of merely possible people seem to enter into her calculations. She says, for example, that the parties behind the veil of ignorance should compare how people would fare under rule X with how people would fare under rule Y and select the rule under which people would fare better (2002: 407, 410; see also Walker (Forthcoming) for a similar argument, though one whose scope is limited to already existing embryos). But since the people who would exist under rule X are not the same people as those who would exist under rule Y, this decision procedure can reject a given society's selection of rule X if rule X proves sub-optimal only by pointing out that things would have been better for a different set of people had rule Y instead been chosen. Since Y was not, in fact, chosen, the people whose interests are appealed to in order to reject the selection of rule X on this decision procedure are merely possible people. To the extent that her argument is therefore a form of the actual and possible people approach, it should be rejected for the reasons given in this section. To the extent that her argument should instead be understood as a form of the actual people approach, it should be rejected for the reasons given in the previous section. Either way, it fails to ground a satisfactory fairness-based solution to the non-identity problem.

is independent of the fact that requiring them to do so might enable us to avoid the Implausible Conclusion. The justification for including the interests of all actual people behind the veil of ignorance is simple: excluding any person who will actually be affected by the adoption of a rule from having their interests considered in deciding whether to adopt the rule is unfair to that person. Suppose, for example, that a white person reaches the conclusion that it is morally acceptable for black people to be enslaved by white people. And suppose that in reaching this conclusion, he takes into account the fact that he is white and as a result ignores the interests of those who are black. Here there is a straightforward answer to the question of to whom it is unfair for white people to enslave black people. It is unfair to the black people whose interests were ignored in deciding to enslave them.

But in the case of merely possible people like Rocks, there is no parallel reason for deliberators to include their interests from behind the veil of ignorance. If Wilma conceives Pebbles rather than Rocks, to whom can her act be unfair? Her act isn't unfair to herself or to Pebbles or to any other actual person, because deliberators representing the interests of all of those people would endorse a rule permitting Wilma to conceive Pebbles. And how can Wilma's act be unfair to Rocks? Rocks does not exist, and an act can't treat a person unfairly if that person never exists. The motivation for including the interests of all actual people behind the veil of ignorance regardless of their race, religion, sex, spatial or temporal location, and so on, is that you treat a person unfairly if you ignore their interests in deciding on rules that will affect their interests. But if Rocks is never conceived, then there is no one for Wilma's act to treat unfairly or to have interests that Wilma's decision has ignored. We have an independent reason to include the interests of all actual people behind the veil of ignorance, then, but no reason to add the interests of merely possible people like Rocks other than the fact that doing so might result in the decision to endorse the merits of a rule that Wilma's act turns out to break. As a result, a solution to the non-identity problem that depends on the actual and possible people approach to applying the Veil Principle cannot satisfy the independence requirement.

The second problem with adding merely possible people to the set of people whose interests are represented behind the veil of ignorance is that doing so produces results that are even more implausible then the Implausible Conclusion. A solution to the non-identity problem that depends on such an approach is therefore incapable of satisfying the modesty requirement as well. This can best be seen by assigning some particular values to the total amount of well-being that different people would have over the course of their lives if they were conceived and then considering what the actual and possible people approach to applying the Veil Principle would entail. Supposing that 20 represents a perfectly adequate life and that 100 represents an exceptionally good life, for example, consider the case in which Meredith can either conceive just Alvin or conceive Alvin along with Barbara, Charles, and Dorothy. If she conceives just Alvin, she will be able to devote enough time, care, and resources to him to ensure that Alvin's life will end up having a value of 100. If she conceives all four children and has to divide her time, care and resources among them, she will still be able to ensure that each will have a perfectly adequate life with a value of 20. Either way, Meredith herself will have an exceptionally good life, but she will be just a little bit better off if she conceives only Alvin. The results of her two options can be represented as follows:

	Conceives just Alvin	Conceives all four children
Meredith	101	100
Alvin	100	20
Barbara	——	20
Charles	——	20
Dorothy	——	20

Now suppose that Meredith decides to conceive just Alvin. The actual people approach to applying the Veil Principle directs deliberators to evaluate possible principles from a point of view in which they know that they will turn out to be either Meredith or Alvin or any other actual person but they don't know which one. If I turn out to be Meredith, I will be a little better off if I give Alvin a life worth 100 rather than a life worth 20; if I turn out to be Alvin, I will be much better off being given a life worth 100 rather than a life worth 20; and if I turn out to be any other actual person, I will not be affected one way or the other by Meredith's choice. So the actual people approach to applying the Veil Principle entails that I would favor a principle that permitted Meredith to conceive just Alvin. This result is clearly correct. Conceiving Alvin with a life worth 100 is much better for Alvin than the alternative and a little better for Meredith than the alternative. It is therefore better for all of the people who ever exist. In addition, the state of affairs that results from Meredith's conceiving just Alvin rather than conceiving Alvin, Barbara, Charles, and Dorothy is better overall from an impersonal point of view. The state of affairs consisting of just Meredith and Alvin contains 201 total units of well-being, while the state of affairs consisting of Meredith, Alvin, Barbara, Charles, and Dorothy contains only 180 total units of well-being. The average level of well-being for those who exist in the first state of affairs is 100.5, while the average level of well-being for those who exist in the second state of affairs is 36. By any reasonable standard, the claim that Meredith does nothing wrong by conceiving just Alvin in this case is clearly correct.

But now consider what the actual and possible people approach to applying the Veil Principle entails about the fact that Meredith decided to conceive only Alvin in this case. That approach directs the deliberators to evaluate principles from behind a veil of ignorance in which they know that they will turn out to be representing the interests of one of the actual or merely possible people involved. So rather than simply saying that I will turn out to represent the interests of Meredith or Alvin or any other actual person in this case, as the actual people approach does, the actual and possible people approach says that in deliberating self-interestedly from behind the veil of ignorance,

I must also take into account the interests of merely possible Barbara and Charles and Dorothy. From this point of view, things look worse for me if Meredith is allowed to conceive only Alvin rather than conceiving all four children. The worse-case scenario on this approach if Meredith conceives only Alvin is that I turn out to represent the interests of Barbara, Charles, or Dorothy and as a result get no life at all rather than a perfectly adequate life. The worse-case scenario if she conceives all four children is that I turn out to represent the interests of Alvin and merely live a perfectly adequate life when I would otherwise have had a much better life. If I turn out to be someone whose interests are significantly impacted by Meredith's choice, then, there is a three in four chance on this account that I will prefer a rule requiring Meredith to conceive all four children to one that would permit her to conceive just Alvin.

This means that the actual and possible people approach to applying the Veil Principle entails that it would be morally wrong for Meredith to conceive just Alvin. And this result is almost impossible to believe. How could it be wrong to conceive just Alvin rather than conceiving all four children when conceiving just Alvin is better for Alvin, better for Meredith, better for every single person who ever actually exists, and better from a purely impersonal point of view in terms of both total and average well-being? This result is clearly more implausible than the Implausible Conclusion, and thus provides a second reason to reject the actual and possible people approach to applying the Veil Principle. Combined with the fact that there is no independent reason to accept this approach and that it is not even clear that this approach would entail that Wilma's act of conceiving Pebbles is wrong even if we accepted it, this means that the actual and possible people approach to applying the Veil Principle cannot be used to provide a satisfactory fairness-based solution to the non-identity problem.

5.2.1.3 THE ACTUAL AND *DE DICTO* PEOPLE APPROACH

A final possibility attempts to combine the merits of the actual people approach and the actual and possible people approach while avoiding the features that prevent each from solving the non-identity problem. Like the actual people approach, it limits the people whose interests are represented by the deliberators reasoning self-interestedly from behind the veil of ignorance to those who actually exist at some point in time. In doing so, it is not burdened by the implausible implications of including the interests of merely possible people or the ad hoc nature of doing so, and so avoids the problems encountered by the actual and possible people approach. Like the actual and possible people approach, though, it finds a way to include the interests of people like Pebbles and people like Rocks in the deliberations that take place behind the veil of ignorance. In doing so, it does not limit the interests represented in the way that the actual people approach does and that clearly prevents that approach from entailing that Wilma's act is morally wrong. This third approach does this by having the deliberators consider the interests of Wilma's child in the *de dicto* sense instead of in the *de re* sense. Rather than saying that after the veil of ignorance is lifted I will find that I am either Wilma or Pebbles or some other actual person, that is, this third approach to applying the Veil

Principle says that I will either be Wilma or "Wilma's child" or some other actual person where "Wilma's child" means "whichever child Wilma conceives" instead of "the specific child (Pebbles) that Wilma actually conceived." For this reason, I will refer to this as the actual and *de dicto* people approach to applying the Veil Principle.

This final approach to using the Veil Principle to solve the non-identity problem has been defended in some detail by Reiman. Reiman develops his solution in terms of rights, but since the right that he appeals to in accounting for the wrongness of an act like Wilma's is ultimately derived from considerations about what people would agree to from behind a suitably devised veil of ignorance, I will consider his position here as a version of the fairness-based solution. Reiman's approach to using the Veil Principle is explicitly like the actual people approach in two respects. First, it treats temporal location as a morally irrelevant property that people from behind the veil of ignorance should be unaware of. "Temporal position," as he puts it,

is an arbitrary difference between people from a moral point of view. But, then, as a matter of fairness, temporal position should not change the force of people's rights. The rights of future people should be no weaker than the rights of living people, and the duties of living people to future people should be no weaker than their duties to other living people.[20]

Second, it limits those whose interests are considered by the deliberators behind the veil to the set of all people who will at some point actually exist and excludes the merely possible people who could have existed but who in fact will not: "Because they do not know their generation, the parties in the original position, in effect, represent all and only those people who, from this moment on, will ever exist: people who are currently living, and future people who do not yet exist but who one day will."[21]

But unlike the actual people approach to applying the veil of ignorance to the case of Wilma, and like the actual and possible people approach, Reiman's approach finds a way to represent the interests of people like both Pebbles and Rocks in the deliberations that take place behind the veil. It does this because it deprives those behind the veil of ignorance of more than just knowledge of their temporal location. It deprives them of all knowledge about the particular people that they will turn out to be. As Reiman puts it:

[T]he veil of ignorance deprives the parties in the original position of knowledge of the individual traits of the people they represent. This goes all the way down to which particular individuals, with which birthdays and genomes, they will be. It follows that future people are represented in the original position as the people who will exist in the future whatever particular individual traits they turn out to have, *indeed, whatever particular individuals they turn out to be.* From this it follows that what we owe to future people is not owed to them in virtue of the particular individuals they will be. We owe it to them simply in virtue of the fact that they will be people, as if which particular individuals they will be were irrelevant.[22]

---

[20] Reiman (2007: 89).   [21] Reiman (2007: 79).
[22] Reiman (2007: 82, emphasis in original).

Not only do I not know whether I will be Wilma or Wilma's child, that is, but I don't even know which particular child I will be if I turn out to be Wilma's child.

This final way of characterizing the appropriate veil of ignorance for cases like that of Wilma seems to be well motivated. As Reiman puts it:

Applied to [cases like that of Wilma], before anyone is conceived, the difference in properties between two particular future children—say, between. . . having a disability and not having one—*is morally significant*. However, that they are different particulars as such *is not*. The original position is capturing this moral fact. *It is representing the interests of future people as if which properties they turn out to have is morally important, but which particulars they turn out to be is morally irrelevant.*[23]

These are the interests of people who do not yet exist as particular individuals, but who already count morally insofar as we can affect their fates and thus have moral duties to them. Their morally relevant interests are a function of what we can do now to improve or worsen their lives in the future; and that is a matter of what properties they are born with or into, not which particulars they are apart from that, since they are not yet particular individuals. This makes it appropriate to think of the interests of future people as interests of people considered as if which particular individuals they are is irrelevant.[24]

Since the justification for the veil of ignorance in general is that it is unfair to allow morally irrelevant properties to influence our selection of moral principles, that is, and since the difference between being one particular future person and being another particular future person is itself morally irrelevant, the people deliberating behind the veil of ignorance in non-identity cases should be shielded from knowledge of which particular individuals they would be if, for example, they turned out to be Wilma's child.

In addition to being independently motivated, this actual and *de dicto* people approach to applying the Veil Principle also seems to yield the result that is needed in order to solve the non-identity problem. Reiman argues that understood in this way, the veil of ignorance "is a device that is capable of identifying the rights of future people against currently living people and the correlative duties of currently living people to future people."[25] He therefore puts the relevant principle that people would evaluate from behind the veil of ignorance in terms of the language of rights. Reiman also argues that from behind the veil of ignorance people would be particularly concerned to protect their ability to enjoy what he calls "normal functioning" because "the parties want to safeguard their ability to pursue their goals whatever they turn out to be, and maintenance of normal functioning (including prevention of serious defects) provides such a safeguard."[26] He therefore puts the principle in terms of "a right to normal functioning" in particular.[27] Focusing on the case of Wilma, then, we can

---

[23] Reiman (2007: 84, emphases in original).   [24] Reiman (2007: 85).
[25] Reiman (2007: 80).   [26] Reiman (2007: 81).   [27] Reiman (2007: 81).

put Reiman's argument in terms of what I will call the Right to Normal Functioning Principle:[28]

RNFP: Currently living people have a moral obligation to ensure that future people are capable of normal functioning, at least when ensuring this does not impose any significant burdens on the currently living people.

The question, then, is what people would conclude about the merits of such a principle if they were to deliberate about it from behind the kind of veil of ignorance that Reiman has described.

The answer seems to be simple. When I think about a case like that of Wilma from behind the actual and *de dicto* people version of the veil of ignorance, I know that after the veil is lifted I will find that I am either a woman with a slight preference to conceive a blind child now rather than a sighted child two months from now; the child conceived by that woman, whoever that child turns out to be; or some other present or future person whose interests will in no way be affected by the woman's decision. If I turn out to be the woman, I will have a slight preference to reject Reiman's proposed principle. Accepting the principle would make things a bit more inconvenient for me. If I turn out to be the child, however, I will have a very strong preference to accept the principle. Accepting the principle will ensure that I am sighted rather than incurably blind. And if I turn out to be anyone else, I will be completely indifferent between accepting the principle and rejecting it since in that case the principle will have no effect on me one way or the other. Since the worse-case scenario for me if the principle is rejected is much worse for me than the worse-case scenario for me if the principle is accepted, I conclude that it is rational for me to endorse the principle. Since everyone else will reason in the same way, we will all accept this principle. And since Wilma's act of conceiving Pebbles when she could easily have conceived Rocks instead clearly violates this principle, we will at last have a successful solution to the non-identity problem.

This final approach to applying the Veil Principle as a means of solving the non-identity problem is in some respects more promising than the others. In the end, though, it too must be rejected. The reason for this can best be put in the form of a dilemma: either the actual and *de dicto* people approach treats Pebbles and Rocks as distinct individuals or it does not, and on either understanding, the approach is unable to provide a satisfactory route from the veil of ignorance that it describes to the conclusion that Wilma's act is morally wrong.

---

[28] Reiman argues "that parties in the original position would agree on a principle providing that currently living people have a duty to do what they reasonably can, subject to their needs, rights, and other moral duties, to ensure that future people are capable of normal functioning and live lives with normal life expectancies and normal morbidity rates. If this is current people's duty to future people, then future people have a correlative right to those efforts on the part of currently living people. I shall sum this up by saying that future people have a *right to normal functioning*. Note that this is not strictly a right to normal functioning as such, but to living people's reasonable efforts to ensure that level of functioning; nor is it a right to a certain quality of life, but to living people's reasonable efforts to ensure that future people face normal life expectancies and morbidity rates" (2007: 81).

Suppose first that Pebbles and Rocks are to be understood as two distinct people. After Wilma makes her choice, that is, the world will contain Pebbles or it will contain Rocks, but it will not contain both. On this version of the approach, we can preserve the approach's ability to entail that Wilma's act is morally wrong. If I will either turn out to be Wilma or turn out to be Wilma's child where that child will either be blind Pebbles or sighted Rocks, then I will strongly prefer the principle that requires Wilma to conceive Rocks to the principle that permits her to conceive Pebbles. This is because being Pebbles rather than Rocks if I turn out to be Wilma's child and Wilma is permitted to conceive Pebbles rather than Rocks is much worse for me than being slightly inconvenienced if I turn out to be Wilma and Wilma is required to conceive Rocks rather than Pebbles.

But if we understand the actual and *de dicto* people approach in this first way, then the approach will violate the stipulation that the only people whose interests are represented by the deliberators from behind the veil of ignorance are those who at some point actually exist. As Reiman himself puts it, the individuals behind the veil of ignorance, "in effect, represent all and only those people who, from this moment on, will ever exist: people who are currently living, and future people who do not yet exist but who one day will."[29] If in deliberating from behind the veil of ignorance I take into account both what it would be like to be Pebbles if a certain principle were adopted and what it would be like to be Rocks, and if Pebbles and Rocks are understood as two distinct individuals only one of whom will ever actually exist, then in my deliberations I include the interests of someone who will never actually exist.

This problem, moreover, is no mere technicality. Once we include in our deliberations the interests of people who will never exist but who could have existed, we have abandoned the core feature that rendered the actual and *de dicto* people approach more plausible than the actual and possible people approach in the first place. On this version of the actual and *de dicto* people approach, then, we will be stuck with the very same problems that undermined the actual and possible people approach: we will have no reason to include the interests of the merely possible people that is independent of our desire to avoid the Implausible Conclusion, and our inclusion of merely possible people will have implications that are even more implausible than that conclusion, as it did in the case of Meredith. This first version of the actual and *de dicto* people approach will be able to satisfy the robustness requirement because it will be strong enough to entail that Wilma's act is morally wrong, then, but it will be too ad hoc and have implications that are too implausible to allow it to satisfy either the independence requirement or the modesty requirement.

Suppose instead that Pebbles and Rocks are to be understood as one and the same person. After Wilma makes her choice, that is, the world will contain this person regardless of which choice Wilma makes, but the person will exist either as a blind girl with one genetic makeup or as a sighted boy with a different genetic makeup. This

---

[29] Reiman (2007: 79).

second version of the actual and *de dicto* approach might be justified by appealing to the kind of metaphysical view of personal identity that was discussed in section 2.3. On one version of Lewis's counterpart account, for example, if you are Pebbles and we ask what would have happened if Wilma had delayed conception by two months, the answer would not be that you would never have existed. Rather, the answer would be that you would have existed as Rocks. And this second version of the actual and *de dicto* people approach is sometimes suggested by Reiman's own characterization of the veil of ignorance. He writes, for example, that behind the veil "future people are represented. . . as the people who will exist in the future whatever particular individual traits they turn out to have, *indeed, whatever particular individuals they turn out to be.*[30] If the future people whose interests are being represented from behind the veil of ignorance are people who will definitely exist in the future, but if those very people can turn out to exist in the future as different particular individuals, then by the transitivity of identity, those different particular individuals must in fact be one and the same individual. When in my deliberations I consider the scenario in which I turn out to be Wilma's child, that is, if Wilma's child will definitely exist in the future, and if Wilma's child will be either Pebbles or Rocks, then the scenario I am considering must be one in which I will exist either way, either as Rocks or as Pebbles. But if in one and the same scenario Rocks will be identical to me and Pebbles will be identical to me, then Rocks and Pebbles must be identical to each other. They are simply two different ways of representing the interests of one and the same person: Wilma's child.

On this second version of the actual and *de dicto* people approach, we can avoid the problems that undermined both the first version of that approach and the actual and possible people approach. Those approaches were both undermined by the fact that they ended up including the interests of merely possible people in the deliberations that take place behind the veil of ignorance. But this second version of the actual and *de dicto* people approach does not do this. Since Pebbles and Rocks turn out to be one and the same person—albeit a person who will either exist as a blind girl with one genetic makeup or as a sighted boy with a different genetic makeup—we can include consideration of the interests of both Pebbles and Rocks in our deliberations behind the veil of ignorance while adhering to the stipulation that only the interests of actual people will be considered. When we consider the interests of Pebbles and Rocks, on this version of the approach, we are considering the interests of a single person who will definitely exist in the future as either a blind girl or a sighted boy. Every person whose interests are considered from behind the veil on this approach, then, is someone who actually exists at some point.

In addition, this second version of the actual and *de dicto* people approach also seems to be able to justify the claim that Wilma's act is morally wrong. Indeed, it seems able to justify it just as easily as the first understanding does and for just the same reason: if I will either turn out to be Wilma or turn out to be Wilma's child where that means

---

[30] Reiman (2007: 82, emphasis in the original).

that I will either be a blind girl or a sighted boy, I will strongly prefer the principle that requires Wilma to conceive the sighted boy to the principle that would permit her to conceive the blind girl. This is because being blind if I turn out to be Wilma's child and Wilma is permitted to conceive a blind child is much worse for me than being slightly inconvenienced if I turn out to be Wilma and Wilma is required to conceive a sighted child instead. This second version of the actual and *de dicto* people approach, then, seems to satisfy the independence requirement and the modesty requirement, and it also seems to satisfy the robustness requirement. It seems, in short, to solve the non-identity problem.

The problem with the actual and *de dicto* people approach to applying the Veil Principle on this second version is not that it fails to entail that Wilma's act is morally wrong. The problem is that it entails that Wilma's act is morally wrong only on the assumption that whichever choice Wilma makes, the very same person will be brought into existence as a result. This second version of the actual and *de dicto* people approach produces the desired result, that is, only because it views conceiving blind Pebbles rather than sighted Rocks as making the person who is conceived worse off than that very person would otherwise have been. This means that this version of the approach can justify the claim that Wilma's act is morally wrong only by treating the case as one that is not a non-identity case. But if the approach works only in cases that are not non-identity cases, then it cannot solve the non-identity problem. And this means that even if this second version of the approach can satisfy the independence requirement and the modesty requirement, it cannot satisfy the robustness requirement.

As I pointed out in section 2.3 when I raised the same objection against the solution based on the metaphysical objection to P1 of the non-identity argument, the non-identity problem is ultimately a moral problem, not a metaphysical problem. The problem arises because most people, when presented with a case like that of Wilma, respond with a firm judgment that the act in question is morally wrong. When they think about a case like that of Wilma, moreover, most people do not view it through the lens of the kind of metaphysical system that would be required in order to sustain this second version of the actual and *de dicto* people approach. What they think, that is, is that it is wrong for Wilma to conceive a blind child now rather than a sighted child later even if we assume that the sighted child would be an entirely different person. In order to satisfy the robustness requirement, a reason for rejecting a given premise of the non-identity argument must be strong enough to help us avoid the Implausible Conclusion. The Implausible Conclusion says that Wilma's act of conceiving Pebbles rather than Rocks is not morally wrong. But what rejecting this conclusion really means for most people is showing that Wilma's act of conceiving Pebbles rather than Rocks is wrong even if Pebbles and Rocks really would be different people. And on this second version of the actual and *de dicto* people approach to applying the Veil Principle, the approach can do nothing to establish the truth of this claim. It can help account for the wrongness of Wilma's act if Pebbles and Rocks turn out to be one and the same person and the case turns out not to be a non-identity case, but it can't help account for the wrongness of Wilma's act if Pebbles and Rocks turn out to be different people and the case turns out to be a genuine non-identity case. And so contrary to initial appearances, a solution based on this second version of the actual and *de dicto* people approach is not strong enough to satisfy the robustness requirement and so cannot be used to solve the non-identity problem.

In the end, then, the actual and *de dicto* people approach to applying the Veil Principle to the case of Wilma is no more successful than the other approaches. If the approach treats Pebbles and Rocks as two distinct people, then while it will satisfy the robustness requirement, it will fail to satisfy the independence requirement and the modesty requirement. If the approach treats Pebbles and Rocks as one and the same person, then while it will satisfy the independence requirement and the modesty requirement, it will fail to satisfy the robustness requirement. Either way, it will fail to satisfy all of the requirements that a successful solution to the non-identity problem must satisfy. And so even if the Veil Principle turns out to provide a compelling reason to reject P4 of the non-identity argument, this fact cannot be used to ground a satisfactory solution to the non-identity problem.

5.2.2 *The Principle of Fair Play*

Two other fairness-based approaches also merit attention. One appeals to the principle of fair play. Usami, for example, claims that a solution based on such a principle can succeed at least in cases like that of the risky policy.[31] The principle of fair play maintains that if you benefit from a form of mutual cooperation in which others incur costs, it would be wrong for you not to pay your fair share by incurring the costs involved in sustaining the practice as well. It is wrong, that is, to be a free rider. Given that you benefit from the social order made possible by the constraint that most other people accept in obeying the law even when they don't want to, for example, the principle can be used to try to justify the claim that it would be wrong for you not to accept such a constraint. Usami argues that this principle can be extended from cases of intra-generational cooperation to cases of what he calls "sequential" or "transgenerational" cooperation.[32] We benefit from the resources and relatively clean air that previous generations have conferred on us, that is, and so it would be wrong for us to fail to confer the same sorts of benefits on future generations.

There are a number of reasons to reject this kind of fairness-based solution. First, it is not at all clear that the principle of fair play is a reasonable one even in the case of intra-generational forms of mutually cooperative practices. If you enjoy listening to NPR, for example, you benefit from the fact that other people contribute to NPR, but it is far from clear that this suffices to establish that it would be positively immoral for you to decline to contribute. Second, and more importantly, even if one accepts the principle in intra-generational cases, the grounds for doing so cannot be extended

---

[31] Usami (2011: 242–5).   [32] Usami (2011: 243, 244).

to the kinds of trans-generational cases that generate the non-identity problem. The motivation behind the principle is the thought that it is unfair to enjoy all the benefits of a cooperative scheme without incurring your share of the costs involved in producing it. It is possible to engage in this kind of free ridership in cases that involve your contemporaries: you can let them do all the work while you sit back and enjoy the benefits. But it is not possible to engage in this kind of free ridership in the kinds of cases with which Usami is concerned. The relevant costs involved in producing the resources and clean air that the current members of the wealthy society enjoy today were incurred by previous generations. If the current members of the wealthy society decline to leave comparable goods to future generations, they are not free riding on their society's past members because nothing they do now could involve reducing the costs that the past members incurred. And if the members of the wealthy society select the risky policy, none of the future people who are later killed by the leaking toxic waste can complain that they have been the victim of free riding either. The future people will not suffer a worse cost/benefit ratio as the result of the current generation's declining to make a sacrifice on their behalf because if the current generation had not chosen the risky policy, those particular future people would never have existed in the first place. So the rationale that motivates the principle of fair play in the intra-generational case fails to support it in the inter-generational case.

Finally, and perhaps most importantly, this kind of fairness-based solution can only work, if it can work at all, in cases where the current generation really has benefited from the previous generation's having done its fair share. But anyone who thinks that it would be wrong for the current members of the wealthy society to select the risky policy will think that it would be wrong regardless of how the previous generations of the wealthy society behaved. If a number of current members of the wealthy society are prematurely killed by leaking toxic waste that was produced several generations earlier by a generation that cared not one whit for the future, for example, anyone who agrees that it would be wrong for the current members of the wealthy society to choose the risky policy over the safe policy in the original version of the case will still think that it would be wrong to do so. If our generation fails to do anything to combat global warming, to take an example to which the risky policy case is often compared, anyone who thinks that we have an obligation to combat global warming would still think that the generation that follows us would have an obligation to do so. If Wilma herself has a significant disability, for that matter, and if she has it only because her mother chose to conceive her rather than to wait two months and instead conceive a different child who would not have had the disability, anyone who agrees that it would be wrong for Wilma to conceive Pebbles in the original version of the story will still think that it would be wrong for her to do so. A sufficiently robust solution to the non-identity problem must be able to show that what Wilma and the wealthy society do is wrong regardless of what previous generations of people have done to them. And a solution based on the principle of fair play cannot do this even if it can overcome all of the other problems for it that I have noted here.

5.2.3   *The Principle of Unfair Exploitation*

Finally, one might try to reject P4 by appealing to a principle of unfair exploitation. On at least some views, an act can be wrong because it wrongs a particular person not by harming them or by violating their rights but by unfairly exploiting them. This is the kind of thing that many people seem inclined to say, for example, about companies that pay extremely low wages to sweatshop workers. If a view of this sort is correct, then Wilma's act might wrong Pebbles despite the fact that it doesn't harm Pebbles or violate Pebbles's rights by unfairly treating Pebbles in an exploitative manner. Rendall has proposed a solution along these lines and such an approach is also briefly suggested by Kavka.[33]

Suppose, for example, that Ann will soon die if she does not drink some water, that the only person who can provide her with the needed water in time is Keith, and that Keith knows that Ann's net worth is a little over two million dollars. And suppose that Keith offers to give Ann the water only if she gives him two million dollars and that Ann accepts. In this case, we might well be inclined to say that Keith's act wrongs Ann because it exploits her: it takes advantage of her vulnerability as a means of extracting from her a price that is unfairly high. But then we might say the same sort of thing about the case of Wilma and Pebbles. As we saw in the context of the rights waiver argument in section 5.1.3, even if Pebbles had a right not to be conceived, Wilma's act of conceiving her would not wrong her because Wilma could be sufficiently confident that Pebbles would waive that right if she could or that Pebbles will subsequently waive that right when she can. This posed a serious problem for rights-based solutions because an act can't wrongfully violate a person's rights if the person waives that right. But the proponent of an exploitation-based solution to the non-identity problem can concede that Pebbles would consent to being conceived as a blind person and yet hold that Wilma's act wrongs Pebbles nonetheless. After all, Ann not only would consent but actually does consent to pay Keith two million dollars for the water, but Keith's act still seems to wrong her. If Keith's act wrongs Ann and if the case of Keith and Ann is relevantly similar to the case of Wilma and Pebbles, then Wilma's act wrongs Pebbles. And it may well seem that the two cases are sufficiently similar because the only reason that Pebbles would consent to being blind is the vulnerable position that she is (or would be) in: she must accept blindness as the price for being brought into existence.

It is not clear to me that Keith's act is wrong because it unfairly exploits Ann. It seems plausible to suppose that Ann has a right to be given the water in this case in the same way that a drowning child might have a right to be thrown a life preserver. If that is so, then Keith's act is wrong because refusing to simply give Ann the water (or perhaps to give Ann the water in exchange for reimbursing him for what the water cost him to purchase) violates Ann's rights. And if that is the reason that Keith's act is wrong, then it does nothing to ground an exploitation-based solution to the non-identity problem.

---

[33]   Rendall (2011), Kavka (1982: 106–9). See also Liberto (2014).

But let's suppose that Keith's act really is wrong because it unfairly exploits Ann and that it unfairly exploits Ann because it takes advantage of her vulnerability as a means of extracting from her a price for the water that is unfairly high. Even if this is so, this cannot ground a solution to the non-identity problem because there is a crucial difference between the two cases. Keith could easily give the water to Ann for free or simply require that she reimburse him for the cost he incurred in purchasing it. By charging her two million dollars for the water instead, Keith takes unfair advantage of Ann's dire circumstances and makes her accept a much worse deal than he could easily have offered her. But when blindness is the price that Pebbles must pay, as it were, in order to be conceived, it is not the case that Wilma could easily have offered Pebbles a better deal. Not only could she not have done so easily, she could not have done so at all. There was no way that Wilma could have conceived Pebbles without Pebbles being blind. As a result, the feature of the situation in virtue of which Keith's act unfairly exploits Ann is absent in the case in which Wilma conceives Pebbles. And so even if Keith's act really is wrong because his act unfairly exploits Ann, this cannot be used to show that Wilma's act is wrong because it unfairly exploits Pebbles. Fairness-based solutions to the non-identity problem that are grounded in considerations of exploitation or in the principle of fair play end up faring no better than those that attempt to make use of Rawls's veil of ignorance. If Wilma's act wrongs Pebbles, then, it does not do so because it treats Pebbles unfairly.

5.3 Respect-based Arguments

Suppose that I perform an act that neither harms you nor violates your rights nor treats you unfairly or in a way that you would not agree to be treated. Some people hold that my act might still wrong you if it fails to treat you with an appropriate degree of respect. Many people find this kind of view plausible in the case of prostitution, for example. Even if a man who hires a prostitute does not harm her, on this kind of account, and even if he does not violate her rights or treat her unfairly or in a way that she has not freely consented to be treated, his act nonetheless wrongs her because it fails to respect her as the kind of being that she is. It might therefore be possible to construct a parallel argument as a way of developing a respect-based solution to the non-identity problem. Even if Wilma's act does not harm Pebbles or violate Pebbles's rights, that is, and even if it does not treat her unfairly or in a way that she would not have freely consented to be treated, Wilma's act might still wrong Pebbles by failing to treat Pebbles with the appropriate degree of respect. I will therefore conclude our survey of solutions that might be grounded in the rejection of P4 by considering whether this approach might be able to yield a satisfactory solution to the non-identity problem.

5.3.1 Treating a Person as a Mere Means to an End

Perhaps the most natural way to try to develop such an account derives from the second formulation of Kant's categorical imperative. That principle is based on the claim that people have value as ends in themselves and not merely as means to the purposes of others. It demands, as a result, that we always treat people as ends in themselves and not merely as a means to our own ends. Since Pebbles does not exist at the time that Wilma's act takes place, there is a sense in which Wilma's act does not treat Pebbles in any way at all. But it may seem plausible to modify the principle in a way that takes this fact into account. Kavka, for example, appeals to a modified version of the categorical imperative that "would forbid treating rational beings *or their creation* (that is, their being brought into existence) as a means only, rather than as ends in themselves."[34] I will refer to the relevant part of this rule as the Treating as an End Principle.

TEP: If the act of bringing a person into existence treats that person's creation merely as a means to an end, then the act wrongs that person

It may seem that by refusing to make the minor sacrifice of taking the pills once a day for two months before conceiving, Wilma's act brings Pebbles into existence merely as a means to her own convenience and that it therefore violates this principle. And if Wilma's act violates this principle, the principle itself may serve as a basis for solving the non-identity problem.

There are two problems with trying to solve the non-identity problem by appealing to the Treating as an End Principle. The first is that Wilma's act does not actually violate the principle. Any solution that is based on the principle will therefore fail to satisfy the robustness requirement. One reason that Wilma's act does not violate the Treating as an End Principle is that it is not the creation of Pebbles that Wilma treats as the means to her end. The end that Wilma's act aims at is personal convenience. But it is not the creation of Pebbles itself that makes things more convenient for Wilma. The creation of Pebbles would make things more convenient for Wilma if, for example, she created Pebbles in order to have Pebbles do all of her housework. Rather, it is the throwing away of the pills and conceiving at once that makes things more convenient for Wilma. Pebbles comes to exist as a consequence of Wilma's conceiving now, and Wilma conceives now in order to make things more convenient for herself, but it is the conceiving now rather than the coming into existence of Pebbles that Wilma uses as a means to making things more convenient for herself. The creation of Pebbles is a consequence of the means that Wilma chooses, but it is not the means itself.

---

[34] Kavka (1982: 110, my emphasis). See also Davis (1997: 12), Weinberg and Hurley (Forthcoming), and, in the legal context, Dillard (2010b: 54). Kumar develops a similar respect-based solution that is grounded in a contractarian framework. The principle that Kumar's solution appeals to does not involve treating people as ends rather than means as a general matter but instead maintains that "Those individuals responsible for a child's, or other dependent person's, welfare are morally required not to let her suffer a serious harm or disability or a serious loss of happiness or good, that they could have prevented without imposing substantial burdens or costs or loss of benefits on themselves or others" (2003: 112). His particular respect-based solution is therefore immune to the difficulties I identify in the text with Kavka's approach. Kumar, however, provides no justification for this principle. Given that the only way that Wilma could prevent Pebbles from being blind would be to prevent Pebbles from coming into existence, that is, Kumar provides no reason to think that by conceiving Pebbles, Wilma treats her daughter in a way that fails to show the respect that a parent owes her child. His solution therefore fails to satisfy the independence requirement.

Since the significance of this distinction may not be immediately apparent, an example may prove useful here. So suppose that you are a wealthy business owner and that I would like to acquire a great deal of money that I will use purely as a means to my own personal gratification. And suppose that I am considering two options. One option is to steal all of your money. The other is to open a business that will compete with yours. I know that if my business makes all the money I want it to make, it will drive you out of business and leave you broke. In one sense, these two options are the same. Both involve me ending up rich and you ending up poor. But in another sense, they are importantly different. The first option involves my treating you as a mere means to my acquiring the money. The second involves my creating a new business as a means to my acquiring the money. Your losing your money is simply a consequence of my means, not the means itself. The first option objectionably treats you as a mere means to my ends while the second does not. And it is the second option, rather than the first, that parallels the case of Wilma. Since Wilma does not really use the creation of Pebbles itself as the means to her end, the prohibition against using people and their creation as a mere means cannot be used to account for the presumed wrongness of Wilma's act.

The second reason that Wilma's act does not violate the Treating as an End Principle is that even if Wilma's act is understood as treating the creation of Pebbles as a means, it cannot be understood as treating it merely as a means, or as a means only. The creation of Pebbles could be understood as treating Pebbles as a mere means if Wilma created Pebbles without any regard for the value of Pebbles as an end in herself. If Wilma did not take into account the effects of her act on Pebbles and ignored the question of whether Pebbles would be made worse off by being brought into existence or whether Pebbles could reasonably be expected to consent to the act of bringing her into existence, for example, then if Wilma created Pebbles as a means to her own ends she would treat her not just partly as a means, but entirely as a means. But we are assuming here that Wilma's act does not harm Pebbles and that Pebbles would consent to the principles that would render her creation morally permissible. There is therefore no reason to think that Wilma is insensitive to Pebbles's value as an end. Indeed, we can simply stipulate for the sake of the example that Wilma would not have conceived Pebbles if she had thought that doing so would harm Pebbles or would be something that Pebbles would refuse to consent to. Even if part of Wilma's reason for bringing Pebbles into existence did turn out to be that doing so would serve Wilma's ends, then, this would not be enough to show that Wilma's act treated the creation of Pebbles merely as a means, and so would not be enough to show that her act violated the Treating as an End Principle.

I have argued so far that a solution to the non-identity problem that is based on the Treating as an End Principle is not strong enough to satisfy the robustness requirement. But let's now suppose that I have been mistaken about this and that the principle really is strong enough to rule out the act of creating a person as a means to some end even in those cases where the act is done only after confirming that creating the person will not harm the person or treat them in a way that they would not agree to be treated.

If this is so, then Wilma's act really does violate the principle. But if this is so, then a second problem arises: a solution based on the principle will be unable to satisfy the modesty requirement. This is because virtually every intentional act of conception will turn out to be morally wrong if the principle is understood in this way. When people deliberately choose to conceive a child, they do so for a reason. A couple might think that having a child will bring them closer together, they might conceive a second child so that their first child will have a sibling, they might want to have a child to create a legacy for the future, or simply to experience the distinctive emotional rewards of parenting. In all of these perfectly ordinary sorts of cases, the people in question choose to bring a person into existence because doing so will serve some end that they have. If the Treating as an End Principle entails that Wilma's act of conceiving Pebbles is wrong merely because Wilma chooses to conceive Pebbles as a means to some end of hers, then it will also entail that it is wrong for people to conceive in the perfectly ordinary cases I have described here. But the claim that it is wrong for people to conceive in such cases is even more implausible than the claim that it is not wrong for Wilma to conceive Pebbles. If the Treating as an End Principle is strong enough to satisfy the robustness requirement, therefore, it is too strong to satisfy the modesty requirement. Either way, the claim that it is possible to wrong a person without harming them by treating them as a mere means to one's ends cannot ground a satisfactory solution to the non-identity problem.

5.3.2 Treating a Person as You Would Treat All Persons

A second kind of respect-based argument for the wrongness of Wilma's act is also inspired by Kant. It arises from the first formulation of the categorical imperative. On that formulation, one should act on a maxim that governs one's behavior only if one can at the same time will that it become a universal law. This principle of universalizability is not explicitly cashed out in terms of respecting people, but it is plausible to see it as grounded in such respect. If I give myself a particular liberty to act in certain ways that I would not be willing to give to everyone else, I don't seem to be respecting everyone as an equal in a morally relevant sense. It might therefore seem plausible to suppose that an act can be wrong because it fails to respect people by violating what I will call the Universalizability Principle:

UP: If an act is done according to a maxim that one cannot will to be acted on by everyone, then the act is wrong

And since it is difficult to imagine endorsing a world in which everyone acts in the way that Wilma does, it may also seem that Wilma's act is wrong because it violates this principle.

There are two problems with trying to solve the non-identity problem by appealing to this principle of universalizability. The first arises from a distinction between two ways in which we might think of the maxim that Wilma acts on when she decides to conceive Pebbles rather than Rocks. One way to think of the maxim is in terms that are independent of the context in which Wilma's act takes place. On this way of viewing things, the maxim she acts on is something like this: "Regardless of how other people act and regardless of the consequences for other people, I will conceive a blind child rather than a sighted child whenever doing so is at least a bit better for me overall." A second way to think of the maxim is in terms of the particular context in which Wilma's act takes place. On this way of viewing things, the maxim she acts on is something more like this: "In situations where I know that my act will not harm anyone, I will conceive a blind child rather than a sighted child whenever doing so is at least a bit better for me overall."

If we think of the maxim that Wilma acts on in context-independent terms, then it is at least plausible to conclude that her act violates the Universalizability Principle. This is because it is difficult to imagine willing a world in which everyone conceives blind children rather than sighted children. But if we interpret the maxims that people act on in this context-independent manner when applying the Universalizability Principle, the principle itself will have implications that are even more implausible than the Implausible Conclusion. A woman who decides not to have children, for example, would have to be understood as acting on a maxim to the effect that she will decline to have children regardless of what other people do and regardless of the consequences for other people. Since it is difficult to imagine willing a world in which no one has children under any circumstances, this means that on this way of interpreting the maxims that people act on, the Universalizability Principle would entail that it is morally wrong for anyone to decline to have children. When maxims are understood in this way, then, a solution based on the Universalizability Principle may prove strong enough to satisfy the robustness requirement but it will be too strong to satisfy the modesty requirement.

If we interpret the maxims that people act on in context-dependent terms, we can avoid the problem posed by cases of people who choose not to have children. On this interpretation of the maxim they act on, people who choose not to have children can be understood as simply endorsing a practice in which they refrain from having children when more than enough other people continue to have children to avoid causing any problems and when those who refrain from having children can therefore do so without harming anyone. There is no difficulty in willing that a maxim of this sort be adopted universally, and so no reason to reject the Universalizability Principle on this interpretation of the maxims that the principle refers to. But on this context-dependent interpretation of the maxims the principle refers to, the principle itself is too weak to entail that Wilma's act is morally wrong. On this account, the maxim that Wilma acts on leads people to conceive blind children rather than sighted children only in contexts in which they know that few other people will do so and that doing so will harm no one. There is no reason not to will that everyone act on this very limited maxim, and so no reason to think that Wilma's act would violate the Universalizability Principle on this interpretation. In the end, then, the principle is either too strong to satisfy the modesty requirement or too weak to satisfy the robustness requirement.

The second problem with trying to solve the non-identity problem by appealing to the principle of universalizability arises from a distinction between two different ways in which we might be unable to will that a particular maxim be acted on by everyone. In what I will refer to as the strong sense, we cannot will that a particular maxim be acted on by everyone because universalizing adherence to the maxim involves a logical contradiction. Kant famously maintained that this was so, for example, in the case of a maxim on which I lie when doing so serves my interests. In what I will refer to as the weak sense, universalizing a particular maxim involves no logical contradiction, but we would be unwilling to endorse its universal adoption nonetheless. Kant conceded that there was nothing incoherent about universalizing a maxim like "I will never harm others but I will never assist others," for example, but he maintained that no one could really will that such a maxim be universally adopted.

The distinction between the strong and weak senses in which a maxim might be incapable of universal endorsement corresponds to the distinction between what Kant called perfect and imperfect duties. If a maxim cannot be universalized in the strong sense, then it generates a perfect duty. Acting on such a maxim is always wrong. If a maxim can be universalized in the strong sense but not in the weak sense, then it generates an imperfect duty. Always acting on such a maxim would be wrong, but acting on it from time to time would not be wrong. Simply telling the truth from time to time would not be enough to render it permissible to lie at other times, for example, but provided that one did help people in some instances, it would not be wrong to refrain from helping people in other instances.

The distinction between perfect and imperfect duties, in turn, generates the second problem with the attempt to solve the non-identity problem by appealing to the Universalizability Principle. Even if we interpret the maxim that Wilma acts on in context-independent terms, her maxim will not fail the universalizability test in the strong sense. There is no logical contradiction involved in everyone acting on a maxim such as "regardless of how other people act and regardless of the consequences for other people, I will conceive a blind child rather than a sighted child whenever doing so is at least a bit better for me overall." This is because there is nothing logically contradictory about a world in which everyone conceives blind children. If the maxim that Wilma acts on is incapable of being universalized at all, then, it is only in the weak sense: we might find ourselves simply incapable of willing that such a state of affairs be brought into existence. This failure would be enough to establish an imperfect duty on the part of Wilma, but it would not be enough to establish a perfect duty. It would show that it would be wrong for Wilma to always conceive blind children rather than sighted children, that is, but it would not show that it would be wrong for her to occasionally do so. If Wilma already had three sighted children at the time that she decided to conceive Pebbles, for example, then an argument based on the claim that the maxim she acted on cannot be universalized in the weak sense would not entail that it was wrong for her to conceive Pebbles rather than Rocks. But the Implausible Conclusion is surely just as implausible regardless of whether Wilma already has three sighted children when she decides to conceive Pebbles. No one, when first presented with the case of Wilma, demands to know whether Wilma has already conceived some sighted children before passing moral judgment on her act. And so a solution based on the claim that Wilma's act violates the Universalizability Principle because the maxim she acts on cannot be universalized in the weak sense will not be able to satisfy the robustness requirement.

My first objection maintained that a solution based on the context-independent understanding of Wilma's maxim would fail to satisfy the modesty requirement even if it turned out to satisfy the robustness requirement. But this second objection shows that such a solution cannot satisfy the robustness requirement either. In addition, it should be clear that there is nothing logically contradictory about universalizing the context-dependent version of Wilma's maxim, the version on which she conceives a blind child only in situations where she knows that very few other people will do so and that her act will not harm anyone. It should therefore be clear that no version of the argument based on the Universalizability Principle can provide a satisfactory solution to the non-identity problem. As with the arguments grounded in considerations about rights and about fairness, then, arguments grounded in considerations about respect might turn out to pose some problems for P4. But even if P4 does not turn out to be true, for purposes of generating the non-identity problem, it remains true enough. As proved to be the case with P1, P2, and P3, if we are going to avoid the Implausible Conclusion by rejecting one of the premises of the non-identity argument, we will yet again have to look elsewhere.

6

Rejecting the Fifth Premise

The first four premises of the non-identity argument maintain that Wilma's act does not make Pebbles worse off than she would otherwise have been, that in order for an act to harm a person the act must make that person worse off than they would otherwise have been, that Wilma's act does not harm anyone other than Pebbles, and that if an act does not harm anyone, then the act does not wrong anyone. If all four of these premises are true, then Wilma's act does not wrong anyone. I have not insisted in the previous chapters that all four of these premises are true. But I have argued that, for purposes of generating the non-identity problem, they are true enough: no solution to the problem that is based on an independently motivated rejection of any of these premises satisfies both the robustness requirement and the modesty requirement. The reasons that can be given for rejecting the premises that are independent of the fact that doing so would enable us to avoid the Implausible Conclusion are either so weak that they fail to prevent a modified version of the argument from generating that conclusion or so strong that they generate implications that are even more implausible than the conclusion they are designed to avoid. Let's now suppose that I have been correct about all of this. If I have been correct, then only one claim stands between us and the Implausible Conclusion. This is the claim made by the fifth premise, the claim that if an act does not wrong anyone, then the act is not wrong.

In order to justify rejecting P5, we must identify a property that can make an act wrong even if the act does not wrong anyone. In order to establish that this property is sufficiently robust to be capable of solving the non-identity problem, we must show that it is a property of Wilma's act of conceiving Pebbles. And in order to establish that the property is also sufficiently modest to render the solution based on it a satisfactory one, we must also show that the claim that this property makes acts wrong even when they wrong no one does not have implications that are even more implausible than the Implausible Conclusion. The goal of this chapter is to consider whether there is such a property.

6.1 Producing Suboptimal Consequences

On the face of it, at least, there is one natural candidate for a property that might make Wilma's act wrong even if her act harms no one and wrongs no one: the property of producing suboptimal results. It is a conspicuous feature of Wilma's situation, after all, that the consequences of conceiving Rocks would have been better than the consequences of conceiving Pebbles in terms of the overall amount of human well-being that would have resulted. And the claim that it is wrong to choose one act over another because the act produces worse consequences in terms of something like overall human well-being strikes many people as an attractive one independent of whether the act in question wrongs anyone. So it may seem plausible to suppose that we can solve the non-identity problem by appealing to the claim that Wilma's act is wrong because it produces worse results than the alternative.[1]

6.1.1 The Moderate Principle

One way to produce such a solution would be to appeal to an act-consequentialist principle. According to act consequentialism, the right act is the one that produces, or that can reasonably be expected to produce, the best overall consequences among all of the available alternatives. Since non-identity cases involve an agent choosing between two available options and knowing what the overall consequences of each option would be, we could therefore attempt to solve the problem by appealing to a simple version of the act-consequentialist position, one that ignores cases where there are many options and that sets aside the difference between actual and expected outcomes. The result is what I will call the Act-Consequentialist Principle:

ACP: If you are choosing between Act 1 and Act 2, and if the overall consequences are better if you choose Act 2, then it is wrong for you to choose Act 1

Assuming that overall consequences are measured in terms of something like overall well-being, many people will find the Act-Consequentialist Principle to be well motivated. If the principle so understood is true, then P5 is false: choosing Act 1 over Act 2 will be wrong even if doing so wrongs no one. If the principle is true, moreover, then P5 would appear to be not just false, but false enough to solve the non-identity problem. The overall consequences if Wilma conceives Rocks seem better than the overall consequences if Wilma conceives Pebbles. And so the Act-Consequentialist Principle clearly seems to entail that Wilma's act of conceiving Pebbles is wrong even if the act wrongs no one. The only question that seems to remain is whether the principle nonetheless has further implications that are even more implausible than the Implausible

---

[1] As Neil Levy has put the point in discussing a case virtually identical to that of Wilma, "Since her action is not the best of the alternatives available to her, she acts wrongly" (Levy (2002: 366)). In Levy's example, the woman must take the medication for three months before conceiving rather than two, and she seems to decline to take the medicine for no reason at all, rather than to avoid a minor cost to herself, but aside from this the case is essentially the same as that of Wilma. Levy's solution to the problem involves an appeal to temporal indexing in addition to the principle cited in the text, but the principle itself is needed in order for Levy's solution to succeed, and so if my argument against the principle is satisfactory, it is not necessary to address the question of temporal indexing independently. Singer makes the same suggestion, claiming that an act such as Wilma's is wrong because it "fails to bring about the best possible outcome" (1999: 124–5). See also Persson (2009).

Conclusion that we are trying to avoid. If a solution to the non-identity problem based on the Act-Consequentialist Principle satisfies the independence requirement and the robustness requirement, that is, then all that is left to consider is whether it also satisfies the modesty requirement.

It might seem clear at this point that a solution to the non-identity problem that is based on the fact that Wilma's act produces suboptimal consequences will be unsuccessful precisely because it cannot satisfy the modesty requirement. This is because it is widely believed that act consequentialism has a variety of extremely counterintuitive implications and many of these are likely to strike most people as even more implausible than the Implausible Conclusion. It is often noted, for example, that act consequentialism entails that if you could prevent a person from suffering a very serious harm by incurring a slightly less serious harm yourself, then it would be positively immoral for you to decline to be a Good Samaritan and make the sacrifice. You would be obligated, for example, to lose one of your legs in order to prevent a stranger from losing a leg and a finger. Act consequentialism also seems to entail that it would be permissible—indeed, obligatory—to punish an innocent person whenever doing so would produce social benefits that outweighed the resulting harm, or to kill an innocent person as a means of saving two other innocent people, and so on. But while these sorts of implications may well be enough to establish that a solution to the non-identity problem that is based on accepting the Act-Consequentialist Principle in particular cannot satisfy the modesty requirement, this does not mean that the approach to solving the problem by appealing to the suboptimal consequences of Wilma's act more generally must be rejected. This is because, in several important respects, the Act-Consequentialist Principle is considerably stronger than it needs to be in order to justify rejecting P5.

One way in which the Act-Consequentialist Principle is needlessly strong is that it insists that it is wrong to choose Act 1 over Act 2 in every case in which Act 2 produces better overall consequences. In the case of Wilma, it isn't just that conceiving Rocks would produce better consequences than conceiving Pebbles, but that conceiving Rocks would produce significantly better consequences. And one could agree that it is wrong to choose the act that produces the worse consequences when the difference between the possible outcomes is so significant without accepting that it is also wrong to choose an act that has worse consequences when the difference between the possible outcomes is relatively minor.

A second way in which the Act-Consequentialist Principle is needlessly strong is that it applies even in cases where the cost to you of doing the act with the better consequences is clearly significant. In the case of Wilma, the cost to her of conceiving Rocks rather than conceiving Pebbles is trivial. And one could agree that it is wrong to choose the act that produces the worse consequences when the cost to you of producing the better consequences is trivial without accepting that it is also wrong to do so in cases where the cost to you of producing the better consequences would be quite significant.

Finally, the Act-Consequentialist Principle maintains that it is wrong to choose the act that produces the worse consequences even if the act that produces the better consequences would violate someone's rights. In the case of Wilma, as we saw in Chapter 5, no rights would be violated if she were to wait two months and conceive Rocks rather than conceive now and conceive Pebbles. And one could agree that it is wrong to choose the act that produces the worse consequences when the act that would produce better consequences would not violate anyone's rights without agreeing that it would also be wrong to do so in cases where the act that would produce the better consequences would violate someone's rights.

As a result of these features of the case, one could appeal to the suboptimal consequences of Wilma's choice as a way of explaining the wrongness of her act by appealing to a heavily qualified version of the Act-Consequentialist Principle. Since adding these qualifications to the principle renders it so moderate, I will refer to the results as the Moderate Principle:

MP: If you are choosing between Act 1 and Act 2 and the overall consequences are better if you choose Act 2, then it is wrong for you to choose Act 1 at least in cases where (a) the overall consequences of Act 2 are significantly better than the overall consequences of Act 1, (b) choosing Act 2 rather than Act 1 does not impose a significant cost on you, and (c) choosing Act 2 would not violate anyone's rights

Anyone who accepts the Act-Consequentialist Principle will also accept the Moderate Principle since the Moderate Principle is entailed by the Act-Consequentialist Principle. The Moderate Principle, moreover, does not have many of the counterintuitive implications that the Act-Consequentialist Principle seems to have. Many people who would reject the Act-Consequentialist Principle, therefore, would still accept the Moderate Principle. Yet while the Moderate Principle is therefore considerably more modest than the Act-Consequentialist Principle, it still seems to be sufficiently robust to entail that Wilma's act is wrong. The overall consequences would have been significantly better if Wilma had waited and conceived Rocks, doing so would not have imposed any significant costs on her, and it would not have violated anyone's rights. In trying to determine whether the suboptimal consequences of Wilma's act can ground a satisfactory solution to the non-identity problem, then, the question is not whether the Act-Consequentialist Principle can satisfy the modesty requirement, but whether the considerably more modest Moderate Principle can.

And on the face of it, at least, the Moderate Principle may well look like the most reasonable means of solving the non-identity problem.[2] It seems robust enough to do the job, modest enough to avoid any unacceptable implications, and familiar enough to avoid the appearance of being a merely ad hoc invention. But things appear this way only to the extent that the scope of the principle is restricted to cases in which the

---

[2] See, e.g., DeGrazia (2012: 184): "One need not assume that all impersonal harming is wrong, as pure consequentialism seems required to hold. What is wrong is causing impersonal harm when one can avoid doing so without undue cost to oneself or anyone else, as in [a case like that of Wilma]." DeGrazia refers to this kind of approach as "the most promising" strategy for solving the non-identity problem (2012: 185). See also DeGrazia (2005: 277–8).

same people will exist regardless of which act you choose. If we add a further clause to the principle, that is, and say that it is wrong for you to choose Act 1 over Act 2 at least in cases where the choice between Act 1 and Act 2 does not affect the identity of the people who will exist after the act takes place, then it seems reasonable to suppose that the principle can be plausibly motivated and can avoid generating implications that are more implausible than the Implausible Conclusion. But if we restrict the scope of the Moderate Principle to cases that are not identity-affecting, we will of course be unable to use it to solve the non-identity problem. The non-identity problem arises in the first place precisely because principles that seem plausible in ordinary cases seem to produce implausible results in identity-affecting cases. In order to use the Moderate Principle to solve the non-identity problem, then, the principle must be understood to say that it is wrong to choose Act 1 over Act 2 even in cases where the choice between Act 1 and Act 2 affects the identity of the people who will exist after the act takes place. And when the Moderate Principle is understood in this way, it turns out to have problems satisfying both the independence requirement and the modesty requirement.

I will consider the problem posed by the independence requirement in the subsection that follows and the problem posed by the modesty requirement in the subsection after that. But in order to do so, two distinctions must first be made clear. The first is the distinction between what, for purposes of this discussion, I will call the actual people and the merely possible people who can be identified relative to a particular action. Suppose, for example, that you are choosing between Act 1 and Act 2 and that you choose Act 1. The actual people relative to this choice are the people who actually exist at some point given that you chose Act 1. These include the people who already existed and the people who would have existed regardless of which act you chose as well as the people who exist only because you chose Act 1. The merely possible people relative to this choice are the people who will never actually exist given that you chose Act 1 but who would have existed had you instead chosen Act 2. These include the people who would have been created as a direct result of your choosing Act 2 and the people who would have been created as an indirect consequence of your choosing Act 2.

This distinction between the people who are actual and the people who are merely possible relative to a given act points to an important distinction between two ways that the Moderate Principle can be understood. The principle says that it is wrong to choose Act 1 if the overall consequences would be better if you choose Act 2, and the distinction between actual and merely possible people points to two ways that these overall consequences can be understood, and thus to two different versions of the Moderate Principle. So suppose that you have just done Act 1 and are now wondering whether the overall consequences would have been better if you had instead chosen to do Act 2.[3] One method for answering this question focuses exclusively on what I have

---

[3] Strictly speaking, it is not necessary to suppose that you have in fact already chosen Act 1. We can instead suppose that you have not yet decided what to do and are simply picturing how things would stand after you do Act 1 if you do choose to do Act 1. I discuss the relevant issues in what follows in the former terms rather than the latter merely for ease of exposition.

called actual people and does not include the interests of what I have called merely possible people. Since this method excludes the interests of merely possible people, I will refer to the version of the Moderate Principle that employs this method as the exclusive version of the principle. On the method employed by this version of the principle, you consider all and only the people who actually exist at some point given that you did Act 1. Taking the interests of each of those people into account equally, you then ask: would the interests of this particular group of people have been better served if you had instead done Act 2? If the answer to this question is no, then on this exclusive version of the Moderate Principle, the principle generates no objection to your doing Act 1. The idea is that only the interests of those people who actually exist at some point given the choice to perform a particular act are capable of making that act wrong. If the act produces an outcome that is optimal from the point of view of the interests of everyone who will ever exist given that act, then the Moderate Principle, on what I am calling the exclusive version, finds nothing objectionable about the act.[4]

If the answer to the question of whether the interests of the people who actually exist at some point given that you chose Act 1 would have been better served if you had instead done Act 2 is yes, however, then with the exception of a peculiar kind of case to be discussed below, the exclusive version of the Moderate Principle entails that your act was wrong, at least in cases where conditions (a)–(c) of the principle apply. The idea is that if you could have made things better overall for these very people, then it was wrong for you to fail to do so, at least if doing so would have made things much better for them overall, would not have imposed any significant costs on you, and would not have violated anyone's rights. The peculiar kind of exception case arises because, at least given a fairly common assumption to be noted below, there can be cases in which if you do Act 1 it would have been better for the actually existing people if you had done Act 2, but in which if you do Act 2 it would have been better for the actually existing people if you had done Act 1. There may be cases, that is, in which no matter which act you choose, your act will not produce the best results from the point of view of the people who actually exist given your choice. In peculiar cases of this sort, the results of your act will be suboptimal for the people who actually exist no matter what you do, and so the exclusive version of the Moderate Principle directs you to choose the act that will be the least suboptimal. The idea is that if you can't do an optimal act for the people who actually exist, you should at least come as close to doing so as possible.

A second method for identifying the overall consequences of your act takes into account the interests of both actual and merely possible people. Since this second method is more inclusive than the first, I will refer to the version of the Moderate Principle that employs this method as the inclusive version of the principle. On the method employed by the inclusive version of the Moderate Principle, you begin by considering the interests of all and only the people who actually exist given that you did Act 1. You then calculate their total amount of well-being given that you did Act 1. Next,

---

[4] For a similar principle, see Roberts (1998: e.g. 1–2, 6).

you consider the interests of all and only the people who would have existed if you had instead done Act 2. You then calculate the total amount of well-being that this group of people would have enjoyed if you had instead done Act 2. Finally, you determine which total, if either, is greater. If doing Act 1 produces a total that is greater than or equal to the total that would be produced by doing Act 2, then this inclusive version of the Moderate Principle generates no objection to your doing Act 1. If doing Act 1 produces a total that is smaller than the total that would be produced by doing Act 2, then on this version the principle entails that your act was wrong, at least in cases where conditions (a)–(c) of the principle apply. The idea behind the inclusive version of the principle is that the interests of those who do not and will not exist given that an act has been performed must still be considered if they would have existed had the act not been performed.[5]

The difference between the exclusive version of the Moderate Principle and the inclusive version is important because the two versions yield different results in non-identity cases. Perhaps the simplest way to see this is to assign particular values to the various outcomes in the case of Wilma and then to consider what the two versions of the principle would entail about her choice. We are assuming that if Wilma conceives Pebbles rather than Rocks things will go a little bit better for Wilma, but that if she conceives Rocks rather than Pebbles, Rocks will enjoy a great deal more well-being over the course of his life than Pebbles would have enjoyed over the course of her life. And we are assuming that no one else's well-being is affected one way or the other by Wilma's choice. So suppose that Wilma's choice is represented as follows, where Act 1 is the act of conceiving Pebbles now, Act 2 is the act of conceiving Rocks after taking the tiny pill once a day for two months, and the numbers represent the total amount of well-being that each would enjoy as a result of a given act. For purposes of generating some particular numbers, let's assume that on either choice that she makes, Wilma will live for another forty years and enjoy one thousand units of well-being per year, but that she will lose one unit of well-being if she has to take the pill once a day for two months. And let's assume that Pebbles or Rocks would each live for eighty years, but that while Rocks would also enjoy one thousand units of well-being per year, Pebbles would only enjoy seven hundred units per year. As we will see below, the particular numbers we choose won't matter as long as the difference between the outcomes for Wilma is small and the difference between the outcomes for Rocks and for Pebbles is large. But for purposes of illustration, let's suppose that the payoffs work out like this:

Act 1 (conceive now)	Act 2 (conceive in two months)
Wilma: 40,000	Wilma: 39,999
Pebbles: 56,000	Rocks: 80,000

[5] See, e.g., Attfield (2007). The most thorough and compelling attempt to defend a solution to the non-identity problem of this sort that I am aware of is the unpublished Purves (2013).

And let's now apply the two versions of the Moderate Principle and see what they entail about whether or not Wilma's choosing Act 1 was morally wrong.

The exclusive version tells us to focus our attention on the interests of all and only those people who actually exist given that Wilma conceived Pebbles. These people are Wilma, Pebbles, and everyone else in the world. Taking the interests of each of those people into account equally, the exclusive version directs us to ask: would the interests of this particular group of people have been better served if Wilma had instead taken the pill once a day for two months and then conceived Rocks? Since the interests of everyone else who exists are not affected by Wilma's choice, we can answer this question by simply focusing on the interests of Wilma and Pebbles, and by asking whether their interests would have been better served if Wilma had instead conceived Rocks. If the answer to this question is no, then on the exclusive version of the Moderate Principle, the principle generates no objection to Wilma's act of conceiving Pebbles. If the answer is yes, then on the exclusive version of the Moderate Principle, the principle entails that Wilma's act was wrong.

The answer to the question is no. When Wilma conceives Pebbles, Wilma enjoys 40,000 units of well-being and Pebbles enjoys 56,000 units of well-being, for a total of 96,000 units of well-being. If Wilma had instead conceived Rocks, then Wilma would have contributed 39,999 units of well-being to the total, but Pebbles would not have existed and so would not have contributed any units of well-being at all. 39,999 units of well-being is not greater than 96,000 units of well-being. The interests of Wilma and Pebbles combined, that is, where the interest of each is counted equally, would not have been better served if Wilma had conceived Rocks. And so on the exclusive version of the Moderate Principle, the principle does not entail that Wilma's act of conceiving Pebbles is morally wrong.

The inclusive version of the principle, though, tells us to take into account the interests of both actual and merely possible people. These include all the people who exist given that Wilma conceived Pebbles and all the people who would have existed if she had instead waited two months and conceived Rocks. On this version of the Moderate Principle, we compare the total well-being of all and only the people who actually exist given that Wilma conceived Pebbles with the total well-being of all and only the people who would have existed if she had instead conceived Rocks. If the former total is greater than or equal to the latter, then on this inclusive interpretation of the Moderate Principle, the principle generates no objection to Wilma's conceiving Pebbles. If the latter total is significantly greater than the former, then on this inclusive interpretation of the principle, the principle entails that Wilma's act of conceiving Pebbles was morally wrong. Since, as before, the interests of everyone else in the world are not affected by Wilma's choice, we can set their interests to the side and carry out this comparison simply by focusing on Wilma, Pebbles, and Rocks.

The total amount of well-being enjoyed by all the people who actually exist from this group given that Wilma conceived Pebbles is 40,000 units of well-being for Wilma plus 56,000 units of well-being for Pebbles, for a total of 96,000 units of well-being.

The total amount of well-being that would have been enjoyed by all of the people from this group who would have existed if Wilma had instead conceived Rocks is the 39,999 units of well-being that Wilma would have enjoyed plus the 80,000 units of well-being Rocks that would have enjoyed for a total of 119,999 units of well-being. 119,999 is significantly greater than 96,000. So the total amount of well-being would have been significantly greater if Wilma had conceived Rocks than it is given that she instead conceived Pebbles. And so, on the inclusive version of the Moderate Principle, the Moderate Principle entails that Wilma's act of conceiving Pebbles is morally wrong.

The inclusive version of the Moderate Principle entails that Wilma's act of conceiving Pebbles is morally wrong, then, but the exclusive version of the Moderate Principle does not entail this. In order to solve the non-identity problem by rejecting P5 in favor of the Moderate Principle, therefore, it is not enough simply to endorse the Moderate Principle. It is necessary to endorse the inclusive version of the Moderate Principle in particular. And this is precisely where the problems arise.[6]

6.1.2 The Independence Problem

The first problem arises when we ask whether there is a justification for preferring the inclusive version of the Moderate Principle to the exclusive version that is independent of the fact that the inclusive version would enable us to avoid the Implausible Conclusion while the exclusive version would not. If there is no such justification, then a solution to the non-identity problem that appeals to the inclusive version of the Moderate Principle cannot satisfy the independence requirement.

There are two ways that a defender of the inclusive version of the principle might try to provide such a justification. The first maintains that there are good reasons to endorse the Moderate Principle that are independent of the desirability of avoiding the Implausible Conclusion and claims that these reasons for endorsing the Moderate Principle as a general matter provide reasons for endorsing the inclusive version of the principle in particular. The second maintains that there are objections that undermine the exclusive version of the Moderate Principle that do not apply to the inclusive version. I will consider the first approach in the first two subsections below and the second in the subsection after that. I will argue that the first approach fails to provide an independent justification for the inclusive version and, if anything, provides an independent justification for the exclusive version. And I will argue that the second approach fails to point to any real problems with the exclusive version and, if anything, points to some real advantages of it. The result is that we have no good independent reason to favor the inclusive version of the Moderate Principle and, if anything, have some good independent reasons to favor the exclusive version. And since the inclusive version is the one that is needed in order to use the Moderate Principle to solve the non-identity

---

[6] For a related discussion, see Rivka Weinberg (Forthcoming). Narveson (1967) defends a similar position in the context of a more purely utilitarian principle.

problem, this means that a solution to the problem based on endorsing the Moderate Principle will fail to satisfy the independence requirement.

6.1.2.1 THE ARGUMENT FROM IMPARTIALITY

Perhaps the most familiar argument for adopting a consequentialist moral theory is one that appeals to the ideal of impartiality. The basic idea is that from a purely prudential point of view, my happiness is the good that should be pursued, that the moral point of view is the impartial point of view, that from the impartial point of view, my happiness is neither more nor less important than that of anyone else, and that morality therefore tells me to pursue the happiness of everyone with the interest of each person being given the same weight as the interest of any other. This is the sort of argument that is most closely identified with John Stuart Mill.

Suppose, to try to spell the argument out in a bit more detail, that I am currently eating a tasty apple and am enjoying it a great deal. I begin by evaluating the state of affairs in which I am eating the apple as a good one from my own purely prudential point of view. Why, from this point of view, do I take this state of affairs to be a good one? It is not simply in virtue of any intrinsic properties that the experience itself has. If a qualitatively identical experience were being had by some other person, I would not evaluate the state of affairs in which that person was having that experience as good from my own prudential point of view. Rather, I judge the state of affairs in which I am eating the tasty apple as prudentially good both because the experience has certain kinds of features and because the experience stands in a certain kind of relation to a particular person, namely me. What exactly that relation is may be a subject of dispute. It might be because the experience feels good to me, or satisfies a preference of mine, is objectively good for me, and so on. But the basic point remains: from the purely prudential point of view, the experience itself is not good. What is good is that the experience is being had by me.

Let's now suppose that this is correct, and that the moral point of view really is the impartial point of view. In that case, I should ask whether, from the impartial point of view, there is something particularly special about enjoyable experiences being had by me in particular. From the point of view of God, or of the universe, or of the view from nowhere, that is, is it somehow better that the enjoyable experience be had by me than that it be had by you? The answer to this question is clearly no. Even if I care a great deal about my being able to enjoy the tasty experience and not at all about your being able to enjoy it, I must still admit that from a neutral, impartial point of view, it's no more important that my desires be satisfied than that yours be satisfied. And so if it would be imprudent for me to fail to most efficiently promote my own interests, then it would be immoral for me to fail to most efficiently promote the interests of everyone, treating the interests of each as equally important.

Let's now suppose that I find this kind of argument convincing, and that for this reason I at least endorse the Moderate Principle, regardless of whether I also endorse the stronger Act-Consequentialist Principle. The question that arises is whether appealing to the argument from impartiality as a reason for endorsing the Moderate Principle provides me with any reason to adopt the inclusive version of the principle rather than the exclusive version. When I agree that the ideal of impartiality requires me to put as much weight on the interests of everyone else as I put on my own interests, that is, does this mean the interests of everyone who will actually exist given the act that I choose to perform? Or must I also include the interests of those who will never exist given that choice but who would have existed if I had made a different choice? I believe that the argument from impartiality gives us no reason to prefer the latter answer to the former and that a defense of the Moderate Principle that rests on the appeal to impartiality therefore fails to provide a foundation for solving the non-identity problem in a way that can satisfy the independence requirement.

The best way to see why this is so is to begin by considering more carefully the question of why we are so confident that from an impartial point of view I must put as much weight on promoting your interests as I put on promoting my own. There are two kinds of answer to this question, one of which favors the exclusive version of the Moderate Principle and one of which favors the inclusive version, but there is nothing about the merits of viewing the moral point of view as the impartial point of view that justifies selecting either of these answers over the other. As a result, appealing to the argument from impartiality as a means of justifying the Moderate Principle does nothing to justify adopting the inclusive version of the principle in particular, and thus nothing to help solve the non-identity problem.

One answer to the question of why I must put as much weight on promoting your interests as I put on promoting my own interests appeals to the claim that from the moral point of view you are just as important as I am and so are just as entitled to have your interests considered as I am entitled to have my interests considered. Different reasons might be given for this answer. A defense of the answer might appeal to the claim that you are sentient just like I am, for example, or that you have preferences just like I do, or have interests just like I do, or have the same human nature that I have. These different defenses of this first answer differ at the level of detail, but they have a common structure: they identify some property that I have, maintain that the property accounts for the importance of my interests being promoted, note that you have the very same property, and conclude that it is therefore equally important that your interests be promoted. As a result, all of these defenses of the first answer presuppose one basic fact about you: you, like me, exist. And as a result of this, all of these defenses of the first answer entail that I must give equal weight to the interests of the other people who will actually exist given the choice that I make without entailing that I must give any weight at all to the interests of those merely possible people who will never exist but who would have existed had I chosen differently. Merely possible people, after all, will never be sentient, never have preferences, never have interests, and never have a human nature. And so if the reason that I must put as much weight on promoting your interests as I put on promoting my own interests is that from the moral point of view you are just as entitled to have your interests considered as I am entitled to have mine considered, then the argument from impartiality favors the exclusive version of the Moderate Principle over the inclusive version.

A second answer to the question of why I must put as much weight on promoting your interests as I put on promoting my own interests appeals to the claim that from the moral point of view the positive experiences that you would have if your interests were promoted would themselves be just as valuable as the positive experiences that I would have if my interests were promoted. Different reasons might be given for this answer, too. A defense of this second answer might appeal to the claim that your positive experiences would have the quality of being pleasurable, just like mine would, or that they would have the quality of satisfying the preference of the person experiencing them, or of serving the interests of the person having them, or of being objectively good for the person experiencing them, just like mine would. These different defenses of the second answer, too, differ at the level of detail, but as with the different defenses of the first answer, they have a common structure: they identify some property had not by me, but by the positive experiences that I would have if my interests were promoted, maintain that the property that these positive experiences themselves would have accounts for the importance of my interests being promoted, note that any positive experiences that you would have if your interests were promoted would have the very same property, and conclude that it is therefore equally important that your interests be promoted.

The first answer to the question of why I must put as much weight on promoting your interests as I put on promoting my own interests entailed that I must give equal weight to the interests of other actual people without entailing that I must give any weight at all to the interests of merely possible people. But the second answer to this question entails that the interests of actual and merely possible people must both be considered. The positive experiences that the merely possible people would have had if they had come into existence and had their interests promoted, after all, would have had the same qualities that my positive experiences would have if my interests were promoted. While the first answer to the question of why I must put as much weight on promoting your interests as I put on promoting my own interests supports the exclusive version of the Moderate Principle over the inclusive version, then, the second answer supports the inclusive version over the exclusive version.

The ideal of impartiality itself provides no guidance in choosing between these two answers. The person who thinks that he must put as much weight on promoting your interests as he puts on promoting his own interests because he thinks that you are just as important as he is is thinking just as impartially as the person who thinks that he must put as much weight on promoting your interests as he puts on promoting his own interests because he thinks that your positive experiences would be just as valuable as his positive experiences would be. They are each viewing themselves and their experiences impartially. They simply have different substantive beliefs about the foundation of the prudential imperative to promote their own interests. And so viewing themselves and their interests impartially produces different substantive conclusions about the moral significance of merely possible people. The proponent of the first answer believes that the prudential imperative to promote his own interests is grounded in facts about him that make promoting his interests important. It is only because he is sentient, for example, or has preferences, or interests, that it is important to promote his interests. Since from an impartial point of view he recognizes that these facts hold for other actual people but not for merely possible people, the result of his moving from the partial point of view to the impartial point of view is the adoption of the exclusive version of the Moderate Principle. The proponent of the second answer believes that the prudential imperative to promote his own interests is grounded in facts about the positive experiences that he would have if his interests were promoted. Facts about himself are irrelevant on this second view. The fact that the positive experiences that he would have if his interests were promoted would be pleasurable, for example, or would have the quality of satisfying the preference of the person experiencing them, or of serving the interests of the person having them, is enough by itself to ground the imperative that his interests be promoted. Since from an impartial point of view he recognizes that these facts would have held for the positive experiences of merely possible people if they had instead been brought into existence, the result of his moving from the partial point of view to the impartial point of view is the adoption of the inclusive version of the Moderate Principle. So there is nothing about the argument from impartiality itself that favors the inclusive version of the principle over the exclusive version. And since only the inclusive version of the Moderate Principle can be used to solve the non-identity problem, there is nothing about the argument from impartiality that can be used to solve the non-identity problem. Even if we agree that the appeal to impartiality gives us a reason to reject P5 and to embrace the Moderate Principle as a general matter, that is, the argument from impartiality gives us no reason to embrace the inclusive version of the principle that is independent of the fact that doing so would enable us to avoid the Implausible Conclusion.

6.1.2.2 THE ARGUMENT FROM COMMONSENSE MORAL BELIEFS

A second kind of defense of the Moderate Principle arises from the claim that endorsing the principle is necessary in order to account for the commonsense moral judgments that people are likely to make in a variety of cases. This strategy is deployed most famously in Shelly Kagan's 1989 book, *The Limits of Morality*. Consider, for example, the following two cases drawn from Kagan's work:[7]

Drowning Child: A child is drowning in front of you. You can save her life by throwing her a life preserver. If you do throw the life preserver, it will cause you a slight amount of physical exertion and your clothes will get wet. If you do not throw the life preserver, she will die.

Bird or Child: You are fleeing a burning building. On your way out, you come across a child and a caged bird. You can carry one but only one of them out of the building. The one you carry will live. The one you do not carry will die. It would be a little easier for you to carry the bird.

---

[7] Kagan (1989: 3–4; see also 16).

Kagan assumes that virtually everyone will agree that in both cases it would be mor-ally wrong for you not to save the child. And he argues that "the best explanation" of these judgments "involves the acceptance of a standing, pro tanto reason to promote the good."[8] It would be wrong to let the child die in each of these cases, that is, because in each case more good overall will result if you save the child than if you don't. Kagan argues that this pro tanto reason to promote the good provides a "reason. . . to perform an act simply by virtue of the fact that it will lead to a greater amount of good overall," and he clarifies that "the overall good simply is the overall well-being of individual persons." The claim that there is a pro tanto reason to promote the good, that is, "is a convenient way of asserting that there is a pro tanto reason to promote each individual good."[9]

Kagan goes on to argue that there are no legitimate constraints on our promot-ing the overall good and that there are no legitimate considerations that would jus-tify our opting out of promoting it. As a result, the argument of his book as a whole provides a defense not simply of the Moderate Principle, but of the pure, unqualified Act-Consequentialist Principle. For our purposes here, though, we can set aside the distinction between the Moderate Principle and the Act-Consequentialist Principle and treat the argument from commonsense moral beliefs as an argument that is meant to show that at the very least the Moderate Principle is true. And we can then ask the same question of this second approach to justifying the Moderate Principle that we asked of the first: if you are persuaded to adopt the Moderate Principle for the reasons that the argument provides, should you adopt the exclusive version of the principle or the inclusive version? When Kagan says that our reactions to the cases he discusses are best explained by endorsing a pro tanto reason to promote "each individual good," that is, which individuals should be included in our reasoning in order to best explain our intuitive reactions: the individuals who actually exist given the choices that we have made, or those individuals plus the merely possible individuals who in fact do not exist and who will never exist but who would have existed if we had acted differently?

The particular cases that Kagan discusses cannot help to answer this question. In those cases, the same people will actually exist regardless of which choice you make, and so the exclusive version and the inclusive version of the principle will consistently generate the same recommendations. Since there are no merely possible people who will exist if you make one choice but not the other, that is, the act that is better for all of the actual people is also the act that is better for all of the actual plus the merely possible people. As a result, Kagan's cases cannot provide a reason for favoring one version of the Moderate Principle over the other. But while the particular cases that Kagan appeals to cannot be used to assess the relative merits of the two versions of the Moderate Principle, the general technique that the cases represent can nonetheless provide the needed test. We simply have to modify Kagan's cases so that the results of apply-ing the two versions of the principle to them produce different answers. Once we do

[8] Kagan (1989: 17; see also 47, 50).   [9] Kagan (1989: 18, 58, 57).

this, it becomes clear that the reasons that Kagan provides for endorsing the Moderate Principle as a general matter favor the exclusive version of the principle over the inclusive version in particular. And since only the inclusive version could be used to solve the non-identity problem, this shows that if we favor the Moderate Principle, or even the Act-Consequentialist Principle, for the sorts of reasons that Kagan provides, we will again lack an independent justification for endorsing the only version of the principle that could solve the non-identity problem. Indeed, if anything, we will have good independent reason to favor the version of the principle that is clearly unable to solve it.

In order to change Kagan's cases so that they will produce different results depending on which version of the Moderate Principle we apply to them, we must make it the case that one of the choices in each case comes out as acceptable on the exclusive version but not on the inclusive version. We need a case, that is, in which it is possible to do an act and then find that two things are true: that doing the alternative act would not have produced more good overall for all of the people who actually exist given the act that we did, and that doing the alternative act would have produced more good overall for all of the people who would have existed if we had done the alternative act. So consider these two variants on Kagan's original cases:

Drowning Petri Dish: A Petri dish is drowning in front of you. It contains a human sperm and a human egg. You can prevent the Petri dish from drowning by throwing a life preserver at it. If you do throw the life preserver, it will cause you a slight amount of physical exertion and your clothes will get wet, and the sperm and egg will later come together to form a new human being who will live a happy life. If you do not throw the life preserver, the Petri dish will drown, and the sperm and egg will never come together to form a new human being.

Bird or Petri Dish: You are fleeing a burning building. On your way out, you come across a caged bird and a Petri dish. The Petri dish contains a human sperm and a human egg. You can carry one but only one of them out of the building. If you carry the bird out, the bird will live and the sperm and egg will never come together to create a new human being. If you carry the Petri dish out, the bird will die and the sperm and egg will later come together to create a new human being who will live a happy life. It would be a little easier for you to carry the bird.

In these two cases, the exclusive and inclusive versions of the Moderate Principle produce different results. Suppose, to start with the case of the drowning Petri dish, that you decide not to throw the life preserver. In that case, the sperm and egg will never come together to form a person and so the only actual person affected by the choice is you. Since you are a bit better off not throwing the life preserver than throwing it, the exclusive version of the Moderate Principle generates no moral objection to your act: throwing the life preserver would not have been better for the actual people because it would not have been better for you. But if you had thrown the life preserver, then the sperm and egg would later have come together to form a new person and the amount of well-being that that person would have enjoyed over the course of his or her life would have greatly outweighed the slight loss of well-being that you would have incurred by throwing the life preserver. Unlike the exclusive version of the

Moderate Principle, the inclusive version insists that in determining whether it was wrong to have chosen one act over another, we must take into account the interests of any merely possible people who in fact do not exist and who will never exist but who would have existed had the other act been selected. And so on the inclusive version of the Moderate Principle, it turns out that you have done something seriously immoral by failing to save the drowning Petri dish.

The same divergent results arise in the case of the bird and the Petri dish. Suppose that you decide to save the bird. In that case, the sperm and egg in the Petri dish will never come together to form a person and so the only actual person affected by the choice is again you. Since you are a bit better off carrying the bird rather than the Petri dish, the exclusive version of the Moderate Principle generates no moral objection to your act: carrying the Petri dish would not have been better for the actual people because it would not have been better for you. But if you had saved the Petri dish instead of the bird, then the sperm and egg would later have come together to form a new person and the total amount of well-being that that person would have enjoyed over the course of his or her life would have greatly outweighed the slight loss of well-being that you would have incurred by carrying the Petri dish rather than the bird. Unlike the exclusive version of the Moderate Principle, the inclusive version insists that in determining whether it was wrong to have chosen one act over another, we must take into account the interests of any merely possible people who in fact do not exist and who will never exist but who would have existed had the other act been selected. And so on the inclusive version of the Moderate Principle, it again turns out that you have done something seriously immoral by failing to save the Petri dish.

If we have accepted the Moderate Principle because of the argument from commonsense moral beliefs, then we have accepted it because the principle in general best accounts for our judgments in cases like those involving the drowning child and the choice between the bird and child. In order to determine which particular version of the Moderate Principle to accept, we should therefore ask which version best accounts for our judgments in cases like those involving the drowning Petri dish and the choice between the bird and the Petri dish. And the answer to this question is clear. Commonsense morality insists that you make a modest sacrifice when doing so is necessary in order to save the life of an already existing child. But it does not insist that you make a modest sacrifice when doing so is necessary in order to help to bring a new child into existence. Commonsense morality holds that you do nothing wrong if you decline to get your clothes wet in order to save the Petri dish in the first case or if you decide to save the bird rather than the Petri dish in the second case.[10] Since the exclusive

[10] Since my claim about commonsense morality here might seem to overlook the fact that many people believe that a human zygote has a right to life and that many believe that contraception is immoral, it may be worth stressing that there are no zygotes and no sexual activity involved in these two cases. Even most people who are opposed to both contraception and abortion do not think that it is wrong simply to decline to enable a particular sperm and egg to come together to form a new person, any more than they think it is wrong to decline to engage in sexual intercourse. My claim might also be subject to the worry that these are quite unusual cases and that if people were really to think through the implications of the choices involved,

version of the Moderate Principle is consistent with both of these judgments and the inclusive version is consistent with neither of them, the very reason for endorsing the Moderate Principle provided by the argument from commonsense moral beliefs provides a reason to endorse the exclusive version of the principle rather than the inclusive version. And since the exclusive version of the Moderate Principle is unable to solve the non-identity problem, we again arrive at the same conclusion: the sorts of reasons people have for endorsing the Moderate Principle as a general matter fail to provide a reason to endorse the inclusive version of the principle in particular. Indeed, in this case, they provide a strong reason to endorse the exclusive version of the principle. And without a reason to endorse the inclusive version of the principle over the exclusive version that is independent of the fact that endorsing the inclusive version would enable us to avoid the Implausible Conclusion, a solution to the non-identity problem that is based on appealing to the Moderate Principle is unable to satisfy the independence requirement that a successful solution to the problem must satisfy.

6.1.2.3 THE ARGUMENT FROM OBJECTIONS TO THE EXCLUSIVE VERSION

I have argued so far that the reasons people offer in favor of the Moderate Principle as a general matter fail to provide an independent reason to endorse the inclusive version of the principle in particular. A defender of the inclusive version might accept this conclusion but claim that an independent justification can instead be found by identifying an objection that undermines the exclusive version without undermining the inclusive version. I will consider three such arguments here.

One objection maintains that by leaving the interests of merely possible people out of the equation, the exclusive version of the Moderate Principle makes it not only permissible to ignore their interests but obligatory to do so. And this result is clearly unacceptable. Return, for example, to the case of Wilma, who conceived a blind child when she could instead have easily waited two months and conceived an otherwise comparable sighted child. Given that Wilma in fact conceived Pebbles, the exclusive version of the Moderate Principle maintains that Wilma and Pebbles are the only actual people whose interests must be taken into account in evaluating the moral status of her act. From the standpoint of the interests of Wilma and Pebbles, the state of affairs in which she conceives blind Pebbles contains a significantly greater amount of well-being overall than does the state of affairs in which she waits two months and conceives sighted Rocks. It contains a little more well-being from the point of view of Wilma's interests and a great deal more from the point of view of Pebbles's interests. In addition, conceiving Pebbles rather than Rocks imposes no significant cost on Wilma. Conceiving

---

they would agree that the resulting state of affairs would be much better if you were to save the Petri dish. But even if this is so, this judgment is perfectly consistent with the claim that it would not be positively immoral to refrain from bringing about the better state of affairs in these cases and that is all that is needed to show that the argument from commonsense moral beliefs favors the exclusive version of the Moderate Principle over the inclusive version.

Pebbles, in fact, is a bit easier for her. And conceiving Pebbles does not violate anyone's rights.

But the Moderate Principle says that if you are choosing between two acts and the overall consequences of one of the acts would be significantly better, then it would be wrong not to choose the act with the better consequences, at least if you can do so at little cost to yourself and without violating anyone's rights. And this seems to show more than that the exclusive version of the Moderate Principle does not entail that it would be wrong for Wilma to conceive Pebbles. In addition, it seems to show that the principle entails that it would be wrong for Wilma to wait two months and conceive sighted Rocks instead. This is clearly an unacceptable result. So if the exclusive version of the Moderate Principle really does entail it, then this fact provides an extremely strong reason to reject the exclusive version of the principle, a reason that is independent of the fact that the inclusive version would enable us to avoid the Implausible Conclusion. The inclusive version of the Moderate Principle, moreover, clearly avoids this problem, since it maintains that the interests of merely possible people must also be taken into account. When the interests of merely possible people are taken into account, the result is that Wilma's act of conceiving Pebbles is wrong, and since it is wrong, it is clearly not obligatory.

This first objection is based on a misunderstanding of the exclusive version of the Moderate Principle. Given that Wilma chose to conceive Pebbles, it is true that Rocks is not an actual person and that the exclusive version of the principle therefore says that we must ignore his interests in deciding whether the principle entails that Wilma's act was morally wrong. But this does not mean that the exclusive version entails that Wilma would have acted wrongly if she had instead conceived Rocks. If Wilma had conceived Rocks, then Wilma and Rocks would have been the actual people whose interests the exclusive version would have directed us to focus our attention on, and Pebbles would have been a merely possible person whose interests we would then have been directed to ignore. From the point of view of the interests of Wilma and Rocks, moreover, Wilma's conceiving Rocks produces much more well-being overall than does her conceiving Pebbles. It would produce a little bit less well-being from the point of view of Wilma's interests but far more well-being from the point of view of Rocks's interests. Rather than entailing that it would have been wrong for Wilma to conceive Rocks, therefore, the exclusive version of the Moderate Principle entails that it would not have been wrong for Wilma to conceive Rocks. If she conceives Pebbles and not Rocks, this produces the best results for the actual people, and if she conceives Rocks and not Pebbles, this too produces the best results for the actual people. The exclusive version of the Moderate Principle, then, entails that neither act would be wrong. As a result, this first objection to the exclusive version of the principle must be rejected.

This response to the first objection to the exclusive version of the Moderate Principle, however, might seem to generate a second objection. We want our moral principles to be action guiding and if the exclusive version of the principle entails that neither of Wilma's choices would be wrong, then it can't tell Wilma what to do. The inclusive version of the Moderate Principle, moreover, entails that conceiving Rocks is not wrong and that conceiving Pebbles is wrong, so the inclusive version of the principle, unlike the exclusive version, actually tells Wilma what to do. And this might seem to provide an independent reason to favor the inclusive version of the principle over the exclusive version.

While it is true that the inclusive version of the Moderate Principle is action guiding in cases such as that of Wilma while the exclusive version is not, however, this fact does not provide a reason to prefer the inclusive version over the exclusive version. If the exclusive version is correct, after all, then it would not be wrong for Wilma to make either choice. To favor the inclusive version of the principle over the exclusive version on the grounds that the inclusive version rules out one of Wilma's options while the exclusive version does not would therefore simply beg the question against the exclusive version.

A final kind of problem case for the exclusive version of the Moderate Principle arises on the assumption that there are lives that are worse than no life at all. Consider, for example, the case of Joan:

Joan: Joan has a mild preference to find out what it is like to conceive and give birth to a child. Her doctor tells her that if she conceives and gives birth to a child, the child will inevitably suffer an excruciating amount of pain for every moment of its life. Even though Joan would be a bit better off conceiving and giving birth to the child, since doing so would satisfy her mild preference to have the experience, she decides not do to so.

Surely we think that Joan did the right thing in this case. But, this final objection maintains, the exclusive version of the Moderate Principle cannot account for this judgment, while the inclusive version of the principle can. Given that Joan did not conceive the child who would have suffered horribly, she is the only actual person who is affected by her decision. The exclusive version of the principle tells us to focus our attention on the interests of all and only those people who actually exist given that Joan did not conceive the suffering child. These people are Joan and everyone else in the world. Taking the interests of each of those people into account equally, we then ask: would the interests of this particular group of people have been better served if Joan had instead conceived the suffering child? Since the interests of everyone else who exists are not affected by Joan's choice, we can answer this question by simply focusing on the interests of Joan, and asking whether her interests would have been better served if she had instead conceived the suffering child. If the answer to this question is no, then the exclusive version of the Moderate Principle generates no objection to her decision not to conceive. If the answer is yes, then the exclusive version of the principle entails that Joan's decision not to conceive the suffering child was wrong.

Unfortunately for the proponent of the exclusive version of the Moderate Principle, the answer to this question is yes. Joan would, in fact, have been a bit better off if she had conceived the suffering child. It is true, of course, that this would have been much worse from the point of view of the interests of the suffering child himself. But given that Joan did not conceive him, that child is a merely possible person. Since the exclusive version of the Moderate Principle tells us that only the interests of actual people should count, it seems clear that the exclusive version of the principle entails that Joan's decision not to conceive the suffering child was morally wrong. Since it seems just as clear that Joan's decision not to conceive the suffering child was not morally wrong, it seems clear that the exclusive version of the Moderate Principle is unacceptable. The inclusive version of the principle, moreover, tells us to include the interests of possible as well as actual people. Since conceiving the suffering child is much worse for the child and only a little better for Joan, the inclusive version therefore entails that Joan did the right thing by not conceiving the suffering child. And so the case of Joan gives us a strong reason to prefer the inclusive version of the Moderate Principle over the exclusive version, a reason that is independent of the fact that the inclusive version would help us to avoid the Implausible Conclusion.

The case of Joan may initially seem to represent the strongest objection to the exclusive version of the Moderate Principle. But in fact, it can be easily overcome. This is because the case of Joan is one of those peculiar cases in which no matter which act a person chooses, the act will not produce the best results from the point of view of the interests of the people who actually exist given the choice to do the act. If Joan does not conceive, as we have just seen, her choice is not the best from the point of view of the interests of the people who actually exist, namely Joan. But if she does conceive, her choice will also not be the best from the point of view of the interests of the people who actually exist. Suppose, after all, that Joan conceives the suffering child. Let's call the child Job. In that case, Joan and Job will both be actual people. The exclusive version of the Moderate Principle will then tell us to focus our attention on the interests of both of them and to ask whether the interests of this group of people would have been better served if Joan had instead refrained from conceiving Job. On the assumption that Job's life really is considerably worse than no life at all, the answer to this question is yes. From the standpoint of Joan's interests, things are a bit better if she conceives Job, but from the standpoint of Job's interests, things are much better if she does not conceive Job. On the whole, then, from the point of view of the interests of the people who actually exist if Joan conceives Job, things are much better if she does not conceive Job.

Since Joan's act will be suboptimal for the people who actually exist regardless of which act she chooses, the exclusive version of the Moderate Principle directs her to choose the act that will be the least suboptimal. If she chooses not to conceive Job, things will be a little bit worse overall from the point of view of the interests of the people who actually exist, namely Joan, than they would otherwise have been from the point of view of the interests of those particular people. If she chooses to conceive Job, things will be a great deal worse overall from the point of view of the interests of the people who actually exist, namely Joan and Job, than they would otherwise have been from the point of view of the interests of those particular people. And so contrary to initial appearances, the exclusive version of the Moderate Principle does indeed entail that it would be wrong for Joan to conceive Job. This final attempt to provide an independent reason to favor the inclusive version of the principle over the exclusive version therefore proves no more successful than the others. And in the absence of a reason to endorse the inclusive version of the principle that is independent of the fact that doing so would enable us to avoid the Implausible Conclusion, a solution to the non-identity problem that is based on appealing to the Moderate Principle as a reason to reject P5 cannot satisfy the independence requirement.

6.1.3 The Modesty Problem

I have argued so far that a solution to the non-identity problem that is based on the Moderate Principle must appeal to the inclusive version of that principle rather than the exclusive version and that there is no reason to prefer the inclusive version of the principle to the exclusive version that is independent of the fact that doing so would help us to avoid the Implausible Conclusion. If that is correct, then a solution to the problem that is based on the Moderate Principle will fail to satisfy the independence requirement. But let us now suppose that I have been mistaken about this and that there is some independent reason to favor the inclusive version of the Moderate Principle over the exclusive version. Even if this is so, there remains a further problem: the Moderate Principle in general, but especially the inclusive version of the principle in particular, has implications that are more implausible than the Implausible Conclusion. Even if a solution based on the Moderate Principle turned out to satisfy the independence requirement, then, it would still prove unable to satisfy the modesty requirement. Whether the implications of the inclusive version of the Moderate Principle are more implausible than the Implausible Conclusion, of course, depends on two things: how implausible these implications are and how implausible the Implausible Conclusion is. I will defer discussion of the latter question until Chapter 7. Here I will simply attempt to show that there are three kinds of cases in which the inclusive version of the Moderate Principle has implications that I believe will strike most people as extremely implausible.

6.1.3.1 RESCUE CASES

One kind of problem for the Moderate Principle arises in cases in which more than one person is endangered and not all of them can be saved. Since this kind of case does not involve people who will be merely possible given one choice but actual given the other, it poses a problem for both the exclusive and the inclusive version of the principle. Consider, for example, the case of Fred.

Fred: Fred is walking past a lake in which two young boys, Billy and Timmy, are drowning. Billy is near Fred while Timmy is a bit further away. Fred has one life preserver. He can toss the life preserver to Billy, but by the time that Billy is safely ashore, it will be too late for Fred to save Timmy. He can run down the shore and toss the life preserver to Timmy, but by the time that Timmy is safely ashore, it will be too late to run back and save Billy. So Fred can save only one of the two boys. Since he would have to walk a bit further to save Timmy, it would be a bit more convenient for Fred to save Billy. Billy is incurably blind, and Fred knows this. He also knows that Timmy is not blind and that the two boys are otherwise comparable. Fred decides to save Billy rather than Timmy because it is a bit more convenient for him to do so.

Fred must choose between two acts: the act of saving incurably blind Billy and the act of saving sighted Timmy. The overall consequences of Fred's saving Timmy are significantly better than the overall consequences of his saving Billy for precisely the same reason that we are assuming the overall consequences of Wilma's conceiving Rocks are significantly better than the overall consequences of her conceiving Pebbles: blindness results in a significant loss of well-being for those it affects. The cost to Fred of saving Timmy rather than Billy is not significant. It is simply the burden of having to walk a bit further before throwing someone the life preserver. And if Fred were to save Timmy, this would not violate anyone's rights. Although it would be a bit more convenient for Fred to save Billy, Billy has no right that he be saved instead of Timmy, and no one else has a right that would be violated by Fred's saving Timmy. As a result, the Moderate Principle entails that it would be positively immoral for Fred to save Billy. And, more generally, the Moderate Principle entails that it is always wrong to save the life of a blind person when one can instead, with just a little more effort and without violating anyone's rights, save the life of an otherwise comparable sighted person. But this is an extremely implausible implication.

A defender of the Moderate Principle might attempt to render the implication that it is morally wrong for Fred to save Billy less implausible by asking us to consider a modified version of the story in which Billy has a life that is just barely better than no life at all. It seems reasonable to suppose that many people would think that it would be wrong for Fred to save Billy rather than Timmy in this modified version of the story. And a defender of the Moderate Principle might try to exploit this fact by means of a kind of slippery slope argument: if we agree that it would be wrong for Fred to save Billy rather than Timmy when Billy's life is just barely better than no life at all, then it shouldn't seem implausible to think that it would also be wrong for Fred to save Billy rather than Timmy if Billy's life was just barely better than a life that is just barely better than no life at all. And we can repeat this move as many times as necessary until we arrive at the original version of the story in which Billy's life is as good as Timmy's except for the fact that Billy is incurably blind. Since there seems to be no natural dividing point along the continuum between the life that is just barely better than no life at all and the life of a blind person, the defender of the Moderate Principle might therefore conclude, if we agree that it would be wrong for Fred to save Billy rather than Timmy in the case where Billy's life is just barely better than no life at all, then we should also agree that it would be wrong for Fred to save Billy rather than Timmy in the case where Billy is incurably blind. And if it would be wrong for Fred to save Billy in that case, then the fact that the Moderate Principle entails that it would be wrong poses no problem for the principle.

The problem with this response to the case of Fred is that the slippery slope structure it depends on is unacceptable. From the fact, if it is a fact, that it would be wrong for

Fred to save Billy in the variant case and that there is no clear dividing point along the continuum from the variant case to the original case, it does not follow that it would also be wrong for Fred to save Billy in the original case or even that it should seem plausible to think that it would be wrong for him to do so. All that follows is that there is a gray area within which it is difficult to say whether it would be wrong for Fred to save Billy. Consider, for example, a parallel argument about the moral acceptability of favoring the interests of one's own child over those of a stranger's child. Virtually everyone would agree that it would not be wrong for me to choose to prevent my child from suffering a painful experience rather than to prevent a stranger's child from suffering a slightly more painful experience if I could only prevent one of the painful experiences from happening. But virtually everyone would also agree that it would be wrong for me choose to prevent my child from suffering a tiny amount of pain rather than to prevent a stranger's child from suffering a horrific amount of pain. In this case, as in the case of Fred, there is a continuum between the version in which the act seems wrong and the version in which the act does not seem wrong. And in this case, again as in the case of Fred, there seems to be no clear dividing point along the continuum between the two. We cannot identify a precise difference between the amount of pain facing the two children and say that I may favor my child over the stranger's child if and only if the difference in the amount of pain facing them is precisely this amount or less, just as we cannot identify a precise difference between the quality of life of Billy and Timmy and say that Fred may save Billy rather than Timmy if and only if the difference in the quality of life is precisely this amount or less. The slippery slope argument clearly does nothing to make it plausible to think that it would be wrong for me to prevent my child from suffering a painful experience rather than preventing a stranger's child from a suffering slightly more painful experience. In the same way, and for the same reason, it should be clear that the slippery slope argument does nothing to make it plausible to think that it would be wrong for Fred to save blind Billy rather than sighted Timmy. That claim retains its implausibility despite our inability to draw a precise line in related cases. And its implausibility remains a problem for the Moderate Principle.

6.1.3.2 CREATION CASES

Rescue cases like the case of Fred pose a powerful problem for both the inclusive and the exclusive version of the Moderate Principle. In order to solve the non-identity problem, though, only the inclusive version of the principle will do. And there are two further sorts of cases that pose even greater problems for that version of the principle in particular. One kind of case involves the choice between creating a new person and not creating a new person. Consider, for example, the case of Jane:

Jane: Jane has two happy and healthy children and she knows that any additional child she conceives will also be happy and healthy. After spending a great deal of time trying to decide if she wants to have one more child, she finds that she has a slight preference not to have a third child. She determines that the positive and negative consequences of having a third child would be equal for the two children she already has and for everybody else, but that the negative consequences would slightly outweigh the positive consequences for her. As a result, Jane decides not to conceive a third happy and healthy child.

Virtually everyone would agree that Jane has done nothing immoral by declining to conceive a third child under these circumstances. The exclusive version of the Moderate Principle is consistent with this judgment. Taking into account equally the interests of everyone who actually exists given that Jane did not have a third child, her decision produced better results overall than would have been produced by her conceiving a third child. Not conceiving a third child is just as good as conceiving one in terms of the interests of the two children she already has, and not conceiving a third child is a bit better than conceiving one in terms of her own interests. In terms of the overall interests of everyone who actually exists given her choice, then, Jane could not have produced a better outcome than the one she produced by not having a third child. And since she could not have produced a better outcome by this measure, the exclusive version of the Moderate Principle finds no fault with her choice.

But the inclusive version of the Moderate Principle insists that in determining whether it was wrong to have chosen one act over another, we must also take into account the interests of any merely possible people who in fact do not exist and who will never exist but who would have existed had the alternative act been selected. And on this version of the Moderate Principle, it turns out that Jane has done something seriously immoral. If she had conceived a third child, then, while this would have produced slightly less overall well-being for her, it would have produced a great deal more well-being for the child she would have conceived: the entirety of the well-being that would have been contained in that child's life. This means that on the measure offered by the inclusive version of the Moderate Principle, Jane produced an outcome that was significantly worse. Since the overall cost to her of conceiving the third child would not have been significant, moreover, and since conceiving the third child would not have violated anyone's rights, this means that the inclusive version of the Moderate Principle entails that what Jane did by not conceiving a third child was morally wrong.[11] And this, too, is an extremely implausible result.

6.1.3.3 REPLACEMENT CASES

A final kind of problem for the inclusive version of the Moderate Principle arises from cases in which you can produce an overall better state of affairs by choosing to have one person go out of existence so that they can be replaced by a second person who would be significantly better off than the person they would replace. It is relatively simple to construct such cases as a means of raising problems for the pure and unmodified

---

[11] Since Jane's choice makes a difference to the total number of people who exist, it might be thought more appropriate to appeal to average well-being rather than total well-being in this case. If that is so, we can simply stipulate that if Jane were to have a third child, that child would be happier than the average person with the result that the inclusive version of the Moderate Principle would require Jane to conceive the child regardless of whether we appeal to average or total well-being.

Act-Consequentialist Principle. Suppose, for example, that you can either push a button or not push a button and that pushing the button will impose only the trivial cost of a moment's inconvenience on you. If you push the button, a blind person who is already living will be killed and an otherwise comparable sighted person who will otherwise never exist will be created to replace him. Surely it would be wrong to push the button in this case. But now suppose that you refrain from pushing the button. If we follow the inclusive version of the Act-Consequentialist Principle and take into account the interests not just of those who actually exist but also the interests of those who would have existed had you pushed the button, it is clear that the overall results would have been much better if you had pushed the button. And so the inclusive version of pure, unmodified act consequentialism would entail that it is immoral for you to refrain from killing a blind person when killing the blind person would also bring into existence an otherwise comparable sighted person who would not otherwise exist.

This result is surely more implausible than the Implausible Conclusion and so demonstrates that a solution to the non-identity problem that is based on the Act-Consequentialist Principle fails to satisfy the modesty requirement. But while this result follows from the inclusive version of the Act-Consequentialist Principle, it does not follow from the inclusive version of the Moderate Principle. The Moderate Principle says that it is wrong to fail to produce the better outcome at least in cases where producing the better outcome can be done without violating anyone's rights. And killing a blind person in order to replace him with an otherwise comparable sighted person presumably violates the blind person's rights. So the inclusive version of the Moderate Principle does not entail that it would be wrong to refrain from killing the blind person.

While the inclusive version of the Moderate Principle is not vulnerable to simple replacement cases like the button-pushing case, however, such cases can be used as the basis for devising more complicated replacement cases that undermine the inclusive version of the Moderate Principle as well. Consider, for example, the case of Greg.

Greg: Greg and his wife have two children. After spending a great deal of time trying to decide if they want to have one more child, they find that they have a slight preference to have a third child. They know that if they conceive a third child, the child will not be blind. And they plan to conceive that third child tonight. As Greg is walking home at the end of the day, he passes a burning building in which a child is trapped. The child is incurably blind but is otherwise comparable to the child that Greg and his wife plan to conceive tonight. If Greg walks by and does nothing, the child trapped in the burning building will die. If Greg rushes into the burning building, he will save the child's life, but he also knows that he will incur two costs: he will lose a leg due to severe burning, and he will become infertile. Knowing all of this, Greg decides to sacrifice his leg and his fertility in order to save the blind child's life. As a result, the blind child does not die and Greg and his wife do not conceive an otherwise comparable sighted child.

Virtually everyone will agree that Greg's act is not morally wrong. Indeed, most people will want to go considerably further and say that his act is not simply not wrong, but is positively admirable. The exclusive version of the Moderate Principle is consistent with this judgment. Taking into account equally the interests of everyone who actually exists given that Greg saved the blind child's life and did not conceive a third child, his decision produced better results overall than would have been produced by leaving the blind child to die and then going home and conceiving an otherwise comparable sighted child. In terms of the overall interests of everyone who actually exists, then, Greg could not have produced a better outcome. And since he could not have produced a better outcome by this measure, the exclusive version of the Moderate Principle finds no fault with his decision. Indeed, since Greg made a serious sacrifice in order to produce the better outcome for all of the actual people, the exclusive version of the Moderate Principle would not have deemed it wrong for him to have refused to make the sacrifice, and thus helps to motivate the view that his act was above and beyond the call of duty, not just permissible but positively praiseworthy.

But the inclusive version of the Moderate Principle again insists that in determining whether it was wrong to have chosen one act over another, we must also take into account the interests of any merely possible people who in fact do not exist and who will never exist but who would have existed had the other act been selected. And on this version of the Moderate Principle, it turns out that Greg has done something seriously immoral by saving the blind child's life. If Greg had let the blind child die, he would then have gone home and conceived an otherwise comparable sighted child whose life would have contained significantly more well-being than was enjoyed by the blind child whom the sighted child would have replaced. This means that on the measure offered by the inclusive version of the principle, Greg produced an outcome that was significantly worse. The overall cost to Greg of producing the better outcome, moreover, would not have been significant. Indeed, it actually cost him more to produce the worse outcome because saving the blind child's life cost him his leg and his fertility. And producing the better outcome would not have violated anyone's rights. The blind child did not have a right to be rescued by Greg, given that rescuing him required Greg to make such a serious sacrifice. Since Greg would have conceived a sighted child without incurring any significant costs and without violating anyone's rights if he had let the blind child die, it follows that the inclusive version of the Moderate Principle entails that what Greg did by sacrificing his leg and his fertility in order to save the blind child's life was morally wrong. And this strikes me as an extremely implausible result.

Even if one agrees that the Implausible Conclusion is really quite implausible, then, it is difficult to resist the judgment that the implications of the inclusive version of the Moderate Principle are even more implausible. The claim that morality requires Greg to let the blind child die so that he can go home and conceive a sighted child to replace him, for example, is harder to believe than the claim that morality permits Wilma to conceive a blind child rather than a sighted child, even if the latter claim is itself hard to believe. Even if we should reject P5 in favor of the Moderate Principle, then, creation cases like that of Jane and replacement cases like that of Greg show that we should reject P5 in favor of the exclusive version of the principle and not the inclusive version.

This result is important for two reasons. First, the exclusive version of the Moderate Principle can be used to undermine Parfit's defense of what he calls the No Difference

View. The No Difference View is not itself a solution to the non-identity problem, but for those readers who are interested in Parfit's defense of the view, I explain how the exclusive version of the Moderate Principle can be used to undermine Parfit's defense of it in Appendix F. Second, and of more immediate concern, the exclusive version of the Moderate Principle does not entail that Wilma's act of conceiving Pebbles is wrong. The only version of the principle that might prove sufficiently reasonable to satisfy the modesty requirement, then, is too weak to satisfy the robustness requirement. And this provides a reason to reject a solution to the non-identity problem based on the Moderate Principle that is independent of its inability to satisfy the independence requirement. Even if we agree that some version of the Moderate Principle provides a good reason to reject P5, therefore, this reason for rejecting P5 cannot ground a satisfactory solution to the non-identity problem.

6.2 Following a Suboptimal Rule

The Moderate Principle represents one way to try to show that Wilma's act is morally wrong because of its suboptimal consequences without having to depend on the claim that every act with suboptimal consequences is morally wrong. I argued in the previous section that this approach to solving the non-identity problem is unsuccessful. A second way to use the suboptimal consequences of Wilma's act to solve the problem without depending on something as strong as the Act-Consequentialist Principle involves appealing to rule consequentialism. Even if there prove to be isolated circumstances in which better consequences would be produced by punishing an innocent person to deter others or by killing an innocent person as a means of providing organs to save others, for example, it may well seem plausible to suppose that on the whole things would go better if people adopted a general rule that prohibited such practices. The overall long-term costs involved in letting people punish and kill innocent people on a case by case basis whenever doing so seemed to them to produce better consequences might well outweigh any short-term benefits that could be produced in the relatively rare instances in which such acts would truly be beneficial overall. This sort of thinking strikes a number of people as providing good reason to endorse rule consequentialism over act consequentialism. Understood generally, the idea is that an act is morally wrong if it would be prohibited by a rule that would produce the best results if people followed the rule. This formulation leaves room for different understandings of what it means to follow a rule and of whether the test requires that everyone follow it or only that most people follow it. Put in terms of the simple two-option scenario that characterizes non-identity cases, we can put the view in terms of what I will refer to as the Rule-Consequentialist Principle:

RCP: If you are choosing between Act 1 and Act 2, and if the set of rules that would produce the best consequences overall if it were followed requires you to choose Act 2 over Act 1, then it is wrong for you to choose Act 1

There are, of course, some well-known objections to rule consequentialism. But let's suppose that enough has been said to provide a sufficiently independent rationale for accepting the Rule-Consequentialist Principle. If that is so, then the question is whether the principle is robust enough to entail that Wilma's act is morally wrong and modest enough to avoid having implications that are more implausible than the Implausible Conclusion.

It seems plausible to suppose that the Rule-Consequentialist Principle is robust enough to entail that Wilma's act is morally wrong. This is because it seems plausible to suppose that the set of rules that a rule consequentialist would endorse would include a rule like this: "if the choice between conceiving at one time and conceiving at another time makes very little difference in terms of the overall consequences for you but will make a big difference in terms of the overall consequences for the person who is conceived, then it would be wrong to conceive at the time that would be worse in terms of the overall consequences for the person who is conceived." And Wilma's act clearly violates this rule.

It is not quite obvious that a rule consequentialist would endorse this particular rule. If we place enough weight on the value of individual autonomy, we might think that the overall benefit to people of being free to conceive when they want to outweighs the overall benefit of ensuring that the optimal conception choices are always made. In that case, we might instead think that a rule consequentialist should endorse a rule like this: "as long as the person you will conceive will clearly have a life worth living, then you may conceive whenever you please." And Wilma's act does not violate this rule. But let's go ahead and assume that we do not place that much weight on the value of individual autonomy, so that the rule consequentialist really would endorse the rule requiring Wilma to conceive Rocks instead of Pebbles. If that is so, then a solution to the non-identity problem that rejects P5 in favor of the Rule-Consequentialist Principle can satisfy both the independence requirement and the robustness requirement.

The problem, though, is that if autonomy is not valuable enough to grant Wilma the freedom to conceive Pebbles rather than Rocks, then it is not valuable enough to grant Jane the freedom to refrain from conceiving a third child in the case where she has a slight preference not to have another child. And this means that the rule-consequentialist solution is not modest enough to solve the non-identity problem. If the rule consequentialist should endorse the rule that deems Wilma's act immoral, that is, then the rule consequentialist should also endorse a rule like this: "if the choice between conceiving a child and not conceiving a child makes very little difference in terms of the overall consequences for you but will make a big difference in terms of the overall consequences for the person who would be conceived, then it would be wrong to make the choice that is worse in terms of the overall consequences for the person who would be conceived." And Jane violates this rule by declining to conceive a child.

A defender of the rule-consequentialist solution might respond to this problem by claiming that there is an important difference between Wilma and Jane. Wilma is going to conceive a child either way, and so the choice she makes is not going to have a significant impact on her life. But Jane is making a choice about whether to conceive at all, and so the choice she makes is going to have a dramatic impact on her life. Since Jane's choice is so much more important to her than Wilma's choice is to her, the defender of the rule-consequentialist solution might say, it is much more important to protect the autonomy that would enable Jane to choose as she pleases than to protect the autonomy that would enable Wilma to choose as she pleases. In that way, a rule consequentialist could claim that the set of rules that would produce the best consequences overall if it were followed would include a rule requiring Wilma to conceive Rocks rather than Pebbles but would not include a rule requiring Jane to conceive a third child rather than not conceive a third child.

There are several problems with this response. First, the relevant question is not whether one outcome is significantly different from another, but whether one outcome is significantly better or worse than another. If there will be a large difference between two outcomes but the difference itself will matter very little to the person choosing between them, then it should matter very little whether the person is free to choose either option. Second, the fact that Wilma will conceive either way does not mean that her choice will not have a dramatic impact on her life. Her life as the mother of a blind child will be very different from her life as the mother of a sighted child. It is simply that, on the whole, she finds that neither is better or worse than the other for her, with the result that the convenience of conceiving without first taking the pills for two months tips the scales in favor of conceiving Pebbles. If Jane should be free to choose as she pleases because her choice will have a dramatic impact on her life, that is, then Wilma should be free to choose as she pleases because her choice will have a dramatic impact on her life.

Finally, we can change the case of Jane so that the choice between conceiving and not conceiving will not seem so dramatic. Consider, for example, the case of Claire:

Claire: Alan and Barbara have a modest preference to have a child, but would require the services of a surrogate. They would be willing to pay up to $50,000 to have a child, but would prefer having no child to paying more than $50,000. Claire is the only available surrogate. She would be willing to serve as a surrogate for any price over $50,000, but would prefer not serving as a surrogate to being paid $50,000 or less. Alan and Barbara offer Claire $50,000 to serve as their surrogate, and have a very slight preference that Claire accept. Claire has a very slight preference to reject their offer and so she rejects their offer.

If Claire agrees to serve as a surrogate, she will not be responsible for raising and caring for the resulting child. Her decision will have a much smaller impact on her life than the decision that Jane makes will have on her life. Even if we agree that a rule consequentialist should endorse a rule on which people should be free to conceive or not to conceive only when the choice will have a dramatic impact on their life, then, this response will be unavailable in the case of Claire. The rule consequentialist will therefore have to endorse a rule on which women are not permitted to decline to serve as surrogates in cases where they have only a small preference not to serve as surrogates. And that result, too, is an extremely implausible one. In the end, then, the Rule-Consequentialist Principle does not offer a viable means of solving the non-identity problem.[12]

6.3 Violating a Scope-restricted Optimizing Principle

The Moderate Principle and the Rule-Consequentialist Principle represent two ways of trying to use the suboptimal consequences of Wilma's act to solve the non-identity problem without depending on anything as strong as the Act-Consequentialist Principle. I have argued that both of these approaches are unsuccessful. A final way of trying to accomplish the same task is simply to restrict the scope of the optimizing principle that is appealed to so that it applies to cases like that of Wilma but not to other cases where the imperative to maximize might prove to have unacceptable implications. I will call such principles scope-restricted optimizing principles.

One example of such a principle arises from what Parfit calls the Same Number Quality Claim, or Principle Q: "If in either of two outcomes the same number of people would ever live, it would be bad if those who live are worse off, or have a lower quality of life, than those who would have lived."[13] As I noted in section 1.1.3, this principle refers to worseness rather than wrongness. And since the non-identity problem is a problem about wrongness rather than worseness, this principle cannot be used to solve the non-identity problem. But as I also noted in that section, the fact that claims about wrongness and claims about worseness are distinct does not mean that they are unrelated. In particular, it might seem plausible to say that Wilma's act is wrong *because* it makes things worse in the way that the principle describes. So we could modify Principle Q to say: "If in either of two outcomes the same number of people would ever live, it would be morally wrong to select the outcome in which those who live are worse off, or have a lower quality of life, than those who would have lived." And since this principle would be stronger than necessary in the same ways that the Act-Consequentialist Principle was stronger than necessary, we could modify this modified version of Principle Q still further to produce what I will call Principle Q*:

Q*: If in either of two outcomes the same number of people would ever live, it would be morally wrong to select the outcome in which those who live are worse off, or have a lower quality of life, than those who would have lived, at least in cases where the better outcome would be significantly better and where choosing the better outcome would not impose a significant cost on the person making the choice or violate anyone's rights.

---

[12] It may be worth noting that even Tim Mulgan, perhaps the only rule consequentialist who has explicitly attempted to apply this theory to the non-identity problem, concedes that there is no clear reason to suppose that the ideal moral code would include a prohibition on making choices like the one that Wilma makes if it would also allow people who do not wish to conceive to refrain from doing so (2009: 131).

[13] Parfit (1984: 360). Parfit appeals to a similar principle that he calls (3) in (1982: 122): "(3) If the same number of lives would be lived either way, it would be intrinsically worse if those who live are worse off than those who would have lived."

A second example is the principle that Brock has defended as what he calls Principle N:[14]

N: Individuals are morally required not to let any possible child or other dependent person for whose welfare they are responsible experience serious suffering or limited opportunity if they can act so that, without imposing substantial burdens or costs on themselves or others, any alternative possible child or other dependent person for whose welfare they would be responsible will not experience serious suffering or limited opportunity.

Principles of this sort are clearly robust enough to solve at least the same number version of the non-identity problem. It is clear, for example, that Wilma's act violates both Principle Q* and Principle N. And, at least as far as I can see, such principles are sufficiently limited in their scope that they can satisfy the modesty requirement as well. I, at least, cannot think of an example in which either Principle Q* or Principle N has an implication in another context that is more implausible than the Implausible Conclusion.

But there is a reason that such scope-restricted principles manage so easily to satisfy both the robustness requirement and the modesty requirement. The reason is that they are deliberately formulated to do precisely that. There is no rationale for accepting them, that is, other than the fact that accepting them would enable us to avoid the Implausible Conclusion. Indeed, Parfit himself acknowledges this limitation of appealing to such principles when he writes of the Theory X that he has not yet uncovered that "we need Theory X. Only X will explain how Q should be justified."[15] And he is even more explicit about this in the context of an earlier version of the principle when he writes: "If [the principle] is intuitively plausible, and provides objections [to the acts in cases like Wilma and Risky Policy], does it solve the [non-identity problem]? Only superficially. [The principle] merely restates our intuitions."[16] And so appeals to such principles, while intuitively attractive, fail to satisfy the independence requirement that any satisfactory solution to the non-identity problem must satisfy.

6.4 Producing an Intrinsically Bad Result

The fact that Wilma's choice is in some sense suboptimal seems to provide the most natural basis for trying to show that her act is wrong if we assume that it does not wrong anyone. I have argued so far that this approach is unsuccessful. There are, in

---

[14] Brock (1995a: 273). For a slightly modified version of N, see also Buchanan, Brock, Daniels, and Wikler (2000: 249). See also Brock (1995b: 205; 2005: 79–87). A similar suggestion is also made by Glover (2007: 75), Peters (2009: 325), Steinbock (2009: 172, 174; 2011: 90), and Hammond (2010: 164). See also Peters (2004: 31), McBrayer (2008: 304–5), DeGrazia (2009: 1234), and Dudley (2010: 350). Garraid and Wilkinson (2006) propose a modified version of Parfit's Principle Q that is designed to avoid entailing that it would be wrong to conceive a typical child rather than one with above average abilities.

[15] Parfit (1984: 364).

[16] Parfit (1982: 1213). Wasserman also notes this problem in the context of Principle N (2005: 139–40). Another similar principle is what Savulescu calls the Principle of Procreative Beneficence: "couples (or single reproducers) should select the child, of the possible children they could have, who is expected to have the best life, or at least as good a life as the others, based on the relevant, available information" (2001: 415). But

addition, a few ways that one might try to show that her act is wrong without wronging anyone that do not depend on the claim that her act is suboptimal in any sense at all. One further feature of Wilma's act is simply that it results in the existence of a person with a significant disability. In order to avoid the Implausible Conclusion by rejecting P5, therefore, we could treat the existence of a significant disability as an intrinsically bad thing and maintain that Wilma's act is wrong because it causes this intrinsically bad thing to exist. Kavka, for example, proposes that we can solve the problem, at least in a good number of cases, by appealing in part to some version of a principle on which "conditions of society or the world are intrinsically undesirable from a moral point of view to the extent that they involve people living restricted lives" where this means living "a life that is significantly deficient in one or more of the major respects that generally make human lives valuable and worth living."[17] We could reject P5, in short, by appealing to what I will call the Intrinsic Badness Principle:

IBP: If you are choosing between Act 1 and Act 2, and if choosing Act 1 would result in something intrinsically bad existing and choosing Act 2 would not, then it is wrong for you to choose Act 1

Accepting the Intrinsic Badness Principle would indeed permit us to reject P5. Acts could be wrong without wronging anyone by causing intrinsically bad things to exist. And on the assumption that there is something intrinsically bad about the world containing people living what Kavka calls "restricted lives," it would also provide a robust enough rejection of P5 to entail that Wilma's act is wrong.

Savulescu, too, offers no reason for accepting his principle other than the fact that doing so would enable us to avoid the Implausible Conclusion: "If we object to [an act like choosing the risky policy in the case of the wealthy society] (which most of us would), then we must appeal to some form of harmless wrong-doing. That is, we must claim that a wrong was done, but no one was harmed. We must appeal to something like the Principle of Procreative Beneficence" (2001: 418). The same problem arises for the defense of a slightly modified version of the principle in Savulescu and Kahane (2009: 274, 277). See also Elster (2011) for a defense of a more impersonal variant of the principle. Bennett (Forthcoming) also notes that Savulescu fails to provide an independent argument for his principle. For additional objections to the principle, see de Melo-Martin (2004), Parker (2007), Stoller (2008), Herissone-Kelly (2009), and Bennett (2009) (though see also Herissone-Kelly (2012) for objections to Bennett's objections).

[17] Kavka (1982: 105). Similarly, Feinberg writes of a woman in a case like that of Wilma that she "must be blamed for wantonly introducing a certain evil into the world, not for harming, or for violating the rights of, a person" (1987: 169). Brock (1995) tentatively puts forth a similar proposal in terms of the notion of "limited opportunity" and Huseby has more recently defended the same basic approach by appealing to a form of sufficientarianism on which it is morally bad if a person is not sufficiently well off even if that person's life is well worth living (2010: 205–10). See also Rivera-Lopez (2009) for another variant on this approach. All of these versions of the view are subject to the same basic problems that I raise in the text for Kavka's version in particular.

As noted in section 5.3.1, Kavka also appeals to a modified version of the categorical imperative that "would forbid treating rational beings *or their creation* (that is, their being brought into existence) as a means only, rather than as ends in themselves" as a means of rejecting P5 (1982: 110). But while Kavka characterizes this second principle as "independent" of the first, it in fact works to solve the non-identity problem only if the first principle does. The modified version of the categorical imperative is designed to block "the attempt to justify (or excuse) acts whose immorality would otherwise be evident *because* they lead to the creation of restricted lives, on the grounds that those created are benefited (or not harmed)" (1982: 110–11, emphasis added). It can therefore succeed only if the fact that an act involves the creation of a restricted life is, indeed, a

But if this kind of approach to rejecting P5 is strong enough to satisfy the robustness requirement, it will surely be too strong to satisfy the modesty requirement. The claim that there is something intrinsically bad about the world containing blind people is itself extremely implausible. It entails that every time a blind person is born, the world becomes a worse place, that it would have been better, from the moral point of view, if such people had never existed. This is extremely hard to believe.[18] And the conjunction of this claim with the Intrinsic Badness Principle produces results that are even harder to believe. Suppose, for example, that Wilma's choice had been between conceiving Pebbles and conceiving no one at all. The principle would entail that even in that case it would have been morally wrong for Wilma to conceive Pebbles. It is hard to believe that it would be worse to conceive a blind child than to conceive no child at all, and even harder to believe that doing so would be positively immoral.[19] And, for that matter, the principle would entail that it would be morally wrong to save the life of a blind person since the result of doing so would be intrinsically worse than the result of not doing so. Appealing to the alleged intrinsic badness of the existence of disabled lives, then, gets us no closer to a satisfactory solution to the non-identity problem. If anything, it seems to push us further away from such a solution.

6.5 Wronging a Group

Some people find it plausible to suppose that certain groups can have rights or interests that are not reducible to the rights or interests of the individuals who constitute the groups. A particular culture, for example, might have a right not to be harmed by a particular act even if the act that would harm the culture would not harm or violate the rights of any of the individual members of the culture. If this is so, then an act might be

---

sufficient reason to deem the act immoral, and this is what the first principle maintains. If, as I suggest above, Kavka's first principle is unsuccessful, therefore, so too is the second.

[18] Parfit notes this in response to Kavka (1982: 121).

[19] Rivera-Lopez (2009) positively embraces this implication of his position and seems to be one of the very few people who has explicitly argued that it would be wrong for a woman to conceive a blind child even if the alternative is conceiving no child at all, at least in cases where she has only a mild preference for conceiving. But his argument for this highly counterintuitive claim is unconvincing. Rivera-Lopez argues that accepting the claim is necessary in order to account for the wrongness of choosing to conceive a disabled child when one could instead have easily conceived that very same child without the disability. In response to the natural alternative explanation which maintains that conceiving a disabled child in that kind of case would be wrong because it would harm that child by making that child worse off than he would otherwise have been—an explanation that does not imply that it is wrong to conceive a disabled child when the alternative is conceiving no child at all—Rivera-Lopez maintains that this alternative explanation must be rejected because it implies that it would also be wrong to choose to conceive a typical child if one could instead have conceived that very same child with some kind of enhancement (such as increased immunity to disease or higher than average IQ) that would have led it to enjoy a higher quality of life (2009: 342–7).

This argument depends on the assumption that it is not wrong to deprive a child of, say, increased immunity to disease, when one could easily have provided it. But this assumption strikes me as far less plausible than the claim that it is wrong to conceive a disabled child when the alternative is conceiving no child at all. Rather than taking his argument as a whole to establish that the latter claim is true, then, it is more reasonable to take it as establishing that the former claim is false.

wrong not because it wrongs any particular individual but because it wrongs a group of individuals. And if this is so, then we might be able to solve the non-identity problem by appealing to the rights of groups.

Page offers one kind of consideration in defense of this holistic group rights approach: we are inclined to think that the death of all of the members of a particular community is worse than the death of a comparable number of individuals scattered across a large number of communities.[20] This suggests that we do think that a human culture has a kind of value above and beyond the value of its individual members. And he argues that this approach can be used to solve the non-identity problem, at least in a certain range of cases. Page gives an example based on a particular kind of concern that has recently arisen in the literature on global warming.[21] Suppose that there is a small Pacific island nation with its own distinctive culture. If we curb our carbon emissions now, then at the end of this century, there will still be many people living on the island and their distinctive cultural traditions will continue to flourish. If we do not curb our carbon emissions now, then over the course of the next several decades, global warming will cause the sea level to rise to the point where much of the Pacific island will be submerged or rendered uninhabitable. By the end of the century there will be an entirely different set of people living on the island, and their lives will still clearly be worth living, but as a result of population displacement and other effects of the rising sea level, most of their cultural practices will have been abandoned.

In this kind of case, at least, Page argues that our failing to reduce carbon emissions could be wrong even if it neither wrongs nor harms any of the resulting Pacific islanders on the grounds that it harms the Pacific islanders' culture. Edith Brown Weiss, moreover, has argued that each generation can itself be understood as a group with its own rights that can be claimed against other generations, and this claim would extend the range of cases in which the group rights approach could solve the non-identity problem beyond those in which particular cultures are damaged or destroyed.[22] Any policy that made a given future generation worse off than that generation would otherwise have been would harm that group, and thus possibly wrong it, even if it neither harmed nor wronged any of its individual members. Even on this broader view, the holistic group rights account cannot be used to solve the direct version of the non-identity problem, since cases like that of Wilma do not involve choices that harm identifiable groups of any sort. But it is still worth asking whether the approach can offer a satisfactory solution to the indirect version of the problem or at least to some subset of that version.

The answer is that it cannot, and for two reasons. The first is that the holistic group rights solution fails to satisfy the independence requirement. We lack a good reason for attributing rights to such groups, that is, other than the fact that doing so might enable

---

[20] Page (2006: 153, 157).   [21] Page (2006: 154).

[22] Weiss (1990: 203–5). See also Page (1999), Kramer (2001: 56), and Slobodian (2012).

us to solve some versions of the non-identity problem. Page points to the fact that we tend to think the death of all of the members of a community is worse than the death of a comparable number of individuals scattered across a large number of communities. But the claim that the former outcome would be worse than the latter outcome does not support the claim that the community has any rights above and beyond the rights of the individuals. If two ships were sinking and one contained all the remaining members of a particular community while the other contained a comparable number of individuals belonging to a wide range of communities, for example, it might well be worse if the former ship sank than if the latter ship sank, but it is hard to believe that the former ship would therefore have a right to be saved ahead of the latter ship if one but not both ships could be saved, that saving the latter ship rather than the former ship would be positively impermissible under such circumstances.

Even if an independent reason is discovered for thinking that we would violate the rights of the Pacific islander culture by failing to curb our carbon emissions in Page's example, moreover, there is a second and more fundamental reason for rejecting his solution to the problem in such cases. The reason is that his solution is not capable of satisfying the robustness requirement. That this is so can perhaps best be seen by first distinguishing between two versions of the Pacific islanders case. On one version, the islanders who will exist if we do not curb our carbon emissions will be just as well off as the islanders who will exist if we do curb our carbon emissions, even though their culture will be seriously damaged in the former case but not in the latter. On a second version, the islanders who will exist if we do not curb our carbon emissions will be significantly worse off than the islanders who will exist if we do curb our carbon emissions.

On the first version of the example, the claim that the culture has a right not to be harmed might help to establish that it would be wrong for us not to curb our carbon emissions. But establishing that it would be wrong for us not to curb our carbon emissions on this version of the example would do nothing to help us avoid the Implausible Conclusion. The Implausible Conclusion, after all, is about cases where our choice results in there being significantly less human well-being than there would otherwise have been. On the second version of the example, the islanders who will exist if we do not curb our carbon emissions will be significantly worse off than the islanders who will exist if we do curb our carbon emissions. The Implausible Conclusion says that it would not be wrong for us to refrain from reducing our carbon emissions in this case. And so it might seem that the reason for rejecting P5 that is provided by the holistic rights account is strong enough to help us to avoid the Implausible Conclusion on this second construal of the case.

But what the Implausible Conclusion on this second construal of the case really says is that it would not be wrong for us to refrain from reducing our carbon emissions regardless of whether our refraining from doing so would harm another culture. On this second version of the case, after all, the claim that our failing to reduce carbon emissions is not wrong seems implausible regardless of whether our failure will have a negative impact on the islanders' culture. The fact that the level of human well-being will be so much lower if we fail to reduce our carbon emissions seems to be enough by itself to render our behavior wrong. As I argued in section 1.3.2, in order to satisfy the robustness requirement, a reason for rejecting a given premise of the non-identity argument must be a good enough reason to reject the Implausible Conclusion itself, not merely to reject a qualified version of the Implausible Conclusion that adds a further fact about a case and then uses that further fact to show that the act in question would be morally wrong. Since the reason for rejecting P5 that is based on the existence of group rights can be used to show that our making things worse for future generations would be wrong only in cases where our doing so would harm some culture, the solution that is based on appealing to this reason cannot satisfy the robustness requirement. And so, on either version of the case, the holistic group rights approach fails to satisfy the robustness requirement.

6.6 Acting from a Defective Character

Some people find it plausible to suppose that an act can be wrong because it manifests an objectionable character trait in the person who performs the act even if the act itself does not wrong anyone. This virtue ethics approach represents yet another way in which we could try to solve the non-identity problem by rejecting P5 without having to appeal to the claim that the consequences of Wilma's act are in some way suboptimal. Valentina Urbanek, for example, has argued that an act of the sort that Wilma performs is wrong because it "exemplifies a bad character, the character of someone who is insensitive to suffering."[23] If we construe suffering broadly to include living with a disability and not just experiencing physical or psychological pain, we can say that there is a significant difference between the amount of suffering that will occur if Wilma conceives now and the amount of suffering that will occur if Wilma takes the pill once a day for two months before conceiving, and that Wilma's act is insensitive to the suffering of others because she makes the choice that will result in a significantly greater amount of suffering among other people simply in order to avoid a minor inconvenience to herself. This virtue-based solution to the non-identity problem ultimately rests on three claims: that an act is morally wrong if it exemplifies a bad character trait, that Wilma's act exemplifies the character trait of insensitivity to the

---

[23] Urbanek (2010: 143). See also McDougall (2005), Wasserman (2005; 2009), McDougall (2007), Stoller (2008: 367–8), Davis (2008: 266–8), Heyd (2009: 16–17), DeGrazia (2012: 181, 186), and Delaney (2012: 25). Kahane (2009) defends a related position with respect to parents who deliberately choose to conceive a disabled child because the child will be disabled. I am inclined to think that his position is untenable for the same reasons I provide here in the context of the virtue-based approach. But even if I am mistaken about this, and as Kahane himself acknowledges, his argument will not solve the non-identity problem in cases like that of Wilma (let alone like that of the wealthy society).

suffering of others, and that the character trait of insensitivity to the suffering of others is a bad one.[24]

There is certainly room for doubt about the first claim. There seems to be an important difference between judging an action and judging the person who performs the action. It seems plausible to say that an action might be objectively wrong even if the person who performs the act does so for admirable reasons and that an action might be objectively right even if the person who performs the act does so for objectionable reasons. It therefore seems reasonable to say that Wilma's insensitivity to the suffering of others might reflect badly on her as a person but that it can do nothing to account for the presumed wrongness of her action. And since the Implausible Conclusion claims that Wilma's act is not morally wrong but does not claim that Wilma is not a bad person, this assessment would render the solution based on the virtue-based approach incapable of satisfying the robustness requirement.

But let's suppose that the first claim made by the virtue-based solution is correct and that an act is morally wrong if it exemplifies a bad character trait. Even if this is so, the virtue-based approach will still be unable to solve the non-identity problem. The reason for this can best be seen after drawing two distinctions. The first is a distinction between two kinds of suffering. One kind is suffering that is caused by an act that makes the sufferer worse off than he would otherwise have been. Ordinary cases of suffering fall into this category. If I hit you in the face, or kick you in the shin, or chop off your arm, the pain that you suffer is caused by an act that makes you worse off than you would have been had I not done the act. I will refer to this kind of suffering as harmful suffering. The other kind is suffering that is caused by an act that does not make the sufferer worse off than he would otherwise have been. Cases of preventing greater suffering fall into this category. If a doctor gives you a painful shot to protect you from a terrible disease or amputates your arm to prevent you from dying, the pain or disability that you suffer is caused by an act that makes you better off than you would have been had she not done the act. Procreative cases also fall into this category. If a woman conceives a blind child, the blindness that the child suffers is caused by an act that does not make the child worse off than the child would otherwise have been since the child would otherwise not have existed. I will refer to suffering of the sort that occurs in these cases as harmless suffering.

The second distinction is between two kinds of insensitivity to the suffering of others. One kind of insensitivity extends to both harmless suffering and harmful suffering. When choosing between causing a significantly greater amount of suffering to others and incurring a minor inconvenience to himself, a person who is insensitive to the suffering of others in this sense will put more weight on his trivial inconvenience than on the significant suffering of others regardless of whether their suffering would

---

[24] Insensitivity to one's own suffering might also be viewed as a character flaw. But since claiming that such insensitivity is bad is not necessary in order to generate the virtue-based objection to Wilma's choice, I restrict the claim to the view that insensitivity to the suffering of others is a bad character trait.

be harmless or harmful. I will refer to this kind of insensitivity as unrestricted insensitivity to the suffering of others. The other kind of insensitivity is limited to cases of harmless suffering. When choosing between causing a significantly greater amount of suffering to others and incurring a minor inconvenience to himself, a person who is insensitive to the suffering of others in this sense will put more weight on his trivial inconvenience than on the significant suffering of others in cases where their suffering would be harmless, but will put more weight on the significant suffering of others than on his trivial inconvenience in cases where their suffering would be harmful. I will refer to this kind of insensitivity as restricted insensitivity to the suffering of others.

With these two distinctions in mind, we can now see why the virtue-based approach cannot solve the non-identity problem. The virtue-based argument appeals to the claim that Wilma's act exemplifies the character trait of insensitivity to the suffering of others and the claim that the character trait of insensitivity to the suffering of others is a bad one. But in which sense of insensitivity to the suffering of others are these two claims supposed to be true? There are two possibilities, and neither generates a satisfactory solution to the non-identity problem.

Suppose first that the claim is that Wilma's act reveals an unrestricted form of insensitivity to the suffering of others. On this supposition, Wilma would choose blindness for her child over a minor inconvenience to herself regardless of whether the blindness in her child would be a harmless form of suffering or a harmful form of suffering. She would conceive a blind child rather than a different sighted child if doing so would be a bit more convenient for her, for example, but if she gave birth to a sighted child, she would also decline to prevent that child from later becoming blind if declining to do so would be a bit more convenient for her. This seems to be what Urbanek has in mind by insensitivity to the suffering of others. She claims as a merit of her position that it entails that conceiving a blind child rather than a sighted child and refraining from preventing a sighted child from becoming blind are equally wrong and wrong for the same reason.[25] And her account produces this result only if it appeals to the unrestricted form of insensitivity to the suffering of others.

If the claim is that Wilma's act betrays an unrestricted form of insensitivity to the suffering of others, then it should prove uncontroversial to say that the character that she reveals is a bad one. But the claim that Wilma's act reveals an unrestricted form of insensitivity to the suffering of others is false. The fact that Wilma would be willing to conceive a blind child rather than a different sighted child in order to avoid a mild inconvenience to herself provides no evidence that she would also be willing to allow an already existing sighted child to become blind even if it would cost her a great deal to prevent the blindness. In choosing to conceive a blind child rather than a different sighted child, after all, Wilma could well be moved by the fact that conceiving the blind child would not harm that child or anyone else. Since permitting an already existing

---

[25] Urbanek (2010: 145). In her case of Mary, the child has not yet been born, but this does not affect the point here.

sighted child to become blind would significantly harm that child, the character trait that would lead her to conceive a blind child rather than a different sighted child would not lead her to allow an already existing sighted child to become blind. The virtue-based approach, therefore, cannot solve the non-identity problem by appealing to the claim that Wilma's act reveals an unrestricted form of insensitivity to the suffering of others.

Suppose instead that the claim is that Wilma's act reveals the restricted form of insensitivity to the suffering of others. On this supposition, Wilma would choose blindness for her child over a minor inconvenience to herself in the case where the blindness in her child would represent a harmless form of suffering, but she would not do so in the case where the blindness in her child would be a harmful form of suffering. Since Wilma chooses to conceive a blind child now rather than wait two months and conceive a different sighted child, the claim that her act reveals her character to involve at least this restricted form of insensitivity to the suffering of others is clearly true. But if this is what is meant by the claim that Wilma's act reveals insensitivity to the suffering of others, then the claim that this character trait is an objectionable one is no longer uncontroversial. We need a reason to believe that it is bad to be the sort of person who is insensitive to the harmless suffering of others.

The one plausible reason to believe that restricted insensitivity to the suffering of others is bad is that a person who is insensitive to the suffering of others in this restricted sense is the kind of person who would choose to conceive a blind child rather than a sighted child merely out of convenience. Since making such a choice would be morally wrong, on this account, it would be bad to have the kind of character that would dispose one to making it. It does seem wrong to conceive a blind child rather than a sighted child merely out of convenience. And so this does seem to provide a good reason to believe that restricted insensitivity to the suffering of others is a bad character trait. But it is a good reason to believe that restricted insensitivity is bad only if we have an independent reason to believe that conceiving the blind child rather than the sighted child would be morally wrong in the first place. And this is precisely why a defender of the virtue-based account cannot appeal to this reason. The virtue-based account attempts to show that conceiving the blind child rather than the sighted child would be wrong because it reveals a certain kind of character. If the certain kind of character is bad because it would dispose people to conceive the blind child rather than the sighted child, then the account will be circular and vacuous. The virtue-based approach cannot solve the non-identity problem by appealing to the claim that Wilma's act reveals a restricted form of insensitivity to the suffering of others, then, because we have no reason to believe that this character trait is bad that is independent of our belief that Wilma's act is morally wrong.

In the end, then, the virtue-based solution to the non-identity problem is impaled on the horns of a dilemma.[26] If it depends on the claim that Wilma's act involves

---

[26] The same dilemma undermines the similar but distinct solution offered by Lotz. Lotz argues that "[t]o manifest an indifference to introducing avoidable suffering into one's community, is to show a lack of respect

unrestricted insensitivity to the suffering of others, then it will fail to satisfy the robustness requirement. The Implausible Conclusion says that Wilma's act is wrong regardless of whether she acts from a restricted or unrestricted form of insensitivity to the suffering of others, and a solution that appeals to the badness of the unrestricted form of insensitivity cannot be used to overturn this judgment. If the solution appeals to the claim that Wilma's act involves restricted insensitivity to the suffering of others, then it will fail to satisfy the independence requirement. We have no reason to believe that restricted insensitivity to the suffering of others is a bad character trait that is independent of our belief that Wilma's act is morally wrong. And so, on either account, even if we agree that P5 is false because an act can be wrong merely because it reflects or exemplifies a bad character trait, the virtue-based approach will fail to provide a satisfactory solution to the non-identity problem.

There are still further kinds of cases that can be used to raise problems for P5. Suppose, for example, that I think I see a human being standing by the side of the road and that because I think that what I see is a human being, I point my gun at what I see and pull the trigger. And suppose that what I see turns out instead to be a mannequin. In that case, it seems plausible to say that my act was morally wrong even though no particular person was wronged by it. But while cases of this sort can plausibly be construed as counterexamples to P5, they can't get us far in solving the non-identity problem. If P5 is mistaken because it overlooks acts that involve trying unsuccessfully to wrong someone, after all, we can simply modify the previous premises to make explicit the fact that Wilma's act neither wrongs anyone nor involves trying to wrong anyone. Alternatives to P5 of this sort, that is, will be modest enough to avoid generating implausible conclusions but not robust enough to entail that Wilma's act is wrong. In the end, then, we seem to be stuck with the same conclusion about P5 that we have reached about all of the other premises of the non-identity argument: it may not be true, but for purposes of generating the non-identity problem, it is true enough.

---

for the community itself" (2011: 112). It is clear why this might be so in the case of avoidable harmful suffering, but Wilma's act does not manifest an indifference to suffering in this sense. Her act does manifest an indifference to introducing avoidable suffering that is harmless both to the person conceived and to everyone else, but there is no reason to think that this sort of indifference shows a lack of respect to the community since it limits the introduction of such suffering to cases in which no one in the community will be adversely affected by it.

7

Accepting the Conclusion

The non-identity problem arises from the fact that five premises that seem plausible entail a conclusion that seems implausible. The most natural way to try to resolve this problem is to reject one of the premises of the argument that gives rise to it. Virtually everyone who has tried to solve the non-identity problem has tried to solve the problem in this way. In Chapter 1, I argued that in order to solve the problem in this way, one must provide a reason for rejecting a particular premise that satisfies what I called the independence requirement, the robustness requirement, and the modesty requirement. In Chapters 2–6, I surveyed the various reasons that seem to be available for rejecting each of the premises, and concluded that none of them satisfies all three of these requirements. If I have been correct about this, then we have no way to justify rejecting the Implausible Conclusion without being stuck with other conclusions that are even more implausible.

Let's now suppose that I have been correct about this. Does this mean that we cannot solve the non-identity problem? It does not. It simply means that we cannot solve the problem by rejecting one of the premises of the argument that gives rise to it. But there is a second way that we can solve the problem. We can solve the problem by accepting the argument's conclusion. If we accept the Implausible Conclusion, after all, then the fact that the five premises of the non-identity argument entail it will no longer give rise to a problem. The non-identity argument will remain but the non-identity problem will not. Virtually no one who has tried to solve the non-identity problem has tried to solve the problem in this way. And of the very few who have, almost none have provided any independent reasons to believe that accepting the Implausible Conclusion is more plausible than the alternative and none at all has done so in a detailed and systematic way.[1] But I want to argue in this final chapter that this is precisely how we should solve the non-identity problem.

In some instances, responding to the difficulty of refuting a particular argument by simply accepting the argument's conclusion is plainly unreasonable. If you are unable

---

[1] The very few philosophers who have explicitly endorsed this kind of solution include Schwartz (1978; 1979: 181–6), Heyd (1988; 1992), and Roberts (1998; 2007: 272; 2009: 202, 209–10), and it also seems implicit in Wasserman (2005; 2009). But as I argue in this chapter, a solution to the non-identity problem that involves accepting the Implausible Conclusion must do something to justify accepting the conclusion

to detect any flaws in one of Zeno's paradoxes of motion, for example, it is more reasonable for you to conclude that the argument contains a flaw that you have overlooked than to conclude that motion is impossible. In many other cases, though, it is more reasonable to accept an argument's conclusion than to continue to reject it if after subjecting the argument to sustained critical scrutiny no independent grounds for rejecting the argument are uncovered. Many people, for example, find the claim that a six-week-old human fetus has the same right to life that a typical adult human being has to be extremely implausible. Many have the same reaction to the claim that

beyond appealing to the fact that doing so will solve the problem. In particular, it must do something to help us see that the conclusion is not as implausible as it at first seems. Neither Schwartz nor Heyd do this at all. Schwartz endorses the Implausible Conclusion but does nothing to respond to the objection that the conclusion is objectionably counterintuitive (see also Crespi (2007, 2008)). Heyd does argue that a variety of empirical facts "can remove the sting of repugnance from many of the hypothetical counterintuitive conclusions" that arise if one accepts all of the premises of the non-identity argument (1992: 195; see also 1992: 15, 79, 209). But this shows only that we can generally avoid endorsing the Implausible Conclusion *in practice*, since P3 will generally be false in the world as it is. It does nothing to remove the apparent implausibility of insisting that the conclusion is true in those cases in which P3 is assumed to be true (McMahan (1994: 557) notes this problem with Heyd's position). In addition, Heyd's version of the kind of solution that I endorse in this chapter rests on the claim that choices like the one that Wilma faces lie outside the realm of ethics altogether and in a separate "nonmoral sphere of deliberation" (1992: 66; see also 1992: 23, 25, 64, 70, 76, 82, 88, 126, and 1988: 152). But the claim that Wilma's act lies outside the scope of moral evaluation altogether strikes me as highly implausible, and the version of the solution that I defend in this chapter does not depend on it.

Roberts acknowledges that the Implausible Conclusion strikes many people as implausible, but for the most part she responds to this fact by simply reporting that her own intuitions are different (e.g.: "Here my own intuitions are quite distinct from Parfit's. . . I do not see at any intuitive level that any wrong has been done" (1998: 28; for similar passages, see also 1998: 29, 99, 100, 101, 110, 111, 112), or by asserting that once we really see that no one is harmed in a genuine non-identity case, "any sentiment that we might have that the couple's choice is wrong will itself begin to fade" (2009: 210). At a few points, though, Roberts does very briefly try to justify the claim that we should not think of the Implausible Conclusion as being so implausible by comparing it to other cases where it seems plausible to say that a particular act would not be wrong (1998: 98, 116). As far as I am aware, these few scattered remarks in Roberts's book are the closest that anyone has come to providing a sustained substantive defense of the sort of solution that I offer in this chapter (though see also Greene and Augello (2011: 134–7) for an example that parallels the example I offer below in section 7.4. I was not aware of their article until after I completed a full draft of the manuscript for this book, but the four pages of their article in which they discuss their example may well be the closest thing to a partial defense of my solution that has thus far been published). Häyry (2004: 511) also makes a very brief gesture in the same general direction.

One other philosopher who has endorsed accepting the Implausible Conclusion is Hull, although Hull maintains that while an act such as Wilma's is not wrong, it may still legitimately be criticized as "irresponsible" (2006: 62). Underkoffler (2013) defends a view that is at least compatible with accepting that Wilma's act is not wrong while still conceding that it is morally objectionable in some other sense. Bennett (2009: 269) also accepts the conclusion but she denies that the conclusion is implausible in the first place on the grounds that what seem like the moral intuitions that oppose it are really just non-moral personal preferences. This analysis itself, however, is highly implausible, since our moral intuitions do not always track what we prefer (Herissone-Kelly (2012: 7–8) has recently raised a similar objection to Bennett). In a more theological context, Heller argues that on the best understanding of the Christian moral tradition as a whole, there is nothing wrong with an act like that of Wilma's, but leaves it open that this may constitute "a possible challenge" to that tradition rather than a reason to simply accept the Implausible Conclusion (1997: 82). It may also be worth noting that some other writers (e.g. Zuradzki (2008)) provide a critical survey that rejects a wide range of solutions to the problem, but do not explicitly consider, and so do not explicitly reject, the possibility that we should simply accept the Implausible Conclusion.

eating a hamburger is morally impermissible. But if you encounter an argument in defense of one of these claims and if after careful examination of the argument you can find no fault with it, it strikes me as more reasonable for you to simply accept the argument's conclusion than to continue to reject the argument simply because you initially assumed that the argument's conclusion was mistaken. The claim that motion is impossible seems so implausible that it is more reasonable to assume that any argument that entails it is flawed than to conclude that the claim is true. Even if you find the claim that a fetus or a cow has a right to life to be implausible, though, it strikes me as unreasonable to suppose that it is really that implausible. The question of whether we can successfully solve the non-identity problem by simply accepting the conclusion of the non-identity argument therefore comes down to the question of just how implausible the Implausible Conclusion really is. And the answer I want to offer in this final chapter is this: the Implausible Conclusion isn't really so implausible.

In one sense, of course, the claim that the Implausible Conclusion is not so implausible is plainly false. Virtually everyone who is presented with a case like that of Wilma has an almost immediate, clear, and visceral reaction to the effect that the act is morally wrong. If the question of whether the Implausible Conclusion is highly implausible is the question of whether it does, in fact, initially strike most people as highly implausible, then the answer is clearly yes. But in asking whether the Implausible Conclusion is really so implausible, we can also ask whether, upon reflection, the conclusion of the non-identity argument really should be considered implausible. This is the question we must ask if we want to know whether we can successfully solve the non-identity problem by simply accepting the argument's conclusion. If an argument has an implication that we initially find implausible but that on reflection we agree should not be deemed implausible, then the fact that the argument has the implication poses no problem. It is in this second sense that I want to argue that the Implausible Conclusion turns out not to be so implausible after all.

I will try to show that the Implausible Conclusion really isn't so implausible in this sense by relating it to other claims that are widely regarded as perfectly plausible. My goal will not be to use these other claims as a way of constructing an argument for the truth of the Implausible Conclusion. The argument for the truth of the Implausible Conclusion has already been provided by the non-identity argument itself in conjunction with the objections I have raised against the various attempts to overcome the argument that I have discussed in the previous chapters. Rather, my goal here will be to show that if my arguments in the previous chapters are accepted, then the Implausible Conclusion should no longer seem so implausible to us. The process of coming to see the problems that arise when we try to avoid the Implausible Conclusion, that is, should lead us to see that the conclusion itself is not as implausible as it at first seemed. Indeed, I will argue that if my arguments in the previous chapters are accepted, then the Implausible Conclusion should no longer seem implausible at all.

If the Implausible Conclusion comes to seem perfectly plausible, then we will have no reason left to resist the non-identity argument or to believe that the non-identity argument gives rise to a non-identity problem. And even if the strategy that I employ in the sections that follow fails to render the Implausible Conclusion completely plausible, as long as it at least renders the conclusion less implausible than the various implausible claims entailed by the solutions I considered in the previous chapters, the strategy will still provide good reason to favor my solution over those that I have rejected. In what follows, I will aim to defend the stronger claim that the Implausible Conclusion is actually, upon reflection, perfectly plausible. But the weaker claim that the Implausible Conclusion is at least less implausible than the claims we will be stuck with if we reject it will still be sufficient for my purposes. Either way, my goal here will be to appeal to a variety of claims that are generally recognized as perfectly plausible as a way of showing that my solution to the non-identity problem is ultimately more plausible than any of the available alternatives.

7.1 Famine Relief Cases

Let me start with a relatively simple example. Suppose that Peter comes home from work and finds two envelopes in the mail. The first contains an unexpected windfall: a check for fifty dollars. The second contains a letter from Oxfam correctly and convincingly informing him that if he contributes fifty dollars to their organization, one less child will die prematurely from hunger or disease. After giving it some thought, Peter throws the letter from Oxfam away and instead spends the fifty dollars on dinner and a movie.

Most people agree that it would have been morally better if Peter had donated the money to Oxfam. But they also think that while it would have been morally praiseworthy for him to have given the money to Oxfam, he was within his rights and did not do anything positively immoral by spending it on himself instead. There are, of course, some well-known arguments for the claim that Peter's act really is morally wrong in this case and some of these arguments are quite powerful.[2] But the question here is not whether the claim that Peter's act is not immoral is true. The question is simply whether it is widely agreed to be plausible. And the answer to this question is clearly yes. Even those who argue that it is positively immoral for Peter not to contribute the money to Oxfam under such circumstances clearly and explicitly recognize that they are arguing against the commonsense view of the matter.[3] If someone presented an argument about an unrelated issue and that argument turned out unexpectedly to entail that it

---

[2] See, e.g., Singer (1972), Unger (1996).

[3] In perhaps the most famous such work, for example, Peter Singer's 1972 article "Famine, Affluence, and Morality," Singer writes that "In what follows, I shall argue that the way people in relatively affluent countries react to a situation like [the famine] in Bengal cannot be justified; indeed, *the whole way we look at moral issues—our moral conceptual scheme—needs to be altered*" (1972: 230, emphasis added).

would not be positively immoral for Peter to spend his money on dinner and a movie, virtually no one would take the fact that the argument had this unexpected implication to be a reason to reject the argument.

But now consider that Peter's act and Wilma's act have a good deal in common. Peter and Wilma each choose from two options. In each case, one option would produce slightly better results for them while the other option would produce much better results from the point of view human well-being overall. And in each case, they choose the option that produces slightly better results for them. In the case of Peter, it strikes most people as perfectly plausible to maintain that, while it would have been better if he had chosen the other option, he has done nothing positively immoral by declining to do so. Indeed, this claim strikes most people as not merely plausible, but true. The most natural explanation for the plausibility of this claim seems to be grounded in the plausibility of the more general claim that it is not immoral for you to refrain from making things better for other people, even much better, at least in cases where refraining from doing so would not positively harm anyone or violate anyone's rights. When most people consider the case of Peter, that is, they think that it would have been much better overall if he had donated the money to Oxfam, but that since he didn't violate anyone's rights and didn't cause harm to anyone by spending the money on dinner and a movie instead, his doing so was not positively immoral. At the least, they acknowledge that this is a perfectly plausible thing to say about the case. But if this is a perfectly plausible thing to say about the case of Peter, why shouldn't we simply accept that it is an equally plausible thing to say about the case of Wilma? It would have been much better from the point of view of overall human well-being if Wilma had conceived Rocks rather than Pebbles, that is, but since she didn't violate anyone's rights by conceiving Pebbles and didn't cause harm to anyone by doing so, her act was not positively immoral.

Indeed, if anything, we should take the claim that Wilma's act is not morally wrong to be even more plausible than the claim that Peter's act is not morally wrong. In Peter's case, the people who will be affected by his decision already exist. These are actual people whose welfare is at stake. In the case of Wilma, it is instead a matter of deciding which new person to bring into existence. The only people whose welfare is at stake at the time that she makes her decision are merely possible people. If it is perfectly plausible to say that Peter may choose an act that is much worse from the point of view of the overall interests of actual, living human beings, then we should accept that it is even more plausible to say that Wilma may choose an act that is no worse for any actual human beings at all, although it is worse from a point of view that includes the interests of merely possible people.

In addition, the magnitude of the difference between the good and bad outcomes that they must choose between is considerably greater in the case of Peter than it is in the case of Wilma. Peter chooses that there be one more dead child rather than one more living child, while Wilma merely chooses that there be one more blind child rather than one more sighted child. And from the point of view of overall human well-being, it is much worse that there be a dead child rather than a living child than that there be a blind child rather than a sighted child. If it is perfectly plausible to say that Peter may choose the outcome that is worse in terms of overall human well-being over the outcome that is better in those terms when the worse outcome overall is so very much worse, then we should accept that it is even more plausible to say that Wilma may choose the outcome that is worse in terms of overall human well-being over the outcome that is better in those terms when the worse overall outcome is not nearly as much worse. The claim that Peter's act is not immoral is widely recognized to be perfectly plausible. Reflecting on this case and on its relation to the case of Wilma should therefore help us to see that the Implausible Conclusion is perfectly plausible, too.

To show that the Implausible Conclusion is plausible, of course, is not enough to show that it is true. But to show that the Implausible Conclusion is plausible is enough to show that the fact that the non-identity argument entails the Implausible Conclusion provides no reason to reject the argument itself. And that is enough to solve the non-identity problem. If we have five plausible premises and one plausible conclusion, then we don't have a problem. We simply have an argument.

Someone who wishes to reject the Implausible Conclusion while agreeing that Peter's act is not immoral could try to show that there is a morally relevant difference between the case of Peter and the case of Wilma. Perhaps Wilma harms Pebbles by conceiving her while Peter does not harm anyone by spending his money on dinner and a movie. Perhaps Pebbles has a right not to be conceived with a significant disability while there is no particular person who has a right that Peter give his money to Oxfam. Or perhaps Wilma has a special parental obligation to her own child while Peter has no special obligation of any kind to any of the children to whom Oxfam provides assistance. Such arguments are certainly possible, and so there is nothing inconsistent about believing both that Wilma acts wrongly and that Peter does not.

But the point of the case of Peter is not to give a reason to believe that Wilma's act is not morally wrong. The reason for thinking that Wilma's act is not morally wrong is provided by the non-identity argument in conjunction with the reasons I provided in the previous chapters for rejecting those responses to the argument that depend on rejecting one of the argument's premises. The point of the case of Peter, rather, is to show that if my analysis in the previous chapters is accepted, then we should be able to see that the claim that Wilma's act is not morally wrong is perfectly plausible. If Wilma's act of conceiving Pebbles is wrong because it harms Pebbles or violates Pebbles's rights or because Wilma has a special maternal obligation to conceive the healthiest child she can conceive, then there is a mistake in one of my arguments in the previous chapters, and there really is a way to solve the non-identity problem by rejecting one of the premises of the argument that gives rise to it. But if we accept the claims that Wilma's act does not harm Pebbles or violate her rights and that Wilma has no such special obligation, then the case of Wilma really should not strike us as being all that different from the case of Peter. The claim that it is not positively immoral for Peter to choose the option that is a little bit better for him but far worse from the point of view of overall human well-being strikes most people as perfectly plausible. Unless we have already solved the non-identity problem by successfully rejecting one of the premises of the non-identity argument, then, we should simply accept that the claim that it is not positively immoral for Wilma to choose the option that is a little bit better for her but far worse from the point of view of overall human well-being is perfectly plausible, too. And if we accept that the claim that Wilma's act is not wrong is perfectly plausible, then we can solve the non-identity problem by simply accepting the non-identity argument.

7.2 Rescue Cases

A second kind of case that can be used to reveal the plausibility of the Implausible Conclusion is the kind of rescue case that I discussed in section 6.1.3.1 in the context of the Moderate Principle. So return for a moment to the case of Fred, who can save incurably blind Billy or otherwise comparable sighted Timmy from drowning but cannot save both, and who decides to save Billy rather than Timmy because it is a bit more convenient for him to do so. Most people will agree that Fred does not act immorally by saving Billy rather than Timmy. At the very least, most people will agree that the claim that Fred does not act immorally is a perfectly plausible one. If someone presented an argument about some other issue and the argument unexpectedly turned out to entail that it is not morally wrong to save a blind child rather than an otherwise comparable sighted child when one cannot save both, virtually no one would take the fact that the argument had this implication to be a reason to reject the argument. If anything, it would be widely taken to be a reason to reject an argument if the argument entailed that Fred's act was positively immoral.

But now consider that, again as in the case of Peter, Fred's act and Wilma's act have a good deal in common. Fred and Wilma each choose from two options. In both cases, the choice they make will determine who will exist and who will not exist after their choice has been made. In both cases, if they choose one option, an incurably blind child who will otherwise not exist after they choose will exist after they choose and a sighted child who will otherwise exist after they choose will not exist after they choose. In both cases, if they choose the other option, a sighted child who will otherwise not exist after they choose will exist after they choose and an incurably blind child who will otherwise exist after they choose will not exist after they choose. In both cases, they choose the option that results in an incurably blind child existing after they choose and a sighted child who would otherwise have existed after they choose not existing after they choose. And in both cases, they make this choice simply because it is a bit more convenient for them to do so.

It will strike most people as perfectly plausible to maintain that Fred has done nothing immoral by saving the blind child rather than the sighted child. Indeed, as I have already noted, this claim will strike most people as not merely plausible, but true. But if it is perfectly plausible to say that it is not wrong for Fred to choose that a blind child exist after his choice rather than that a sighted child exist after his choice, why shouldn't we accept that it is equally plausible to say that it is not wrong for Wilma to choose that a blind child exist after her choice rather than that a sighted child exist after her choice? If Fred is morally free to decide which person will exist after his choice without having to make the choice that is better from the point of view of overall human well-being, why shouldn't Wilma be morally free to decide which person will exist after her choice without having to make the choice that is better from the point of view of overall human well-being?

Indeed, if anything, we should take the claim that Wilma's act is not morally wrong to be even more plausible than the claim that Fred's act is not morally wrong. This is because there is an obvious difference between the two cases: Wilma's choice involves choosing which of two lives to create while Fred's involves choosing which of two lives to extend. And this difference makes it even harder to believe that Wilma's act is morally wrong if Fred's act is not morally wrong. When you save a person's life, your act prevents them from suffering a harm. When you create a person's life, your act does not prevent them from suffering a harm, though it enables them to enjoy the benefits that their life makes possible. And since it seems plausible to suppose that there is a stronger duty to minimize the harm to others that results from our choices than there is to maximize the benefits to others that result from our choices, we should take the claim that Wilma's act is not morally wrong to be even more plausible than the claim that Fred's act is not morally wrong.

Suppose, for example, that you have a pill that could either prevent Alice from suffering twenty units of pain or prevent Ben from suffering thirty units of pain and that you also have a candy bar that can either give Carol twenty units of pleasure or give Dan thirty units of pleasure. Even if you think that you are morally obligated to give the pill to Ben rather than to Alice since doing so would prevent a greater amount of harm, you may well agree that you are still morally permitted to give the candy to Carol rather than to Dan. If this is so, then it should seem even more plausible to say that Wilma is free to give life to Pebbles rather than to Rocks than it is to say that Fred is free to prevent the death of Billy rather than the death of Timmy. The claim that Fred's act is not immoral will surely strike most people as perfectly plausible. Reflecting on this case and on its relation to the case of Wilma should therefore provide a second way for us to see that the Implausible Conclusion is perfectly plausible, too. As before, the plausibility of the Implausible Conclusion does not show that the Implausible Conclusion is true. But it does show that the fact that the Implausible Conclusion is entailed by the non-identity argument is not enough to generate the non-identity problem. Five plausible premises and one plausible conclusion constitute an argument, not a problem.

Someone who wishes to reject the Implausible Conclusion while agreeing that Fred's act is not immoral could try to show that there is a morally relevant difference between the case of Fred and the case of Wilma. They might argue, for example, that in the case of Wilma, she will be the mother of the child who exists after her choice is made while in the case of Fred, he will be unrelated to the child who exists after his choice is made.

Since it is commonly believed that we have stronger duties to our own children than we have to other people's children, it might seem that Wilma has an obligation to ensure that the child she chooses be as healthy as possible, while Fred has no such obligation.

But there are two problems with this response. First, the point of the case of Fred is not to give a reason to believe that Wilma's act is not morally wrong. The point is simply to show that if my analysis in the previous chapters is accepted, then we should recognize that the Implausible Conclusion is perfectly plausible. If Wilma has a special obligation as a parent to conceive Rocks rather than Pebbles, then there is a mistake in one of my arguments in the previous chapters and there really is a way to solve the non-identity problem by rejecting one of the premises of the argument that gives rise to it. But if we accept the claim that Wilma has no such special obligation, then the case of Wilma really should not strike us as being all that different from the case of Fred. The claim that Fred's act is not immoral will strike most people as perfectly plausible. We should therefore simply accept that the claim that Wilma's act is not immoral is perfectly plausible, too. And if we accept that the claim is perfectly plausible, then we can solve the non-identity problem by simply accepting the non-identity argument's conclusion.

The second problem with this response is that we can simply revise the case of Fred to make it more like the case of Wilma with respect to the parent–child relationship. And when we do, we find that the claim that Fred's act would not be wrong remains just as plausible. Suppose, for example, that the two children drowning in the lake are his own children, that Fred can save only one of the two, and that it is easier for him to save his blind child. Virtually no one would insist that Fred is morally obligated to let his blind child die so that he can go out of his way to save his sighted child. They would find the claim that it is not positively immoral for Fred to save his blind child rather than his sighted child not just perfectly plausible, but true. But if this is correct, then we can simply use this version of the case of Fred to motivate the plausibility of the Implausible Conclusion. If it is perfectly plausible to maintain that it is not immoral for Fred to save the blind child rather than the sighted child when both children are his own children, then why shouldn't we also accept that it is perfectly plausible to maintain that it is not immoral for Wilma to conceive a blind child rather than a sighted child when both children would be her own children?

A second way to try to establish a difference between the case of Fred and the case of Wilma appeals to the existence of rights. The claim, more specifically, is that people who exist have a right to assistance, at least in cases where the assistance will prevent them from suffering a great harm and will cost very little to the people who could assist them, but that people who do not yet exist have no right to be brought into existence. If this is correct, then Billy and Timmy each have a right to assistance in the case of Fred, while neither Pebbles nor Rocks have a right to be brought into existence in the case of Wilma. This claim seems plausible enough, but it does nothing to undermine the strategy that I have been employing here. Since Billy and Timmy both have the right to assistance and Fred cannot save both of them, their rights simply cancel each other out. Billy's right to assistance gives Fred no greater reason to save Billy than Timmy's right to assistance gives him to save Timmy. If it is not immoral for Fred to make the choice that is a bit more convenient for him but much worse from the point of view of overall human well-being when there are two rights that cancel each other out, then why shouldn't it also not be immoral for Wilma to make the choice that is a bit more convenient for her but much worse from the point of view of overall human well-being when there are no rights at stake in the first place? The claim that Fred's act is not positively immoral strikes most people as perfectly plausible. We should there-fore simply accept that the claim that Wilma's act is not positively immoral is perfectly plausible, too. And if we accept that the claim is plausible, then, again, we can solve the non-identity problem by simply accepting the non-identity argument's conclusion.

7.3 The Transitivity Argument

A third way to show that the Implausible Conclusion is not so implausible involves appealing to a pair of further cases.[4] The first is like the case of Wilma except that there is nothing that the doctor can do to change the fact that her child will be incurably blind. So consider the case of Betty. Betty has a slight preference to have a child. She goes to her doctor for a pre-conception checkup and the doctor tells her that if she has a child, no matter when the child is conceived, the child will be incurably blind. Knowing this, Betty decides to conceive and, as a result, she has an incurably blind child. Assuming, as I will assume here, that her choice will have no negative conse-quences for anyone else, the claim that it is positively immoral for her to conceive a blind child rather than to conceive no child at all strikes me as extremely implausible. So it seems perfectly plausible to me to say that Betty has not done anything wrong. Some people may not share this reaction to the case of Betty. For those people, the strategy that I want to develop in this section will prove ineffective. But for those who react to the case of Betty in the way that I do, and I suspect that most people who are initially inclined to reject the Implausible Conclusion will react in this way, the case of Betty can serve as the foundation for a powerful additional defense of the plausibility of the Implausible Conclusion.

This is so because we can combine the case of Betty with a second case. So return for a moment to the case of Jane, which I introduced in section 6.1.3.2 as a problem for the inclusive version of the Moderate Principle. Jane already has two healthy and happy children and knows that if she conceives a third child, that child will be healthy and

---

[4] See McMahan (2001: 467–9) for a similar argument, though McMahan's argument is designed to raise problems for a particular kind of solution to the non-identity problem that involves rejecting P5 while mine is designed to raise problems for any solution that involves rejecting any of the premises of the non-identity argument. See also McMahan (2005: 147). Petersen (2002: 360–1) also discusses a similar argument, though his is concerned with the relation "is as morally good as" rather than "is permissible to choose instead of" and, like McMahan's, is only designed to raise problems for a narrow range of responses to the non-identity argument.

happy, too. But after giving it a great deal of thought, Jane has decided that she has a slight preference not to have a third child, and so chooses not to conceive a third child. Virtually everyone will find the claim that Jane's act is not immoral to be perfectly plausible. Indeed, most people will agree that it is not simply plausible, but true. But if it is perfectly plausible to say that it is not wrong for Betty to conceive a blind child rather than no child and perfectly plausible to say that it is not wrong for Jane to conceive no child rather than a sighted child, then we have a further reason to agree that it is perfectly plausible to say that it is not wrong for Wilma to conceive a blind child rather than a sighted child. Considering the case of Wilma in the context of the cases of Betty and Jane, that is, should help us to see Wilma's choice in a new light: by conceiving Pebbles, she adds to the total amount of human well-being in the world when it would not have been immoral for her to add no amount of human well-being to the world by conceiving no child at all. Since it would not have been wrong for her to add nothing at all to the total amount of human well-being in the world, the fact that she could easily have added even more of it than she did because she could easily have conceived Rocks rather than Pebbles doesn't make it wrong for her to have conceived Pebbles. If it wouldn't have been wrong for Wilma to add no human well-being to the world at all, that is, how can it be wrong for her to have added something that was better than nothing?

This third approach to defending the plausibility of the Implausible Conclusion appeals to a kind of transitivity principle. Before subjecting the defense to scrutiny, then, it may help to make the principle and its role in the overall approach explicit. So consider what I will call the Transitivity Argument:

P1: If you must choose between conceiving a blind child and conceiving no child, it is not immoral to choose to conceive a blind child

P2: If you must choose between conceiving no child and conceiving a sighted child, it is not immoral to choose to conceive no child

P3: If it is not immoral to choose A over B when those are the only two options and it is not immoral to choose B over C when those are the only two options, then it is not immoral to choose A over C when those are the only two options

C: If you must choose between conceiving a blind child and conceiving a sighted child, it is not immoral to choose to conceive a blind child

The Transitivity Argument is clearly valid. P1 and P2 represent plausible responses to the cases of Betty and Jane. P3 is what I will refer to as the Transitivity Principle. And C represents the Implausible Conclusion. If the Transitivity Principle is sufficiently plausible, then, the cases of Betty and Jane provide a further way to reveal the plausibility of the seemingly Implausible Conclusion.

Someone who wishes to reject the Implausible Conclusion while agreeing that neither Betty's act nor Jane's act is immoral can do so by rejecting the Transitivity Principle. And they can justify rejecting the Transitivity Principle if they can find a clear counterexample to it. One possibility arises from considering the following three cases.[5] Suppose first that a goldfish is trapped in a burning building. You can enter the burning building and suffer serious harm, and if you do, you will be able to save it. Here it seems clear that it is not immoral to choose saving the goldfish over not entering the building. Morality certainly does not require you to save the goldfish. But if you decide to save it nonetheless, you just as clearly do nothing wrong, at least if we assume, as I will assume here, that the serious harm you will suffer will not prevent you from discharging any of your other moral obligations. Now suppose that a man is trapped in the building rather than a goldfish. Here it again seems clear that morality does not require you to enter the burning building and that it is therefore not immoral for you to choose to refrain from entering the building. It would be morally praiseworthy for you suffer serious harm in order to rescue the person in the burning building, but given the great harm to you, it would not be positively immoral for you to decline to do so. And now finally, suppose that a man and a goldfish are both trapped in the building and that for some reason you must choose between entering and saving the goldfish and entering and saving the man. Here it seems extremely plausible to say that it would be immoral for you to save the goldfish rather than the man. But if this is so, then we have a genuine counterexample to the Transitivity Principle, and thus a rebuttal to the defense of the plausibility of the Implausible Conclusion that is grounded in it. For consider this argument:

P1: If you must choose between going into a burning building to save a goldfish and not going into a burning building at all, it is not immoral to choose to go into the burning building to save a goldfish

P2: If you must choose between not going into a burning building at all and going into a burning building to save a man, it is not immoral to choose to not go into a burning building at all

P3: If it is not immoral to choose A over B when those are the only two options and it is not immoral to choose B over C when those are the only two options, then it is not immoral to choose A over C when those are the only two options

C: If you must choose between going into a burning building to save a goldfish and going into a burning building to save a man, it is not immoral to choose to go into a burning building to save a goldfish

P1 and P2 are extremely plausible. P1–P3 jointly entail C. C is extremely implausible. This seems to provide a powerful reason to reject P3. And P3 is the Transitivity Principle.

The case of the man, the goldfish, and the burning building does indeed pose a problem for the Transitivity Principle. But this does not mean that the strategy for revealing the plausibility of the Implausible Conclusion that the principle represents must be abandoned. It simply means that the principle must be modified. And the principle can easily be modified because there is a natural explanation for the failure of transitivity in this particular instance. When you must choose between saving the goldfish and

---

[5] Parfit provides a somewhat similar case (1982: 131).

not going into the burning building at all, there is an enormous difference between the two options in terms of the effect your choice will have on your own well-being. The same is so when you must choose between saving the man and not going into the burning building at all. It is plausible to suppose that it is in virtue of this particular feature of those two cases that you are morally free to enter the building or not enter the building as you choose. But when you must choose between going into a burning building to save a goldfish and going into a burning building to save a man, there is no difference between the two options in terms of the effect your choice will have on your own well-being. Since you must go into the burning building and suffer serious harm either way, it seems plausible to suppose that the man, but not the goldfish, will have a right to your assistance once you get there. The man has no right that you make a great sacrifice in order to save him, that is, and so no right that you enter the building in the first place. But if you must enter the building no matter which option you choose, then the cost to you of saving him once you are in the building becomes trivial, and it seems plausible to suppose that this means that he does have a right to your assistance and that this is why it would then be wrong for you to save the goldfish instead of saving him.

If this is the correct account of why it would not be wrong to save the goldfish rather than save no one, not be wrong to save no one rather than save the man, but nonetheless wrong to save the goldfish rather than save the man, then we can see what kind of revision the Transitivity Principle requires. The change from the A/B choice (goldfish or no one) and the B/C choice (no one or man) to the A/C choice (goldfish or man) generates a change in the difference the choice between the two options makes in terms of your own well-being, from an enormous difference in the A/B and B/C choices to virtually no difference in the A/C choice. This change accounts for the failure of transitivity. And so the Transitivity Principle must be modified to make clear that the transitivity holds only if the difference in cost to the agent is held constant in all three choice situations. The resulting formulation of the principle would read:

TP: If it is not immoral to choose A over B when those are the only two options and it is not immoral to choose B over C when those are the only two options, and if the change from choosing between A and B and between B and C to choosing between A and C makes no difference in terms of the effects of the choices on the person making them, then it is not immoral to choose A over C when those are the only two options

This revision to the Transitivity Principle is not ad hoc. It is motivated by the independently plausible claim that differences in terms of cost to the agent are morally relevant. Once the revision is made, moreover, it becomes clear that the case of the man, the goldfish, and the burning building no longer poses a problem for the principle. Since there is a big difference in terms of effects on the agent between the "goldfish or no one" and "no one or man" choices on the one hand and the "goldfish or man" choice on the other, this case simply falls outside the scope of the revised version of the Transitivity Principle. And while the revised version of the principle is therefore more limited in scope, it is still broad enough to reveal the plausibility of the seemingly

Implausible Conclusion. Betty is just a little better off having a blind child rather than no child, Jane is just a little better off having no child rather than a sighted child, and Wilma is just a little better off conceiving a blind child now rather than taking the pills once a day for two months and then conceiving a sighted child. Since it is clearly plausible to say that it is not wrong for Betty to conceive a blind child rather than no child and that it is not wrong for Jane to conceive no child rather than a sighted child, even the restricted version of the Transitivity Principle should be enough to help us see that it is also plausible to say that it is not wrong for Wilma to conceive Pebbles rather than Rocks. The problem with the initial formulation of the Transitivity Principle, then, is not enough to undermine the general strategy of using transitivity to see that the Implausible Conclusion really isn't so implausible.

The case of the man, the goldfish, and the burning building, however, is really just one instance of a more general problem with the Transitivity Principle, a problem that is not fully addressed by the revision to the principle that I have thus far offered. The problem in this particular case is that the change from the A/B and B/C choices to the A/C choice generates a change in terms of effects on the person making the choice. But this is a problem for the Transitivity Principle only because the effects on the person making the choice seem to be morally relevant. The more general problem, then, is that a change from the A/B and B/C choices to the A/C choice can generate a change in terms of some morally relevant factor. The effects on the person making the choice are simply one morally relevant factor. There could be others. And so there could be other kinds of cases in which the change from the A/B and B/C choices to the A/C choice turns out to be morally relevant and to undermine the appeal to transitivity. It might be that choosing A over B and B over C would not be immoral but that choosing A over C would break a promise you had made to someone, for example, or would cause harm to innocent people, or would violate someone's rights. To fully respond to the problem represented by the case of the man, the goldfish, and the burning building, then, requires a more significant revision to the Transitivity Principle. The result would be something more like this:

TP: If it is not immoral to choose A over B when those are the only two options and it is not immoral to choose B over C when those are the only two options, and if the change from choosing between A and B and between B and C to choosing between A and C makes no difference in terms of any morally relevant properties, then it is not immoral to choose A over C when those are the only two options

This formulation of the Transitivity Principle will be immune to any of the possible counterexamples referred to above. It is, moreover, extremely plausible. The question that remains is whether it is still robust enough to lend plausibility to the Implausible Conclusion.[6]

---

[6] It is also worth noting that this version of the Transitivity Principle can be used to undermine Hare's ingenious "morphing" argument (2009), which attempts to establish that if it is wrong to choose blind Pebbles over sighted Pebbles then it must also be wrong to choose blind Pebbles over sighted Rocks. Imagine

The answer depends on whether the change from choosing between a blind child and no child and choosing between no child and a sighted child, on the one hand, and choosing between a blind child and a sighted child, on the other, introduces a change in some morally relevant property. If it does, then this version of the Transitivity Principle does not apply to this case and so does not support the conclusion that Wilma's act is not immoral. But if it doesn't, then as long as we find it plausible to say that what Betty and Jane do is not immoral, we should also find it plausible to say that what Wilma does is not immoral.

There is one obvious difference between the A/B and B/C choices and the A/C choice in this case. Betty and Jane are each deciding whether to have a child at all, while Wilma has already decided that she will have a child and is deciding which child to have. Someone who wishes to reject the Implausible Conclusion and accept the revised version of the Transitivity Principle while agreeing that neither Betty's act nor Jane's act is immoral, then, could try to show that this difference is a morally relevant one. One way they could do this would be to argue that the difference between having a child and not having a child is significant in terms of the costs to the person making the choice, while the difference between having one particular child and having a different particular child is not. Since a change in the magnitude of the cost to the person making the choice seems clearly to be morally relevant, this would show that the change from the A/B and B/C choices to the A/C choice really does generate a change in a morally relevant factor in this case. But this argument overlooks the stipulation that Betty, Jane, and Wilma are each only slightly better off making the choice that they make. So in

---

a continuum of cases with Pebbles on the left, Rocks on the right, and a spectrum of cases in between such that the difference between any given child and the child just to the right of that child on the spectrum is so infinitesimal that there is no reason to believe that that they are two different children rather than one and the same child in two very slightly different conditions. In short, imagine a spectrum along which Pebbles very gradually morphs into Rocks. At any point along the spectrum, it should be clear that it would be wrong to conceive any given child in a blind condition rather than the child just to the right of that child in a sighted condition. Doing so would amount to creating a blind child rather than creating that very same child as a sighted child. So it would be wrong to choose blind A over sighted B, wrong to choose blind B over sighted C, blind C over sighted D, blind D over sighted E, and so on, all the way to the end where it would be wrong to choose the penultimate child blind rather than the final child sighted. But A is clearly Pebbles and the final child is clearly Rocks, and so by transitivity it follows that it would be wrong to choose blind Pebbles over sighted Rocks.

The problem with this morphing argument is that it depends on the unrestricted version of the Transitivity Principle on which if it is wrong to choose A over B and B over C, then it is wrong to choose A over C even if there is a morally relevant difference between the A/B and B/C choices on the one hand and the A/C choice on the other. This is the version of the principle that runs into problems in cases like that of the goldfish, man, and burning building. But once we restrict the Transitivity Principle to account for such cases, it no longer suffices to generate Hare's conclusion. In the choices between A/B, B/C, C/D, and so on up to the penultimate/final child, there is no reason to think that the blind child and the sighted child are different people, but in the choice between Pebbles and Rocks they are clearly different people. This difference is a relevant difference. And so on the corrected version of the Transitivity Principle, it does not follow that if it would be wrong to choose the first child in any given pair as a blind child over the second child in that pair as a sighted child for all of the pairs of cases along the spectrum that it would be wrong to choose blind Pebbles over sighted Rocks.

this case, at least, the change from the A/B and B/C choices to the A/C choice does not generate a change in this morally relevant factor.

A second way to argue that the change from the A/B and B/C choices to the A/C choice generates a morally relevant change in this case appeals to the intuitively plausible claim that parents have special obligations to their children. Because Wilma is going to have a child regardless of which choice she makes, on this account, she has already decided to become a parent. Because Betty and Jane are each choosing between having a child and not having a child, neither of them has yet decided to become a parent. Someone who wishes to reject the Implausible Conclusion and accept the revised version of the Transitivity Principle while agreeing that neither Betty's act nor Jane's act is immoral could therefore argue that Wilma has already acquired a special kind of parental duty that neither Betty nor Jane have acquired and that this special duty commits Wilma to conceiving a sighted child rather than a blind child. A parent has a special obligation to do what is best for her child, that is, and it will be better for her child if her child is sighted than it will be if her child is blind. This is essentially the argument defended by Hare that I discussed in section 2.2. If that argument is sound, then there really is a morally relevant difference between the choices that Betty and Jane confront and the choice that Wilma confronts: Betty harms no one by conceiving a blind child rather than no child and Jane harms no one by conceiving no child rather than a sighted child, but Wilma does harm someone by conceiving a blind child rather than a sighted child: she harms "her child," at least in the *de dicto* sense. And because of the special parental obligations that Wilma has, on this account, the *de dicto* sense of harming someone is morally relevant.

Hare's argument certainly shows that there is nothing inconsistent about accepting the revised version of the Transitivity Principle and believing that Betty's act and Jane's act are not wrong while at the same time believing that Wilma's act is wrong. One can consistently accept the principle and believe all three claims about Betty, Jane, and Wilma if one believes that Wilma's act is wrong because it harms her child in a morally relevant sense. But the point of conjoining the principle with the examples of Betty and Jane is not to provide an argument for the conclusion that Wilma's act is not wrong. The argument for the conclusion that Wilma's act is not wrong is the non-identity argument itself combined with the reasons I gave in the previous chapters for thinking that any attempt to overcome the argument by rejecting one of its premises either fails to avoid entailing the conclusion or entails an even more implausible conclusion. The point of conjoining the revised version of the Transitivity Principle with the examples of Betty and Jane, rather, is to show that if my arguments in the previous chapters are accepted, then we shouldn't find the claim that Wilma's act is not wrong to be so implausible. And if my arguments in the previous chapters are correct, then Wilma does not harm her child in a morally relevant sense by conceiving Pebbles rather than Rocks, nor does she violate any special maternal obligation she might have to conceive Pebbles rather than Rocks. If that is correct, then we really have no reason to think that the change from the A/B choice of Betty and the B/C choice of Jane to the A/C choice of

Wilma generates a morally relevant change in their choice situations. And if the change from the choices that Betty and Jane confront to the choice that Wilma confronts does not generate a morally relevant change in the nature of their choice situations, then the revised version of the Transitivity Principle really should make it perfectly plausible to say that Wilma's act is not morally wrong. If it is perfectly plausible to agree that isn't wrong for Betty to conceive a blind child rather than no child or for Jane to conceive no child rather than a sighted child, and if there isn't a morally relevant difference between their choice situations and the choice Wilma faces between conceiving a blind child and a sighted child, then why shouldn't it be just as plausible to agree that it would not be wrong for Wilma to conceive a blind child rather than a sighted child? And if we accept that this claim is perfectly plausible, then, once more, we can solve the non-identity problem by simply accepting the non-identity argument's conclusion.

7.4 Different Species Cases

A fourth kind of case that can be used to reveal the plausibility of the Implausible Conclusion points to a particular feature of the conclusion that may be responsible for making it initially seem so implausible to so many people. This is the fact that Pebbles does not simply enjoy less well-being than Rocks would have enjoyed but has a disability that Rocks would not have had. The way in which the fact that Pebbles is disabled may distract us from the ultimate plausibility of the Implausible Conclusion can perhaps best be seen by first considering a variation on the case of Wilma in which the child suffers from a mental rather than a physical disability.[7] And to make the point as forcefully as possible, it is useful to focus on a case where the disability would be quite serious. So suppose first that Wilma had been told that if she did not take the pill once a day for two months before conceiving, her child would have a mental disability so severe that her child would have a mental life equivalent to that of an ordinary horse. Surely if it would be wrong for Wilma to conceive right away in the original version of the story, it would be wrong for her to conceive right away in this version.

But now consider the case of Mary:

Mary: Mary lives on a farm with her two children and four horses. After deciding that she wanted to conceive one more child or breed one more horse but not both, she consulted with a

---

[7] The same point is also sometimes made by appealing to a case in which Wilma can either conceive an ordinary child now or wait two months and conceive a child with extraordinary mental or physical abilities (e.g. Lillehammer (2005: 33)). To the extent that people think it would not be wrong for Wilma to have the ordinary child rather than the extraordinary child, this, too, lends support to the claim that it is not so implausible to think that it would not be wrong for her to have a disabled child rather than an ordinary child and that our initial intuitions to the contrary are unduly framed by the unwarranted thought that there is something intrinsically bad about living a disabled life. Since people's intuitions do not seem to be particularly strong or uniform on this case, however, and since I think they can be challenged by potentially forceful debunking responses, I present a different kind of case in the text, one that I believe makes the same point more effectively.

doctor and a veterinarian. The doctor assured her that if she conceived a child, the child would be perfectly healthy and the veterinarian assured her that if she bred another horse, the horse would be perfectly healthy. After spending a long time considering whether she would rather have one more child or breed one more horse, she decided that she had a slight preference to breed one more horse. As a result, she bred one more horse and did not have any more children.

Most people will think that Mary has done nothing morally wrong. At the very least, they will surely agree that it is perfectly plausible to maintain that it is not immoral to bring an additional healthy horse into the world rather than an additional healthy child. But now consider that Mary's act has a good deal in common with Wilma's act in the version of the story where Wilma conceives a child with the mental life of a horse instead of waiting two months and conceiving a healthy child. Mary and Wilma each choose from two options. In each case, one option would produce slightly better results for them than the other. In each case, the option that would produce slightly better results for them involves bringing into existence a new being with the mental life of a horse: an ordinary horse in Mary's case and a human being with the mental life of a horse in Wilma's case. In each case, the option that would produce slightly worse results for them involves bringing into existence a healthy human being. And in each case, they choose to bring into existence a being with the mental life of a horse rather than a healthy human being because doing so produces slightly better results for them. Mary finds it slightly better for her to bring into existence an ordinary horse rather than an ordinary child and Wilma finds it slightly better for her to bring into existence a child with the mental life of a horse rather than an ordinary child. In the case of Mary, it will strike most people as perfectly plausible to maintain that she has done nothing immoral. Indeed, this claim will likely strike most people as not merely plausible, but true. But if this is a perfectly plausible thing to say about the case of Mary, why shouldn't we simply accept that it is an equally plausible thing to say about the case of Wilma? If it is not immoral for Mary to create a being with the mental life of a horse rather than creating an ordinary human being, then why should it be immoral for Wilma to create a being with the mental life of a horse rather than creating an ordinary human being? The case of Mary, then, provides yet another way to see that the Implausible Conclusion isn't so implausible after all.

There is, of course, an obvious difference between the case of Mary and the revised case of Wilma. The being with the mental life of a horse that Mary brings into existence is a horse. The being with the mental life of a horse that Wilma brings into existence is a human being. Someone who wishes to reject the Implausible Conclusion while agreeing that Mary's act is not immoral could maintain that this difference between the two cases is morally relevant. And so it is not strictly speaking inconsistent to maintain that Wilma's act is morally wrong while maintaining that Mary's act is not morally wrong.

The problem with this response to the case of Mary can best be put in the form of a dilemma. Either a mere difference in species membership is morally relevant or it is not morally relevant. Suppose first that it is not morally relevant. If two beings have the same kind of mental life, on this account, then the fact that one is a member of the human species and the other is a member of some other species does not, by itself, make any moral difference. The two beings have the same moral value. Killing or inflicting pain on one of them, for example, would be just as wrong as killing or inflicting pain on the other. This view strikes many people as not merely plausible, but true. If this account is correct, then the child with the mental life of a horse that Wilma brings into existence has precisely the same value as the horse with the mental life of a horse that Mary brings into existence. If it isn't wrong for Mary to bring into existence the being that she chooses to bring into existence rather than a healthy human being, and if the being that Mary brings into existence has precisely the same value as the being that Wilma brings into existence, then this really should make it plausible to suppose that it isn't wrong for Wilma to bring into existence the being that she chooses to bring into existence rather than a healthy human being. And so if species membership is morally irrelevant, then reflecting on the case of Mary really should help us to recognize the plausibility of the seemingly Implausible Conclusion.

Suppose on the other hand that a difference in species membership is morally relevant. In that case, even though a horse and a human being with the mental life of a horse have the same kind of mental experiences, the fact that one of them is a member of the human species and the other is not makes a moral difference. One of them counts for more than the other even though from the point of view of what it is like to be them, there is no significant difference between the two. This view, too, strikes many people as not merely plausible, but true. But what strikes them as true, or at least as highly plausible, is the view that a human being with the mental life of a horse counts for more than a horse, not the view that a horse counts for more than a human being with the mental life of a horse. They would say that that killing or inflicting pain on a human being with the mental life of a horse would be morally worse than killing or inflicting pain on a horse, for example, not that killing or inflicting pain on a horse would be worse than killing or inflicting pain on a human being with the mental life of a horse. If a difference in species membership is morally relevant, then a human being with the mental life of a horse has more value than a horse, not less.

But if this account is correct, then the being that Wilma brings into existence has even more value than the being that Mary brings into existence. Mary merely brings a horse into existence, after all, but Wilma brings a human being into existence, albeit a human being with the mental life of a horse. But if it isn't wrong for Mary to bring a mere horse into existence rather than a healthy human being, then the view that species membership is morally relevant should make it even more plausible to suppose that it isn't wrong for Wilma to bring into existence a human being with the mental life of a horse rather than a healthy human being. If it isn't wrong for Mary to choose creating a mere horse over creating a healthy human being, that is, then how could it be wrong for Wilma to choose creating something with even more value than a mere horse over creating a healthy human being? And so if a difference in species membership really is morally relevant, then reflecting on the case of Mary should do more, not less, to reveal the plausibility of the Implausible Conclusion. Whether species membership is morally relevant or not, then, the case of Mary provides a powerful further reason to simply accept the plausibility of the Implausible Conclusion.

There is, however, a second way that the claim that species membership is morally relevant might be used to try to undermine the appeal to the case of Mary. On this second account, the species membership of a particular being is relevant not to the moral value of the being, but to the total amount of welfare that the being enjoys. The welfare of a particular being, that is, is at least in part a function of the kind of being that it is. The fact that a particular horse is unable to enjoy the pleasures of reading poetry, for example, does not count against how well the horse is doing because a horse is not the kind of being that can read and enjoy poetry. But the fact that a particular human being with the mental life of a horse is unable to enjoy the pleasures of reading poetry does count against how well he is doing because a human being is the kind of being that can read and enjoy poetry. There is something sad about a human being who cannot read and enjoy poetry in a way that there is not in the case of a horse that cannot read and enjoy poetry. And so, on this second account, there is still a relevant difference between Mary's bringing a horse into existence and Wilma's bringing into existence a human being with the mental life of a horse.

Even if we accept this second account of the relevance of species membership, however, it will be unable to undermine the argument from the case of Mary. It will simply force us to modify the already modified version of the case of Wilma. If the fact that a human being with the mental life of a horse is a member of the human species really does count against the level of well-being that he enjoys relative to the level of well-being that an ordinary horse enjoys, that is, then we can instead say that if Wilma conceives a child now, the child will have a significantly less severe mental disability. Because the disability will be much less severe, the child will be able to enjoy a variety of experiences that are unavailable to a horse. In this respect, the child will be better off than a horse. But because the child will still be unable to enjoy some of the experiences that a typical human being is able to enjoy, while the horse will be able to enjoy all of the experiences that a typical horse is able to enjoy, the child will in this second sense be worse off than the horse, at least on the assumption that species membership really is relevant to a being's welfare level in the way that is being assumed here. We can then simply stipulate that the magnitude of the mental disability that the child will have if Wilma conceives now will be such that the welfare advantage relative to the horse of the child's being able to do things that the horse cannot do and the welfare disadvantage relative to the horse of the child's being unable to do some things that a typical human being can do while the horse can do all of the things that a typical horse can do precisely cancel each other out. Perhaps this means that the child would have some form of Down syndrome. Perhaps it means it would have a mental life equivalent to that of a dolphin or a great ape. Perhaps it would be somewhere in between, or below this level but above the mental life of a horse. Whatever degree of mental disability has to be stipulated, though, the result will be the same: that once we adjust for the presumed fact that species membership is relevant to determining a particular being's level of welfare, this particular disabled child would have a life that on the whole is no better and no worse for him than the life of a typical horse is for it. And once the case has been reformulated in this way, the argument based on the case of Mary will continue to retain its initial force. If it is not immoral for Mary to create a horse rather than a healthy human being, then why should it be immoral for Wilma to create a human being with an overall level of welfare identical to that of a horse rather than a healthy human being? In the end, then, whether species membership is morally irrelevant or is relevant in either of the ways that I have identified, the case of Mary provides an additional reason to conclude that the Implausible Conclusion is not really so implausible. Combined with the responses that most people will have to the cases of Peter, Fred, Betty, and Jane that I discussed in the previous sections, we have good reason to conclude that, upon reflection, we should deem the Implausible Conclusion to be perfectly plausible. And once we accept that the Implausible Conclusion is actually quite plausible, we can solve the non-identity problem by simply accepting the non-identity argument's conclusion.

7.5 The Three Distinctions Revisited

In sections 1.1.1–1.1.4, I drew distinctions between the direct version of the non-identity problem and the indirect version, between same number cases and different number cases, and between bad condition cases and bad outcome cases. These three distinctions combine for a total of eight kinds of case that can give rise to the non-identity problem: direct same number bad condition cases, direct same number bad event cases, direct different number bad condition cases, direct different number bad event cases, indirect same number bad condition cases, indirect same number bad event cases, indirect different number bad condition cases, and indirect different number bad event cases. The case of Wilma is a direct same number bad condition case. I have argued so far in this chapter that we can solve the non-identity problem in this kind of case by simply accepting the non-identity argument's conclusion. And I have attempted to show that doing so is plausible by appealing to the cases of Peter, Fred, Betty, Jane, and Mary. In this section, I want to argue that if my solution is successful in the direct same number bad condition case of Wilma, then it is also successful in all of the other kinds of cases that give rise to the non-identity problem. If this is so, and if my arguments in Chapters 2 through 6 are correct, then while none of the other approaches in the literature provides even a partial solution to the non-identity problem, my approach provides a complete solution. I will assume for the purposes of this section that the cases of Peter, Fred, Betty, Jane, and Mary really do help to show that the Implausible Conclusion is sufficiently plausible in the direct same number bad condition case of Wilma and will try to show that if this is so, then variants of at least some of these cases can be used to show that the Implausible Conclusion is also sufficiently plausible in all of the other kinds of case in which the non-identity problem can arise.

Let's begin with the distinction between same number cases and different number cases. The case of Wilma is a same number case. The world will contain the same number of people regardless of which option Wilma chooses. The only difference is whether that number will include Pebbles or Rocks. One way we can change the Wilma case into a different number case is by saying that if she conceives now she will have blind twins and that if she takes the pill once a day for two months before conceiving she will have a single sighted child. The Implausible Conclusion that would follow from the non-identity argument in this different number version of the Wilma case would be that it would not be morally wrong for Wilma to conceive the blind twins rather than the sighted single child. And the response to the non-identity problem that my solution would offer in this different number case would again be to accept the conclusion.[8]

If the cases that I appealed to in the context of the original same number Wilma story succeeded in rendering the same number version of the Implausible Conclusion sufficiently plausible, then suitably modified versions of those cases should render the different number version of the Implausible Conclusion sufficiently plausible in this case, too. If it is plausible to say that it is not morally wrong for Fred to save a blind child rather than a sighted child, for example, then it is surely plausible to say that it is not morally wrong for Fred to save two blind children rather than a sighted child. If it is plausible to say that it is not morally wrong for Betty to conceive a blind child rather than no child and for Jane to conceive no child rather than a sighted child, then it is surely plausible to say that it is not morally wrong for Betty to conceive two blind children rather than no child and for Jane to conceive no child rather than a sighted child. And if it is plausible to say that it is not morally wrong for Mary to breed one more horse rather than to conceive one more child, then it is surely plausible to say that it is not morally wrong for Mary to breed two more horses rather than to conceive one more child. But if it is plausible to say that it is not morally wrong for Fred to save two blind children rather than one sighted child, not morally wrong for Betty to conceive two blind children rather than no child and for Jane to conceive no child rather than a sighted child, and not morally wrong for Mary to breed two more horses rather than to conceive one more child, then at least on the assumption that the original versions of the cases sufficed to establish the plausibility of the original version of the Implausible Conclusion, the revised versions of the cases should suffice to establish the plausibility of

---

[8] We can also change the case so that if Wilma conceives now she will conceive one blind child and if she conceives two months from now she will conceive two sighted children. The same strategy that I use in the text to render it plausible to suppose that it would not be wrong for Wilma to conceive two blind children rather than one sighted child can also be used to render it plausible to suppose that it would not be wrong for Wilma to conceive one blind child rather than two sighted children. It is plausible, for example, to say that it would not be wrong for Betty to conceive a blind child rather than conceive no child and not be wrong for Jane to conceive no child rather than conceive sighted twins. And it is plausible to say that it would not be wrong for Mary to breed one more healthy horse rather than conceiving two more healthy children. If the original cases of Betty, Jane, and Mary make it plausible to say that it would not be wrong for Wilma to conceive Pebbles rather than Rocks, then the revised versions of these cases will in the very same way make it plausible to say that it would not be wrong for Wilma to conceive one blind child rather than conceiving two sighted children.

saying that it is not morally wrong for Wilma to conceive two blind children rather than to conceive one sighted child. If the original versions of these cases render the Implausible Conclusion sufficiently plausible in direct same number bad condition cases like the original case of Wilma, then, these revised versions should render the Implausible Conclusion sufficiently plausible in direct different number bad condition cases like this revised case of Wilma. If my solution succeeds in direct same number bad condition cases, it should therefore succeed in direct different number bad condition cases, too.

Consider next the distinction between bad condition cases and bad event cases. The original case of Wilma is a bad condition case. If she makes the choice that is a bit more convenient for her in that case, she will conceive a child who is blind rather than a different child who would have been sighted. Blindness, we are assuming, is a bad condition to be in, but we need not assume that anything bad will happen to her blind child as a result of Wilma conceiving her that would not also have happened to her sighted child if she had conceived him instead. We can change the Wilma case into a bad event case by saying that if Wilma conceives now rather than two months from now, this will have no effect on the health of the child she would conceive but will somehow cause Wilma's body to produce a toxic substance that would leak out several years later and unavoidably cause her child to become blind and that if she takes the pill once a day for two months before conceiving, she would conceive a different healthy child and would not produce a toxic substance that would later cause that child to become blind. The Implausible Conclusion that would follow from the non-identity argument in this bad event version of the Wilma case would be that it would not be morally wrong for Wilma to conceive the child who would later become blind rather than the child who would never become blind. And the response to the non-identity problem that my solution would offer in this bad event case would again be simply to accept the conclusion.

If the cases that I appealed to in the context of the original bad condition version of the Wilma story succeeded in rendering the bad condition version of the Implausible Conclusion sufficiently plausible, then suitably modified versions of those cases should render the bad event version of the Implausible Conclusion sufficiently plausible as well. If it is plausible to say that it is not morally wrong for Fred to save a blind child rather than a sighted child, for example, then it is surely plausible to say that it is not morally wrong for Fred to save a sighted child who he knows will later become blind rather than a sighted child he knows will never become blind. If it is plausible to say that it is not morally wrong for Betty to conceive a blind child rather than no child and for Jane to conceive no child rather than a sighted child, then it is surely plausible to say that it is not morally wrong for Betty to conceive a child who will later become blind rather than no child and for Jane to conceive no child rather than a child who will never become blind.[9] But if it is plausible to say that it is not morally wrong for

---

[9] The case of Mary, who chooses to breed one more horse rather than to conceive one more child, is a bit more difficult to adapt for use in bad event cases. This is because while there are animals whose lives are like those of human beings in certain bad conditions, there are no animals whose lives are like those of human beings who begin life in a healthy condition and who later suffer a loss that leaves them with a disability. But

Fred to save a sighted child who he knows will later become blind rather than a sighted child he knows will never become blind, not morally wrong for Betty to conceive a child who will later become blind rather than no child, and not morally wrong for Jane to conceive no child rather than a child who will never become blind, then at least on the assumption that the original versions of the cases sufficed to establish the plausibility of the original version of the Implausible Conclusion, the revised versions of the cases should suffice to establish the plausibility of saying that it is not morally wrong for Wilma to conceive a child who will later become blind rather than a different child who would never become blind. If the original versions of these cases render the Implausible Conclusion sufficiently plausible in direct same number bad condition cases like the original case of Wilma, then these revised versions should render the Implausible Conclusion sufficiently plausible in direct same number bad event cases like this revised version of the case of Wilma. If my solution succeeds in direct same number bad condition cases, it should therefore succeed in direct same number bad event cases as well.

In addition, since we have already seen that the difference between same number and different number cases makes no difference to the merits of my solution, it follows that my solution succeeds in direct different number bad event cases as well. If it is plausible to say that it is not morally wrong for Fred to save a blind child rather than a sighted child, to save two blind children rather than a sighted child, or to save a sighted child who will later become blind rather than a sighted child who will never become blind, for example, then surely it is plausible to say that it is not morally wrong for Fred to save two sighted children who will both later become blind rather than a single sighted child who will never become blind. If it is plausible to say that it is not morally wrong for Betty to conceive a blind child rather than no child and for Jane to conceive no child rather than a sighted child, not morally wrong for Betty to conceive two blind children rather than no child and for Jane to conceive no child rather than a sighted child, and not morally wrong for Betty to conceive one child who will later become blind rather than no child and for Jane to conceive no child rather than a sighted child who would never become blind, then surely it is plausible to say that it is not morally wrong for Betty to conceive two children who will later go blind rather than no child and for Jane to conceive no child rather than a sighted child who would never become blind. And if the original versions of these cases were enough to render it plausible to say that it is not morally wrong for Wilma to conceive one blind child rather than one

---

if we don't mind making the case a bit more fanciful, we can modify it, too, in a way that can help reveal the plausibility of the Implausible Conclusion in bad event cases. Suppose, for example, that we have discovered life on Mars and that the Martians are rational beings who are exactly like us except that after a number of years they invariably lose their vision. And suppose also that Mary has already conceived two children of her own, has helped to create four Martian children, and has now decided that she has a slight preference to help create one more Martian rather than to conceive one more human. If it is plausible to say that it is not morally wrong for Mary to breed one more horse rather than conceive one more child, it is plausible to say that it is not morally wrong for Mary to decide to help create one more Martian rather than to conceive one more human child.

sighted child, these revised versions of the cases should be enough to render it plausible to say that it is not morally wrong for Wilma to conceive two children who will later become blind rather than one child who would never become blind. If my solution is successful in direct same number bad condition cases like the original version of Wilma, then, it is successful in direct different number bad condition cases, direct same number bad event cases, and direct different number bad event cases.

Finally, there is the distinction between the direct and indirect version of the non-identity problem. The original case of Wilma is an example of the direct version of the problem. Her choice to conceive now rather than two months later directly determines which particular person will exist after her choice is made. In examples of the indirect version of the problem, a person's choice has consequences that initiate a complex chain of events that eventually have an equally decisive effect on which particular people exist after the choice is made. In Chapter 1, I introduced the wealthy society's choice of the risky policy as an example of the indirect version of the non-identity problem. I will return to that case in more detail and explain how my solution can satisfactorily address it in section 7.7.3 below. Here, I will more briefly complete my discussion of the eight forms that the non-identity problem can take by starting with the fact that we can also change the Wilma case into an example of the indirect version of the non-identity problem by having her choose between two options whose identity-affecting consequences will occur hundreds of years in the future. Suppose that if she chooses the first option, things will be a little more convenient for her and that if she chooses the second option, then hundreds of years from now everything will be exactly the same as it will be if she chooses the first option except that one blind person who would exist if she chooses the first option will not exist if she chooses the second option and one sighted person who would not exist if she chooses the first option will exist if she chooses the second option. The Implausible Conclusion that would follow from the non-identity argument in this indirect version of the Wilma case would be that it would not be morally wrong for Wilma to choose the first option rather than the second option. And the response to the non-identity problem that my solution would offer in this indirect version of the case would once again be simply to accept the conclusion.

If the cases that I appealed to in the context of the direct version of the Wilma story succeeded in rendering the direct version of the Implausible Conclusion sufficiently plausible, then suitably modified versions of those cases should render the indirect version of the Implausible Conclusion sufficiently plausible in this modified version of the story as well. If it is plausible to say that it is not morally wrong for Fred to save a blind child rather than a sighted child, for example, then it is surely plausible to say that it is not morally wrong for Wilma to choose an option that will indirectly lead to Fred's saving a blind child rather than a sighted child hundreds of years in the future. If it is plausible to say that it is not morally wrong for Betty to conceive a blind child rather than no child and for Jane to conceive no child rather than a sighted child, then it is surely plausible to say that it is not morally wrong for Wilma to choose an option that will indirectly lead to Betty's conceiving a blind child rather than no child and to Jane's conceiving no child rather than a sighted child hundreds of years in the future. And if it is plausible to say that it is not morally wrong for Mary to breed one more horse rather than to conceive one more child, then it is surely plausible to say that it is not morally wrong for Wilma to choose an option that will indirectly lead to Mary's breeding another horse rather than conceiving another child hundreds of years in the future. If the original cases render the Implausible Conclusion sufficiently plausible in direct same number bad condition cases like the original case of Wilma, then, these revised versions should render the Implausible Conclusion sufficiently plausible in indirect same number bad condition cases like this revised case of Wilma. If my solution succeeds in the former kind of case, it therefore succeeds in the latter kind of case as well. And since, as we have already seen, my solution works equally well in same and different number cases and in bad event and bad condition cases, it can be applied to the indirect version of all of these cases as well. In short, I have argued that my solution works in direct same number bad condition cases, and that if it does work in such cases, then it works in all of the sorts of cases that give rise to the non-identity problem. If this is correct, then while other approaches fail to provide even a partial solution to the non-identity problem, my approach offers a complete solution.

7.6 Implications

I began this book by summarizing what the non-identity problem is, explaining the significance of the problem, and identifying three requirements that any solution to the problem must satisfy in order to count as a successful one. It therefore seems appropriate to conclude the book by summarizing what my solution to the problem is, explaining the significance of the solution, and considering whether the solution satisfies the three requirements with which I began.

Summarizing the solution that I have defended in this book is simple: we solve the problem that is generated by the inconsistency between accepting the five plausible premises and rejecting the Implausible Conclusion by recognizing that we have no good reason to reject the Implausible Conclusion. Once we agree to accept the Implausible Conclusion, the non-identity argument no longer gives rise to the non-identity problem.

Explaining the significance of the solution that I have defended here is also a relatively straightforward matter. As I explained in Chapter 1, the non-identity problem has important implications across a broad range of practical moral controversies and also puts pressure on a set of more general theoretical claims that most people seem inclined to accept. In the case of the theoretical beliefs that are challenged by the problem, the significance of the problem is that it seems to show that at least one of our current beliefs is mistaken. If we are right in thinking that Wilma's act is immoral, that is, then we must be wrong about what it is for a condition to make a person worse off, wrong about the relationship between making a person worse off and harming a person, wrong about the relationship between harming a person and wronging a person, or wrong about the relationship between wronging a person and doing something wrong. The significance of the solution that I have defended here in terms of these theoretical beliefs is therefore simple. Since the solution involves accepting the claim that Wilma's act is not immoral, the solution demonstrates that we need not be wrong about any of those beliefs. This is not to insist that all of the premises of the non-identity argument are true. There may well turn out to be good reasons for rejecting them. It is simply to say that the fact that they jointly entail that Wilma's act is not immoral gives us no reason to reject any of them. Every other proposed solution to the non-identity problem requires a significant revision to at least one of our initial theoretical beliefs. My solution does not.

In the case of the practical implications that I identified in Chapter 1, the significance of the non-identity problem arises from the fact that Wilma's act seems to be symmetric with a number of other acts that are the subject of significant moral controversy. Choosing to conceive a blind child now rather than a sighted child two months later, for example, seems relevantly similar to choosing to reproduce by cloning rather than by ordinary conception, at least on the assumption that cloning would result in a significant disability, that ordinary conception would not, and that the clone would still clearly have a life that is not worse than no life at all. Given certain other familiar assumptions about what is and is not good for children, choosing to conceive a blind child now rather than a sighted child two months later is also relevantly similar to a number of other potentially controversial acts, like conceiving a child out of wedlock rather than within it, having children with someone of a different faith or race rather than with someone of the same faith or race, or having a child when one is very young or very old rather than when one is somewhere in between.

The significance of the solution that I have defended here in the context of such cases is also fairly straightforward. Accepting that Wilma's act is not immoral means accepting that those other acts are not immoral either, at least on the assumption that there are no morally relevant differences between those other acts and Wilma's act. This need not mean that reproductive cloning, for example, would not be wrong. It might turn out that reproductive cloning would have negative consequences for third parties in a way that Wilma's act by stipulation does not, for example, and this fact might be used to argue against the practice. But it does mean that all of the arguments against reproductive cloning that appeal to the claim that cloning would be in some way bad for the child produced by cloning must be rejected. And since these seem clearly to be the most powerful arguments against cloning, this would make it far harder to argue against the practice. Every other solution to the non-identity problem involves rejecting the Implausible Conclusion and maintaining that what Wilma does is morally wrong, while my solution to the problem involves accepting the Implausible Conclusion and maintaining that what Wilma does is not morally wrong. Every other solution to the problem therefore makes it much easier to argue against reproductive cloning, while my solution makes it much harder. And the same would go for all of the other practices that might seem to be morally symmetric with Wilma's. While every other solution to the non-identity problem therefore tends in the direction of less reproductive moral freedom, my solution tends in the direction of more.

What about the case of the wealthy society? Here, too, the implications of my solution stand in stark contrast to the implications of all of the alternative solutions. To whatever extent our current failure to curb our consumption of natural resources or to reduce our levels of carbon emission proves to be morally on a par with the wealthy society's adopting the risky policy, for example, then to that extent my solution to the non-identity problem will make it harder to argue against our current behavior while every other solution will make it easier to argue against it. This does not mean that our current behavior is not wrong. But it does mean that we must reject any argument against our current behavior that depends on the claim that our current practices are wrong because they will have bad consequences for future people whose lives will clearly be worth living and who will never exist at all if we change our current behavior.

The practical significance of this particular implication may well prove to be quite modest. When I pollute, I impose costs on people who already exist. If a society opens up a nuclear power plant, it risks imposing costs on a great many people who already exist. My individual act of polluting and a society's act of opening a particular nuclear power plant, moreover, cannot reasonably be expected to alter the identity of every single person who is conceived after the act and who might be adversely affected by it. There is therefore no reason to think that ordinary cases of pollution and of risking pollution are sufficient to generate the non-identity problem and therefore no reason to think that my solution to the non-identity problem raises doubts about the claim that such acts can be wrong because they harm people or expose people to unwarranted risks of harm.[10] But if there do turn out to be particular cases in which we act in ways that are worse for no one but that will cause bad things to happen to people in the distant future in the way that the risky policy does in the case of the wealthy society, then the solution to the non-identity problem that I have advanced here would make it harder to argue against those practices while every other solution would make it easier to do so. And the same is true in the case of obligations to make amends for historical injustices. My solution to the non-identity problem does not make it impossible to sustain a case for slave reparations, for example, but it does make it more difficult.[11] None of the other solutions to the problem automatically generates a successful defense of slave reparations, but all of them make it much easier to do so. These results further distinguish the solution that I have defended here from all of the alternatives.

---

[10] Carter (2001: 444–5) notes this as well.

[11] I argue that the slave reparations position can be sustained while accepting the conclusion of the non-identity argument in Boonin (2011: 109–12). For other attempts to establish this, see, e.g., Meyer (2006: 409–10), Herstein (2008a; 2008b), Sepinwall (2006: 226–8), Sher (2005), Shiffrin (2009), and Simmons (1995: 178 n. 41).

7.7 The Three Requirements Revisited

Finally, let me turn to the question of whether the solution that I have defended in this book satisfies the three requirements that I set forth at the outset. Here things become a bit more complicated.

7.7.1 The Independence Requirement

When I first introduced the independence requirement, I characterized the requirement as saying that the reason provided for rejecting a given premise of the non-identity argument must be independent of the fact that rejecting the premise would enable us to avoid the Implausible Conclusion. Since my solution to the problem does not involve rejecting any of the premises of the non-identity argument, it might seem a straightforward matter to say that my solution satisfies this requirement. Indeed, since my solution is precisely that we should accept the Implausible Conclusion, it should be obvious that my solution in no way depends on accepting any claim at all merely because accepting the claim would help us to avoid the Implausible Conclusion. So it may seem obvious that my solution satisfies the independence requirement.

But this doesn't get things quite right. The independence requirement is reasonable because it arises from a more general requirement that a solution to the non-identity problem not be ad hoc. Whatever claims a solution to the problem rests on, that is, those claims must be justified by something other than the fact that if they are accepted they will help to solve the problem. Seen in this more general light, the question is not whether my solution depends on accepting any claims just in order to avoid the Implausible Conclusion—clearly it does not—but rather whether my solution depends on accepting any claims just in order to avoid being unable to solve the problem. And since my solution involves accepting the Implausible Conclusion, this means that what the independence requirement must really demand is that my solution provide reasons to accept the Implausible Conclusion that are independent of the fact that accepting the conclusion would enable us to solve the non-identity problem.

Once the independence requirement is recast in this way, it should become clear that my solution to the problem does, in fact, satisfy it. I have not argued that we should accept the Implausible Conclusion merely because doing so enables us to resolve the tension between the plausibility of the non-identity argument's premises and the apparent implausibility of its conclusion. Rather, and unlike the few other philosophers who have urged us to solve the problem by accepting the conclusion, I have given a number of distinct reasons to believe that the Implausible Conclusion is not so implausible and these reasons are all completely independent of the fact that accepting the plausibility of the Implausible Conclusion would help us to solve the non-identity problem. Independent of any desire to solve the non-identity problem, for example, most people find it perfectly plausible to say that it is not positively immoral for Peter to spend his fifty dollars on dinner and a movie rather than donating it to Oxfam. In the same way, they find it independently plausible to say that it is not immoral for Fred to save blind Billy rather than sighted Timmy, not immoral for Betty to conceive a blind child rather than no child, not immoral for Jane to conceive no child rather than a sighted child, and not immoral for Mary to breed another horse rather than conceive another child. In all of these cases, the reasons I have given for accepting that the Implausible Conclusion is not so implausible are completely independent of the fact that accepting the plausibility of the Implausible Conclusion enables us to solve the non-identity problem. And so even when the independence requirement is adapted to fit the nature of the solution I have defended here, it should be clear that my solution does indeed satisfy it.

7.7.2 *The Robustness Requirement*

The second requirement that I said any solution to the non-identity problem must satisfy is what I called the robustness requirement. When I introduced this requirement, I described it by saying that in order to underwrite a successful solution to the problem, a reason for rejecting a given premise of the non-identity argument must be strong enough to warrant rejecting any weakened version of the premise that would still be strong enough to generate the Implausible Conclusion. This was because if a reason for rejecting a particular premise is not sufficiently robust, it will show that the non-identity argument as I initially formulated it is mistaken, but it will not prevent a suitably revised version of the argument from yielding precisely the same Implausible Conclusion. Here it may seem clear that my solution to the problem fails to satisfy the requirement. The robustness requirement says that a solution must prevent us from being forced to accept the Implausible Conclusion, after all, and my solution depends precisely on our accepting the Implausible Conclusion.

But this, too, doesn't get things quite right. The robustness requirement is reasonable because it arises from a more general requirement that a solution to the non-identity problem be strong enough to prevent the problem from simply reemerging in a modified form. Whatever claims a solution to the problem rests on, that is, those claims must be strong enough to ensure that the tension between the premises and the conclusion is truly eliminated, and not simply relocated. Seen in this more general light, the question is not whether my solution is strong enough to avoid the Implausible Conclusion— clearly it is not—but rather whether it is strong enough to avoid the problem generated by the tension between that conclusion and the premises of the argument that gives rise to it. And since my solution involves accepting the Implausible Conclusion, this means that what the robustness requirement must really demand is that the reason for accepting the plausibility of the Implausible Conclusion be strong enough to prevent a modified version of the premises from generating the same tension all over again.

When the robustness requirement is recast in this way, it should become clear that my solution to the problem also satisfies this requirement. The reasons I have given for accepting the plausibility of the Implausible Conclusion have nothing to do with the particular premises of the argument that gives rise to it. They instead have to do with the plausibility of the claims I have made about the acts involved in the cases of Peter,

Fred, Betty, Jane, and Mary. No matter what version of the premises the non-identity argument uses to generate the Implausible Conclusion, then, my solution will be strong enough to prevent those premises from generating a problem because it will be strong enough to show that the conclusion generated by those premises is not implausible enough to generate a problem.

7.7.3 The Modesty Requirement

Finally, there is the modesty requirement. When I introduced the modesty requirement, I characterized the requirement as saying that the reason provided for rejecting a given premise of the non-identity argument must not be so strong that it generates implications that are even more implausible than the Implausible Conclusion that the reason is deployed to help us avoid. This is what I meant by saying that the cure to the non-identity problem must not be worse than the disease. As in the case of the independence requirement, it might again seem a simple matter to show that my solution satisfies this requirement. My solution to the non-identity problem does not give a reason for rejecting a premise of the non-identity argument that is too strong because my solution to the non-identity problem does not give a reason for rejecting a premise of the non-identity argument at all.

But, once again, this doesn't get things quite right. The modesty requirement is reasonable because it arises from a more general requirement that the cure to the non-identity problem not be worse than the disease. Whatever claims a solution to the problem rests on, that is, those claims must not saddle us with a bigger problem than the problem we are trying to solve. Seen in this more general light, the question is not whether my solution gives too strong a reason for rejecting one of the premises of the non-identity argument—clearly it does not—but rather whether it gives a reason of any kind that is so strong that it creates bigger problems than it solves. And since my solution involves giving reasons to accept the plausibility of the Implausible Conclusion, this means that what the modesty requirement really demands is that my reasons for accepting the Implausible Conclusion not be so strong that they would also justify accepting other conclusions that pose even bigger problems.

7.7.3.1 THE EVEN MORE IMPLAUSIBLE CONCLUSION

When the modesty requirement is recast in this way, it poses two final challenges to the solution that I have defended in this book. The first challenge arises from a case that I introduced in Chapter 1 but to which I have returned only sporadically since: the case of the wealthy society. In that example, the current members of the society select a risky energy policy that will make things a little bit better for them than the alternative but that will also cause toxic waste to leak five hundred years later, killing tens of thousands of innocent people at the age of forty. Since the choice between the two energy policies will determine which set of people will exist five hundred years later, and since the people who will be killed by the toxic waste will still clearly have lives that are worth living, the argument that entails that Wilma's act of conceiving Pebbles is not immoral also entails that the wealthy society's act of selecting the risky policy is not immoral. This means that my solution to the non-identity problem commits me to accepting this further conclusion. And this may well seem to show that my solution to the problem cannot satisfy the modesty requirement. Even if we are willing to accept that it is not wrong to conceive a blind child rather than a sighted child, after all, will we really be willing to accept that it is not wrong to kill tens of thousands of innocent people just in order to enjoy a slightly higher standard of living? Although I have to this point considered both claims to be simply different versions of the same Implausible Conclusion, we may well find the latter claim to be even more implausible than the former claim. For my purposes here, I will therefore refer to the claim that the wealthy society's act is not wrong as the Even More Implausible Conclusion. If my solution to the non-identity problem commits us to accepting this Even More Implausible Conclusion, then my solution may very well seem too strong.

It is not obvious that my solution to the non-identity problem commits me to accepting the Even More Implausible Conclusion. This is because the case of Wilma involves principles of individual morality while the case of the wealthy society involves principles of public policy. One could argue that consequentialist considerations should play a greater role in public policy deliberations than in cases of individual morality and then argue that such considerations would make the choice made by the wealthy society wrong without making the choice made by Wilma wrong.[12] This is one way that my solution might be protected from the charge that the Even More Implausible Conclusion prevents it from satisfying the modesty requirement.

But let's assume that my solution does commit me to accepting the Even More Implausible Conclusion. Even if this is so, this does not mean that my solution must fail to satisfy the modesty requirement. This is because the strategies that I have employed in this chapter to show that the Implausible Conclusion about Wilma is not really so implausible can be modified to show that the Even More Implausible Conclusion about the wealthy society is not really so implausible either. And if the Even More Implausible Conclusion is not really so implausible, then the fact that my solution commits me to accepting it, if it is a fact, provides no reason to think that my solution fails to satisfy the modesty requirement.

Consider, for example, the case of Peter. Virtually everyone will agree that although it would be better for Peter to donate his fifty dollars to Oxfam, it would not be positively immoral for him to spend it on dinner and a movie instead. At the least, they will agree that this claim is a perfectly plausible one. I argued that the case of Peter is not so different from the case of Wilma and that this helped to show that the Implausible Conclusion was not so implausible either. But the case of Peter can be easily modified to make it more like the case of the wealthy society. The United States, after all, currently contributes billions of dollars each year in the form of international humanitarian aid. But it could increase the amount that it spends by enough to save tens of

---

[12] See, e.g., Lillehammer (2009: 232, 245), Herissone-Kelly (2009: 256).

thousands of additional lives, and if it did so, the increased cost would have only a mar-
ginal effect on the overall well-being of its population. As with the case of Peter, most
people would agree that it would be praiseworthy for the United States to increase its
already considerable humanitarian aid spending. But, again as with the case of Peter,
they would reject the claim that it would be positively immoral for the United States
to instead continue giving at its current level. At the very least, they would have to
agree that it is plausible to say that it is not positively immoral for the United States to
refrain from giving even more than the billions of dollars it already gives each year.
Even those who argue that it is positively immoral for the United States not to spend
more money on humanitarian aid than it currently does clearly recognize that they are
arguing against the deeply embedded conventional view of the matter. But the case of
the United States declining to increase its level of humanitarian aid in this way is similar to the case of the wealthy society's adopting the risky policy in just the same way
that the case of Peter is similar to the case of Wilma. In both cases, an affluent society
makes the choice that is a little bit better for itself even though it could prevent tens of
thousands of innocent people from dying prematurely if it instead made the choice
that was a little bit worse for it. If it is plausible to say that it is not positively immoral
for the United States not to donate even more than the billions of dollars it already
contributes in humanitarian aid each year, then why shouldn't it also be plausible to
say that it is not positively immoral for the wealthy society to choose the energy policy
that makes things a bit better for it?

Someone who wishes to reject the Even More Implausible Conclusion while agreeing that it is not immoral for the United States to refrain from increasing the amount
of money it already contributes to humanitarian aid could try to show that there is a
morally relevant difference between the United States example and the wealthy society
example. They could argue, for example, that the wealthy society has a special obligation to its own future citizens while the United States does not have a special obligation to the citizens of other countries. Or they could argue that declining to increase
humanitarian aid merely allows some innocent people to be harmed while adopting
the energy policy that produces the toxic waste actively harms innocent people. As
in the case of Peter and Wilma, such arguments are certainly possible, and so there
is nothing inconsistent about believing both that the wealthy society acts wrongly by
adopting the risky policy and that United States does not act wrongly by not increasing
its current level of humanitarian aid.

But, as before, the point of the case of United States humanitarian aid policy is not
to give a reason to believe that the wealthy society's act is not morally wrong. The reason for thinking that the wealthy society's act is not morally wrong is provided by the
non-identity argument in conjunction with the reasons I provided in the previous
chapters for rejecting those responses to the argument that depend on rejecting one of
the argument's premises. The point of the humanitarian aid example, rather, is to show
that if my analysis in the previous chapters has been correct, then we should accept that
even the Even More Implausible Conclusion is perfectly plausible. If adopting the risky

policy really does harm the innocent people who are later killed when the toxic waste leaks, for example, then the objection I raised against the argument made by Matthew Hanser in section 3.2.1 must be mistaken, in which case we can solve the non-identity problem by rejecting P2 of the non-identity argument. Similarly, if adopting the risky policy really does violate a special civic obligation that the society has to those future people as fellow citizens, then there must be a mistake in one of the other arguments I made in the previous chapters and again a way to solve the non-identity problem by rejecting one of the premises of the argument that gives rise to it. But if I have been correct in maintaining that the wealthy society's act does not harm those future people and that it does not violate any special obligation it has to them, then the case of the wealthy society adopting the risky policy really should not strike us as being much different from the case of the United States deciding not to increase the amount of money it already contributes to humanitarian aid. The claim that it is not positively immoral for the United States to make that decision strikes most people as perfectly plausible. Unless we have already solved the non-identity problem by successfully rejecting one of the premises of the non-identity argument, then, we should simply accept that the claim that the wealthy society's act is not positively immoral is perfectly plausible, too. And if we accept that the claim is plausible, then even if my solution to the non-identity problem commits us to accepting the Even More Implausible Conclusion, this does nothing to show that the solution fails to satisfy the modesty requirement.

The same strategy that I have used in modifying the case of Peter, moreover, can also be applied to other cases that I used to defend the plausibility of the Implausible Conclusion. For ease of exposition, it may help to suppose that five hundred years from now the average life expectancy will be eighty and to remember that all of the tens of thousands of people who will be killed by the leaking toxic waste generated by the wealthy society will be killed when they are forty. With that in mind, we can change the case of Fred so that neither Billy nor Timmy is blind but Billy has a genetic condition that will cause him to die at the age of forty while Timmy will be sure to live until the age of eighty. If it is plausible to say that it is not immoral for Fred to save Billy rather than Timmy when Billy is blind and Timmy is not, then it should be plausible to say that it is not immoral for Fred to save Billy rather than Timmy when Billy has this genetic condition and Timmy does not.

But if it is not immoral for Fred to save Billy rather than Timmy in this revised version of the story, then it would not be immoral for tens of thousands of people to each save a child with the life-shortening condition rather than save a different child without the life-shortening condition under the same set of circumstances. If it would not be wrong for tens of thousands of people to each save a child with the life-shortening condition rather than save a different child without the life-shortening condition under the same set of circumstances then it would not be wrong for a society to adopt a policy that would predictably lead to tens of thousands of people each saving a child with the life-shortening condition rather than saving a different child without the life-shortening condition under the same set of circumstances. And adopting such a policy is similar to the wealthy society's adopting the risky policy in just the same way that the original version of Fred was like the original version of Wilma. The original version of Fred was like the original version of Wilma in that Wilma chooses to bring into existence a blind child rather than a sighted child while Fred chooses to sustain the existence of a blind child rather than a sighted child. In just the same way, the new policy case is like the original policy case in that the wealthy society chooses a policy that ends up causing to come into existence tens of thousands of people who will die at the age of forty rather than causing to come into existence tens of thousands of different people who would instead have lived to the age of eighty, while the society in the new policy case chooses a policy that ends up sustaining the existence of tens of thousands of people who will die at the age of forty rather than sustaining the lives of tens of thousands of different people who would instead have lived to the age of eighty. If the plausibility of the claim that Fred's act is not wrong in the original version of Fred makes it plausible to say that Wilma's act is not wrong, then, the plausibility of the claim that it would not be wrong for a society to adopt a policy that would predictably lead to tens of thousands of people each saving a child with the life-shortening condition rather than saving a different child without the life-shortening condition should make it plausible to say that it would not be wrong for the wealthy society to adopt the risky policy. A modified version of a case that shows that the Implausible Conclusion is not so implausible again shows that even the Even More Implausible Conclusion is not so implausible either.

And the same goes for the cases of Betty and Jane. We can change the case of Betty so that she must choose between conceiving no child and conceiving a child with a life expectancy of forty. And we can change the case of Jane so that she must choose between conceiving a child with a life expectancy of eighty and conceiving no child. If it is plausible to say that it is not immoral for Betty to conceive a blind child rather than no child, then it is clearly plausible to say that it is not immoral for Betty to conceive a child with a life expectancy of forty rather than no child. If it is plausible to say that it is not immoral for Jane to conceive no child rather than conceiving a sighted child, then it is clearly plausible to say that it is not immoral for Jane to conceive no child rather than conceiving a child with a life expectancy of eighty. And if the transitivity argument succeeds in showing that the original versions of Betty and Jane make it plausible to say that it would not be immoral for a woman to conceive a blind child rather than conceiving a different sighted child, then when applied to these modified versions of Betty and Jane, the very same transitivity argument will make it plausible to say that it would not be immoral for a woman to conceive a child with a life expectancy of forty rather than conceiving a different child with a life expectancy of eighty. If the plausibility of the claim that it would not be immoral to choose A over B and not immoral to choose B over C makes it plausible to say that it would not be immoral to choose A over C in the original cases of Betty and Jane, that is, then it will also make it plausible to say this in the modified cases of Betty and Jane. And in the modified versions of the cases of Betty and Jane, the claim that it would not be immoral to choose A over C is the claim that it would not be immoral to conceive a child with a life expectancy of forty rather than conceiving a different child who would have had a life expectancy of eighty.

But if it is not immoral for one woman to conceive a child with a life expectancy of forty rather than conceiving a different child who would instead have had a life expectancy of eighty, then it would not be immoral for tens of thousands of women to each conceive a child with a life expectancy of forty rather than conceiving a different child who would instead have had a life expectancy of eighty. If it would not be immoral for tens of thousands of women to make this choice, then it would not be immoral for a society to adopt a policy that would predictably lead to tens of thousands of women making this choice. And adopting such a policy is relevantly similar to the wealthy society's adopting the risky policy: the wealthy society chooses to predictably cause to come into existence tens of thousands of people who will die at the age of forty rather than to predictably cause to come into existence tens of thousands of different people who would instead have lived to the age of eighty, while the society in the new case adopts a policy that predictably leads to tens of thousands of women each conceiving one child who will die at the age of forty rather than conceiving a different child who would instead have died at the age of eighty. If it would not be immoral for a society to adopt a policy that predictably leads to tens of thousands of women each choosing to conceive a child with a life expectancy of forty rather than conceiving a different child who would instead have had a life expectancy of eighty, therefore, it would not be immoral for the wealthy society to adopt the risky policy. So if the original versions of the cases of Betty and Jane show that it is plausible to say that it is not immoral for Wilma to conceive a blind child rather than a sighted child, then the modified versions of the cases of Betty and Jane show that it is plausible to say that it is not immoral for the wealthy society to adopt the risky policy. Modified versions of the cases that show that the Implausible Conclusion is not so implausible once again show that even the Even More Implausible Conclusion is not so implausible either.

As was true with the original cases of Fred, Betty, and Jane, someone who wishes to reject the Even More Implausible Conclusion while agreeing that the choices made are not immoral in the modified versions of the cases that I have appealed to here could try to show that there is a morally relevant difference between these cases and the case of the wealthy society. But, again as in those cases, this strategy will fail to undermine the approach that I have adopted here. If they identify a morally relevant difference between the cases, this will be because of some mistake I overlooked in one of the previous chapters. If there are no such mistakes, then the case of the wealthy society really should not strike us as being much different from these other cases. Unless we have already solved the non-identity problem by successfully rejecting one of the premises of the non-identity argument, then, these additional cases should give us even more reason to simply accept that the claim that the wealthy society's act is not positively immoral is perfectly plausible. And if we accept that the claim is plausible, then, again, even if my solution does commit us to accepting the Even More Implausible

Conclusion, this does nothing to show that my solution fails to satisfy the modesty requirement.

The case of Mary, who chooses to breed one more horse rather than to conceive one more child, is a bit more difficult to render comparable to the case of the wealthy society. This is because there are no other animals whose lives are like that of a typical human being with a forty-year life expectancy. But if we don't mind making the case a bit more fanciful, we can modify it, too, in a way that helps to further reveal the plausibility of the Even More Implausible Conclusion. Suppose, for example, that we have discovered life on Mars and that Martians are rational beings who are exactly like us except that the natural life span for their species is forty years while the natural life span for our species is eighty years. And suppose also that Mary has already conceived two human children of her own, has helped four Martian women with fertility problems to each create one Martian child, and has now decided that she has a slight preference to help create one more Martian rather than to conceive one more human. Surely it is plausible to say that it is not immoral for Mary to decide to help create one more Martian rather than to conceive one more human child. And if that is right, then it is just as surely plausible to say that it is not immoral for a society to permit tens of thousands of its citizens to make that choice. But a society whose choice results in tens of thousands of additional Martians coming into existence and dying at the age of forty rather than tens of thousands of additional humans coming into existence and dying at the age of eighty is like the wealthy society's choosing the risky policy rather than the safe policy in just the same way that the original case of Mary was like the original case of Wilma. If the original case of Mary successfully helps to uncover the plausibility of the Implausible Conclusion, then this revised version of the case of Mary should once again help to uncover the plausibility of the Even More Implausible Conclusion. The combination of all of these modified cases, then, gives us good reason to conclude that, upon reflection, the Even More Implausible Conclusion should be deemed perfectly plausible. And if we accept that the Even More Implausible Conclusion is actually quite plausible, then, once again, the fact that my solution commits us to accepting the Even More Implausible Conclusion, if it is a fact, does nothing to show that my solution fails to satisfy the modesty requirement.

7.7.3.2 THE MOST IMPLAUSIBLE CONCLUSION

The case of the wealthy society poses one challenge to the claim that my solution to the non-identity problem satisfies the modesty requirement. A second challenge emerges from a further kind of case, one that I have not to this point discussed. When I introduced the non-identity problem at the outset of this book, I began with the case of Wilma. And while I stipulated that the disability that Wilma's child would have if she conceived right away was the kind of disability that clearly has a substantially negative impact on a person's quality of life, I also stipulated that the disability would clearly not be serious enough to render the child's life worse than no life at all. In short, I stipulated that while the child would be disabled, the child's life would nonetheless clearly be worth living. I went on to use the example of a child born with incurable blindness, in part because blindness is one of the most common examples discussed in the literature on the non-identity problem. But I also used this example in part because while blindness is widely regarded as having a significantly negative impact on a person's quality of life, whether due to features of blindness itself or to the way that society typically treats or fails to accommodate blind people, it is also clearly not seen as something that could plausibly make a life worse than no life at all. This last part of the description of the case was crucial because the non-identity problem does not arise in cases, if there are any, in which conceiving a person makes that person worse off than they would otherwise have been. But, a critic of my solution might point out, a typical blind person doesn't have a life that is just barely better than no life at all. A typical blind person is perfectly capable of enjoying a very high quality of life, even if the deprivations resulting from the blindness or from the way that blind people are treated make that high quality of life significantly lower than it would be for an otherwise comparable sighted person. It may be, then, that if I have succeeded in rendering the Implausible Conclusion plausible in this chapter, I have done so only because I have focused on the example of a blind person and because blind people can typically live quite happy lives. And so the final challenge to the claim that my solution can satisfy the modesty requirement arises from the fact that my solution seems to commit us to accepting the claim that Wilma's act would not have been wrong even if she had known that her child would have a life whose quality was much lower than that of a typical blind person and that would by the thinnest of margins be just barely worth living.

It is difficult to provide an uncontroversial example of a life that is just barely worth living. So let me start by modifying the case of Wilma and saying that if she conceives now, she will have a girl named Sandy, and that whatever kind of life strikes you as one that by the thinnest of margins is just barely worth living, that is precisely the life that Sandy will have. The final challenge to my solution consists of two claims: that my solution entails that it would not be wrong for Wilma to conceive Sandy rather than waiting two months and conceiving Rocks, and that if this is so, then my solution fails to satisfy the modesty requirement. Since the claim that it would not be wrong for Wilma to conceive Sandy rather than Rocks may well seem to be the most implausible implication that my solution might be said to have, I will refer to this claim as the Most Implausible Conclusion.

As with the case of the Even More Implausible Conclusion, it is not clear that my solution to the non-identity problem commits me to accepting the Most Implausible Conclusion. There might turn out to be a morally relevant difference between conceiving Pebbles and conceiving Sandy. Some people might argue, for example, that the life of a blind person has the same moral value as the life of an otherwise comparable sighted person but that the life of a person whose life is just the slightest bit better than no life at all does not. Or they might argue that the amount of well-being in the life of a blind person is close enough to the amount of well-being in the life of an otherwise comparable sighted person to justify treating the amount as equal for decision-making purposes but that the amount of well-being in the life of a person whose life is just the slightest bit better than no life at all is not. A proponent of either sort of account, or of any other account on which there proves to be a morally relevant difference between Pebbles and Sandy, could therefore consistently hold that while it would not be wrong to save a blind child rather than a sighted child, as in the case of Fred, it would be wrong to save a child whose life is just barely worth living rather than saving an ordinary child. Or they might hold that while it would not be wrong to conceive a blind child rather than no child at all, as in the case of Jane, it would be wrong to conceive a child whose life is just barely worth living rather than conceiving no child at all. Indeed, I suspect that many people will respond to these pairs of cases in just this way. On this sort of account, the arguments I have given for the claim that it would not be wrong for Wilma to conceive Pebbles rather than Rocks would not commit me to the claim that it would not be wrong for Wilma to conceive Sandy rather than Rocks because there would be a morally relevant difference between conceiving Pebbles and conceiving Sandy. So my argument for simply accepting the Implausible Conclusion would not entail that we should also accept the Most Implausible Conclusion. And if my argument does not entail that we should accept the Most Implausible Conclusion, then it will not matter if the Most Implausible Conclusion really is most implausible. This is one way that my solution to the non-identity problem might be defended from the charge that the Most Implausible Conclusion prevents it from satisfying the modesty requirement.

But let's suppose that there really is no morally relevant difference between Pebbles and Sandy. If this is so, then my proposal that we solve the non-identity problem by accepting the Implausible Conclusion really does commit me to accepting the Most Implausible Conclusion. But even if my solution does commit me to accepting the Most Implausible Conclusion on this assumption, this does not mean that my solution fails to satisfy the modesty requirement. This is because the same strategies that I employed to show that the Implausible Conclusion is not so implausible can be modified to show that the Most Implausible Conclusion is not so implausible either, at least if we assume that there really is no morally relevant difference between Pebbles and Sandy. And if the Most Implausible Conclusion is not so implausible on the assumption that there is no morally relevant difference between Pebbles and Sandy, then the fact that my solution commits me to accepting the Most Implausible Conclusion on that assumption provides no reason to think that my solution fails to satisfy the modesty requirement.

I suspect that many people will be inclined to reject this second response out of hand. This is because they will think that it is virtually self-evident that it would be wrong, for example, to conceive a child whose life would be just barely worth living even if the alternative was conceiving no child at all.[13] And if it is virtually self-evident that this would be wrong, then it would be pointless to try to make the Most Implausible Conclusion seem less implausible by appealing, for example, to the claim that it would not be wrong for Betty to conceive a child like Sandy if the alternative was conceiving no child at all. Before trying to render this second response to the objection to my

[13] See, e.g., Steinbock (2009: 163–4).

solution plausible by revising the cases I have appealed to so that they can be compared with Wilma conceiving Sandy rather than with Wilma conceiving Pebbles, then, I want to say something to try to blunt the force of this likely initial resistance.

So go back to what I said when I introduced the case of Sandy. Rather than providing any details about Sandy's condition, I simply said that whatever kind of life strikes you as one that by the thinnest of margins is just barely worth living, that is the life that Sandy would have. And now ask yourself what kind of life you pictured. I suspect that you pictured a person whose life contains a great deal of suffering and hardship, but who also enjoys just enough positive experiences to barely outweigh the negative ones. If this is the way that you were picturing Sandy's life, and if you find it clear that it would be wrong for Betty to conceive a child like the one you were picturing even if the alternative were conceiving no child at all, I suspect that this is because the way you were picturing Sandy's life is too unreliable to make for a fair test of your intuitions about this question. Even if you try to assure yourself by explicit stipulation that the positive experiences in Sandy's life will just barely outweigh the negative experiences, you are imagining a life with so many and such serious negative experiences that the picture in your mind may easily slip over into that of a life that is what some have called "worth not living," a life where the negatives outweigh the positives and that is actually worse than no life at all. If that is what you are picturing when you are picturing Sandy, then it may well be the thought that creating Sandy would actually make things worse for Sandy that accounts for your belief that creating Sandy would be morally wrong. And if that is why you think that it would be wrong to create Sandy, then the fact that you think it would be wrong to create Sandy, if you do think this, will do nothing to show that you think it would be wrong for Betty to conceive a child whose life really would be worth living, even if only barely, rather than no child at all.

We can test this hypothesis about your intuitions by picturing a life that is just barely worth living but that contains no hardship or suffering. Suppose, to take an admittedly fanciful example, that you must press one of two buttons and that it would be a little bit more convenient for you to press Button One rather than Button Two. If you press Button Two, nothing will happen, but if you press Button One, a brand new, fully-formed adult human being named Ted will instantaneously pop into existence, sit down in a mildly comfortable seat, watch one mildly amusing television show, fall asleep, and then die painlessly before awakening without experiencing any fear or regret and without having formed any plans or preferences that will be frustrated by his sudden demise. This life that contains no unpleasant experiences or frustrated desires and one mildly pleasant experience strikes me, at least, as just barely better than no life at all. I find it difficult to see anything bad in Ted's life and difficult to deny that it contains at least a little bit that is at least a little bit good. And when I then think about the situation you find yourself in with the two buttons, I also find it difficult to see what could be wrong about your pushing Button One and bringing Ted into existence. It seems clear to me, in fact, that your doing so would not be morally wrong. So, at least to me, the case of Ted makes it extremely plausible to say that it would not be wrong to create a person whose life will just barely be worth living when the alternative is creating no life at all.

If your response to the case of Ted is the same as mine, and if you thought that it would clearly be wrong for Betty to create a child whose life would be barely worth living rather than create no child at all when you were picturing that child's life as including a great deal of hardship and suffering, then this is evidence that the child's life that you were picturing was not providing an accurate test of your intuitive response to the question of whether it would be wrong to create a child whose life really was worth living, even if only barely, rather than creating no child at all. If you agree that Ted's life would be just barely worth living and that it would not be wrong to create Ted, that is, this shows that you thought it would be wrong for Betty to create the child whose life you were imagining only because you were not fully convinced that that child's life would be worth living in the first place. If that's right, then the fact that you thought that it would be wrong for Betty to create the child whose life you initially thought was a good example of a life that is just barely worth living provides no reason for you to think that it would be wrong for Betty to create a child whose life really would be just barely worth living. And the fact that you think that it would not be wrong to push Button One and create Ted, if you do think that, provides you with a reason to think that it would not, in fact, be wrong for Betty to create a child whose life would be just barely worth living when the alternative was creating no child at all. And if it would not be wrong for Betty to create such a child, then this modified version of the case of Betty may well prove useful in trying to show that even the Most Implausible Conclusion is actually perfectly plausible.

But suppose that your response to the case of Ted is different from mine. It seems clear to me that it would not be wrong to create Ted when the alternative is creating no one at all, but let's suppose that it seems clear to you that doing so really would be wrong. And now ask yourself this: why do you think that it would it be wrong to create Ted in this case? There are two possibilities. One is that you agree with me that Ted's life really would be worth living but you think that it would be wrong to create him despite this fact. The other is that you think that even though Ted's life would contain no negative experiences or frustrated desires, it still would not be worth living and you think that it would be wrong to create him because of this fact. I suspect that most people who think it would be wrong to create Ted would endorse the second answer rather than the first. It is easy enough to make sense of the thought that Ted's life is not worth living. Even though it contains no unpleasant experiences or frustrated desires, it falls so far short of what a human being is capable of that it might well strike some people as being unworthy of a human being. And if Ted's life really would not be worth living for this reason, it is easy enough to make sense of the thought that this could make it wrong to bring him into existence. But I, at least, find it difficult to make sense of the thought that it could be wrong to create Ted if Ted's life really would be worth living. If pushing Button One rather than Button Two wouldn't be bad for Ted or for anyone else and if it would actually result in a slightly higher total amount of well-being in the world, what kind of consideration could justify the conclusion that doing so would be wrong? So if it really would be wrong to create Ted, it seems far more plausible to me to suppose that this would be because Ted's life really would not be worth living than to think that it would be wrong despite the fact that his life really would be worth living. And if your reaction to the case of Ted is different from mine because you don't really think that Ted's life would be worth living in the first place, then the fact that you think it would be wrong to create Ted rather than to create no one does nothing to show that you think it would be wrong to create someone whose life really would be worth living, even if just barely, rather than to create no one.

If you agree with me that Ted's life is barely worth living and that it would not be wrong to create Ted, then nothing more is needed to convince you that it is not wrong to create someone whose life is barely worth living when the alternative is creating no life at all.[14] If you remain confident that Ted's life really is worth living and that it really would be wrong to create Ted, then while I remain puzzled about how this could be the case and skeptical that many people will think that it is, I admit that I have nothing further to say in response to you and that the strategy I will deploy below to try to render the Most Implausible Conclusion plausible will not work on you.[15] But suppose that you think that it would be wrong to create Ted and that, as seems more likely, this is because you do not agree with my claim that Ted's life really would be worth living, even if just barely. In that case, your response to the case of Ted does not give you a reason to reject my claim that it would not be wrong to create someone whose life is just

---

[14] One other case might be worth briefly noting. Suppose that if you push a button, a fully formed adult human being named Bill will instantaneously pop into existence. Bill will be in a deep coma from the first moment of his existence and he will live for many years without ever becoming at all conscious before he dies. This life that contains no experiences at all strikes me as not being worth living but also as not being "worth not living." I don't think it's better for Bill to be brought into existence than never to exist but I also don't think it's worse for Bill to be brought into existence than never to exist. And while I can't see any point in your pushing the button in this case, it doesn't seem to me that it would be morally wrong if you did. If pushing this button does not seem wrong to you either, and if you thought that it would obviously be wrong for Betty to create a child whose life would be barely worth living when you were picturing that child's life as including a great deal of suffering and hardship, then this second case provides additional evidence that your version of the case of Sandy was not providing an accurate test of your intuitive response to the question of whether it would be wrong to create a child whose life really was worth living, even if only barely, rather than creating no child at all. After all, if it would not be wrong to create Bill rather than create no one, and if by stipulation the child that Betty would conceive if she conceives a child would have a life that was at least a tiny bit better than Bill's, how could it be wrong for Betty to conceive such a child rather than to conceive no child at all?

[15] If I am unable to render the Most Implausible Conclusion plausible to you, this does not mean that you are justified in rejecting my solution to the non-identity problem. It simply means that you will have to consider whether the claim that it would not be wrong to create Ted is even more implausible than the implausible implications of the various alternative solutions I have identified in the previous chapters. Is the claim that it is not wrong to create Ted rather than no one, for example, more implausible than the claim that it is wrong for Betty to create a blind child rather than no one or for Jane to create no one rather than a sighted child? I am inclined to think that the answer is no. If you think that the answer is yes, then you will think that at least some other solution does a better job of satisfying the modesty requirement than mine does, though this is no guarantee that it will also satisfy the robustness and independence requirements.

barely worth living when the alternative is creating no life at all, but it also gives you no reason to accept it.

If this is your reaction to the case of Ted, then I can try to give you a reason to accept the claim by asking you to modify the case of Ted in the following way. First, add just a little bit to the amount of good things in Ted's life without adding anything bad. Perhaps you let him watch a bit more or a bit better television. Perhaps you let him take a brief walk, or read a short story, or have a quick conversation with another person. Now ask whether you think this slightly better life is worthy of a human being. If the answer is still no, then continue to add more and better things to his life until you get to the point where you are now convinced that the life you are picturing really is a life that is worthy of a human being, even if by a very thin margin. And once you get to this point, ask yourself whether you think it would be wrong to create Ted rather than create no one if Ted would have the life you are now picturing. At this point, I can do no more than state my suspicion that if you really are convinced that you have improved Ted's life enough to make it worth living, then you will not think that it would be wrong to create Ted. And if I'm correct about that, then once the case of Ted is properly calibrated to align with your own sense of what kind of a life is worth living, it really does turn out to vindicate the claim that I have been trying to render plausible here: that if the choice is between creating a person whose life really will be just barely worth living and creating no person at all, it would not be wrong to create that person.

If we picture Sandy's life as containing a great deal of hardship and suffering, we make it difficult to picture a life that we are confident is worth living. If instead we picture a life that is more like some version of Ted's, we make it easier to do so. And my suspicion, at least, is that once we think of cases that make it easier for us to be confident that we are picturing a life that really is better than no life at all, even if just barely, the claim that it would not be wrong for Betty to conceive a child who would have such a life rather than to conceive no child will not seem so implausible after all. For purposes of the discussion that follows, then, let me stipulate that the life of Sandy will be the one that, after reflecting on all of these considerations, you find to do the best job of representing a life that really does strike you as worth living, even if just barely. And returning to the cases that I initially appealed to in the context of Wilma and Pebbles, I will now try to show that the same strategies that I used to render the Implausible Conclusion plausible can be applied to the case of Wilma and Sandy as a way of rendering even the Most Implausible Conclusion plausible, too.

I argued, for example, that if it is plausible to say that it is not positively immoral for Peter to spend his fifty dollars on dinner and a movie rather than donating it to famine relief, then we should accept that it is plausible to say that it is not positively immoral for Wilma to conceive Pebbles rather than Rocks. If it is not wrong for Peter to make the choice that leaves things worse in terms of overall human well-being but a little bit better for him, I asked, then why should it be wrong for Wilma to make the choice that leaves things worse in terms of overall human well-being but a little bit better for her? If I was right about this, and if, as we are now supposing, the very same non-identity argument that applies to Pebbles also applies to Sandy, then why shouldn't we simply say the same thing about the Most Implausible Conclusion? If the case of Peter helps us to see the plausibility of the claim that it is not wrong for Wilma to conceive Pebbles rather than Rocks, that is, then why shouldn't it also help us to see the plausibility of the claim that it is not wrong for Wilma to conceive Sandy rather than Rocks? In the case of Peter, the plausibility of the claim that his act is not wrong seemed to arise from the fact that although he could have produced a better outcome in terms of overall human well-being, his act did not harm anyone or violate anyone's rights. If the case in which Wilma conceives Sandy really is on a par with the case in which Wilma conceives Pebbles, and if I was right to maintain that Wilma's act does not harm anyone or violate anyone's rights in the case in which Wilma conceives Pebbles, then we should simply say the same thing about the case in which Wilma conceives Sandy: Wilma would have produced a much better outcome in terms of overall human well-being by conceiving Rocks rather than conceiving Sandy, but her act of conceiving Sandy did not harm anyone or violate anyone's rights. And once we come to see the case of Wilma and Sandy in this way, why should we find it so hard to accept the claim that, even on this version of the case, Wilma's act was not wrong?

In defending the plausibility of the Implausible Conclusion, I also appealed to the case of Fred. If it is not wrong for Fred to save blind Billy rather than sighted Timmy, I asked, then why shouldn't we simply accept that it is also not wrong for Wilma to conceive blind Pebbles rather than sighted Rocks? But if I was right about this, and if we continue to assume that there is no morally relevant difference between Pebbles and Sandy, then why shouldn't we simply accept the same judgment about the case of Sandy? If it would not be wrong for Fred to save a child like Sandy rather than a child like Rocks, that is, then why shouldn't we simply accept that it would not be wrong for Wilma to conceive a child like Sandy rather than a child like Rocks?

The transitivity argument, too, can be easily modified to reveal the plausibility of the Most Implausible Conclusion. As long as Sandy's life will at least be worth living, it is hard to see why it would be wrong for Betty to conceive a child like Sandy rather than to conceive no child at all if those were her only two options, and it remains just as hard to see why it would be wrong for Jane to conceive no child rather than to conceive an ordinary child like Rocks if those were her only two options. But if it is not wrong to conceive a child like Sandy rather than no child and not wrong to conceive no child rather than a child like Rocks, then the very same argument that helped to reveal the plausibility of saying that it would not be wrong for Wilma to conceive Pebbles rather than Rocks should also help to reveal the plausibility of the claim that it would not be wrong for Wilma to conceive Sandy rather than Rocks. And the case of Mary the horse breeder can be easily modified for the same purposes, too. If it would not be wrong for Mary to breed one more flea rather than to conceive one more child, for example, then why would it be wrong for Wilma to conceive a child whose life would be as worthwhile as a flea's rather than conceiving Rocks?

In all of these cases, there are two ways in which a critic of my solution might try to respond to the strategy that I have employed here in defending my solution from the claim that it fails to satisfy the modesty requirement. One would be to deny that the cases I have appealed to here are sufficiently analogous to the case of Wilma and Sandy. If there proves to be a morally relevant difference between the cases of Peter, Fred, Betty, Jane, and Mary, on the one hand, and the case of Wilma and Sandy on the other, then the fact that we find it plausible to say that the acts are not wrong in the cases of Peter, Fred, Betty, Jane, and Mary will do nothing to support the plausibility of the Most Implausible Conclusion. But we are assuming here that the case of Wilma and Pebbles is morally on a par with the case of Wilma and Sandy. If the cases involving Pebbles and Sandy really are morally on a par, then the claim that the modified versions of Peter, Fred, Betty, Jane, and Mary are not sufficiently parallel to the case in which Wilma conceives Sandy simply amounts to the claim that the unmodified versions of Peter, Fred, Betty, Jane, and Mary are not sufficiently parallel to the original case in which Wilma conceives Pebbles. And I already responded to this concern at length in the previous sections, when I first introduced those cases in the context of the Implausible Conclusion. If those cases are sufficiently parallel to the case in which Wilma conceives Pebbles rather than Rocks, and if the case in which Wilma conceives Pebbles rather than Rocks really is morally on a par with the case in which Wilma conceives Sandy rather than Rocks, then the modified versions of those cases are sufficiently parallel to the case in which Wilma conceives Sandy rather than Rocks. If the original cases of Peter, Fred, Betty, Jane, and Mary are sufficient to show that the Implausible Conclusion is not so implausible, that is, and if the case of Wilma and Sandy really is relevantly similar to the case of Wilma and Pebbles, then the modified versions of Peter, Fred, Betty, Jane, and Mary are sufficient to show that the Most Implausible Conclusion is not so implausible either.

The other response to the strategy that I have employed here would be to agree that the modified versions of Peter, Fred, Betty, Jane, and Mary are sufficiently analogous to the case in which Wilma conceives Sandy rather than Rocks, but to maintain that the acts in question really would be morally wrong in these cases. Someone might agree, for example, that the modified version of the case of Fred, or of Betty, really is sufficiently analogous to the case in which Wilma conceives Sandy, just as the original cases of Fred and Betty were sufficiently analogous to the case in which Wilma conceives Pebbles, but then maintain that while it would not be wrong in the original case for Fred to save a blind child rather than a sighted child or for Betty to conceive a blind child rather than to conceive no child, it would be wrong in the revised case for Fred to save a child like Sandy rather than a healthy child, or wrong for Betty to conceive a child like Sandy rather than to conceive no child. If the acts in question in the modified versions of the cases of Peter, Fred, Betty, Jane, and Mary would be morally wrong, after all, then far from establishing the plausibility of the Most Implausible Conclusion, the claim that the acts in those cases are sufficiently analogous to Wilma's act of conceiving Sandy rather than Rocks would simply reinforce the initial impression that conceiving Sandy rather than Rocks really would be wrong and that the Most Implausible Conclusion is therefore mistaken.

But if the acts in question are not wrong in the original cases of Peter, Fred, Betty, Jane, and Mary and are wrong in the modified versions of those cases, and if the acts in question in the original cases are sufficiently parallel to Wilma's conceiving Pebbles while the acts in question in the modified versions of the cases are sufficiently parallel to Wilma's conceiving Sandy, then there must be a morally relevant difference between Wilma's conceiving Pebbles rather than Rocks and Wilma's conceiving Sandy rather than Rocks. And if there is a morally relevant difference between Wilma's conceiving Pebbles rather than Rocks and Wilma's conceiving Sandy rather than Rocks, then my solution to the non-identity problem does not commit me to accepting the Most Implausible Conclusion in the first place. Accepting the Implausible Conclusion's claim that it is not immoral for Wilma to conceive Pebbles entails accepting the Most Implausible Conclusion's claim that it would not be immoral for Wilma to conceive Sandy only if there is no morally relevant difference between the case in which Wilma conceives Pebbles and the case in which Wilma conceives Sandy. If, as this second response to my defense of my solution requires us to believe, the difference between Pebbles and Sandy really does make a moral difference, then accepting the Implausible Conclusion does not entail accepting the Most Implausible Conclusion in the first place and I need not defend the plausibility of the Most Implausible Conclusion in order to establish that my solution satisfies the modesty requirement. If we view the cases of Pebbles and Sandy as being morally on a par, in short, then my solution to the non-identity problem does commit me to accepting the Most Implausible Conclusion, but accepting the Most Implausible Conclusion does not prevent my solution from satisfying the modesty requirement. If we view the cases as being morally different, then accepting the Most Implausible Conclusion might well prove to be too great a price to pay in order to solve the non-identity problem, but it is a price that the defender of my solution need not pay. Either way, we have no reason to deny that the solution to the problem that I have offered at the end of this book satisfies all three of the requirements for a successful solution that I set out at the beginning of the book.

I have been thinking on and off about the non-identity problem for a number of years now. When I first encountered the problem, I assumed that there must be a satisfactory way to avoid the Implausible Conclusion by modifying one of the premises of the argument that gives rise to it. The only question seemed to be which premise to target and how, precisely, to modify it. After a number of years of false starts and dashed hopes, though, it occurred to me one day to wonder whether the most reasonable response to the problem might simply be to give up and bite the bullet. I didn't find this a particularly satisfactory response at the time, but I came to think of it as less unsatisfactory than any of the alternatives. As I continued to hold this view over the years that followed, moreover, the Implausible Conclusion came to strike me as less and less implausible. Indeed, what eventually came to strike me as implausible is the claim that it is positively immoral to conceive a child whose life will be worth living simply because you could instead have easily conceived a different child whose life would have gone even better. As a result, the solution to the problem that I have defended here now strikes me not simply as less unsatisfactory than the alternatives, but as perfectly satisfactory in its own right. I have tried, in this final chapter, to use the cases of Peter, Fred, Betty, Jane, and Mary as a way of inculcating this attitude in the reader. If I have succeeded, then the strategy that I have employed in this chapter should make it easy to accept the solution that I have defended in this book. But even if this strategy has failed, and the solution that I have defended here seems difficult to accept, it remains, I believe, less difficult to accept than the alternative.

Appendices

Appendix A: Two More Problems with the Incoherence Objection (2.1)

The incoherence objection rests on two claims: that we cannot coherently make judgments about whether existing or not existing is better or worse for Pebbles, and that coherently making such judgments is necessary in order for P1 to be true. I am inclined to reject both claims.

The reason I am inclined to reject the first claim, the claim that such comparisons are incoherent, is that there are other cases in which we seem to be able to compare how existence and non-existence would be for someone without lapsing into incoherence. One kind of case is that in which it seems intelligible to say of some already existing person that he would be better off dead. Suppose, for example, that Fred is on fire, that he is suffering excruciating pain, and that he will either die right away or will die after suffering five additional hours of unfathomable agony. In this case, it seems to make sense to say that Fred would be better off dying now rather than surviving only to endure another five hours of unimaginable suffering. And this seems to make sense not because it means that if Fred dies now he will then be in a condition that is better for him than the condition of being alive and suffering horribly, but rather because it means that from the point of view of his own interests, Fred should prefer not to exist in any condition at all for the next five hours rather than to exist in excruciating pain.

But if we can make sense of the claim that Fred would be better off dead without comparing how things would be for Fred existing and not existing, then we can also make sense of the claim that Pebbles would be better off being alive without comparing how things would be for Pebbles existing and not existing. Just as it can make sense to say of a particular person that it is better for him that he no longer exist than that he continue to exist given that his existence involves a certain amount of pain, so it can make sense to say of a person who would otherwise not exist that it is better—and better *for her*—to exist with a certain disability than not to exist at all. In both cases, what is meant is simply that from the point of view of the interests of the person who would exist in one but not the other of two possible states of affairs, one state of affairs is rationally preferable to the other.

A critic of this first response to the incoherence objection might claim that we can account for our ability to make this judgment in the case of Fred without comparing existence and non-existence. On this alternative account, what we really mean when we say that Fred would be better off dead is that Fred's life, when taken as a whole, will turn out to have gone better for Fred if he dies right now than Fred's life as a whole will turn out to have gone for Fred if he goes on living for another five hours in terrible pain. This explanation of the judgment that we make when we say that Fred would be better off dead does not involve comparing existence and non-existence in terms of how they would be for Fred. It simply involves comparing two different ways that things could go for Fred over the course of the period during which he does exist in terms of which would be better for Fred. And so, on this account, the fact that we can coherently say that Fred would be better off dead provides no support for the claim that we can coherently compare existence and non-existence in the way that P1 seems to require us to do. I'm inclined to reject this alternative explanation of the judgment we make in the case of Fred. There is a difference between asking what would make Fred's life on the whole turn out to have gone better and asking what would be better for Fred from here on out. In ordinary cases, these two criteria go hand in hand. Whatever makes the rest of a person's life go better typically makes that person's life overall go better, too. But in idiosyncratic cases, the two criteria can come apart. In such cases, most people seem to care about what will make the rest of a person's life go better rather than what will make the person's life as a whole turn out to have gone better. It thus seems plausible to suppose that this is the kind of judgment most people really mean to be making in the case of Fred.

Suppose, for example, that you wake up in a hospital with no memory of how you got there. A doctor then tells you that you are one of two new patients, that she doesn't know which one you are, but that she knows that either one or the other of the following is true: (1) yesterday, you underwent a terribly painful procedure that caused you 1,000 units of pain and you were then given a drug to make you forget this horrible experience, or (2) tomorrow you will undergo a somewhat less painful procedure that will cause you 800 units of pain, after which you will be given a drug to make you forget this very bad but not quite horrible experience.[1] As the doctor is examining your chart to determine which situation is the one that you are in, you ask yourself which answer you should rationally prefer. If what you should prefer is the answer that will mean that your life as a whole will turn out to have gone better, you should prefer the second answer: suffering 800 units of pain tomorrow rather than 1,000 units of pain yesterday will be better for you by that measure. If what you should prefer is the answer that will mean that things will go better for you from here on out, then you should prefer the first answer: suffering 1,000 units of pain yesterday rather than 800 units of pain tomorrow will be better for you by that measure.

Virtually everyone, I suspect, would strongly prefer to receive the first answer. They would much rather have the 1,000 units of pain behind them than the 800 units of pain in front of them. And I suspect that this would be true even if they could be given a pill in the meantime that would let them forget that they have the 800 units of pain in

---

[1] This is a modified version of an example taken from Parfit (1984: 165–6).

front of them. If that's right, then when the two criteria come apart, what most people really care about when they make judgments about what would be in a person's interest is what would be best for them from here on out, rather than what would make their life as a whole turn out to have gone best. And this, in turn, undermines the alternative explanation of the judgment that most people would make in the case of Fred. When we ask which state of affairs would be better for Fred one hour from now, the state of affairs in which he is suffering horribly or the state of affairs in which he does not exist, we are not asking which state would make it the case that his life as a whole turns out to have gone better. We are asking which would be better from that point on. This is the judgment that strikes most people as coherent, and if it is coherent, then so is the comparison between existing and not existing that seems to be required by P1 of the non-identity argument.

But let's suppose that I'm wrong about this and that the alternative explanation of our judgment in the case of Fred really does prevent that example from undermining the first claim made by the incoherence objection to P1. Even if it does, there is a second kind of case that is not subject to this kind of response: cases where we think someone would have been better off never having existed. Suppose, for example, that a single sperm and egg are in a Petri dish and will shortly come together to form a zygote. If they do, it is inevitable that the zygote will eventually develop into a child who will experience nothing but excruciating pain from the moment he first becomes conscious until he dies at the age of three. And for ease of exposition, let's suppose that the prospective parents have already decided on a name: they will call their child Barney. It seems just as clear that Barney would be better off never being conceived as it does that Fred would be better off dead. If you were trying to make a decision from the point of view of the interests of the person who would come into existence if the sperm and egg came together, that is, it seems clear that the right thing to do would be to prevent the conception from occurring, rather than to say that the idea of making a decision from that point of view was incoherent. But the alternative explanation that interpreted our judgment about Fred in terms of which option would make Fred's life as a whole go best can't be applied to the case of Barney. In the case of Barney, we really do seem to be coherently comparing existence and non-existence. And so even if the case of Fred fails to show that we can coherently compare existence and non-existence in the way that P1 seems to require us to do, the case of Barney can still establish this and can thus undermine the first claim made by the incoherence objection.

Before turning to the objection's second claim, it is worth briefly considering a further response that might be offered to my argument against the first. A proponent of the incoherence objection might agree that the first claim made by the objection is incompatible with the judgments that virtually everyone would make in the cases of Fred and Barney. But rather than saying so much the worse for the incoherence objection, this critic might say so much the worse for the judgments that most people would make. We might think we are saying something coherent when we say that Fred would be better off dead and that Barney would be better off never coming into existence, that is, but perhaps we are mistaken about this. And if we are mistaken about this, then the conflict between these common judgments and the claim made by the incoherence objection fails to count against the objection.

I don't see how we could decisively establish that our judgments in the cases of Fred and Barney are coherent, and so I don't think that this response to my argument can be decisively overturned, though the burden of proof clearly lies with those who claim that the judgments are incoherent. But I don't think that overturning the response is necessary in order to establish that the response would fail to ground a satisfactory solution to the non-identity problem. As I noted in section 1.3.3, a solution is not satisfactory if it eliminates the non-identity problem by replacing it with an even bigger problem. Such a solution would fail what I called the modesty requirement. And that, it seems to me, is what would happen if we were to rest a solution to the non-identity problem on the incoherence objection and rest the incoherence objection on the claim that our judgments about cases like Fred and Barney are mistaken. Even if such a solution had no further problems, and as I argue below and in section 2.1 it does have further problems, it would enable us to say that it is wrong for Wilma to conceive a blind child rather than a sighted child only by compelling us to deny that Fred would be better off dead and that Barney would have been better off never being conceived. These implications strike me as more implausible than the Implausible Conclusion that the solution is attempting to help us avoid. And so it seems, at least to me, that this approach to salvaging the incoherence objection is unsatisfactory.

I've argued so far that we should reject the first claim made by the incoherence objection. But let's now suppose that the first claim made by the objection is correct and that it really is incoherent to insist that Pebbles is better off existing than not existing. Even if this is so, I'm inclined to think that the incoherence objection should still be rejected. This is because I'm inclined to think that the second claim made by the objection is false. The second claim maintains that P1 requires us to compare Pebbles existing and Pebbles not existing in terms of one being better or worse for her than the other. But P1 does not require this. P1 does not maintain that Pebbles is positively better off existing than not existing. It merely claims that it is not the case that she is worse off existing. And it seems to me that the claim that it is not the case that she is worse off existing can be true even if the claim that she is better off existing is incoherent. Consider, for example, the claim that "green is smaller than justice." That claim strikes me as incoherent. It maintains that the relation "is smaller than" obtains between green and justice, and they are not the kinds of things between which that relation can obtain. But now consider the claim that "it is not the case that green is bigger than justice." This claim strikes me as perfectly coherent. It does not maintain that a particular relation obtains between green and justice. It simply claims that it is not the case that a particular relation, the relation of being bigger than, does obtain between them. And it seems true that it is not the case that that relation obtains between them. In the same way, and for the same reason, the claim that it is incoherent to say that Pebbles is better off existing than not existing does nothing to undermine the truth of the claim that it is not the case that Pebbles is worse off existing than not existing. And that is all that P1 says: Wilma's act has not, in fact, made Pebbles worse off than she would otherwise have been.[2] Even if the first claim made by the incoherence objection is true, then, its second claim seems to be false.

Appendix B: A Further Problem with Benatar's Argument (2.5)

Benatar's argument depends on the claim that his Relational Asymmetry Principle (RAP) provides the best explanation for the moral asymmetry between cases like that of the Blessed Couple and the Cursed Couple. I will reject this claim here by arguing that we can identify an alternative principle that does a better job of explaining the asymmetry than does Benatar's principle and that produces a different result in the case of Wilma.[3] We can do this if we start by appealing to a symmetric version of Benatar's principle, one in which (1)–(3) are the same as in RAP but in which the claim made about the absence of pleasure in (4) is symmetric to the claim made by RAP (3) about the absence of pain. What I will call the Relational Symmetry Principle (RSP), then, amounts to taking RAP (1)–(3) and conjoining them with:

(4) the absence of pleasure is worse than the presence of pleasure if either (a) there is an actual person whose interests are better served by the presence of the pleasure or (b) the absence of the pleasure would require the absence of a person who would otherwise exist and whose potential interests are better served by the presence of the pleasure

If RAP (3) is logically coherent, then surely RSP (4) is logically coherent as well. If the absence of pain can be better than the presence of pain even when there is no actual person who enjoys the absence of pain, that is, then the absence of pleasure can be worse than the presence of pleasure even when there is no actual person who is deprived of the absent pleasure. Benatar himself concedes this much.[4] My claim here will be not only that RSP is as coherent as RAP, but that RSP can be used to undermine Benatar's argument.

---

[2] On some accounts of negation, there might prove to be an important difference between the claim "it is not the case that Pebbles is worse off existing than not existing" and the claim "Pebbles is not worse off existing than not existing." If that is correct, then it does not follow from the claim that the former claim is coherent that the latter claim is as well. And this would mean that the coherence of the former claim would not be enough to establish the coherence of P1's claim that Wilma's act has not made Pebbles worse off than she would otherwise have been. But even if this is so, it poses no problem for my response to the incoherence objection. We could simply revise P1 to read: "It is not the case that Wilma's act makes Pebbles worse off than she would otherwise have been" and revise P2 to read: "If A's act harms B, then it is the case that A's act makes B worse off than B would otherwise have been." An objection to my response to the incoherence objection that depends on this distinction would therefore fail to be sufficiently robust to ground a satisfactory solution to the non-identity problem.

[3] This appendix is a modified version of Boonin (2012).   [4] Benatar (2006: 31 n. 23).

To see how this can be accomplished, let's begin by considering what my Relational Symmetry Principle would entail about the case of the Cursed Couple and the Blessed Couple. If the Cursed Couple conceives, the resulting child's life on the whole will contain zero units of pleasure and a million units of pain. RSP (3b) is identical to RAP (3b). It says that the absence of pain is better than the presence of pain if the presence of the pain would require the existence of a person who would not otherwise exist and whose potential interests are better served by the absence of the pain. And so RSP, just like RAP, makes it plausible to say that by conceiving, the Cursed Couple would make things worse for the Cursed Child. If the Blessed Couple conceives, on the other hand, the resulting child's life on the whole will contain a million units of pleasure and zero units of pain. RAP (4) entailed that by not conceiving, the Blessed Couple would not make things worse for the Blessed Child. But RSP (4b) maintains that the absence of pleasure is worse than the presence of pleasure even if the absence of the pleasure would require the absence of a person who would otherwise exist and whose potential interests are better served by the presence of the pleasure. So my RSP, unlike Benatar's RAP, entails that the Blessed Couple would make things worse for the Blessed Child by not conceiving.

Does this mean that the Relational Symmetry Principle is unable to account for the asymmetry between the Blessed Couple and the Cursed Couple? It does not. The asymmetry between the Blessed Couple and the Cursed Couple can be accounted for by appealing to an asymmetry between pleasure and pain that is different from the asymmetry that Benatar appeals to and that is fully consistent with affirming the Relational Symmetry Principle. The asymmetry is that with respect to pleasure, no actual person is made worse off by the decision about whether to conceive them regardless of whether the better or worse outcome is selected, but with respect to pain, whether an actual person is made worse off by the decision about whether to conceive them depends on whether the better or worse outcome is selected.

If the Blessed Couple decides to conceive the Blessed Child, for example, then things will be better from the point of view of the interests of the Blessed Child, and the Blessed Child will therefore not be made worse off by the decision. If the Blessed Couple decides not to conceive the Blessed Child, then things will be worse from the point of view of the interests of the Blessed Child, but the Blessed Child will not exist and so will not be an actual person who has been made worse off by the decision. Regardless of which choice the Blessed Couple makes, then, no actual person will be made worse off by their decision. But pain is different from pleasure in this respect. Whether an actual person will be made worse off by the Cursed Couple's decision about whether to conceive depends on the choice they make. If the Cursed Couple decides not to conceive the Cursed Child, then things will be better from the point of view of the interests of the Cursed Child. No actual person will be made worse off by their decision both because there will be no actual person to be affected by their decision and because their decision made things better rather than worse. But if the Cursed Couple decides to conceive the Cursed Child, then things will be worse from the point of view of the interests of the Cursed Child, and the Cursed Child will exist to be made worse off by this fact. There will therefore be an actual person who has been made worse off by their decision. While in the case of pleasure no actual person is made worse off regardless of whether the Blessed Couple chooses the better or worse outcome, then, in the case of pain, whether or not an actual person will be made worse off depends on whether the Cursed Couple chooses the better or worse outcome.

Because of this asymmetry between pleasure and pain, the Relational Symmetry Principle that I am proposing as an alternative to Benatar's Relational Asymmetry Principle can account for the claim that it would be wrong for the Cursed Couple to conceive the Cursed Child but not wrong for the Blessed Couple not to conceive the Blessed Child. The Relational Symmetry Principle can do this by appealing to what I will call the Actual Persons Principle (APP), where by an "actual person" I mean a person who actually exists at some point in time:

APP: When choosing between two options, it is prima facie wrong to make the choice the acting on which will result in its being the case that there is an actual person for whom your act made things worse.

RSP entails that if the Cursed Couple conceives the Cursed Child, this will make things worse for the Cursed Child. Since the Cursed Child will exist, the Actual Persons Principle entails that this will make the Cursed Couple's act prima face wrong. RSP also entails that if the Blessed Couple does not conceive the Blessed Child, this will make things worse for the Blessed Child. But since if the Blessed Couple does not conceive the Blessed Child, the Blessed Child will never exist, and since the Actual Persons Principle focuses only on the harmful effects on people who actually exist at some point in time, the principle will not entail that the Blessed Couple's act is prima facie wrong. Thus, while Benatar's Relational Asymmetry Principle can account for the asymmetry between the Blessed Couple and the Cursed Couple, my Relational Symmetry Principle can account for it as well, provided that it is conjoined with the Actual Persons Principle.

As we saw in section 2.5, Benatar's RAP entails that Wilma harms Pebbles by conceiving her. What does my RSP entail about this case? Suppose, as we did in that section, that if Wilma conceives Pebbles, Pebbles's life on the whole will contain 500,000 units of pleasure and 20,000 units of pain. As in the case of RAP, we can follow Benatar and see how the case looks from the point of view of RSP by considering the relevance of the pain that Pebbles would suffer and of the pleasure that Pebbles would enjoy independently. With respect to the 20,000 units of pain that Pebbles will suffer if Wilma conceives her, RSP entails that existing will be worse for Pebbles than not existing. RSP (3b), just like RAP (3b), maintains that the absence of pain is better than the presence of pain even if the presence of the pain would require the existence of a person who would not otherwise exist and whose potential interests are better served by the absence of the pain. So, with respect to the choice between existing and not existing,

RSP, just like RAP, treats the 20,000 units of pain as counting against bringing Pebbles into existence.

With respect to the 500,000 units of pleasure that Pebbles will enjoy if Wilma conceives her, RAP (4) maintains that the absence of pleasure is worse than the presence of pleasure only if there is an actual person whose interests are better served by the presence of the pleasure. Since if Pebbles is not conceived there will be no actual Pebbles who is deprived by the absence of the 500,000 units of pleasure, RAP maintains that the absence of pleasure does not make it worse for Pebbles not to exist than to exist. But my RSP is crucially different from Benatar's RAP in precisely this respect. RSP (3) is identical to RAP (3), but where RAP (4) maintains that the absence of pleasure is worse than the presence of pleasure only if there is an actual person who is harmed by the absence of pleasure, RSP (4b) maintains that the absence of pleasure is worse than the presence of pleasure even if there is no actual person who is harmed by the absence of the pleasure because the absence of the pleasure requires the absence of the person who would otherwise exist with the pleasure. So RSP maintains that the absence of pleasure does make it worse for Pebbles not to exist than to exist. With respect to the choice between existing and not existing, the 500,000 units of pleasure does count in favor of bringing Pebbles into existence according to my RSP, while it does not count in favor of bringing Pebbles into existence according to Benatar's RAP.

Regarding the 20,000 units of pain, then, RSP maintains that existence is worse than non-existence, and regarding the 500,000 units of pleasure, RSP maintains that existence is better than non-existence. Since the total amount of pleasure clearly outweighs the total amount of pain in this case, the magnitude of the advantage that existence has over non-existence is greater than the magnitude of the advantage that non-existence has over existence. And so, in the end, RSP entails that in the case of Pebbles, the advantages of existence clearly outweigh the advantages of non-existence. Benatar's RAP entails that Wilma harms Pebbles by conceiving her. But my RSP does not entail this.

We now have two principles that are capable of accounting for our asymmetric judgment in the case of the Blessed Couple and the Cursed Couple: Benatar's Relational Asymmetry Principle and my Relational Symmetry Principle. The question, then, is which principle provides the better account. There are three reasons to conclude that my Relational Symmetry Principle does.

The first reason to favor RSP over RAP is that RAP entails that Wilma harms Pebbles by conceiving her while RSP entails that Wilma does not harm Pebbles by conceiving her. It may seem that I am begging the question here. It may seem that I am saying, "We should believe that Wilma does not harm Pebbles by conceiving her because RSP entails that she doesn't, and we should believe RSP because RSP entails that Wilma does not harm Pebbles by conceiving her." That would, indeed, be circular. But that is not what I am saying. What I am saying is this: Benatar provides, as a reason for endorsing RAP, the claim that RAP accounts for the difference between the Blessed Couple and the Cursed Couple. Accepting the deeply counterintuitive claim that Wilma harms Pebbles by conceiving her is simply the price we have to pay in order to preserve our judgments about the cases of the Blessed and Cursed Couples. But RSP shows that we can account for the judgments in these two cases without paying that price. If, among two competing explanations for the same set of judgments, one has fewer counterintuitive implications in additional cases than the other, then that is a legitimate, non-circular reason for preferring it. The case of Wilma and Pebbles therefore provides a legitimate, non-circular reason to prefer RSP over RAP. And, of course, once we have selected RSP over RAP for this legitimate, non-circular reason, there is no longer any reason to doubt our initial judgment that Wilma does not make Pebbles worse off by conceiving her.

A second reason to prefer my RSP over Benatar's RAP is independent of RSP's implications for the case of Wilma and Pebbles. Instead, it arises from the fact that while both RSP and RAP involve affirming the existence of an asymmetry between pleasure and pain, the asymmetry that RSP appeals to is perfectly straightforward while the asymmetry that RAP appeals to is quite counterintuitive. The asymmetry that my RSP appeals to arises directly from the fact that pleasure is good and pain is bad. Since pleasure is good, the worse outcome regarding pleasure is when it is absent. Since pain is bad, the worse outcome regarding pain is when it is present. There is nothing surprising or mysterious about this. In order for an actual person to be made worse off by something, they must actually exist at some point in time. There is nothing surprising or mysterious about this, either. But these two perfectly straightforward observations are enough to ground the asymmetry between pleasure and pain that my RSP appeals to in accounting for the asymmetry between the Blessed Couple and the Cursed Couple: since existing is the worse outcome in the case of the Cursed Child, there is an actual person who is made worse off if the Cursed Couple makes the worse choice. Since not existing is the worse outcome in the case of the Blessed Child, there is no actual person who is made worse off if the Blessed Couple makes the worse choice.

But the asymmetric claim that Benatar's RAP appeals to should seem quite surprising. It seems odd to say that the absent pain of non-existence makes it better for the Cursed Child not to exist but that the absent pleasure of non-existence does not make it worse for the Blessed Child not to exist. How can the absence of something have an effect on the would-be child's welfare in one case but not in the other? Benatar, of course, provides a reason for accepting this asymmetry: the claim that accepting it is necessary in order to account for the asymmetry between our moral judgments in the case of the Blessed Couple and the Cursed Couple. But my RSP shows that Benatar's RAP is not necessary in order to account for this feature of our moral judgments. Once we see this, we lose our reason to endorse the asymmetry that Benatar appeals to. And once we lose our reason to endorse the asymmetry that is appealed to by RAP, the fact that the asymmetry itself is intuitively less plausible than the asymmetry appealed to by RSP provides a second independent reason to prefer my RSP over Benatar's RAP.

A final reason to prefer RSP over RAP is also independent of its implications for the case of Wilma and Pebbles. It arises from the fact that while both RSP and RAP can produce the intuitively correct answers in the case of the Blessed Couple and the

Cursed Couple, there is an important difference between the two principles in terms of the additional assumptions that have to be accepted in order for them to be able to do so. Neither RSP nor RAP by themselves yield any conclusions about what it would be right or wrong to do. Neither principle makes any reference to right or wrong, obligatory or impermissible, should or should not. Instead, they make judgments about which states of affairs are good or bad, or better or worse. Without some sort of bridging principle, therefore, neither can justify any conclusions about what should or should not be done. And this is what generates the third reason to prefer my RSP over Benatar's RAP: the bridging principle needed in order for RSP to account for our judgments in the Blessed Couple and Cursed Couple cases is superior to the bridging principle needed in order for RAP to do so.

As I noted earlier, RSP can account for the asymmetry between the Blessed Couple and the Cursed Couple by appealing to what I called the Actual Persons Principle.

APP: When choosing between two options, it is prima facie wrong to make the choice the acting on which will result in its being the case that there is an actual person for whom your act made things worse.

In order to account for the asymmetry between the Blessed Couple and the Cursed Couple by appealing to RAP, however, we must instead depend on what I will call the Actual and Possible Persons Principle (APPP), where by a "possible person" I mean a person who will never actually exist, but who would have actually existed had the other option been selected:

APPP: When choosing between two options, it is prima facie wrong to make the choice the acting on which will result in its being the case that there is an actual or possible person for whom your act made things worse.

That Benatar's argument requires us to assume the Actual and Possible Persons Principle is clear from the following considerations. Benatar claims that we must say that the absent pleasures if the Blessed Child is not conceived do not make it worse for the child that he not be conceived. He claims that we must say that it is not worse for the Blessed Child that he not be conceived so that we can avoid having to say that it would be wrong for the Blessed Couple not to conceive the Blessed Child. But the claim "not conceiving the Blessed Child does not harm the child" is necessary to sustaining the claim "not conceiving the Blessed Child is not morally wrong" only if it would be morally wrong for the Blessed Couple to harm the Blessed Child by not conceiving him. The Actual Persons Principle does not entail that this would be wrong: even though not conceiving the Blessed Child would make things worse for the Blessed Child, not conceiving the Blessed Child would not be wrong because it would not result in an actual person for whom refraining from conceiving the Blessed Child had made things worse. Only if we include merely possible people in the scope of our considerations can Benatar's argument for RAP succeed. And so Benatar's argument requires us to accept the Actual and Possible Persons Principle.

But there are two reasons to prefer the bridging principle required by my RSP to the bridging principle required by Benatar's RAP. The first is that the RSP bridging principle is simpler. The Actual Persons Principle posits only one kind of entity whose interests we must consider: people who at some point actually exist. The Actual and Possible Persons Principle includes this kind of entity plus a second and very different kind of entity: those people who do not exist and who will never exist but who would have existed had a different choice been made. All else being equal, a simpler principle should be preferred to a more complex principle, and this provides one reason to prefer the bridging principle required by RSP to the bridging principle required by RAP.

The second reason to prefer the RSP bridging principle to the RAP bridging principle is that the RSP bridging principle appeals to a consideration whose moral salience is less controversial. The fact that an act would harm an actual person is generally recognized as relevant to the question of whether the act would be wrong. But the fact that an act would be worse for the interests of a merely possible person who will never exist if the act is performed is not already accepted to be relevant in the same way. Indeed, to say that we must consider the interests of people who will never exist is quite controversial. All else being equal, a principle whose salience is less controversial should be preferred to a principle whose salience is more controversial. And this provides a second reason to prefer the bridging principle required by my RSP to the bridging principle required by Benatar's RAP.

Benatar, of course, might maintain that all else is not equal, that RAP itself has a great amount of explanatory power because it can account for our asymmetric moral judgments in the case of the Blessed Couple and the Cursed Couple. But, as I have already argued, RSP can account for these cases as well. If the bridging principle required by RSP is simpler and less controversially salient than that required by RAP, and if RSP has at least as much explanatory power as RAP, then we have a third and final reason to prefer RSP to RAP. Combined with the fact that RAP implausibly entails that Wilma makes Pebbles worse off by conceiving her while RSP more plausibly entails that she does not, and with the fact that the asymmetry that RSP appeals to is more plausible than the asymmetry that RAP appeals to, we have three good reasons to prefer RSP over RAP. And by justifying the choice of RSP over RAP, we justify rejecting Benatar's argument for the claim that Wilma's act of conceiving Pebbles makes Pebbles worse off than she would otherwise have been.

I have argued that we can justify rejecting Benatar's argument by showing that RSP better accounts for our intuitions about the Blessed Couple and the Cursed Couple than does RAP and by showing that RSP entails that Wilma does not make Pebbles worse off than she would otherwise have been by conceiving her. I want now to consider two responses that might be offered on Benatar's behalf. The first response arises from the fact that Benatar's defense of RAP as a whole appeals to its ability to explain our asymmetric intuitions in four kinds of cases, not just the kind of case involved in the Blessed and Cursed Couples. Even if RSP proves superior to RAP in the context of the first kind of case, then, Benatar's RAP might still prove superior overall. The second response arises from the fact that Benatar briefly responds to an objection that is in some respects similar to the one that I have developed here. One might then ask whether his response would apply to my objection as well.

Let us begin with the supplemental cases that Benatar appeals to in supporting RAP. The first such case is this: "Whereas it is strange (if not incoherent) to give as a reason for having a child that the child one has will thereby be benefited, it is not strange to cite a potential child's interests as a basis for avoiding bringing a child into existence."[5] RAP accounts for this asymmetry by maintaining that bringing a happy child into existence does not really make the child better off whereas bringing an unhappy child into existence really does make the child worse off. But RSP can account for this asymmetry just as easily. It can explain why it is not strange to cite a potential child's interests as a reason not to conceive, as in the case of the Cursed Couple. It can explain this because it maintains that creating an unhappy child causes harm to an actual person and because it is not strange to cite the negative impact on the interests of an actual person as a reason not to bring the child into existence. And it can also explain why it is strange to give as a reason for conceiving a happy child that the child will thereby be benefited. The reason that giving this as a reason is strange is not that it involves saying something that isn't true. According to RSP, it is true that a happy child benefits from being brought into existence. And so it is true that the Blessed Couple would benefit its child by conceiving it. The reason it would be strange for the Blessed Couple to give this as a reason for conceiving the Blessed Child is that, if they don't bring him into existence, there won't be any actual child whom they have failed to benefit. In cases where it clearly does make sense to cite as a reason for doing a particular action the fact that doing the action would benefit someone, that is, it makes sense because there is an actual person who stands to benefit from the action being done and who will have to do without the benefit if the action is not done. But when the Blessed Couple is deciding whether or not to conceive, there is no actual person who stands to benefit from their deciding to conceive and no actual person who will have to do without a benefit if they decide not to conceive. And there is nothing about RSP that prevents us from appealing to this consideration in explaining our intuitions in the first supplemental case that Benatar appeals to.

Benatar's second supplemental case involves reasons for regret rather than reasons for action.[6] If we bring an unhappy person into existence, we can later regret this for the sake of the unhappy person himself. If we decline to bring a happy person into existence, on the other hand, we may regret this for our own sake, but we cannot really regret it for the sake of the person we could have conceived. RAP is again able to account for this asymmetry. We have harmed the unhappy person by creating him, and so regret for this for his sake is appropriate, but we have not harmed the potential but not actual happy person by not creating him, and so regret for his sake is not appropriate. As Benatar puts it, "The reason why we do not lament our failure to bring

---

[5] Benatar (2006: 34).   [6] Benatar (2006: 34–5).

somebody [happy] into existence is because absent pleasures [unlike existing pains] are not bad."[7]

But RSP can account for this asymmetry just as well, too. If the Cursed Couple conceives the Cursed Child, then RSP entails that they have made things worse for this child, just as RAP does. Since their child will be an actual person, there will therefore be an actual person they have harmed and thus an actual person for whose sake they can appropriately regret their action. If the Blessed Couple does not conceive the Blessed Child, then RSP, unlike RAP, does entail that they have made things worse for the Blessed Child. But since in that case the Blessed Child does not exist, there exists no one for whose sake they can regret their decision. And so, as on the RAP account, they can regret their choice for their own sake, but not for the sake of any actual person that they have harmed. The case of asymmetric sources of regret then, like the case of asymmetric reasons for action, provides no reason to prefer RAP over RSP.[8]

Finally, Benatar appeals to an asymmetry between our response to distant places where people are suffering and our response to distant places that are uninhabited.[9] When we learn of a distant place where people are suffering, we are sad for those people. But when we learn, say, of an uninhabited island, we are not sad for the people who, if they had existed, would have happily lived there. RAP is once more able to account for this asymmetry: the suffering people are worse off because of their suffering but the non-existent people are not worse off because of their not existing. And so we are right to feel bad about the existing pains and not feel bad about the absent pleasures. But RSP can once again account for the asymmetry, too. We feel bad for the suffering of actual people not just because their suffering makes things worse for them but because their suffering is something bad that is actually happening to them. And while the non-existing happy people really would have benefited from being brought into existence, according to RSP, it is nonetheless the case that nothing bad is happening to them by their not having been brought into existence—indeed, nothing at all is happening to them since they don't exist—and so their absent pleasures, while worse than existing pleasures, give us no reason to feel bad for them. There is simply no them for whom we can feel bad.

The result of considering all four cases that Benatar presents in defense of his argument, then, is that we have three reasons to favor RSP over RAP—the reason arising from the case of Wilma and Pebbles, the reason arising from the more plausible

---

[7] Benatar (2006: 35).

[8] It may also be worth noting that if the example of regret really does pose a problem for my RSP, then a parallel example poses the same problem for Benatar's RAP. If the Cursed Couple does not conceive, then there is no one for whom they can feel pleased about their decision. If the fact that there is no one for whom the Blessed Couple can feel regret if they do not conceive means that conceiving the Blessed Child would not have made things better for him, then the fact that there is no one for whom the Cursed Couple can feel pleased if they do not conceive would mean that conceiving the Cursed Child would not have made things worse for him. But RAP and RSP both agree that conceiving the Cursed Child would make things worse for him (McMahan (2009: 63) makes a similar point).

[9] Benatar (2006: 35).

asymmetry that RSP appeals to, and the reason arising from the more parsimonious and more salient bridging principle that RSP depends on—and no reason to favor RAP over RSP, since all the cases that RAP can account for can also be accounted for by RSP. The first kind of response to my objection to Benatar's argument, then, should be rejected.

The second kind of response to my objection arises from something that Benatar says about the distinction between positive and negative duties. Immediately after arguing that RAP is supported by its ability to explain our intuitions in cases like the Blessed and Cursed Couples, Benatar notes that someone might propose an alternative explanation that does not involve the asymmetry between RAP (3) and RAP (4). Specifically, he anticipates someone suggesting that the difference can be accounted for by appealing to the distinction between a negative duty not to cause harm and a positive duty to actively "bring about happiness." If we have a duty of the former sort but not of the latter sort, then this might explain why the Cursed Couple has a duty not to conceive while the Blessed Couple does not have a duty to conceive. And it could explain this without appealing to the sort of asymmetry that Benatar's principle involves. Benatar responds to this possibility as follows: "I agree that for those who deny that we have any positive duties, this would indeed be an alternative explanation to the one I have provided. However, even of those who do think that we have positive duties only a few also think that amongst these is a duty to bring happy people into existence."[10] Since virtually everyone who believes in positive duties will still deny that it would be wrong for the Blessed Couple not to conceive, that is, a response to Benatar's argument that depends on denying the existence of such duties will prove unsatisfactory.

It may seem that this alternative account of why it is not wrong for the Blessed Couple not to conceive is the same as the alternative explanation that I have provided here, and that the objection that I have raised here is therefore one that Benatar has already satisfactorily answered. But this is not so. It is true that the RSP-based response that I have endorsed maintains that the Blessed Couple's child will be better off if they conceive it than if they don't. And it is also true that the RSP-based response maintains that the Blessed Couple nonetheless has no moral obligation to conceive the child. It is therefore true that the objection to Benatar that I have defended here maintains that the Blessed Couple has no moral obligation to do the act that would be better for the child they would conceive.

But it does not follow from this that the RSP-based objection to Benatar's argument depends on the claim that we have no positive moral duties. The RSP-based account is compatible with the claim that we have a great many positive duties, provided only that they are positive duties that we have to other actual people, people with actual lives that will go worse for them in various ways if we refrain from benefiting them. If there is a child drowning in front of you, or an injured motorist lying by the side of the road,

---

[10] Benatar (2006: 32).

or a person starving in some distant country, for example, the RSP-based objection to Benatar's argument can allow that it would be morally wrong for you not to provide assistance. Indeed, even in cases where your assistance would simply make already happy people even happier, the RSP-based objection to Benatar's argument is consistent with the claim that it would be morally wrong for you not to provide it. If an already very happy child is about to enjoy a delicious ice cream sundae, for example, and if it would taste even better if you were to let him have one of your extra cherries to put on top of it, then the RSP-based account could allow that it would be morally wrong for you not to donate the extra cherry you happen to have to the child.

The RSP-based account can allow that you would have positive duties in any or all of these cases because in these cases there is an actual person whose life will go less well if you do not benefit them. If the Blessed Couple declines to conceive, by contrast, there will be no actual person whose life will go less well as a result. And so the claim made by the RSP-based account that I have offered here, the claim that it is not immoral for the Blessed Couple to refrain from conceiving since doing so does not result in there being an actual person who is made worse off as a result, is consistent with (but does not require us to accept) the claim that we have a prima facie positive duty to benefit actual people and not just a negative duty not to harm them. It is not the fact that the Blessed Couple would (merely) benefit the Blessed Child by conceiving it that renders it morally acceptable for them not to conceive the child on this account. It is the fact that if they don't conceive the child, there will be no actual person whose life will go less well as a result: no actual person that they have harmed and no actual person that they have failed to benefit.

Appendix C: Three More Problems with Harman's Argument (3.3.1)

(1) Harman's claim that the rape and Nazi prisoner cases pose a problem for the Counterfactual Account of harm depends on our accepting the claim that the victims are harmed by the acts described in these cases despite the fact that they are not made worse off by the acts than they would otherwise have been. But given that they are not made worse off than they would otherwise have been, it is not clear why we must accept the claim that they have been harmed by the acts that wronged them. Harman claims that in each of the two cases three things are true: that the subject of the act has a legitimate complaint about the act's having been performed, that the act was morally impermissible, and that the act harmed the victim. Although she is not explicit about this, the argument for the claim that the acts harmed the victims seems to assume that everyone will agree with the first two claims, and that this will lead them to accept the third claim as a result: if we don't think the person was harmed, after all, then how could we think that they have a legitimate complaint about the act and how could we think that the act was morally impermissible? But there is a reasonable answer to this

question, and thus a way that a defender of the Counterfactual Account could deny that the two cases Harman appeals to involve acts that harm their victims.

The answer to the question of how the acts could be impermissible if they do not harm their victims is that some acts are impermissible not because they are harmful, but because they are done without consent. If a patient refuses to consent to a given operation, for example, this can make it impermissible for the doctor to perform the operation and can give the patient a legitimate complaint if the operation is performed against his will, and this can be so even if the doctor and the patient both know that the operation will be beneficial to the patient. In the same way, and for the same sort of reason, if a woman refuses to consent to sexual intercourse with a particular man, this can make it impermissible for the man to have sexual intercourse with her and can give her a legitimate complaint if he has intercourse with her against her will, and this can be so even if the man's act turns out to be beneficial to the woman rather than harmful and even if both of them knew that this would be the case. Since the absence of consent is sufficient to account for the wrongness of the acts in the rape and Nazi prisoner cases, and since the acts would therefore be impermissible regardless of whether they end up harming their victims, the fact that we take them to be impermissible does nothing to support the claim that we should also take them to be harmful.

Harman anticipates this objection. She responds as follows:[11]

I agree with the objector that lack of consent plays a crucial explanatory role in both cases. But I affirm that harm also plays a crucial explanatory role. Part of the explanation of why it is wrong to rape, and why it is wrong to imprison someone as the Nazis did, is how awful it is for the victim to go through, and to have gone through, these experiences. Part of what makes these experiences awful to go through is that [they] were not consented to. I claim that consent does play a crucial explanatory role, but that the harm to someone of going through these experiences also plays an important role in explaining what is wrong with these experiences.

But this response is unsatisfactory for two reasons.

First, Harman provides no reason to believe that harm plays a crucial role in explaining the wrongness of the acts in question. She does "affirm" and "claim" that harm plays such a role, but she offers no argument to show that it does. Second, the claim that harm plays a crucial role in accounting for the wrongness of the acts is either too strong to be plausible or too weak to support Harman's conclusion. If the claim that harm plays a crucial role means that the presence of harm is necessary in order for the acts in question to be wrong, then the claim would be strong enough to support Harman's conclusion. The acts in question are clearly wrong and so if harm is necessary in order for the acts to be wrong, then the acts are clearly harmful. But the claim that harm is necessary in order for the acts to be wrong entails that harmless variants of the acts would be permissible even in the absence of consent. And this result is unacceptable. It would be wrong for a doctor to perform a procedure on a competent adult patient

---

[11] Harman (2004: 100).

if the patient refused to consent to it, even if it was clear that the procedure would benefit the patient and even if the patient acknowledged that this was so. In the same way, it would be wrong to have sexual contact with an unwilling person or to confine a person against their will even in circumstances in which it was clear that the behavior in question would benefit them and even if they acknowledged that this were so. If, on the other hand, the claim that harm plays a crucial role in the wrongness of the acts in Harman's cases means something other than that the presence of harm is necessary in order for the acts in question to be wrong, then our agreeing that the acts are wrong in these cases gives us no reason to agree that the acts are harmful. If the acts are wrong regardless of whether they are harmful, after all, then the fact that they are wrong provides no reason to believe that they are harmful.

(2) I believe that there is an additional reason to reject the Non-Comparative Account. The reason rests on a presumption that killing is a form of harming. If this is so, then a successful analysis of harming should be symmetric with a successful analysis of killing. This presumption might turn out to be mistaken. But in the absence of a good reason to think that killing and harming should turn out to have structurally different analyses, the fact that a proposed analysis of harming would generate an implausible parallel analysis of killing should count at least somewhat in favor of rejecting the proposed analysis of harming. And the Non-Comparative Account of harm has precisely this feature.

To see that this is so, consider what the analyses of killing would look like if they were parallel to the Non-Comparative Account and the Counterfactual Account. The Counterfactual Account treats harming as an essentially comparative matter: to harm a person is to put that person in a state that is worse for him in terms of how much well-being he has than the state that he would otherwise be in. A parallel analysis of killing would therefore be comparative in a parallel manner: to kill a person is to put that person in a state that is worse for him in terms of how alive he is than the state that he would otherwise be in. The Non-Comparative Account, on the other hand, is fundamentally non-comparative. It says that some states are simply bad states for people to be in, and that an act that causes a person to be in that state harms that person, regardless of what would have been the case had the act not been performed. A parallel analysis of killing would therefore be non-comparative in a parallel manner: to kill a person is to cause it to be the case that the person is dead, regardless of what would have been the case had the act not been performed. I will call the first account the Counterfactual Account of killing and the second account the Non-Comparative Account of killing. The question, then, is whether there is a difference in terms of the plausibility of these two accounts.

The Counterfactual Account of killing says that to kill a person is to cause him to be "less alive" than he would otherwise be. This certainly has a strange sound to it. But it sounds strange only if we take it to mean that being alive comes in degrees. Once we realize that the account does not require this to be the case, what the Counterfactual Account of killing says should seem perfectly straightforward: an act kills a person if it causes that person to be dead when he would otherwise be alive. The Non-Comparative Account of killing, on the other hand, says that an act kills a person if it causes it to be the case that the person is dead, regardless of what would have been the case had the act not been performed. And this analysis has strongly counterintuitive implications in cases involving conception, at least if we follow Harman in assuming that "counterfactual dependence is sufficient for causation: I assume that if an action is such that if it had not been performed, a particular event would not have occurred, then the action causes the event."[12] For every death that occurs, after all, there is an act of conception such that if that act of conception had not occurred, the death would not have occurred. This means that the Non-Comparative Account of killing entails that the act of conceiving a person kills that person. And this strikes me as an implausible result. Since the Counterfactual Account of killing is therefore more plausible than the Non-Comparative Account of killing, and since there is a reasonable presumption in favor of there being a structural symmetry between the best analyses of harming and of killing, we have a good independent reason to prefer the Counterfactual Account of harm over the Non-Comparative Account of harm.

(3) The moral principle that Harman defends in her 2004 paper entails that it would be morally impermissible for you to give the ice cream sundae to Sally. In order to avoid this kind of result, Harman introduces a modified version of the principle in her 2009 paper, appealing to what she refers to there as (4) rather than (4*). And referring to a case that is structurally identical to my ice cream sundae case, she responds to the worry that the revision to her earlier principle is ad hoc as follows:[13]

I think this case does establish that (4*) is false. But it helps to motivate the possibility that (4) is true while (4*) is false. What strikes us about the case is that if we don't harm Sally, then Sally loses out on the benefit. What moves us to think it may be permissible to harm Sally is the thought of what is bad for her about our not harming her. This brings out an important difference between actions that affect whether people exist and those that do not. If an action benefits someone who exists independently of the action, then there are two kinds of considerations in favor of the action:

– the action benefits the person
– if the action is not performed, the person is deprived of the benefits (that is, she exists but doesn't get some benefits she could have had)

When a non-identity action benefits someone, only the first of these two considerations is available to tell in favor of the action; the second does not apply. But the second seems to play a crucial role in how, sometimes, the fact that we benefit someone can play a role in making harming that person permissible—and it plays a crucial role in why (4*) is false. Since the second consideration doesn't apply to non-identity actions, this suggests that the reasons (4*) is false just don't apply to (4).

Harman's reply, in short, is that restricting the scope of (4*) is independently justified by the difference between cases like that of the ice cream sundae and cases like that of

---

[12] Harman (2009: 140).   [13] Harman (2009: 147–8).

Wilma. If you cause Sally to have a stomach ache by giving her the sundae, there are two kinds of consideration that will favor your act: she will benefit from the sundae if you give it to her and she will be deprived of it if you don't. But if Wilma causes Pebbles to be blind by conceiving her, there will only be one kind of consideration in favor of her act: Pebbles will benefit from the good experiences her existence will make possible if Wilma conceives her, but she won't be deprived of those experiences, or of anything else, if Wilma doesn't conceive her.

But this response to the objection only pushes the question back a step. Rather than asking why the difference between (4^*) and (4) is morally relevant, that is, the question now becomes why the difference between cases where both kinds of consideration favor a harmful act and cases where only the first kind of consideration favors a harmful act is morally relevant. Harman's response is to claim that in the kind of case where both considerations are present, it is the second that is actually doing the work in accounting for the permissibility of the harmful act. Put in terms of the ice cream sundae case, she says that "what strikes us" about the case is that Sally will lose out on the ice cream if we don't give it to her, not that Sally will greatly enjoy the ice cream if we do give it to her. She says that "what moves us to think it may be permissible" to give Sally the ice cream is "the thought of what is bad for her about our not" giving it to Sally, rather than the thought of what is good for her about our giving it to her. And she says that the fact that Sally would be deprived of a benefit if we don't give her the ice cream "seems to play a crucial role" in making the act of giving her the sundae permissible. If Harman is correct about all of this, then there is indeed a reason to treat the difference between the two kinds of cases as morally relevant. If the second kind of consideration is needed in order to justify a harmful act, and if the second kind of consideration applies in ordinary cases but not in non-identity cases, then there is an independent justification for limiting the scope of the Alternative Possibility Principle in the way that (4) does so that it only covers non-identity cases.

But why should we think that Harman is correct about this? Why should we think that the benefit to Sally of enjoying the ice cream is not enough, by itself, to make it permissible for us to give it to her? Harman gives no reason for us to think this. She simply asserts that we do think it. But this is an unsatisfying response for three reasons. First, simply saying that people think this does not provide a justification for their thinking it. Why should the difference make a difference? Second, the claim that most people think this is implausible. Suppose, for example, that a mother takes her child on a roller coaster ride knowing that it will be exhilarating for him but also knowing that it will cause him to become a bit nauseated. If we asked the mother afterwards why she took the child on the ride, we would surely expect her to say something like this: "because I knew he would have such a great time on the roller coaster and that the benefits to him would far outweigh the costs." It would be quite surprising if she instead said something like this: "because I knew it would be very bad for him to not go on the roller coaster, much worse for him than suffering a bit of nausea." Rather than thinking that people would primarily appeal to the second sort of consideration in cases where both considerations apply, then, it seems much more likely that most people would naturally appeal to the first.

But finally, and most importantly, there is no reason to treat the two considerations in the ice cream sundae case as if only one of them could provide a sufficient justification for the permissibility of performing the harmful act. Even if someone really is initially moved to think that it would be permissible to give Sally the ice cream by considering how bad it would be for Sally if she were deprived of the ice cream, this would provide no reason for them to doubt that the fact that Sally would benefit from getting the ice cream would also be a sufficient justification for the claim that it would be permissible to give it to her. There is no reason, that is, to deny that the ice cream sundae case is simply one in which the permissibility of the act is overdetermined. Suppose, to take a different kind of example, that I promise you that I will not murder Sally. In this case, you might well be moved to think that it would be impermissible for me to murder Sally by considering how bad it would be for Sally if I were to murder her. The fact that I promised you that I would not murder Sally would likely play no role in your thinking. But this would do nothing to undermine the claim that the fact that an act would break a promise I made to you could also be a sufficient reason to deem it impermissible.

Appendix D: One More Case to Test the Preventative Benefit Principle (3.3.2)

In the case where Richie's dropping the gold cube on Joe confers a pure benefit on Joe, the harms and benefits are strikingly incommensurable: a broken arm on the one hand, a great deal of money on the other. So we can change the case where Larry's rescuing Moe confers a preventative benefit on Moe by making it one in which the harms and benefits are equally incommensurable. Here is an example:

Drowning Money: Moe is asleep next to a large open box that contains a great deal of his money. A strong wind starts blowing, and the money will soon be blown into a nearby lake, where it will be ruined. Larry is unable to close the box, but Moe will be able to close it if Larry wakes Moe up. In order to wake Moe up, Larry will have to break Moe's arm. Larry wakes Moe up. As a result, Moe is spared the loss of a great deal of his money and suffers a broken arm.

In this case, as in the original drowning case, Larry confers a preventative benefit on Moe. But in this case, unlike the original drowning case, the harm that Larry causes is not at all commensurable with the benefit he confers.

Virtually everyone, I assume, agrees that it is permissible for Larry to break Moe's arm in the case where Moe himself is drowning. What about the case where it is Moe's money that will drown if Larry doesn't break Moe's arm? I suspect that a number of people will think that it would be permissible for Larry to break Moe's arm in this case as well. But that is not enough to help vindicate the Preventative Benefit Principle. After all, a number of people will probably think that it is permissible for Richie to break

Joe's arm in the original gold cube case, too. The significance of changing the drowning case into the drowning money case rests on the answer to this question: to whatever extent you think the original drowning case is different from the gold cube case in terms of the permissibility of the acts in question, does changing the drowning case to the drowning money case eliminate that disparity? If you think that there is no difference in permissibility between the original drowning case and the gold cube case, after all, then Shiffrin's argument won't be able to get off the ground in the first place: there will be no difference in permissibility for either the difference in commensurability or the difference between pure and preventative benefits to be accounting for.

Suppose, though, that you think it's just obvious that it is permissible for Larry to break Moe's arm in the original drowning case but that while you are inclined to think that it is probably permissible for Richie to break Joe's arm in the gold cube case, you don't really think it's just obvious that it would be permissible. In that case, you should consider whether this relatively small discrepancy between the two cases is eliminated by changing the drowning case to the drowning money case. If the change leaves you thinking that it is probably permissible for Larry to break Moe's arm in the drowning money case but less obviously so than in the original drowning case, then the change in the drowning story again shows that it was the difference in terms of commensurability, not the difference in terms of pure and preventative benefits, that was making the original cases seem somewhat different to you. If you think it is clear that it is permissible for Larry to break Moe's arm in the original drowning case and also clear that it is positively impermissible for Richie to break Joe's arm in the gold cube case, then you should consider whether this large disparity is eliminated by changing the drowning case to the drowning money case. If the change leaves you thinking that it is clearly impermissible for Larry to break Moe's arm in the drowning money case, then the change from the original drowning story again shows that it was the difference in terms of commensurability, not the difference in terms of pure and preventative benefits, that was making the original cases seem so different to you.

The argument at this point must rest on the particular reactions that it generates, but I find it hard to believe that many people will think that there is a significant difference between the permissibility of Larry's breaking Moe's arm in the drowning money case and Richie's breaking Joe's arm in the original gold cube case. And if that's right, then this second way of testing my claim should produce the same result as the first: Shiffrin's cases fail to provide sufficient warrant for endorsing the Preventative Benefit Principle.

Appendix E: Rejecting Five Objections to the Rights Waiver Argument (5.1.3)

The rights waiver argument maintains that even if Pebbles has a right that Wilma's act would directly or indirectly violate, the existence of the right cannot be used to ground a satisfactory solution to the non-identity problem because Pebbles would waive that right at the time of Wilma's act if she could or because she will later waive the right when she comes to understand the choice that Wilma faced. Several objections have been raised against the rights waiver argument, but none of them is successful.

Jeffrey Reiman, for example, argues that

the choices in the non-identity cases are not analogous to the choice to perform life-saving surgery on an unconscious person. Consider that when we assume that the unconscious person would waive his right not to have surgery performed on him without his consent, we assume that the waiver releases us from wrongdoing at the moment we made the choice to operate. Such a waiver is a retroactive permission, not an after-the-fact pardon. It is tantamount to saying that had the person been conscious at the moment when the choice to operate had been made, he would *then* have consented to surgery. No such retroactive consent is possible, however, in the case of the people negatively affected by the choices made in the non-identity cases, because they did not exist when those choices were made. Since particular individuals only care about existing as those particulars once they already are alive, the argument that they would waive their rights fallaciously assumes that particular people have an interest before they are alive that they only can have once they are alive.[14]

There are three problems with this objection. First, the fact that we take the waiver in the surgery case to be effective at the moment that we act does nothing to favor a hypothetical present consent account of waivers over a subsequent actual consent account. When a parent has a child vaccinated, for example, she could appeal to the claim that the child would consent right now if he understood the relevant details, but she could just as easily appeal to the claim that the child will later come to consent once he understands the relevant details. At the time that she acts, it is just as true that the child will later consent as it is that the child would at that time consent. The fact that the waiver is operative at the time that she acts therefore does nothing to favor appealing to the latter consideration over the former. And if subsequent actual consent is sufficient to generate a valid rights waiver, then the fact that the unconscious patient already exists when the surgery is performed but the not-yet-conceived Pebbles does not exist when Wilma conceives her does nothing to undermine the rights waiver argument. The fact that Pebbles will later exist and consent to what Wilma has done is enough to make Wilma's act permissible at the time that she does it.

But suppose that Reiman is correct in maintaining that a waiver of rights is valid only in cases where the person would actually consent to it at the time that the relevant act was performed. And suppose that he is also correct in maintaining that people have no interest in living until they already exist. If this is so, then a second problem arises. If Pebbles has no interest in her existence prior to the point at which she is conceived, then she presumably has no rights relating to her existence prior to that point either. But if Pebbles has no rights relating to her existence prior to the point at which she exists, then Wilma can appeal to the waiver of Pebbles's rights to justify conceiving her even if only hypothetical actual consent is good enough to render a waiver of rights valid. Before she exists, Pebbles has no rights that could be violated by Wilma's act. As soon as she exists, she may have such rights, but as soon as she exists Wilma can appeal to the fact that she would consent to waive those rights given that she now exists. And so there is no point in time either before Wilma's act or after it at which Pebbles has a right that she would not waive and that is violated by Wilma's act.

Finally, Reiman's objection rests on the claim that pre-existing Pebbles would waive whatever right Wilma's act might be thought to violate only if she had a positive interest in being brought into existence. But this claim, too, can be challenged. Consider, for example, the case of trespassing. If you are unconscious and bleeding to death on your living room floor, it seems reasonable to suppose that you would waive your right against my trespassing so that I could walk into your house and save your life. If you are peacefully sleeping in your bed, it seems reasonable to suppose that you would not waive your right against my trespassing so that I could walk into your house and kill you. You would waive your right against my trespassing in cases where doing so would serve your interests, that is, but not in cases where doing so would hinder them. But what about cases in which you are completely indifferent to my trespassing? Suppose, for example, that I am walking home and that it would be a bit more convenient for me to take a few extremely light and gentle steps across your front lawn. Suppose that any harm that my act might cause to your interests would be precisely offset by corresponding benefits. If I very slightly damage a few blades of grass, for example, then I also help to kill a few weeds that were competing with the grass for nutrients. And suppose that there was no other reason that you would not want me to walk across a small part of your lawn, so that you are truly and completely indifferent between my briefly trespassing and my not trespassing at all. In this case, it seems reasonable to suppose that you would not object to my trespassing on your property and so would waive your right against my doing so. But if this is correct, then the fact that Pebbles has no positive interest in being brought into existence—if this is a fact—does not mean that Pebbles would not waive her right against Wilma conceiving her. She would still waive that right since she would have no reason to object to Wilma's conceiving her, just as you would waive your right since you would have no reason to object to my briefly walking across your lawn. And this provides one final reason to reject Reiman's first objection to the rights waiver argument.

Reiman has a second objection to the rights waiver argument. It runs as follows:

[I]t is unjust to make the price of some particular individual's existing that that person waive his or her right not to be negatively affected. Then it is clear, however, that such a waiver would be obtained under duress: that is, by an unjust albeit retroactive threat, namely, the threat of not existing. Parfit is certainly right to think that the people produced as a result of the negative actions in the non-identity cases might be tempted to waive their rights since the alternative is not existing at all. A person who waives a right in the face of an unjust threat of not existing, however, does not make a free and morally binding choice. Thus, even if the future people in the non-identity cases would waive their rights, that waiver would not be valid.[15]

The foundation of Reiman's second objection seems reasonable. Suppose, for example, that I tell you that I will kill you unless you waive your right not to have your eyes cut out and that, as a result of my telling you this, you explicitly waive your right not to have your eyes cut out. In this case, it seems clear that your rights waiver would not be valid and that my act of cutting your eyes out would be morally wrong despite the fact that you had explicitly waived your right against my doing so. Or suppose that I cut your eyes out while you are under heavy sedation and that when you later confront me about it, I defend my act by saying that I would have killed you if I hadn't cut your eyes out and that I knew that you would have agreed to waive your right not to have your eyes cut out given that the alternative was my killing you. Again, this rights waiver would not be valid. So Reiman is presumably right to say that a rights waiver made in the face of an unjust threat is not binding.

The case in which I will either cut your eyes out or kill you, moreover, is in one important respect similar to the case of Wilma and Pebbles. After I make my choice, either you will exist as a blind person or you will not exist at all. After Wilma makes her choice, either Pebbles will exist as a blind person or Pebbles will not exist at all. If the fact that you would waive your right not to be deprived of vision given the choices available to you is not enough to make your rights waiver a valid one, then, it may well seem that the fact that Pebbles would waive her right not to be deprived of vision given the choices available to her is not enough to make her rights waiver a valid one either. And if her rights waiver would not be a valid one, then Reiman's second objection to the rights waiver argument must be accepted.

But now suppose that a diabolical villain has injected a lethal poison into your eyes, that you are fully conscious, that I tell you that you will die unless you let me cut your eyes out and that, as a result of my telling you this, you explicitly waive your right not to have your eyes cut out. In this case, it seems clear that your rights waiver would be valid and that my act of cutting your eyes out would not be morally wrong. It seems clear that my act would not be morally wrong, moreover, precisely because you had explicitly waived your right against having your eyes cut out. And your rights waiver would also seem to be perfectly valid in the case where you are under heavy sedation and I appeal to the fact that you would waive your right not to have your eyes cut out if you could or that you will waive it after the fact. These considerations, too, seem to show that my act would not be morally wrong under those circumstances.

Yet the diabolical villain case is like the case of Wilma and Pebbles in just the same way that the case in which I will either cut your eyes out or kill you is like the case of Wilma and Pebbles. After I make my choice in the case where a diabolical villain has injected poison into your eyes, either you will exist as a blind person or you will

---

[15] Reiman (2007: 88). The same objection is also pressed by Hudson (1986: 100–1).

not exist at all. After Wilma makes her choice in our original non-identity case, either Pebbles will exist as a blind person or Pebbles will not exist at all. And the fact that you would waive your right not to be deprived of vision given the choices available to you in the diabolical villain case really does seem to be enough to make your rights waiver a valid one in that case. In order to sustain Reiman's second objection to the rights waiver argument, then, it is not enough to show that the Wilma case is in one way like the case in which I will either cut your eyes out or kill you. The objection would have to show that the Wilma case is more like that case than it is like the case of the diabolical villain. But in the end, it is the diabolical villain case that proves more like the case of Wilma. And this is why, in the end, Reiman's second objection must also be rejected.

In order to see this, it is important first to be clear about the main difference between the case in which I will either cut your eyes out or kill you and the case in which the diabolical villain has injected the poison into your eyes. In both cases, I tell you that you will die if I don't cut your eyes out. But in the former case, it is my fault that these are your only two options. In the latter case, it is not my fault. Prior to my arriving on the scene in the first case, there was a third option available to you: living and not being blind. This third option would have been better for you. I took that option away from you by threatening to kill you if you did not let me cut your eyes out. Removing this third option thus harmed you. And I had no right to take this third option away from you. Removing this third option thus wrongfully harmed you. But prior to my arriving on the scene in the second case, living and not being blind was not an option for you. Because the diabolical villain had already injected the poison into your eyes, living as a blind person or dying were the only two options you had when I arrived on the scene. When I tell you in that case that you will die if I don't cut your eyes out, then, I am simply stating the facts as they exist independent of my actions. My doing so neither harms you nor wrongs you.

This difference between the two cases explains why your rights waiver is invalid in the first case but valid in the second. When you agree to let me cut your eyes out in the first case, you do this only because I have made this the best option available to you by unjustly eliminating a third option that would have been even better. When you agree to let me cut your eyes out in the second case, you do this because this is the best option available to you regardless of what I do and regardless of what I have done. I unjustly coerce you into agreeing to waive your rights in the first case, then, but I do not unjustly coerce you into agreeing to waive your rights in the second case. This is why your rights waiver is valid in the case of the diabolical villain but not in the case in which I threaten to kill you if you don't let me cut your eyes out.

But given this understanding of the difference between the two cases, we can now see that the case of Wilma is like the case of the diabolical villain and unlike the case in which I threaten to kill you if you don't let me cut your eyes out. Prior to Wilma's making her decision about when to conceive, that is, living and not being blind was not an available option for Pebbles. Because of a medical condition that was not Wilma's fault and basic facts about human reproduction that were beyond Wilma's control, the only two options available to Pebbles were being conceived in an incurably blind condition and never being conceived at all. To put things in the terms that Reiman uses in pressing his objection, Wilma does not make it the price of Pebbles's existing that she waive her right not to be conceived as a blind person. That price was set by factors that were beyond Wilma's control. This makes the case of Wilma like the case in which the diabolical villain has injected poison into your eyes and unlike the case in which I threaten to kill you if you don't let me cut your eyes out. I do not make it the price of your continued existence that you let me cut your eyes out in the former case. I simply recognize that this is the price given the facts as they are. But I do make it the price of your continued existence that you let me cut your eyes out in the latter case, since in that case it is only my unjust threat to kill you that makes losing your eyes the price of existence for you. Since your rights waiver is valid in the case of the diabolical villain, and since Pebbles's rights waiver in the Wilma case is morally on a par with your rights waiver in the case of the diabolical villain, Pebbles's rights waiver in the Wilma case is valid as well. Reiman's second objection to the rights waiver argument, then, like his first, is ultimately unsuccessful.

David Velleman has also raised two objections to the rights waiver argument. Both are presented in terms of the case of a fourteen-year-old girl who conceives a child and who, because she is so young, is unable to give her child as good a start in life as she would have given her child if she had waited to conceive until she was older. Velleman argues that this girl's act of conceiving at such a young age violates her child's right to be given the best start in life that that child's parents are capable of providing. And he presents two objections to the claim that the girl's act is rendered morally acceptable by the fact that the child would or will waive that right. I will discuss Velleman's two objections to the rights waiver argument in terms of the particular right that he endorses, but the points I raise in response to his objections would apply to other rights as well.

Velleman's first objection is similar to Reiman's second objection:

Ordinarily, the prospect of waiving a right arises in the context of three possible outcomes. We can (1) retain the right in order to ensure either (a) that it will be fulfilled or (b) that we will have legitimate grounds to protest its nonfulfillment; or we can (2) waive the right. Entertaining all three outcomes, we may prefer to retain the right, even though we would prefer to waive it if outcome (1)(a) were excluded. That is, we may think that retaining the right for the sake of possibly having it fulfilled would be sensible, but that retaining it merely for the sake of having grounds for protest would be petty and foolish. Given our preferences, the party against whom we hold the right can induce us to waive it if he can manage to take outcome (1)(a) off the table. But surely a waiver obtained by such means would not be normatively valid. He cannot gain release from fulfilling our right by confronting us with the fact that he isn't going to fulfill it, so that our only alternative to waiving the right is to retain it for the petty purpose of lodging a protest. To be sure, the child of a fourteen-year-old mother cannot exactly claim that she has taken outcome (1)(a) off the table: it was never *on* the table for this particular child. And yet the child may still waive his birthright because his only alternative is to complain that it cannot be fulfilled. And such a waiver is granted less voluntarily, because it is granted in the presence of fewer relevant alternatives, than the waiver of a right that can still be fulfilled. Its validity is therefore questionable.[16]

If you try to waive a given right only because that right will not be fulfilled no matter what happens, in short, then the waiver of your right will not be valid. The fourteen-year-old girl's child will not have his right to the best start in life that his parents could provide fulfilled no matter what happens. And so the child's waiver of this right will not be valid.

There are two reasons to reject this objection. The first is that it rests on a mistaken view of the nature of the right that the child could have against his mother. Velleman describes the right as a right to the best start in life that the particular parents of a particular child could provide. This right can be understood in two ways. One is as a positive right. On this interpretation, you have the right to be given the best start in life that your parents can provide you. The other is as a negative right. On this interpretation, you have the right not to be given a start in life that is less than the best that your parents can provide you. Velleman's objection to the rights waiver argument depends on the claim that the girl's child has this right in the positive sense. This is because the objection depends on the claim that fulfilling the right is not a possibility in the case of this particular child and because this is true in the positive sense of the right but false in the negative sense of the right. In the positive sense of the right, it is true that there is nothing the girl can do that will fulfill the child's right. If she conceives the child, he will not get the best start in life that she can provide, and if she doesn't conceive the child, he will not get the best start in life that she can provide, or indeed any start in life at all. But in the negative sense of the right, there is something that the girl can do to fulfill the child's right. If she refrains from conceiving this particular child, then this particular child will not be given a start in life that is less than the best that she would be able to provide because he will not be given any start in life at all. If the right is simply the negative right not to be conceived unless you will be given the best start in life that your parents can provide, that is, then the claim that Velleman's objection rests on—the claim that there is no way for the girl to fulfill the right—is false. She could fulfill this right in the negative sense by not conceiving until she is older.[17]

---

[16] Velleman (2008: 277 n. 12).

[17] Strictly speaking, we might say that there is a distinction between positively fulfilling a right and simply not violating a right. We might then say that the girl can ensure that she does not violate the child's right in the negative sense by not conceiving when she is fourteen but that she cannot actually fulfill the right in the negative sense in this way because a person's right to something can't be fulfilled if they don't exist. If this is so, then my claim that Velleman's argument depends on construing the right in the positive sense is mistaken. It could also be construed in the negative sense and my first objection to Velleman's argument only applies to the positive sense. But even if we accept this distinction, it cannot vindicate Velleman's first argument. This is because if we agree with Velleman that it makes sense to retain a right when there is a chance of appealing to the right as a way of having it fulfilled, we will also think that it makes sense to retain a right when there is a chance of appealing to it as a way of simply preventing it from being violated. The fact that the negative sense of the right is one that the girl can at least avoid violating by not conceiving when she is fourteen will therefore still be enough to show that Velleman's argument depends on the positive sense of the right.

So Velleman's first objection can succeed only if we attribute the right to this girl's child in the positive sense. But even if children do have a right to the best start in life that their parents could provide, they can have this right only in the negative sense. This is because if a child has a particular right against his mother, then the mother has a corresponding obligation not to violate that right. If she has an obligation not to violate that right, then she ought to refrain from violating it. But if she ought to refrain from violating it, then it must be the case that she can refrain from violating it. If it is impossible for her to refrain from violating it, then it cannot be the case that she ought to refrain, and if it is not the case that she ought to refrain from violating it, then it is not the case that it is a right that the child has in the first place. But the fourteen-year-old girl cannot refrain from violating her child's right to be given the best start in life that she can provide on the positive interpretation of that right. No matter what she does, this child will not be given such a start in life. Therefore, the child does not have this right in the positive sense.

My argument for this conclusion requires only two uncontroversial claims: that rights entail correlative duties and that ought implies can. Indeed, the claim that ought implies can is enough by itself to undermine Velleman's objection here. Even if we were to allow that the girl's child really can have a right that it is impossible for the girl not to violate, the fact that it would be impossible for the girl not to violate it would still be enough to show that it can't be the case that she ought not to violate it. And if it is not the case that she ought not to violate it, then the fact that conceiving the child violates his rights—even if it is a fact—won't be enough to justify the claim that conceiving the child is something she ought not to do. I'm inclined to favor the view on which the impossibility of fulfilling the purported right means that there is no such right. But either way, the appeal to such a right cannot ground a successful objection to the rights waver argument. And either way, the problem with the objection will arise in the case of any purported right that might be violated in non-identity cases. Pebbles cannot have a right to be born with vision since it is impossible for Wilma to refrain from violating that right, for example, but Pebbles can have a right not to be born without vision, since Wilma can refrain from violating that right by refraining from conceiving Pebbles. The future members of the wealthy society cannot have a right to be born and then not killed by the leaking toxic waste since it is impossible for them to be conceived and for the toxic waste not to leak, but they can have a right not to be born at all if they can only be born into a world in which toxic waste will subsequently leak and kill them. But if these are the rights that Pebbles and the future members of the wealthy society can have, then Velleman's objection to the validity of the waiver of their rights will again be unsuccessful. In the only sense in which they can have the right in question, their waiver of the right will prove valid because they would waive it or will waive it in a context in which the right really could have been fulfilled.

But let's suppose that Velleman is correct and that the only options available to the child in non-identity cases are waiving the right in question or retaining it solely in order to have legitimate grounds to protest its nonfulfillment. Even if this is so, there is a second problem with Velleman's first objection. Velleman claims that under such circumstances, "such a waiver is granted less voluntarily, because it is granted in the presence of fewer relevant alternatives, than the waiver of a right that can still be fulfilled." But the fact that a person chooses between fewer options rather than more options does not make the choice he makes any less voluntary or the waiver of rights that results from his choice any less valid. If I buy a car from you when I have only two cars to choose from, the waiver of my right to the money I give you is just as voluntary and just as valid as it is if I buy a car from you when I have hundreds of cars to choose from.

Perhaps Velleman thinks the second option in the non-identity case is not a genuine option because "retaining [the right] merely for the sake of having grounds for protest would be petty and foolish." This would mean that the fourteen-year-old girl's child has only one real option, which really would make his "choice" involuntary. But this assertion is unjustified. Suppose a thief announces that he is going to take your money no matter what you do and that once he takes it, you will never get it back. Before taking it, though, he asks if you would voluntarily waive your right to the money. I suspect that most people would refuse to waive the right to their money if they found themselves in such circumstances and that they would think their reasons for doing so neither petty nor foolish. Even if retaining the grounds for a legitimate protest would not have any practical consequences, a fundamental matter of principle would be at stake. It is wrong for the thief to take your money and by waiving the right to it you would in effect be endorsing his behavior and rendering it permissible. If the fourteen-year-old girl's child would waive his right to the best start in life his mother could provide even though the only alternative to waiving it was retaining it just so that he could have a moral complaint about his situation, then, this would still be enough to make the waiver of his right voluntary and valid, and thus enough to sustain the rights waiver argument.

Velleman's second objection to the rights waiver argument is more fundamental. He denies that the child in question would waive his rights in the first place. Parfit at times motivates the rights waiver argument by appealing to the claim that if he is glad that someone did something to him, then he waives or would waive his right that the person not do that thing.[18] But Velleman rejects this inference:

The fact that a child would be glad to have been born does not entail that he would excuse his mother from her procreative obligations. He can reasonably say to his mother, "I'm glad that *I* was born, but you were wrong to have a child in my case." Not only can he reasonably say this; he probably *will* say it, once he realizes that other children have been given, and sensibly regard themselves as entitled to, the best start in life that their parents could provide to a child. He will continue to assert his birthright, despite being glad that he was born.[19]

---

[18] "[S]ince I am glad that you act as you do, with respect to you I *waive* this right" (1984: 364). See also Parfit (1984: 373).

[19] Velleman (2008: 277).

If being glad that he was conceived does not mean that he would waive the right that was violated by conceiving him, then the rights waiver argument seems to be cut off at its foundation.

Velleman is certainly right to insist that a person can be glad that he was conceived while believing that it was wrong for him to have been conceived. A person who was conceived in an act of rape, for example, could be glad to be alive while recognizing that the act of conceiving him was morally wrong. And, more generally, a person can be glad that an act was performed while believing that it was wrong for the act to have been performed. If I wake up and discover that you performed life-saving surgery on me last night, for example, I will be glad that you did so. If I discover that the surgery involved your killing innocent people and removing their organs in order to save me, I will think that your act was morally wrong but I could still feel glad that I was the person who was saved by your wrongful behavior given that someone was saved by your wrongful behavior. Velleman is therefore right to say that the fact that a child would be glad to have been conceived does not entail that the child would excuse his mother from her moral obligations. And so the mere fact that the fourteen-year-old girl's child will be glad to be born if she conceives him does not mean that he would waive whatever right her act of conceiving him would otherwise violate.

But there is an important difference between the rape and surgery cases and the case of the fourteen-year-old girl. In the former cases, the act in question is wrong for reasons that are independent of their effect on the person whose existence depends on the act. It is wrong to rape a person in order to conceive a person and wrong to kill people in order to save a person regardless of whether the person who ends up existing as a result of the wrongful act turns out to be glad that the act happened, and it is wrong because the act wrongs people other than person who now exists as a result of the wrongful act. This is why it can be coherent for the person who now exists as a result of the act in those cases to be glad that the act happened while agreeing that it was wrong that it happened. The act was wrong because it wronged other people. But the fourteen-year-old girl's act of conceiving her child did not wrong any other people. The rights-based solution claims that her act was nonetheless wrong because it wronged her child and that it wronged her child by violating her child's rights. Since her act did not wrong anyone else, on this account, it will be wrong only if it violates her child's rights, and it will violate his rights only if he does not or would not waive them. But if, once he is alive, the child will be glad that his mother conceived him, then the only reason he could have for not waiving the right in question would be if he thought that doing so would amount to tacitly approving of behavior that was immoral for other reasons. This can be so in the rape and surgery cases because those acts are wrong for other reasons. But if the only reason that conceiving the child would be wrong would be because it would violate his rights, and if he will be glad that he was conceived, then he will have no moral or prudential reason not to waive the right in question. Waiving his right will not, as Velleman puts it, excuse his mother from her procreative obligations, because waiving his right will make it the case that her act violated no such obligations. Her only obligation in this case was not to violate any unwaived rights and by waiving whatever right her act would otherwise violate he will ensure that she satis-fies her obligation. Since he has no moral or prudential reason not to waive his right, he will waive it. And since he will waive it, her act will not be wrong. The fact that a person is glad that someone did a particular act cannot be enough to prevent the act from being wrong as a general matter because it cannot be enough to prevent the act from being wrong in cases where it wrongs other people. But the fact that a person is glad that someone did a particular act can be enough to prevent the act from being wrong in cases where there would be no reason for the act to be wrong other than that person's not wanting it to have occurred and where the person will therefore happily waive the right in question as a result. In the end, then, Velleman's second objection to the rights waiver argument is also unsuccessful.

A final objection to the rights waiver argument is suggested, though only tentatively endorsed, by Parfit himself. Referring to a case in which if Jane conceives now rather than later, her child will be born with a life-shortening condition, Parfit writes that if he were the child that Jane conceived with the life-shortening condition, "I would not regret that my mother caused me to exist. And I would deny that her act was wrong because of what it did to me. If I was told that it *was* wrong, because it caused me to exist with a right that cannot be fulfilled, I would *waive* this right." But he then adds: "though *I* would waive this right, I cannot be certain that, in all such cases, this is what such a child would do. If Jane's child does not waive his right, an appeal to this right may perhaps provide some objection to her choice."[20]

In order to see whether this possibility points to a genuine problem with the rights waiver argument, it may help to begin by assigning specific probabilities to the case. So let's suppose that Jane knows that if she conceives a child now, there is a one in twenty chance that the child will grow up to resent her decision and to refuse to waive his right not to have been conceived in such a condition. And now consider the following case: you are a doctor and I am brought unconscious into your emergency room. You can save my life only by performing surgery on me, but even if you do, I will be perma-nently paralyzed below the waist and significantly disfigured. You must decide what to do before I wake up and thus before I can have an opportunity to tell you whether I waive my right not to have you cut into my body. Based on your experience in similar cases, you are confident that I would want you to save my life, but you also recognize that there is a one in twenty chance that I would rather die than live on in such a condi-tion. If that turns out to be the case, then when I wake up, I will resent your decision and refuse to waive my right not to have you cut into my body.

It is clear that it would not be morally wrong for you to operate on me in this case. The mere fact that there is a modest chance that I will later refuse to waive my right not to be operated on is therefore not enough to make operating on me wrong. But given

---

[20] Parfit (1984: 375).

that this is so, we must say the same thing about the case of Jane. The mere fact that there is a modest chance that her child will later refuse to waive his right not to have been conceived is not enough to make conceiving him wrong. In order for the rights waiver argument to succeed, then, it is not necessary to insist with certainty that the fourteen-year-old girl's child will later waive his rights. It is enough to maintain that it is highly likely that he will. And there is no good reason to doubt this assumption.

Appendix F: Rejecting Parfit's Defense of the No Difference View (6.1.3)

Wanda is planning to conceive a child tonight. Her doctor tells her that as things now stand, the child she conceives tonight will be incurably blind. But if she takes a handful of tiny pills this afternoon, then when she conceives that child tonight, the child will not be blind. The pills are easy to take, have no side effects, and will be paid for by her health insurance. And since taking the pills this afternoon will have no effect on the timing of the conception that will occur tonight, she will conceive the same child tonight regardless of whether she takes the pills this afternoon. So either that child will be incurably blind or that very same child will be sighted. Like Wilma, Wanda decides that having to deal with a bunch of pills is a bit too much of a bother. So she tosses the pills away, goes home, and conceives Patty who is born incurably blind. Like Wilma, Wanda ends up conceiving a blind child rather than a sighted child when she could easily have conceived a sighted child rather than a blind child. But unlike Wilma, Wanda was going to conceive the same child regardless of which choice she made. Wanda made Patty worse off than Patty would have been if Wanda had taken the pills, that is, but Wilma did not make Pebbles worse off than Pebbles would have been if Wilma had taken the pills. Wanda's act harmed someone. Wilma's act did not. Does this difference between the two cases make a moral difference?

One view maintains that this difference does not make a moral difference. This is what Parfit calls the "No Difference View."[21] On the No Difference View, Wilma's act is just as morally wrong as Wanda's act is, and is morally wrong for just the same reason. On a second view, what Parfit calls the "Two-Tier View," the difference between the two cases does make a moral difference. Parfit puts the second view this way: "Though we always have reasons not to cause future lives to be less worth living, these reasons would be weaker if, because these lives would be lived by different people, these acts would not be worse for any of these people."[22] On this second view, Wanda's reasons for not causing her future child to be blind Patty rather than sighted Patty are stronger than Wilma's reasons for not causing her future child to be blind Pebbles rather than sighted Rocks. On the first view, Wilma's act is just as morally wrong as Wanda's act.

---

[21] E.g. Parfit (1984: 367; 2011: vol. 2, 219).   [22] Parfit (2011: vol. 2, 219).

On the second view, Wilma's act is less morally wrong than Wanda's act or perhaps not even morally wrong at all.

Parfit argues that we should accept the No Difference View. His argument for this claim is indirect. Rather than providing reasons that support the view, he attempts to establish that denying the view has unacceptable implications. Two cases, in particular, serve as the basis for this *reductio ad absurdum* argument. The first case involves our choosing between two medical programs.[23] Program A would test millions of pregnant women for Disease A and cure the women who tested positive for it before their illness could cause their children to be born with a life-shortening condition. Program B would test millions of women for Disease B before they became pregnant and cure the women who tested positive for it before their illness could cause them to conceive a child who would be born with a similar life-shortening condition. The cure for Disease B would cause the women to postpone conception by two months. The women who currently have Disease A, then, will give birth to the very same children regardless of whether Program A cures their disease before they give birth. The women who currently have Disease B, though, will conceive and give birth to one set of children if Program B cures them before they conceive and will conceive and give birth to a different set of children if Program B does not cure them before they conceive. Program A and Program B would affect the same number of women and would prevent the same number of children from being born with a similar life-shortening condition.

One way to picture the difference between Program A and Program B is to look at a representative sample of the children who would be born under either program. Ann and Arnold are currently being gestated in mothers infected with Disease A. Ann and Arnold will thus be born in a few months regardless of whether their mothers are tested and cured by Program A. If their mothers are cured, they will be spared the life-shortening condition. Beth and Beverly are currently infected with Disease B and plan to become pregnant later this year. If Program B does not test and cure them, Beth will soon conceive Bob and Beverly will soon conceive Becky. Bob and Becky will both have the life-shortening condition. If Program B does test and cure Beth and Beverly, thus delaying their acts of conception by two months, they will instead conceive Bill and Barbara who will be spared the life-shortening condition. We can represent the number of years that each child would live under the two programs as follows:

| Program A: | Ann 70 | Arnold 70 | Bob 50 | Becky 50 |
| Program B: | Ann 50 | Arnold 50 | Bill 70 | Barbara 70 |

And we can simply assume that for every additional case like Ann and Arnold there would be an additional case like Bob or Bill and Becky or Barbara.

23 Parfit (1984: 367; 2011: vol. 2, 221). There are some differences between the two versions. The version I give here follows the 2011 version.

Parfit finds that when he considers this sort of case, the two programs seem to be morally on a par. Neither would be better or worse than the other. The No Difference View entails that this judgment is correct. This is because the No Difference View says that the fact that Ann and Arnold will be better off under Program A and worse off under Program B while there is no one who will be better off under Program B and worse off under Program A does not matter morally. But the Two-Tier View entails that Program A is better than Program B. This is because the Two-Tier View says that our reason for adding twenty years of life to a particular person like Ann or Arnold is stronger than our reason for adding twenty years of life that will simply be lived by some person or other by having someone like Bill or Barbara live seventy years rather than having someone like Bob or Becky live fifty years. The argument that Parfit grounds in this first case, in short, is that the two programs are morally on a par, that the No Difference View accounts for this and that denying the No Difference View is incompatible with this.

Let's suppose that Parfit is correct that Program A and Program B are morally on a par.[24] He is certainly correct that the No Difference View entails that this judgment is true and that the Two-Tier View entails that it is false. But the Two-Tier View is not the only alternative to the No Difference View. The exclusive version of the Moderate Principle that I defend in section 6.1 is another alternative. Unlike the No Difference View, the exclusive version of the Moderate Principle entails that there is a moral difference between the cases of Wilma and Wanda. And unlike the Two-Tier View, the exclusive version of the Moderate Principle does not entail that there is a moral difference between Program A and Program B. The exclusive version of the Moderate Principle, therefore, defeats Parfit's argument from the claim that the two medical programs are morally on a par to the conclusion that we should accept the No Difference View.

Consider first what the exclusive version of the Moderate Principle entails about the cases of Wanda and Wilma. Assuming that the total amounts of well-being that Wanda and her child would enjoy on each of the two options available to Wanda are the same as the total amounts of well-being that Wilma and her child would enjoy on each of the two options available to Wilma, we can appeal to the numbers that I appealed to in Chapter 6 and represent the two cases as follows:

Wilma	Don't take pills first	Take pills first
	Wilma: 40,000	Wilma: 39,999
	Pebbles: 56,000	Rocks: 80,000
Wanda	Don't take pills first	Take pills first
	Wanda: 40,000	Wanda: 39,999
	Patty: 56,000	Patty: 80,000

[24] Though see Justin Weinberg (2013) for a powerful attempt to explain away this common intuition by identifying several potentially distorting features of the way that Parfit presents the case. See also Hope and McMillan (2012: 25–6).

As I showed in section 6.1.1, the exclusive version of the Moderate Principle does not entail that Wilma's act of conceiving Pebbles is morally wrong. Conceiving Pebbles does not make things worse for Wilma and Pebbles than they would otherwise be where the interests of Wilma and Pebbles are counted equally. What about the case of Wanda?

The exclusive version of the Moderate Principle tells us to focus our attention on the interests of all and only those people who actually exist given that Wanda decided not to take the pills before conceiving Patty. These people are Wanda, Patty, and everyone else in the world. Taking the interests of each of those people into account equally, the principle directs us to ask: would the interests of this particular group of people have been better served if Wanda had instead taken the pills before conceiving Patty? Since the interests of everyone else who exists are not affected by Wanda's choice, we can answer this question by simply focusing on the interests of Wanda and Patty, and by asking whether their interests would have been better served if Wanda had taken the pills before conceiving Patty. If the answer to this question is no, then the principle generates no objection to Wanda's choice. If the answer is yes, then the principle entails that Wanda's act was morally wrong.

The answer to the question is yes. When Wanda conceives Patty without first taking the pills, Wanda enjoys 40,000 units of well-being and Patty enjoys 56,000 units of well-being, for a total of 96,000 units of well-being. If Wanda had instead taken the pills before conceiving Patty, then Wanda would have enjoyed 39,999 units of well-being and Patty would have enjoyed 80,000 units of well-being, for a total of 119,999 units of well-being. 119,999 units of well-being is greater than 96,000 units of well-being. The interests of Wanda and Patty combined, that is, where the interests of each are counted equally, would have been better served if Wanda had taken the pills before conceiving Patty. And so while the exclusive version of the Moderate Principle does not entail that Wilma's act of conceiving blind Pebbles rather than sighted Rocks is morally wrong, it does entail that Wanda's act of conceiving blind Patty rather than sighted Patty is morally wrong. The exclusive version of the Moderate Principle, that is, rejects the No Difference View.

Let's now turn to the two medical programs. If we choose Program A, Ann and Arnold will live for seventy years, Bob and Becky will live for fifty years, and Bill and Barbara will never exist. If we choose Program B, Ann and Arnold will live for fifty years, Bob and Becky will never exist, and Bill and Barbara will exist and will live for seventy years. Parfit's argument maintains that we must endorse the No Difference View because doing so is necessary in order to account for the judgment that the two programs are morally on a par. But the exclusive version of the Moderate Principle enables us to reject the No Difference View without rejecting this judgment.

Suppose, for example, that we choose Program B. If we choose Program B, then Ann and Arnold are each made worse off than they would otherwise have been. Since no one would be made worse off than they would otherwise be if we chose Program A, the Two-Tier View entails that choosing Program A is morally better than choosing Program B. But the exclusive version of the Moderate Principle directs us to ask an importantly different question. It tells us to focus our attention on the interests of all and only those people who actually exist given that we chose Program B. These people are Ann, Arnold, Bill, Barbara, and everyone else in the world. Taking the interests of each of those people into account equally, the principle directs us to ask: would the interests of this particular group of people have been better served if we had instead chosen Program A? Since the interests of everyone else who exists are not affected by our choice, we can answer this question by simply focusing on the interests of Ann, Arnold, Bill, and Barbara, and by asking whether their interests would have been better served if we had instead chosen Program A. If the answer to this question is no, then the principle generates no objection to our choice. If the answer is yes, then the principle entails that our choice was morally wrong.

The answer to the question is no. When we choose Program B, Ann and Arnold each enjoy fifty years of life and Bill and Barbara each enjoy seventy years of life, for a total of 240 years of life. If we had instead chosen Program A, then Ann and Arnold would have each enjoyed seventy years of life, but Bill and Barbara would never have existed and so would have enjoyed no years of life at all. The total number of years of life enjoyed by Ann, Arnold, Bill, and Barbara would then have been only 140 years. 140 years is not greater than 240 years. And so the exclusive version of the Moderate Principle generates no objection to our choosing Program B. By the same reasoning, the principle also generates no objection to our choosing Program A. If we choose Program A, Ann and Arnold will live for seventy years and Bob and Becky will live for fifty years. In order to evaluate this choice, the exclusive version of the Moderate Principle therefore requires us to focus our attention on the interests of Ann, Arnold, Bob, and Becky, and to ask whether their interests would have been better served if we had instead chosen Program B. And the answer to this question is also no. When we choose Program A, Ann, Arnold, Bob, and Becky enjoy a total of 240 years of life. If we had instead chosen Program B, Ann and Arnold would each have enjoyed fifty years of life, and Bob and Becky would never have existed and so would have enjoyed no years of life at all. The total number of years of life enjoyed by Ann, Arnold, Bob, and Becky would then have been only one hundred years. And one hundred years is not greater than 240 years. So the exclusive version of the Moderate Principle generates no objection to our choosing Program A either.

The exclusive version of the Moderate Principle, then, unlike the Two-Tier View, does not entail that there is a moral difference between Program A and Program B. Parfit's argument maintains that if there is no moral difference between Program A and Program B, then we should accept the No Difference View. But this is a mistake. If there is no moral difference between Program A and Program B, we can account for this by appealing to the exclusive version of the Moderate Principle. And if we accept the exclusive version of the Moderate Principle, then we must reject the No Difference

View. The claim that there is no moral difference between Program A and Program B, then, fails to support the No Difference View.

Parfit has more recently appealed to a second case in arguing for the No Difference View in *On What Matters*. This is what Parfit refers to simply as Case Six:[25]

We choose A	Adam lives for 70 years	Bernard lives for 40 years	———	———
We choose B	———	Bernard lives for 90 years	Charles lives for 10 years	———
We choose C	———	———	Charles lives for 50 years	David lives for 20 years

In this case, Parfit argues that even the most defensible version of the Two-Tier View entails that we ought to choose C.[26] This is because while A would be worse for Bernard than B and B would be worse for Charles than C, C would be worse for no one than A or than B. But if we were to choose C rather than A, we could cause two people to live for only fifty years and twenty years when we could instead have caused two entirely different people to live for seventy years and forty years. It is virtually impossible to believe that we ought to choose C rather than A, far harder to believe than to believe that the two medical programs are not really morally on a par. And the No Difference View easily accounts for the claim that we ought to choose A rather than C. On the No Difference View, choosing C rather than A would be morally on a par with choosing that two people live for only fifty years and twenty years rather than that those very same two people live for seventy years and forty years. And that would clearly be wrong. For this reason, Case Six provides a potentially much stronger foundation for Parfit's argument. If denying the No Difference View means believing that C really is morally better than A, then we should almost certainly accept the No Difference View.

But denying the No Difference View does not mean believing that C is morally better than A. Accepting the Two-Tier View means believing that C is morally better than A, but as I have already noted, denying the No Difference View does not require us to accept the Two-Tier View. We can instead account for the fact that C is not morally better than A by appealing to the exclusive version of the Moderate Principle. And the exclusive version of the Moderate Principle entails that we should reject the No

---

[25] Parfit (2011: vol. 2, 228).

[26] Parfit (2011: vol. 2, 228–9). Strictly speaking, there are weighted versions of the Two-Tier View that can avoid the problem in this particular case, but the numbers in the case can be revised to generate the same basic problem for any version of the Two-Tier View. Since the argument I develop in the text concedes that Case Six (or at least a case very much like it) provides a decisive reason to reject the Two-Tier View, the details are not relevant to the discussion. I therefore omit them.

Difference View, not that we should accept it. We can therefore deny the No Difference View without having to insist that C is morally better than A.

To see what the exclusive version of the Moderate Principle entails about Case Six, it may help to start by supposing that we have chosen A and that Adam is now beginning his seventy-year life and Bernard is now beginning his forty-year life. Have we done something morally wrong by selecting A? The exclusive version of the Moderate Principle directs us to answer this question by focusing our attention on the interests of all and only those people who actually exist given that we chose A. These people are Adam, Bernard, and everyone else in the world. Taking the interests of each of those people into account equally, the exclusive version directs us to ask: would the interests of this particular group of people have been better served if we had instead selected B or C? On the assumption that the interests of everyone else who exists are not affected by our choice, we can answer this question by simply focusing on the interests of Adam and Bernard, and by asking whether their interests would have been better served if we had instead selected B or C. If the answer to this question is no, then the principle generates no objection to our choosing A. If the answer is yes, then the principle entails that our choice was morally wrong.

The answer to the question is no. When we choose A, Adam enjoys seventy years of life and Bernard enjoys forty years of life, for a total of 110 years of life between them. If we had instead selected B, then Bernard would have contributed ninety years of life to the total, but Adam would not have existed and so would not have contributed any years of life at all. The total number of years lived by Adam and Bernard would then have been ninety. Ninety years is not more than 110 years, and so selecting B instead of A would not have been better for Adam and Bernard where their interests are treated equally. If we had instead selected C, moreover, neither Adam nor Bernard would have existed and so neither would have contributed any years of life to the total lived between them. The total number of years lived by Adam and Bernard would have been zero. And zero years is also not more than 110 years. So the exclusive version of the Moderate Principle does not entail that it would be morally wrong for us to choose A.

For the same reasons that applied in the case of the two medical programs, of course, the principle also does not entail that it would be morally wrong for us to choose B or C. Choosing B will not make things worse for Bernard and Charles than they would be if we chose A or C, and choosing C will not make things worse for Charles and David than they would be if we chose A or B. The exclusive version of the Moderate Principle, in short, does not entail that any of the available choices would be morally wrong. But this is not a problem for the claim that the principle successfully undermines Parfit's argument. Parfit's argument maintains that we should accept the No Difference View so that we can avoid the conclusion that C would be better than A. And we can avoid that conclusion without accepting the No Difference View by accepting the exclusive version of the Moderate Principle regardless of what that principle implies about whether any of the choices would be morally wrong. Parfit concludes his discussion of the cases I have discussed here by saying that "these various cases show, I believe, that we should reject the Two-Tier View and accept the No Difference View."[27] But even if they do show that we should reject the Two-Tier View, they do not show that we should accept the No Difference View. They provide no reason to reject the exclusive version of the Moderate Principle, and if we accept the exclusive version of the Moderate Principle, then we must reject the No Difference View.

Two objections might be raised against my response to Parfit's argument for the No Difference View.[28] The first objection concedes that my response may succeed as a response to the argument as Parfit states it, but maintains that Parfit's argument can easily be modified to overcome the response. The second objection maintains that my response does not succeed even as a response to the argument as Parfit states it. The first objection focuses on Case Six. It acknowledges that the exclusive version of the Moderate Principle does not entail we ought to choose C rather than A, and thus acknowledges that we can reject the claim that C is better than A without accepting the No Difference View. But the objection maintains that Case Six can still be used to undermine the exclusive version of the Moderate Principle because the principle has a different unacceptable implication in that case. This is the implication that it would not be morally wrong for us to choose C rather than A. That claim, too, is likely to strike most people as highly implausible.

---

[27] Parfit (2011: vol. 2, 231).
[28] A third objection may also be worth noting. A critic might point out that in responding to the first objection to P5, I did not simply provide reasons to favor the exclusive version of the Moderate Principle over the inclusive version. In section 6.1.3.1, I also gave one reason to reject both versions of the principle, the reason based on the case of Fred. If it is not wrong for Fred to save blind Billy rather than sighted Timmy when saving blind Billy is a bit more convenient for him and he cannot save both, then even the exclusive version of the Moderate Principle should be rejected. And if the exclusive version of the Moderate Principle is false, then it cannot be used to undermine Parfit's argument for the No Difference View.

I do, in fact, think that the case of Fred provides a good reason to reject the Moderate Principle on either formulation. So I do, in fact, think that even the exclusive version of the Moderate Principle should be rejected. But the reason that I find to be a good reason for rejecting the exclusive version of the Moderate Principle is not available to a defender of the No Difference View. This is because the No Difference View entails that the case of Fred is morally no different from what I will call the case of Frank: Frank walks by a pond in which Bobby is drowning. Bobby is sighted and there are two different ways in which Frank could save Bobby. One way would be a bit more convenient for Frank, but it would cause Bobby to become incurably blind. The other way would be a bit less convenient for Frank, and it would enable him to rescue Bobby intact.

It is clear that it would be wrong for Frank to choose the option in which Bobby survives and is incurably blind rather than the slightly less convenient option in which Bobby survives and is sighted. The No Difference View entails that the case of Fred is morally on a par with the case of Frank. This means that if the No Difference View is true, then it would be wrong for Fred to choose the option in which Billy survives and is incurably blind rather than the slightly less convenient option in which Timmy survives and is sighted. Since a proponent of the No Difference View must therefore insist that it really is wrong for Fred to save blind Billy rather than sighted Timmy, the proponent of the No Difference View cannot endorse my objection to the exclusive version of the Moderate Principle. If my objection to the exclusive version of the Moderate Principle is correct, then, we should reject the No Difference View because it is clear that it would be wrong for Frank to save Bobby in a manner that causes him to become incurably blind. And if my objection to the exclusive version of the Moderate Principle is not correct, then we can use the principle to undermine Parfit's argument in defense of the No Difference View. So either we have no reason to accept the No Difference View or we have a positive reason to reject the No Difference View.

This objection should be rejected because it is mistaken in claiming that the exclusive version of the Moderate Principle entails that it would not be morally wrong for us to choose C rather than A. The principle does not entail that choosing C rather than A would be morally wrong, but this is not the same as entailing that choosing C rather than A would not be morally wrong. Choosing C rather than A might still be morally wrong for some other reason. For example, choosing C rather than A might be wrong because it violates an optimizing principle on which it is wrong to make the suboptimal choice in different person cases. This optimizing principle is consistent with the exclusive version of the Moderate Principle. The Moderate Principle simply says that it is wrong to make one choice over another *at least* in cases where a certain set of conditions are satisfied. It leaves it open that there might be other conditions that can also make a choice wrong. And the optimizing principle is also consistent with rejecting the No Difference View. Nothing about the optimizing principle can be used to reject the claim that Wanda's act is morally worse than Wilma's act. And so the claim that it would be wrong to choose C rather than A in Parfit's Case Six cannot be used to ground a modified version of his defense of the No Difference View.

The second objection claims that my response rests on a misinterpretation of Parfit's argument. I have been characterizing Parfit's argument as maintaining that if the two medical programs are morally on a par or if it is not the case that we ought to choose C in Case Six, then we should accept the No Difference View. As I pointed out, Parfit concludes his discussion of these cases in *On What Matters* by saying that "these various cases show, I believe, that we should reject the Two-Tier View and accept the No Difference View." But, this objection points out, Parfit also prefaces his discussion of the cases by identifying and rejecting what he calls the "Narrow Person-Affecting View": "one of two outcomes cannot be worse, nor can one of two acts be wrong, if this outcome or act would be worse for no one."[29] And it is only after setting the Narrow Person-Affecting View to the side that he says that "there are now two possibilities": the No Difference View and the Two-Tier View.[30] What Parfit's argument therefore really maintains, according to the second objection, is that if the two medical programs are morally on a par (or if it is not the case that we ought to choose C in Case Six), *and if we reject the Narrow Person-Affecting View*, then we should accept the No Difference View. And, the objection maintains, my response cannot undermine this version of Parfit's argument because my response appeals to the exclusive version of the Moderate Principle and the exclusive version of the Moderate Principle is simply a version of the Narrow Person-Affecting View. If Parfit's argument is based on the assumption that the Narrow Person-Affecting View is false and if my response to Parfit's argument depends on the assumption that the Narrow Person-Affecting View is true, then my response to Parfit's argument, once that argument is properly understood, turns out to simply beg the question.

---

[29] Parfit (2011: vol. 2, 219).   [30] Parfit (2011: vol. 2, 219).

The principle that I have appealed to in responding to Parfit's argument is in some respects very close to the Narrow Person-Affecting View. It is therefore understandable that my response might seem to beg the question against Parfit's argument. But the principle that I have appealed to is nonetheless distinct from the Narrow Person-Affecting View. And so, in the end, this second objection to my response to Parfit's argument must also be rejected. The Narrow Person-Affecting View says that if one of two acts would not be worse for anyone, then the act cannot be wrong. Making things worse for someone, on this view, is a necessary condition in order for an act to be wrong. If one of two acts would not be worse for anyone, then the exclusive version of the Moderate Principle will generate no moral objection to it. Making things worse for someone, in other words, is necessary in order for an act to violate the exclusive version of the Moderate Principle. But the Moderate Principle does not maintain that there are no other moral principles. Nor does it maintain that there are no other moral principles on which an act might be wrong despite that fact that it is worse for no one. The Moderate Principle, for example, is consistent with the claim that an act can be wrong because it violates someone's rights even if the act does not make things worse for anyone. This is one reason that one can accept the exclusive version of the Moderate Principle without accepting the Narrow Person-Affecting View.

Second, and more importantly, the Narrow Person-Affecting View claims that if one of two outcomes would be worse for no one, then it cannot be *the worse outcome*. The outcome in which Wilma conceives Pebbles rather than Rocks, for example, is not worse for Pebbles or for anyone else, and so the Narrow Person-Affecting View entails that the outcome is not worse when Wilma conceives Pebbles than it would have been if she had instead conceived Rocks. But the exclusive version of the Moderate Principle says nothing at all about which outcomes are better or worse. Accepting the principle therefore entails nothing about which outcomes are better or worse than others. One can accept the principle while agreeing that it would be better for Wilma to conceive Rocks. One would simply have to deny that the fact that it would be better for Wilma to conceive Rocks means that it would be positively immoral for her to conceive Pebbles. This is a second reason that one can accept the exclusive version of the Moderate Principle without accepting the Narrow Person-Affecting View. And since one can accept the principle without accepting the view, the fact that my response to Parfit's argument appeals to the principle does not mean that my response requires us to accept the view.

There is one final interpretive wrinkle. Immediately after referring to the Narrow Person-Affecting View, Parfit writes:

Most of us would rightly reject this view. We would believe that (D) it would be in itself worse if some of the lives that will later be lived will be less worth living, and that (E) we have reasons not to act in ways that would have such effects, and if these effects would predictably be very bad, and we could avoid them at little cost to ourselves, such acts would be wrong.[31]

---

[31] Parfit (2011: vol. 2, 219).

And it is immediately after this passage that he says that we are now left with two possibilities: the No Difference View and the Two-Tier View. Parfit's argument for the No Difference View might therefore be understood as saying not just that if the two medical programs are morally on a par (or if it is not the case that we ought to choose C in Case Six), and if we reject the Narrow Person-Affecting View, then we should accept the No Difference View, but rather that if the two medical programs are morally on a par (or if it is not the case that we ought to choose C in Case Six), *and if we accept (D) and (E)*, then we should accept the No Difference View. These are not simply two ways of stating the same argument. One can reject the Narrow Person-Affecting View without accepting both (D) and (E). Accepting (D) and the first part of (E), for example, would be sufficient for rejecting the Narrow Person-Affecting View.

If Parfit's argument presupposes not only that we reject the Narrow Person-Affecting View but also that we accept (D) and (E), then my response to the argument might seem to be subject to the second objection after all. The second part of (E) maintains that it would be wrong to produce an outcome that would be much worse than the outcome that would otherwise have been produced even if the outcome was worse for no one, and this claim might seem to be incompatible with the principle that I have appealed to in responding to Parfit's argument. But the exclusive version of the Moderate Principle is not incompatible with the conditional claim made by (E). The Moderate Principle does not say that acts of the sort identified in the second part of (E) are not wrong. It simply says that they do not violate the Moderate Principle. We could therefore reject the Narrow Person-Affecting View and accept both (D) and (E) and Parfit's claims about the two medical programs and Case Six while still appealing to the exclusive version of the Moderate Principle as a reason for rejecting the No Difference View. Wanda's act would still have a wrong-making property that Wilma's act lacked. The No Difference View would still be false.

Works Cited

Adams, Robert M. 1979. "Existence, Self-Interest, and the Problem of Evil." *Noûs*, vol. 13, pp. 53–65.

Anstey, K. W. 2002. "Are Attempts to Have Impaired Children Justifiable?" *Journal of Medical Ethics*, vol. 28, pp. 286–8.

Archard, David. 2004. "Wrongful Life." *Philosophy*, vol. 79, no. 309, pp. 403–20.

Attfield, Robin. 2007. "Beyond the Earth Charter: Taking Possible People Seriously." *Environmental Ethics*, vol. 29, pp. 359–67.

Bayles, D. M. 1976. "Harm to the Unconceived." *Philosophy and Public Affairs*, vol. 5, no. 3 (Spring), pp. 292–304.

Benatar, David. 1997. "Why It Is Better Never to Come into Existence." *American Philosophical Quarterly*, vol. 34, no. 3, pp. 345–55.

Benatar, David. 2000. "The Wrong of Wrongful Life." *American Philosophical Quarterly*, vol. 37, no. 2, pp. 175–83.

Benatar, David. 2006. *Better Never to Have Been: The Harm of Coming into Existence*. Oxford: Clarendon Press.

Bennett, Rebecca. 2009. "The Fallacy of the Principle of Procreative Beneficence." *Bioethics*, vol. 23, no. 5, pp. 265–73.

Bennett, Rebecca. Forthcoming. "When Intuition is not Enough: Why the Principle of Procreative Beneficence Must Work Much Harder to Justify Its Eugenic Vision." *Bioethics*.

Bernstein, Stacey Scriven. 2006. "Washington's 2002 Parentage Act: A Step Backward for the Rights of Nonmarital Children." *Seattle University Law Review*, vol. 30, pp. 195–243.

Boonin, David. 2008. "How to Solve the Non-Identity Problem." *Public Affairs Quarterly*, vol. 22, no. 2, pp. 127–57.

Boonin, David. 2011. *Should Race Matter? Unusual Answers to the Usual Questions*. Cambridge: Cambridge University Press.

Boonin, David. 2012. "Better to Be." *South African Journal of Philosophy*, vol. 31, no. 1, pp. 10–25.

Bradley, Ben. 2012. "Doing Away with Harm." *Philosophy and Phenomenological Research*, vol. 85, no. 2, pp. 390–412.

Brock, Dan W. 1995a. "The Non-Identity Problem and Genetic Harms: The Case of Wrongful Handicaps." *Bioethics*, vol. 9, nos. 3–4, pp. 272–5.

Brock, Dan W. 1995b. "Procreative Liberty" [review of John A. Robertson, *Children of Choice: Freedom and the New Reproductive Technologies*]. *Texas Law Review*, vol. 74, pp. 187–206.

Brock, Dan W. 2005. "Preventing Genetically Transmitted Disabilities while Respecting Persons with Disabilities." In David Wasserman, Jerome Bickenbach, and Robert Wachbroit, eds., *Quality of Life and Human Difference: Genetic Testing, Health Care, and Disability*. Cambridge: Cambridge University Press, pp. 67–100.

Bruhl, Aaron-Andrew P. 2002. "Justice Unconceived: How Posterity Has Rights." *Yale Journal of Law & the Humanities*, vol. 14, pp. 393–439.

Buchanan, Allen, Dan W. Brock, Norman Daniels, and Daniel Wikler. 2000. *From Chance to Choice: Genetics and Justice*. Cambridge: Cambridge University Press.

Burley, Justine and John Harris. 1999. "Human Cloning and Child Welfare." *Journal of Medical Ethics*, vol. 5, pp. 108–13.

Caney, Simon. 2006. "Cosmopolitan Justice, Rights and Global Climate Change." *Canadian Journal of Law and Jurisprudence*, vol. 19, no. 2, pp. 255–78.

Carter, Alan. 2001. "Can We Harm Future People?" *Environmental Values,* vol.10, pp. 429–54.

Carter, Alan. 2002. "On Harming Others: A Response to Partridge." *Environmental Values*, vol. 11, pp. 87–96.

Chambers, Clare. 2009. "Inclusivity and the Constitution of the Family." *Canadian Journal of Law and Jurisprudence*, vol. 22, no. 1, pp. 135–51.

Cohen, I. Glenn. 2008. "Intentional Diminishment, the Non-Identity Problem, and Legal Liability." *Hastings Law Journal*, vol. 60, pp. 347–75.

Cohen, I. Glenn. 2011. "Regulating Reproduction: The Problem with Best Interests." *Minnesota Law Review*, vol. 96, no. 2, pp. 1187–274.

Cohen, I. Glenn. 2012. "Rethinking Sperm-Donor Anonymity: Of Changed Selves, Non-Identity, and One-Night Stands." *Georgetown Law Journal*, vol. 100, no. 2, pp. 431–47.

Cohen, I. Glenn. 2013. "Of Modest Proposals and Non-Identity: A Comment on the Right to Know Your Genetic Parents." *The American Journal of Bioethics*, vol. 13, no. 5, pp. 45–7.

Cooley, D. R. 2007. "Deaf by Design: A Business Argument against Engineering Disabled Offspring." *Journal of Business Ethics*, vol. 71, pp. 209–27.

Coons, Christian. 2012. "The Best Expression of Welfarism." In Mark C. Timmons, ed., *Oxford Studies in Normative Ethics* (Vol. 2). Oxford: Oxford University Press.

Crespi, Gregory Scott. 2007. "What's Wrong with Dumping Radioactive Wastes in the Ocean? The Surprising Ethical and Policy Analysis Implications of the Problem of Person-Altering Consequences." *Environmental Law Reporter*, vol. 37.

Crespi, Gregory Scott. 2008. "Would it be Unethical to Dump Radioactive Wastes in the Ocean? The Surprising Implications of the Person-Altering Consequences of Policies." *Ecology Law Currents*, vol. 35, pp. 43–52.

Crespi, Gregory Scott. 2010a. "How Recognizing the Endogeneity of Identity Renders the Discounting Debate Largely Irrelevant." *Journal of Land, Resources & Environmental Law*, vol. 30, no. 1, pp. 75–94.

Crespi, Gregory Scott. 2010b. "The Endogeneity Problem in Cost-Benefit Analysis." *The Georgetown Journal of Law & Public Policy*, vol. 8, pp. 91–145.

Davidson, Marc D. 2008. "Wrongful Harm to Future Generations: The Case of Climate Change." *Environmental Values*, vol 17, pp. 471–88.

Davis, Dena S. 1997. "Genetic Dilemmas and the Child's Right to an Open Future." *The Hastings Center Report*, vol. 27, no. 2, pp. 7–15.

Davis, John. 2008. "Selecting Potential Children and Unconditional Parental Love." *Bioethics*, vol. 22, no. 5, pp. 258–68.

DeCamp, Matthew. 2012. "A Sufficient Limit to 'Reasonable' Choices." *The American Journal of Bioethics*, vol. 12, no. 8, pp. 36–8.

DeGrazia, David. 2005. *Human Identity and Bioethics*. Cambridge: Cambridge University Press.

DeGrazia, David. 2009. "Just(ice) in Time for Future Generations: A Response to Hockett and Herstein. *The George Washington Law Review*, vol. 77, pp. 1216–36.

DeGrazia, David. 2012. *Creation Ethics: Reproduction, Genetics and Quality of Life.* Oxford: Oxford University Press.

Delaney, James J. 2011. "Possible People, Complaints, and the Distinction between Genetic Planning and Genetic Engineering." *Journal of Medical Ethics*, vol. 37, pp. 410–14.

Delaney, James J. 2012. "Revisiting the Non-Identity Problem and the Virtues of Parenthood." *American Journal of Bioethics*, vol. 12, no. 4, pp. 24–6.

de Melo-Martin, Inmaculada. 2004. "On Our Obligation to Select the Best Children: A Reply to Savulescu." *Bioethics*, vol. 18, no. 1, pp. 72–83.

de Shalit, Avner. 1997. "Down to Earth Environmentalism: Sustainability and Future Persons." In Nick Fotion and Jan C. Heller, eds., *Contingent Future Persons: On the Ethics of Deciding Who Will Live, or Not, in the Future*. Dordrecht: Kluwer Academic Publishers, pp. 123–35.

de Wert, Guido. 1998. "The Post-menopause: Playground for Reproductive Technology? Some Ethical Reflections." In John Harris and Soren Holm, eds., *The Future of Human Reproduction: Ethics, Choice and Regulation*. Oxford: Clarendon Press, pp. 221–37.

Dillard, Carter J. 2007. "Rethinking the Procreative Right." *Yale Human Rights & Development Law Journal*, vol. 10, pp. 1–63.

Dillard, Carter J. 2010a. "Procreation, Harm, and the Constitution." *Northwestern University Law Review Colloquy*, vol. 105, pp. 5–17.

Dillard, Carter J. 2010b. "Future Children as Property." *Duke Journal of Gender, Law & Policy*, vol. 17, pp. 47–79.

Doran, Michael. 2008. "Intergenerational Equity in Fiscal Policy Reform." *NYU Tax Law Review*, vol. 61, pp. 241–93.

Dudley, Taylor Irene. 2010. "A Fair Hearing for Children." *Whittier Journal of Child and Family Advocacy*, vol. 9, no. 2, pp. 341–65.

Elliot, Robert. 1989. "The Rights of Future People." *Journal of Applied Philosophy*, vol. 6, no. 2, pp. 159–69.

Elsner, D. 2006. "Just Another Reproductive Technology? The Ethics of Human Reproductive Cloning as an Experimental Medical Procedure." *Journal of Medical Ethics*, vol. 32, pp. 596–600.

Elster, Jakob. 2011. "Procreative Beneficence: Cui Bono?" *Bioethics*, vol. 25, no. 9, pp. 482–8.

Fahmy, Melissa Seymour. 2011. "On the Supposed Moral Harm of Selecting for Deafness." *Bioethics*, vol. 25, no. 3, pp. 128–36.

Feinberg, Joel. 1987. "Wrongful Life and the Counterfactual Element in Harming." *Social Philosophy and Policy*, vol. 4, pp. 145–77.

Feldman, Fred. 1991. "Some Puzzles about the Evil of Death," *The Philosophical Review*, vol. 100, no. 2, pp. 205–27.

Fisher, Fleur and Ann Sommerville. 1998. "To Everything There Is a Season? Are There Medical Grounds for Refusing Fertility Treatment to Older Women?" In J. Harris and S. Holm, eds., *The Future of Human Reproduction*. Oxford: Oxford University Press, pp. 203–20.

Garraid, Eve and Stephen Wilkinson. 2006. "Selecting Disability and the Welfare of the Child." *The Monist*, vol. 89, no. 4, pp. 482–504.

Glover, Jonathan. 2007. *Choosing Children: Genes, Disability, and Design*. Oxford: Oxford University Press.

Goold, Imogen and Julian Savulescu. 2009. "In Favour of Freezing Eggs for Non-Medical Reasons." *Bioethics*, vol. 23, no. 1, pp. 47–58.

Govier, Trudy. 1979. "What Should We Do about Future People?" *American Philosophical Quarterly*, vol. 16, pp. 105–13.

Green, Ronald M. 1997. "Parental Autonomy and the Obligation Not to Genetically Harm One's Child Genetically." *Journal of Law, Medicine & Ethics,* vol. 25, pp. 5–15.

Greene, Mark and Steven Augello. 2011. "Everworse: What's Wrong with Selecting for Disability?" *Public Affairs Quarterly,* vol. 25, no. 2 (April), pp. 131–9.

Greene, Richard. 2004. "Does the Non-Identity Problem Block a Class of Arguments against Cloning?" *International Journal of Applied Philosophy,* vol. 18, no. 1, pp. 95–101.

Hammond, Jessica. 2010. "Genetic Engineering to Avoid Genetic Neglect: From Chance to Responsibility." *Bioethics,* vol. 24, no. 4, pp. 160–9.

Hanser, Matthew. 1990. "Harming Future People." *Philosophy and Public Affairs,* vol. 19, no. 1 (Winter), pp. 47–70.

Hanser, Matthew. 2008. "The Metaphysics of Harm." *Philosophy and Phenomenological Research,* vol. 77, no. 2 (September), pp. 421–50.

Hanser, Matthew. 2009. "Harming and Procreating," in Melinda A. Roberts and David T. Wasserman, eds., *Harming Future Persons: Ethics, Genetics and the Nonidentity Problem.* New York: Springer, pp. 179–99.

Hanser, Matthew. 2011. "Still More on the Metaphysics of Harm. *Philosophy and Phenomenological Research* vol. LXXXII No. 2 (March), pp. 459–69.

Haramia, Chelsea. 2013. "Our Responsibility to the Non-Existent." *Southwest Philosophy Review,* vol. 29, no. 1, pp. 249–56.

Hare, Caspar. 2007. "Voices from Another World: Must We Respect the Interests of People Who Do Not, and Will Never, Exist?" *Ethics,* vol. 117, no. 3, pp. 498–523.

Hare, Caspar. 2009. "The Ethics of Morphing." *Philosophical Studies,* vol. 145, no. 1, pp. 111–3.

Harman, Elizabeth. 2004. "Can We Harm and Benefit in Creating?" *Philosophical Perspectives,* 18, pp. 89–113.

Harman, Elizabeth. 2009. "Harming as Causing Harm." In Melinda A. Roberts and David T. Wasserman, eds., *Harming Future Persons: Ethics, Genetics and the Nonidentity Problem.* New York: Springer, pp. 137–54.

Havstad, Joyce C. 2010. "Human Reproductive Cloning: A Conflict of Liberties." *Bioethics,* vol. 24, no. 2, pp. 71–7.

Häyry, Matti. 2004. "There Is a Difference Between Selecting a Deaf Embryo and Deafening a Hearing Child," *Journal of Medical Ethics,* vol. 30, no. 5, pp. 510–12.

Heller, Jan C. 1997. "Deciding the Timing of Children: An Ethical Challenge Only Indirectly Addressed by the Christian Tradition." In Nick Fotion and Jan C. Heller, eds., *Contingent Future Persons: On the Ethics of Deciding Who Will Live, or Not, in the Future.* Dordrecht: Kluwer Academic Publishers, pp. 71–84.

Heller, Jan C. 1998. "Religious Perspectives on Human Cloning: Revisiting Safety as a Moral Constraint." *Valparaiso University Law Review,* vol. 32, pp. 661–78.

Herissone-Kelly, Peter. 2009. "Two Varieties of 'Better-For' Judgements." In Melinda A. Roberts and David T. Wasserman, eds., *Harming Future Persons: Ethics, Genetics and the Nonidentity Problem.* New York: Springer, pp. 249–63.

Herissone-Kelly, Peter. 2012. "Wrongs, Preferences, and the Selection of Children: A Critique of Rebecca Bennett's Argument against the Principle of Procreative Beneficence." *Bioethics,* vol. 26, no. 8, pp. 447–54.

Herstein, Ori. 2008a. "Historic Injustice, Group Membership and Harm to Individuals: Defending Claims for Historic Justice from the Non-Identity Problem." *Columbia Law School Public Law and Legal Theory Working Paper Group,* Paper Number 08-174 (version of March 3).

Herstein, Ori. 2008b. "Historic Injustice and the Non-Identity Problem: The Limitations of the Subsequent-Wrong Solution and Towards a New Solution." *Law and Philosophy*, vol. 27, pp. 505–31.

Herstein, Ori. 2009. "The Identity and (Legal) Rights of Future Generations." *The George Washington Law Review*, vol. 77, pp. 1173–215.

Heyd, David. 1988. "Procreation and Value: Can Ethics Deal with Futurity Problems?" *Philosophia*, vol. 18, pp. 151–70.

Heyd, David. 1992. *Genethics: Moral Issues in the Creation of People.* Berkeley: University of California Press.

Heyd, David. 2009. "The Intractability of the Nonidentity Problem. In Melinda A. Roberts and David T. Wasserman, eds., *Harming Future Persons: Ethics, Genetics and the Nonidentity Problem.* New York: Springer, pp. 3–25.

Holtug, Nils. 2003. "Good for Whom?" *Theoria*, vol. 69, nos.1–2, pp. 4–20.

Hope, Tony and John McMillan. 2012. "Physicians' Duties and the Non-Identity Problem." *The American Journal of Bioethics*, vol. 12, no. 8, pp. 21–9.

Hudson, James L. 1986. "Rights and the Further Future." *Philosophical Studies*, vol. 49, pp. 99–107.

Hull, Richard J. 2006. "Cheap Listening? Reflections on the Concept of Wrongful Disability." *Bioethics*, vol. 20, no. 2, pp. 55–63.

Huseby, Robert. 2010. "Person-Affecting Moral Theory, Non-Identity and Future People." *Environmental Values*, vol. 19, pp. 193–210.

Jecker, Nancy S. 1987."Reproductive Risk Taking and the Nonidentity Problem." *Social Theory and Practice*, vol. 13, no. 2, pp. 219–35.

Jecker, Nancy S. 2012. "The Right Not to Be Born: Reinterpreting the Nonidentity Problem." *The American Journal of Bioethics*, vol. 12, no. 8, pp. 34–5.

Kagan, Shelly. 1989. *The Limits of Morality.* Oxford: Oxford University Press.

Kahane, Guy. 2009. "Non-Identity, Self-Defeat, and Attitudes to Future Children." *Philosophical Studies*, vol. 145, pp. 193–214.

Kamm, F. M. 2000–1. "Cloning and Harm to Offspring." *N.Y.U. Journal of Legislation and Public Policy*, vol. 4, pp. 65–76.

Kass, Leon. 2001. "Preventing a Brave New World." *The New Republic*, May 21. Reprinted in David Boonin and Graham Oddie, eds., *What's Wrong? Applied Ethicists and Their Critics.* Oxford: Oxford University Press, 2005, pp. 682–5.

Kavka, Gregory S. 1982. "The Paradox of Future Individuals," *Philosophy and Public Affairs*, vol. 11, no. 2, pp. 93–112.

Klocksiem, Justin. 2012. "A Defense of the Counterfactual Comparative Account of Harm." *American Philosophical Quarterly*, vol. 49, no. 4, pp. 285–300.

Kobayashi, Masaya. 1998. "Holistic Self and Future Generations: A Revolutionary Solution to the Non-Identity Problem." In Tae Chang Kim and Ross Harrison, eds., *Self and Future Generations: An Intercultural Conversation between East and West.* Cambridge: White Horse Press, pp. 131–214.

Kramer, Matthew H. 2001. "Getting Rights Right." In Matthew H. Kramer, ed., *Rights, Wrongs and Responsibilities.* Basingstoke: Palgrave, pp. 28–95.

Kumar, Rahul. 2003. "Who Can Be Wronged?" *Philosophy and Public Affairs*, vol. 31, no. 2, pp. 99–118.

Lane, Robert. 2006. "Safety, Identity and Consent: A Limited Defense of Reproductive Human Cloning." *Bioethics*, vol. 20, no. 3, pp. 125–35.

Levy, Neil. 2002. "The Apology Paradox and the Non-Identity Problem," *The Philosophical Quarterly*, vol. 52, no. 208 (July), pp. 358–68.

Liberto, Hallie. 2014. "The Exploitation Solution to the Non-Identity Problem." *Philosophical Studies*, vol. 167, no. 1, pp. 73–88.

Lillehammer, Hallvard. 2005. "Benefit, Disability and the Non-Identity Problem." In Nafsika Athanassoulis, ed., *Philosophical Reflections on Medical Ethics*. New York: Palgrave Macmillan, pp. 24–43.

Lillehammer, Hallvard. 2009. "Reproduction, Partiality, and the Non-identity Problem." In Melinda A. Roberts and David T. Wasserman, eds., *Harming Future Persons: Ethics, Genetics and the Nonidentity Problem*. New York: Springer, pp. 231–48.

Locke, Don. 1987. "The Parfit Population Problem." *Philosophy*, vol. 62, no. 240, pp. 131–57.

Lotz, Mianna, 2011. "Rethinking Procreation: Why it Matters Why We Have Children." *Journal of Applied Philosophy*, vol. 28, no. 2, pp. 105–21.

McBrayer, Justin Patrick. 2008. "Rights, Indirect Harms and the Non-Identity Problem." *Bioethics*, vol. 22, no. 6, pp. 299–306.

McCarthy, David. 2001. "Why Sex Selection Should Be Legal." *Journal of Medical Ethics*, vol. 27, pp. 302–7.

McDougall, Rosalind. 2005. "Acting Parentally: An Argument against Sex Selection." *Journal of Medical Ethics*, vol. 31, pp. 601–5.

McDougall, Rosalind. 2007. "Parental Virtue: A New Way of Thinking about the Morality of Reproductive Actions." *Bioethics*, vol. 21, no. 4, pp. 181–90.

MacLean, Douglas. 1983. "A Moral Requirement for Energy Policies." In Douglas MacLean and Peter G. Brown, eds., *Energy and the Future*. Totowa, NJ: Rowman & Littlefield, pp. 180–97.

McMahan, Jeff. 1994. Review of David Heyd, *Genethics: Moral Issues in the Creation of People*. *The Philosophical Review*, vol. 103, no. 3, pp. 557–9.

McMahan, Jeff. 2001. "Wrongful Life: Paradoxes in the Morality of Causing People to Exist." In John Harris, ed., *Bioethics*. Oxford: Oxford University Press, pp. 445–75.

McMahan, Jeff. 2005. "Preventing the Existence of People with Disabilities." In David Wasserman, Jerome Bickenbach, and Robert Wachbroit, eds., *Quality of Life and Human Difference: Genetic Testing, Health Care, and Disability*. Cambridge: Cambridge University Press, pp. 142–71.

McMahan, Jeff. 2009. "Asymmetries in the Morality of Causing People to Exist." In Melinda A. Roberts and David T. Wasserman, eds., *Harming Future Persons: Ethics, Genetics and the Nonidentity Problem*. New York: Springer, pp. 49–68.

McMahan, Jefferson. 1981. "Problems of Population Theory." *Ethics*, vol. 92, no. 1, pp. 96–127.

Malek, Janet. Unpublished-a. "The Non-Identity Nonproblem."

Malek, Janet. Unpublished-b. "The Possibility of Being Made Worse Off by One's Own Conception."

Malek, Janet. 2008. "Disability and the Duties of Potential Parents." *Saint Louis University Journal of Health Law & Policy*, vol. 2, pp. 119–34.

Malek, Janet and Judith Daar. 2012. "The Case for a Parental Duty to Use Preimplantation Genetic Diagnosis for Medical Benefit." *The American Journal of Bioethics*, vol. 12, no. 4, pp. 3–11.

Markie, P. J. 2005. "Nonidentity, Wrongful Conception and Harmless Wrongs." *Ratio*, vol. 18, no. 3, pp. 290–305.

Martin, Angela K. and Bernard Baertschi. 2012. " In Favor of PGD: The Moral Duty to Avoid Harm Argument." *American Journal of Bioethics*, vol. 12, no. 4, pp. 12–13.

Meachem, Christopher J. G. 2012. "Person-affecting Views and Saturating Counterpart Relations." *Philosophical Studies*, vol. 158, no. 2, pp. 257–87.

Meyer, Lukas H. 1997. "More Than They Have a Right To: Future People and Our Future-Oriented Projects." In Nick Fotion and Jan C. Heller, eds., *Contingent Future Persons: On the Ethics of Deciding Who Will Live, or Not, in the Future*. Dordrecht: Kluwer Academic Publishers, pp. 137–56.

Meyer, Lukas H. 2004. "Historical Injustice and the Right of Return." *Theoretical Inquiries in Law*, vol. 5, pp. 305–15.

Meyer, Lukas H. 2006. "Reparations and Symbolic Restitution." *Journal of Social Philosophy*, vol. 37, no. 3, pp. 406–22.

Morriem, E. Haavi. 1988. "The Concept of Harm Reconceived: A Different Look at Wrongful Life." *Law and Philosophy*, vol. 7, no. 1, pp. 3–33.

Mulgan, Tim. 2009. "Rule Consequentialism and Non-Identity." In Melinda A. Roberts and David T. Wasserman, eds., *Harming Future Persons: Ethics, Genetics and the Nonidentity Problem*. New York: Springer, pp. 115–34.

Narveson, Jan. 1967. "Utilitarianism and New Generations." *Mind*, vol. 76, no. 301, pp. 62–72.

Norcross, Alastair. 2005. "Harming in Context." *Philosophical Studies*, 123, pp. 149–73.

Page, Edward A. 1999. "Intergenerational Justice and Climate Change." *Political Studies*, vol. 47, pp. 53–66.

Page, Edward A. 2006. *Climate Change, Justice and Future Generations*. Northampton, MA: Edward Elgar Publishing, Inc.

Palmer, Clare. 2011. "Animal Disenhancement and the Non-Identity Problem: A Response to Thompson." *Nanoethics*, vol. 5, no. 1, pp. 43–8.

Parfit, Derek. 1976a. "On Doing the Best for Our Children." In Michael Bayles, ed., *Ethics and Population*, Cambridge, MA: Schenkman, pp. 100–15.

Parfit, Derek. 1976b. "Rights, Interests and Possible People." In Samuel Gorovitz, et al., eds., *Moral Problems in Medicine*. Englewood Cliffs, NJ: Prentice-Hall, Inc., pp. 369–75.

Parfit, Derek. 1982. "Future Generations: Further Problems." *Philosophy and Public Affairs*, vol. 11, no. 2, pp. 113–72.

Parfit, Derek. 1983. "Energy Policy and the Further Future: The Identity Problem." In Douglas MacLean and Peter G. Brown, eds., *Energy and the Future*. Totowa, NJ: Rowman and Littlefield, pp. 166–79.

Parfit, Derek. 1984. *Reasons and Persons*. Oxford: Oxford University Press.

Parfit, Derek. 1986. "Comments." *Ethics*, vol. 96, no. 4, pp. 832–72.

Parfit, Derek. 2011. *On What Matters*. Oxford: Oxford University Press.

Parker, Michael. 2007. "The Best Possible Child." *Journal of Medical Ethics*, vol. 33, pp. 279–83.

Parsons, Josh. 2003. "Why the Handicapped Child Case is Hard." *Philosophical Studies*, vol. 112, no. 2, pp. 147–62.

Partridge, Ernest. 2002. "The Future: For Better or Worse. *Environmental Values*, vol. 11, pp. 75–85.

Pattinson, Shaun D. 1999. "Wrongful Life Actions as a Means of Regulating Use of Genetic and Reproductive Technologies." *Health Law Journal*, vol. 7, pp. 19–32.

Persson, Ingmar. 2009. "Rights and the Asymmetry between Creating Good and Bad Lives." In Melinda A. Roberts and David T. Wasserman, eds., *Harming Future Persons: Ethics, Genetics and the Nonidentity Problem*. New York: Springer, pp. 29–47.

Peters, P. G. 1999. "Harming Future Persons: Obligations to the Children of Reproductive Technology." *Southern California Interdisciplinary Law Journal*, vol. 8, pp. 375–400.

Peters, P. G. 2004. *How Safe is Safe Enough? Obligations to the Children of Reproductive Technology*. Oxford: Oxford University Press.

Peters, P. G. 2009. "Implications of the Nonidentity Problem for State Regulation of Reproductive Liberty." In Melinda A. Roberts and David T. Wasserman, eds., *Harming Future Persons: Ethics, Genetics and the Nonidentity Problem*. New York: Springer, pp. 17–31.

Petersen, Thomas Sobirk. 2002. "The Claim from Adoption." *Bioethics*, vol. 16, no. 4, pp. 353–75.

President's Council on Bioethics. 2002. *Human Cloning and Human Dignity: An Ethical Inquiry*. Washington, DC.

Purves, Duncan. 2013. *Who Should Exist: A Welfare-based Solution to the Non-identity Problem*. Ph.D. dissertation, Department of Philosophy, University of Colorado.

Purves, Duncan. Forthcoming. "Accounting for the Harm of Death." *Pacific Philosophical Quarterly*.

Rachels, Stuart. 2001. "A Set of Solutions to Parfit's Problems." *Noûs*, vol. 35, no. 2, pp. 214–38.

Rakowski, Eric. 2002. "Who Should Pay for Bad Genes?" *California Law Review*, vol. 90, no. 5, pp. 1345–414.

Reiman, Jeffrey. 2007. "Being Fair to Future People: The Non-Identity Problem in the Original Position." *Philosophy and Public Affairs*, vol. 35, no. 1, pp. 69–92.

Rendall, Matthew, 2011. "Non-identity, Sufficiency, and Exploitation." *The Journal of Political Philosophy*, vol. 19, no. 2, pp. 229–47.

Rivera-Lopez, Eduardo. 2009. "Individual Procreative Responsibility and the Non-Identity Problem." *Pacific Philosophical Quarterly*, vol. 90, pp. 336–63.

Rivera-Lopez, Eduardo. 2009. "The Nonidentity Problem and the Two Envelope Problem: When is One Act Better for a Person than Another?" In Melinda A. Roberts and David T. Wasserman, eds., *Harming Future Persons: Ethics, Genetics and the Nonidentity Problem*. New York: Springer, pp. 201–28.

Roberts, Melinda A. 1998. *Child Versus Childmaker: Future Persons and Present Duties in Ethics and the Law*. New York: Rowman & Littlefield Publishers, Inc.

Roberts, Melinda A. 2007. "The Nonidentity Fallacy: Harm, Probability and Another Look at Parfit's Depletion Example. *Utilitas*, 9, pp. 267–311.

Roberts, Melinda A. 2009. "The Non-Identity Problem and the Two Envelope Problem: When Is One Act Better for a Person than Another?" In Melinda A. Roberts and David T. Wasserman, eds., *Harming Future Persons: Ethics, Genetics and the Nonidentity Problem*. New York: Springer, pp. 201–28.

Roberts, Melinda A. 2012. "Does the Non-Identity Problem Imply a Double Standard for Physicians and Patients?" *The American Journal of Bioethics*, vol. 12, no. 8, pp. 38–9.

Robertson, John A. 2004. "Gay and Lesbian Access to Assisted Reproductive Technology." *Case Western Reserve Law Review*, vol. 55, pp. 323–71.

Savulescu, Julian. 2001. "Procreative Beneficence: Why We Should Select the Best Children." *Bioethics*, vol. 15, no. 5/6, pp. 414–26.

Savulescu, Julian and Guy Kahane. 2009. "The Moral Obligation to Create Children with the Best Chance of the Best Life." *Bioethics*, vol. 23, no. 5, pp. 274–90.

Schiavone, Karen E. 2009. "Playing the Odds or Playing God? Limiting Parental Ability to Create Disabled Children Through Preimplantation Genetic Diagnosis." *Albany Law Review*, vol. 73, no. 1, pp. 283–328.

Schwartz, Thomas. 1978. "Obligations to Posterity." In Richard Sikora and Brian Barry, eds., *Obligations to Future Generations*. Philadelphia: Temple University Press, pp. 3–13.

Schwartz, Thomas. 1979. "Welfare Judgments and Future Generations." *Theory and Decision*, vol. 11, pp. 181–94.

Sepinwall, Amy J. 2006. "Responsibility for Historical Injustices: Reconceiving the Case for Reparations." *Journal of Law & Politics*, vol. 22, pp. 183–229.

Shapiro, Michael H. 1996. "Illicit Reasons and Means for Reproduction: On Excessive Choice and Categorical and Technological Imperatives." *Hastings Law Journal*, vol. 47, pp. 1081–221.

Shaw, David. 2008. "Deaf by Design: Disability and Impartiality." *Bioethics*, vol. 22, no. 8, pp. 407–13.

Sher, George. 2005. "Transgenerational Compensation." *Philosophy and Public Affairs*, vol. 33, no. 2, pp. 181–200.

Shiffrin, Seana Valentine. 1999. "Wrongful Life, Procreative Responsibility, and the Significance of Harm." *Legal Theory*, 5, pp. 117–48.

Shiffrin, Seana Valentine. 2009. "Reparations for U.S. Slavery and Justice Over Time." In Melinda A. Roberts and David T. Wasserman, eds., *Harming Future Persons: Ethics, Genetics and the Nonidentity Problem*. New York: Springer, pp. 333–9.

Simmons, A. John. 1995. "Historical Rights and Fair Shares." *Law and Philosophy*, vol. 14, no. 2, Special Issue on Rights (May, 1995), pp. 149–84.

Singer, Peter. 1972. "Famine, Affluence, and Morality." *Philosophy and Public Affairs*, vol. 1, no. 3, pp. 229–43.

Singer, Peter. 1999. *Practical Ethics*, 2nd ed. Cambridge: Cambridge University Press.

Slobodian, Lydia N. 2012. "Obligations to Transgenerational Groups: A Justification for Sustainable Environmental Policy." *The Georgetown International Environmental Law Review*, vol. 24, pp. 387–411.

Smolensky, Kirsten Rabe. 2008. "Creating Children with Disabilities: Parental Tort Liability for Preimplantation Genetic Intervention." *Hastings Law Journal*, vol. 60, pp. 299–345.

Smolkin, Doran. 1994. "The Non-Identity Problem and the Appeal to Future People's Rights." *The Southern Journal of Philosophy*, vol. 32, pp. 315–29.

Smolkin, Doran. 1999. "Toward a Rights-Based Solution to the Non-Identity Problem." *Journal of Social Philosophy*, vol. 30, no. 1, pp. 194–208.

Spriggs, M. 2002. "Lesbian Couple Create a Child who is Deaf Like Them." *Journal of Medical Ethics*, vol. 28, p. 283.

Steinbock, Bonnie. 2009. "Wrongful Life and Procreative Decisions." In Melinda A. Roberts and David T. Wasserman, eds., *Harming Future Persons: Ethics, Genetics and the Nonidentity Problem*. New York: Springer, pp. 155–78.

Steinbock, Bonnie. 2011. *Life Before Birth: The Moral and Legal Status of Embryos and Fetuses*, 2nd ed. Oxford: Oxford University Press.

Steinbock, Bonnie and Ron McClamrock. 1994. "When Is Birth Unfair to the Child?" *Hastings Center Report*, vol. 24, no. 6, pp. 15–21.

Stoller, Sarah E. 2008. "Why We Are Not Morally Required to Select the Best Children: A Response to Savulescu." *Bioethics*, vol. 22, no. 7, pp. 364–9.

Streiffer, Robert. 2008. "Animal Biotechnology and the Non-Identity Problem." *American Journal of Bioethics*, vol. 8, no. 6, pp. 47–8.

Taylor, Edward M. 2010. "Procreative Liberty and Selecting for Disability: Section 14(4) Human Fertilisation and Embryology Act 2008." *King's Student Law Review*, vol. 71, pp. 71–86.

Thomson, Judith Jarvis. 2011. "More on the Metaphysics of Harm." *Philosophy and Phenomenological Research*, vol. 82, no. 2, pp. 436–58.

Tooley Michael. 1983. *Abortion and Infanticide*. Oxford: Clarendon Press.

Tooley Michael. 1998. "Value, Obligation, and the Asymmetry Question." *Bioethics*, vol. 12, pp. 111–24.

Trent, Justin. 2006. "Assisted Reproductive Technologies." *The Georgetown Journal of Gender and the Law*, vol. 7, pp. 1143–63.

Underkoffler, Keith. 2013. "Aretaic Assessment and the Non-Identity Problem." M.A. thesis, University of Alberta.

Unger, Peter. 1996. *Living High and Letting Die*. Oxford: Oxford University Press.

Urbanek, Valentina Maria. 2010. "The Non-Identity Problem." Ph.D. dissertation, Department of Linguistics and Philosophy, MIT.

Usami, Makoto. 2011. "Intergenerational Justice: Rights versus Fairness." *Philosophy Study*, vol. 1, no. 4, pp. 237–46.

Vanderheiden, Steve. 2006. "Conservation, Foresight, and the Future Generations Problem." *Inquiry*, vol. 49, no. 4, pp. 337–52.

van der Zee, Boujke and Inez de Beaufort. 2011. "Preconception Care: A Parenting Protocol. A Moral Inquiry Into the Responsibility of Future Parents Towards Their Future Children." *Bioethics*, vol. 25, no. 8, pp. 451–7.

Velleman, J. David. 2008. "Persons in Prospect, Part III: Love and Nonexistence." *Philosophy and Public Affairs*, vol. 36, no. 3, pp. 266–88.

Walker, Mark. Forthcoming. "Eugenic Selection Benefits Embryos." *Bioethics*.

Wasserman, David. 2005. "The Nonidentity Problem, Disability, and the Role Morality of Prospective Parents." *Ethics*, vol. 116, no. 1, pp. 132–52.

Wasserman, David. 2008. "Hare on De Dicto Betterness and Prospective Parents." *Ethics*, vol. 118, no. 3, April, pp. 529–35.

Wasserman, David. 2009. "Harms to Future People and Procreative Intentions." In Melinda A. Roberts and David T. Wasserman, eds., *Harming Future Persons: Ethics, Genetics and the Nonidentity Problem*. New York: Springer, pp. 265–85.

Wax, Amy L. 1996. "The Two-Parent Family in the Liberal State: The Case for Selective Subsidies." *Michigan Journal of Race & Law*, vol. 1, no. 2, pp. 491–550.

Weinberg, Justin. 2013. "Non-Identity Matters, Sometimes." *Utilitas*, vol. 26, no. 1, pp. 1–11.

Weinberg, Rivka M. 2002. "Procreative Justice: A Contractualist Account." *Public Affairs Quarterly*, vol. 16, no. 4, pp. 405–25.

Weinberg, Rivka M. 2008. "Identifying and Dissolving the Non-Identity Problem." *Philosophical Studies*, vol. 137, pp. 3–18.

Weinberg, Rivka M. 2013. "Existence: Who Needs It? The Non-Identity Problem and Merely Possible People." *Bioethics*, vol. 27, no. 9, pp. 471–84.

Weinberg, Rivka and Paul Hurley. Forthcoming. "Whose Problem is Non-Identity?" *The Journal of Moral Philosophy*.

Wolf, Clark. 2009. "Do Future Persons Presently Have Alternate Possible Identities?" In Melinda A. Roberts and David T. Wasserman, eds., *Harming Future Persons: Ethics, Genetics and the Nonidentity Problem*. New York: Springer, pp. 93–114.

Woodward, James. 1986. "The Non-Identity Problem." *Ethics*, vol. 96, no. 4, July, pp. 804–31.

Woodward, James. 1987. "Reply to Parfit." *Ethics*, vol. 97, no. 4, pp. 800–16.

Woollard, Fiona. 2012. "Have We Solved the Non-Identity Problem?" *Ethical Theory and Moral Practice*, vol. 15, pp. 677–90.

Weiss, Edith Brown. 1990. "Our Rights and Obligations to Future Generations for the Environment." *The American Journal of International Law*, vol. 84, no. 1, pp. 198–207.

Wrigley, Anthony. 2006. "Genetic Selection and Modal Harms." *The Monist*, vol. 89, no. 4, pp. 505–25.

Wrigley, Anthony. 2012. "Harm to Future Persons: Non-Identity Problems and Counterpart Solutions." *Ethical Theory and Moral Practice*, vol. 15, no. 2, pp. 175–90.

Zuradzki, Tomasz. 2008. "Genetic Engineering and the Non-Identity Problem." *Diametros*, 16, pp. 63–79.

Index